Advanced Higher Physics
New Revised Syllabus

Questions & Solutions

P D Burnett

Published by MathsGroundWork
http://www.mathsgroundwork.co.uk

© PD Burnett 2015

This publication is copyright. No reproduction of any part may take place without the written permission of the publisher.

First published 2014
Printed in the United Kingdom
Typeface Frutiger Neue 11pt

The publisher has used its best endeavours to ensure that URL's for external websites referred to in this book are correct and active at the time of going to press. However, we have no responsibility for external or third-party websites referred to in this publication and can make no guarantee that any such content will remain active or that the content will remain accurate and appropriate.

Thanks to Tiago da Silva for the front cover illustration of Valles Marineris on Mars, and to xkcd at http://xkcd.com/ for the cartoon on page 22.

Physical Constants

Quantity	Symbol	Value
speed of light in a vacuum	c	299792458 m s^{-1}
permittivity of free space	ε_o	8.854 187 817.. x 10^{-12} F m^{-1}
permeability of free space	μ_o	4π x 10^{-7} H m^{-1}
universal gravitation constant	G	6.674 x 10^{-11} m^3 kg^{-1} s^{-2}
Planck's constant	h	6.626 070 x 10^{-34} J s
elementary charge (like electron)	e	1.602 176 x 10^{-19} C
fine structure constant	α	7.297 352 57 x 10^{-3}
Böhr radius		0.529 177 211 x 10^{-10} m
electron mass	m_e	9.109 383 x 10^{-31} kg
proton mass	m_p	1.672 622 x 10^{-27} kg
neutron mass	m_n	1.674 927 x 10^{-27} kg
alpha particle mass	m_α	6.644 657 x 10^{-27} kg
atomic mass unit	u	1.660 5389 x 10^{-27} kg
Stefan-Boltzmann constant	σ	5.670 37 x 10^{-8} W m^{-2} K^{-4}
Boltzmann's constant	k	1.380 650 x 10^{-23} J K^{-1}
Avogadro's constant	N_A	6.022 141 x 10^{23} mol^{-1}

Earth, Moon, Sun

Earth's Mean Radius	6372.797 km
Earth's Mass	5.9737 x 10^{24} kg
Period of Earth's Orbit (the sidereal year)	365.25636042 days = 3.155815 x 10^7 s
Earth's Rotation Period (sidereal day)	23 hr 56min 04.0905s
Radius of Moon (equatorial)	1737.4 km
Mass of Moon	7.3477 x 10^{22} kg
Radius of Sun (equatorial)	6.955 x 10^8 m
Mass of Sun	1.989 x 10^{30} kg
Mean Earth-Moon distance	3.844 x 10^8 m
Astronomical Unit (A.U.)	1.49597870696 x 10^{11} m
Distance of 1 light-year	9.4605284 x 10^{15} m

Solar System

Object	Mass (kg)	Mean Distance to Sun (m)	Mean radius (km)	Rotation period (days)	Orbital Period (days)
Mercury	3.303 x 10^{23}	5.791 x 10^{10}	2439.7	58.6462	87.97
Venus	4.869 x 10^{24}	1.082 x 10^{11}	6051.8	-243.0187	224.7
Earth	5.974 x 10^{24}	1.496 x 10^{11}	6373	0.99727	365.26
Mars	6.419 x 10^{23}	2.279 x 10^{11}	3394	1.025957	686.97
Jupiter	1.899 x 10^{27}	7.785 x 10^{11}	71492	0.41354	4333
Saturn	5.688 x 10^{26}	1.433 x 10^{12}	60268	0.44401	10759
Uranus	8.681 x 10^{25}	2.877 x 10^{12}	25559	-0.71833	30799
Neptune	1.024 x 10^{26}	4.503 x 10^{12}	24550	0.67125	60190
Pluto	1.303 x 10^{22}	5.914 x 10^{12}	1187	-6.3872	89866
Eris	1.67 x 10^{22}	1.012 x 10^{13}	1163	≈ 1	204870

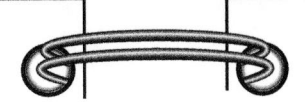

Rotational Motion & Astrophysics
5.....Kinematic relationships.....94
7.....Motion in a circle.....95
9.....Equations of Motion.....96
12.....Centripetal forces.....98
15.....Moment of Inertia.....99
17.....Torque.....100
18.....Moment of Inertia & Torque.....101
19.....Rotational kinetic energy.....102
21.....Angular momentum.....103
22.....Gravitation.....105
26.....Space & Time.....108
30.....Stellar Physics.....112

Quanta and Waves
33.....Quantum Theory.....118
40.....Particles from Space.....125
47.....Simple Harmonic Motion.....131
51.....Waves.....135
55.....Interference by division of amplitude.....138
59.....Interference by division of the wavefront.....141
61.....Polarisation.....143

Electromagnetism
63.....Electric Fields.....145
66.....Electrostatic potential.....148
71.....Magnetic Fields.....154
76.....Capacitors.....158
82.....Inductors.....163
87.....Electromagnetic Radiation.....168

88.....**Units & Uncertainties**.....169

Equations for Unit 1

$v = \dfrac{ds}{dt}$ $\qquad$ $a = \dfrac{dv}{dt} = \dfrac{d^2s}{dt^2}$ $\qquad$ $v = u + at$ $\qquad$ $s = ut + \dfrac{1}{2}at^2$ $\qquad$ $v^2 = u^2 + 2as$

$\omega = \dfrac{d\theta}{dt}$ $\qquad$ $\alpha = \dfrac{d\omega}{dt} = \dfrac{d^2\theta}{dt^2}$ $\qquad$ $\omega = \omega_o + \alpha t$ $\qquad$ $\theta = \omega_o t + \dfrac{1}{2}\alpha t^2$ $\qquad$ $\omega^2 = \omega_o^2 + 2\alpha\theta$

$s = r\theta$ $\qquad$ $v = r\omega$ $\qquad$ $a_t = r\alpha$ $\qquad$ $a_r = \dfrac{v^2}{r} = r\omega^2$ $\qquad$ $F = \dfrac{mv^2}{r} = mr\omega^2$

$T = rF$ $\qquad$ $T = I\alpha$ $\qquad$ $L = mvr = mr^2\omega$ $\qquad$ $L = I\omega$ $\qquad$ $E_K = \dfrac{1}{2}I\omega^2$

$F = \dfrac{GMm}{r^2}$ $\qquad$ $V = -\dfrac{GM}{r}$ $\qquad$ $v = \sqrt{\dfrac{2GM}{r}}$ $\qquad$ $b = \dfrac{L_{um}}{4\pi r^2}$ $\qquad$ $W = \sigma T^4$

$L_{um} = 4\pi r^2 \sigma T^4$ $\qquad$ $r_{Sch} = \dfrac{2GM}{c^2}$

Equations for Unit 2

$E = hf$ $\qquad$ $\lambda = \dfrac{h}{p}$ $\qquad$ $mvr = \dfrac{nh}{2\pi}$ $\qquad$ $\Delta x \Delta p_x \geq \dfrac{h}{4\pi}$ $\qquad$ $\Delta E \Delta t \geq \dfrac{h}{4\pi}$

$F = qvB$ $\qquad$ $\omega = 2\pi f$ $\qquad$ $\phi = \dfrac{2\pi x}{\lambda}$ $\qquad$ $\Delta x = \dfrac{\lambda l}{2d}$ $\qquad$ $d = \dfrac{\lambda}{4n}$

$\Delta x = \dfrac{\lambda D}{d}$ $\qquad$ $n = \tan i_p$ $\qquad$ $y = A\sin\omega t$ $\qquad$ $a = \dfrac{d^2y}{dt^2} = -\omega^2 y$ $\qquad$ $v = \pm\omega\sqrt{(A^2 - y^2)}$

$E_K = \dfrac{1}{2}m\omega^2(A^2 - y^2)$ $\qquad$ $E_P = \dfrac{1}{2}m\omega^2 y^2$ $\qquad$ $y = A\sin 2\pi\left(ft - \dfrac{x}{\lambda}\right)$

Equations for Unit 3

$F = \dfrac{Q_1 Q_2}{4\pi\varepsilon_o r^2}$ $\qquad$ $E = \dfrac{Q}{4\pi\varepsilon_o r^2}$ $\qquad$ $V = \dfrac{Q}{4\pi\varepsilon_o r}$ $\qquad$ $F = qE$ $\qquad$ $V = Ed$

$F = BIL\sin\theta$ $\qquad$ $B = \dfrac{\mu_o I}{2\pi r}$ $\qquad$ $c = \dfrac{1}{\sqrt{\varepsilon_o \mu_o}}$ $\qquad$ $t = CR$ $\qquad$ $X_C = \dfrac{V}{I} = \dfrac{1}{\omega C} = \dfrac{1}{2\pi fC}$

$V = -L\dfrac{dI}{dt}$ $\qquad$ $E = \dfrac{1}{2}LI^2$ $\qquad$ $X_L = \dfrac{V}{I} = \omega L = 2\pi fL$

Where units have not been given for a quantity, assume that they are in S.I. units. Questions requiring deeper understanding are numbered with a bold typeface.

Unit 1 Kinematic Relationships

1. From empty, a bucket fills up with 20 litres of water in 5s.

   (a) What is the change in volume per second?

   (b) If the change in volume per second was constant, how much would it contain after 3s?

   (c) Using 'V' for volume and 't' for time, write down an equation for the volume at time 't' if it had started with 6 litres of water.

   (d) Deduce what you can about the water in this bucket if its volume is described by:
   $$V = 36 - 1.2t$$

2. The speed of a car is given by: $v = 40 + 1.5t$

   (a) What do the 40 and the 1.5 represent?

   (b) Does the speed change at a constant rate?

3. The mathematical symbol for rate of change with time is $\frac{d}{dt}$.

   (a) What would $\frac{ds}{dt}$ represent and what units is it usually measured in?

   (b) Suppose $\frac{ds}{dt} = 3$. What value would 's' have after 7s if s = 0 at t = 0?

   (c) In part (b), was it important to be told that s = 0 at t = 0? If so, why?

4. The displacement 's' of a bicycle is given by: $s = 0.8t + 20$

   (a) What does the '20' tell you and what units does it have?

   (b) What does the '0.8' represent and what units does it have?

   (c) Calculate $\frac{ds}{dt}$ and describe the motion of the bicycle.

5. The displacement of a second bicycle moving in one dimension is given by: $s = 0.2t^2 + 0.8t + 20$

   (a) What word describes what this bicycle is doing compared with the one in Q(4)?

   (b) Calculate $\frac{ds}{dt}$ and $\frac{d^2s}{dt^2}$.

   (c) What does '0.2', '0.8' and '20' represent? What symbol is used for the second one?

6. A car had a constant acceleration of 2.4m s^{-2} and an initial speed of 5m s^{-1}. A timer was started when the car's displacement was +30m. Write down an equation for its displacement at any time 't'.

7. An aeroplane increases its speed uniformly from the take-off point on the end of a runway and reaches s = 96m after 4s and s = 480m after 10s. Calculate its acceleration.

8. The velocity of an object in terms of its displacement is given by: $v = \sqrt{12s + 225}$. Calculate its velocity at the origin and its acceleration.

9. A spacecraft's acceleration is not constant. During a certain stage of the launch, its acceleration is given by: $a = 0.06t + 3$. At t = 0, s = 0 and v = 0.

   (a) Calculate its acceleration at t = 2s and t = 40s.

   (b) Use $\frac{dv}{dt}$ for the acceleration 'a' and derive an expression for the velocity.

5

(c) Now use $\frac{ds}{dt}$ for the velocity and derive an expression for the displacement.

(d) Calculate the velocity and displacement after 40s.

10. Willy and Wally are two Australian cyclists. They have a race. Wally sets-off first and accelerates uniformly at 1.5m s^{-2} for 6s then continues at constant speed. Willy set-off 30s after Wally and accelerated uniformly at 1.75m s^{-2} for 8s, then continued at constant speed. How much time did it take for Willy to catch Wally (from when Wally started) and how far was this from the start line?

11. Calculate the velocity, acceleration and displacement at points 'A', 'B' and 'C' on the graph below.

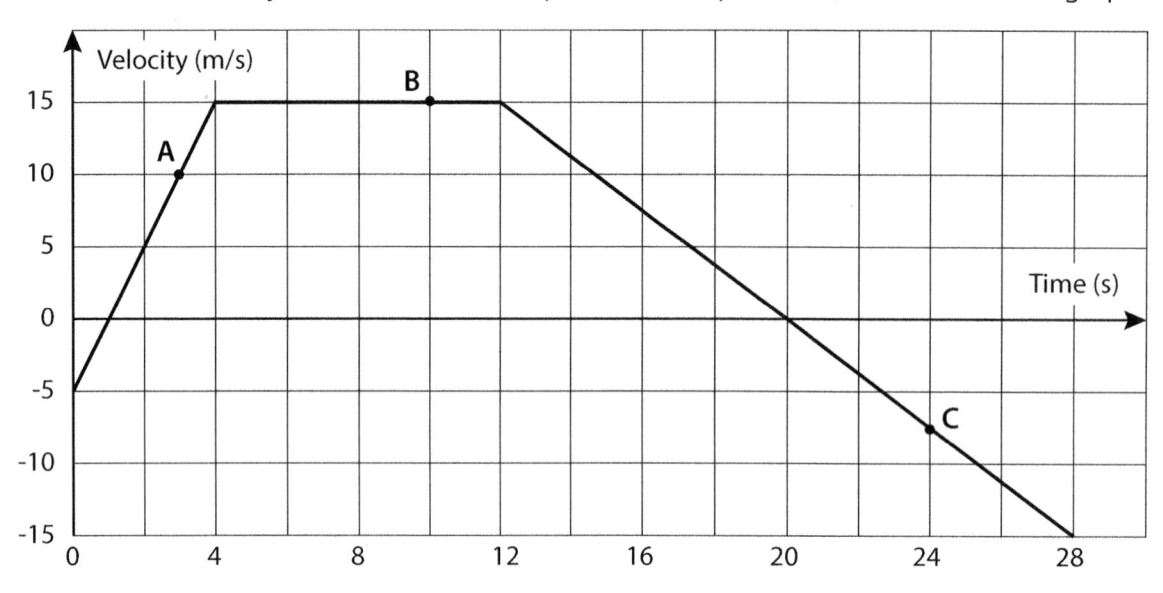

12. Starting from rest, the acceleration of a particle is given by $a = 3t + 5$. It follows this motion for a time of 12s. It then decellerates uniformly to rest in a time of 8s. Calculate the total distance travelled.

13. The star Epsilon Eridani has been considered as a target for sending spaceships from Earth. It is at a distance of 3.22 parsecs and is moving away from us at a speed of 15.5km/s. If a spaceship was launched from Earth in the year 2040 with an average speed of 150,000mph, when would it reach Epsilon Eridani? (1 parsec is a distance of 3.262 lightyears).

14. The displacement-time graphs on the right show the motions of three separate objects 'A', 'B' and 'C'.

(a) Which object(s) travelled the greatest distance after 1s?

(b) Which object is fastest at a time of 2s. Explain your reasoning.

(c) The displacement 's' for each object can be quantified by a polynomial expression in time 't'. Using values from both axes, derive expressions for the displacement of each motion as a function of time.

(d) Calculate $\frac{d^2s}{dt^2}$ for each object.

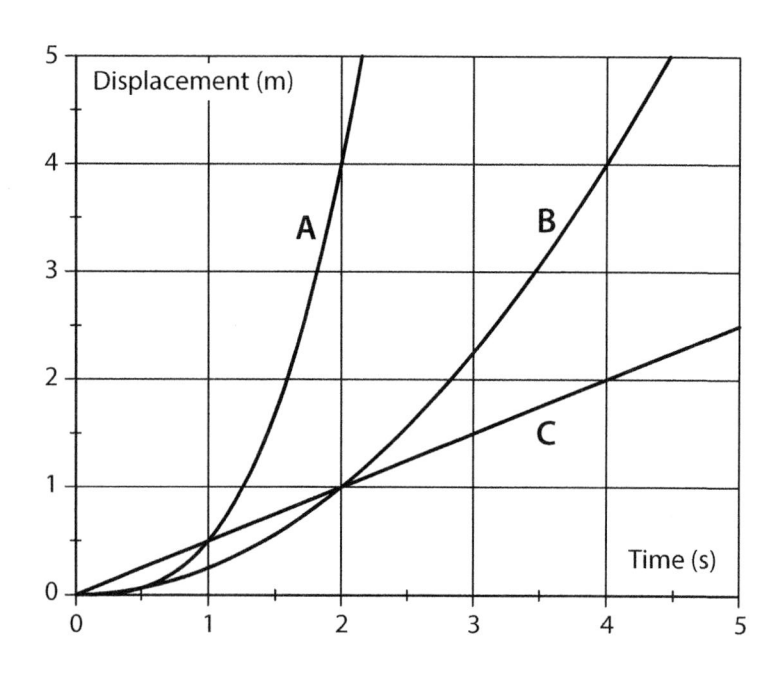

6

Unit 1 Motion in a Circle

Angles are measured in 'degrees'. There are 360 of them in one complete turn so one degree is quite a small angle. Let's practice using a different unit for our angles. This one is much bigger, with 6 of them not quite enough to make one turn. It's the radian.

1. The diagram on the right shows an angle of one radian. For an angle of one radian, the length of the arc is the same as the radius.

    (a) The circumference of the circle is $2\pi r$, so how many radians make up one complete turn?

    (b) How many radians would make up two complete turns?

    (c) How many complete turns is $4\pi n$ radians, where 'n' is any integer?

    (d) Why would **aliens** be more likely to use radians than degrees?

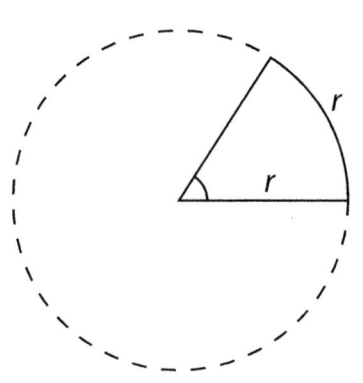

2. 2π radians is the same angle as 360 degrees. Convert 2π to decimal form then calculate how many degrees there are in 1 radian. Compared with the above diagram, does it seem about right?

3. Convert these angles in radians into degrees:

    (a) π (b) $\pi/2$ (c) $\pi/4$ (d) $\pi/3$ (e) $3\pi/2$

4. Convert these angles in radians into number of turns.

    (a) 4π (b) 5π (c) π (d) $\pi/4$ (e) $3 \times 10^8 \pi$

5. Two small spheres chase each other at a constant rate along the circumference of a circle as shown. They start 120 degrees apart. Sphere 'B' moves through an angle of $\pi/12$ radians each second.

    (a) Convert 120 degrees into radians.

    (b) How many radians each second does sphere 'A' move through if it catches 'B' in a time of 4s?

    (c) Calculate the period (T) for sphere 'A' and for sphere 'B'.

    (d) Where is 'A' when it catches 'B'?

    (e) If you were looking down on the diagram and rotating anti-clockwise at a rate of $\pi/12$ radians each second anticlockwise, what would you see happening?

    (f) Describe the motion of an observer who sees sphere 'A' moving clockwise with a period of 8s. How much time would this observer record for 'A' to catch 'B'?

6. Starting from mid-day, the hour hand of an analogue clock goes through an angle ('angular displacement') of $\pi/6$ radians. What is the new time on the clock?

7. If two waves destructively interfere at a point, what must be the phase difference between the waves in radians? Why are there many possible answers for the phase difference?

8. How much time does it take to make one complete turn at a constant angular velocity of 15degrees per second?

9. A satellite called 'Gravity Probe 'B'' was launched to test one of the lesser known predictions of General Relativity (an effect known as 'frame dragging').

    (a) During the science gathering phase of the mission its rotation rate was 0.7742rpm. What was its period of rotation?

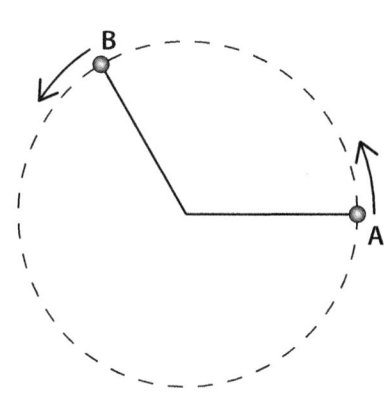

(b) Liquid helium was required for the instruments to operate properly. After it was all used up, the rotation rate was reduced to 0.4898rpm. Calculate its new period.

10. A type of star known as a pulsar spins at a high rate. The highest spin rate is a pulsar discovered in 2004 called PSR J1748-2446ad with a period (T) of 0.00139595482 seconds.

   (a) Calculate its spin frequency (f) in Hz and its angular velocity (ω) in rad s^{-1}.

   (b) What is the speed (in m s^{-1}) of a point on the equator of the pulsar if its radius is 16km?

11. Planet Earth takes 1 year to complete an orbit about the Sun. The left-hand diagram below shows its position at the start of one of its circuits. The dotted line from 'B' to 'A' points straight towards the Sun. A person standing at the dotted line from 'A' would observe the Sun to be at its highest point in the sky; it would be 'midday'. The right-hand diagram shows the Earth 23 hours and 56 minutes later after it has rotated through exactly 360° (note position of line AB).

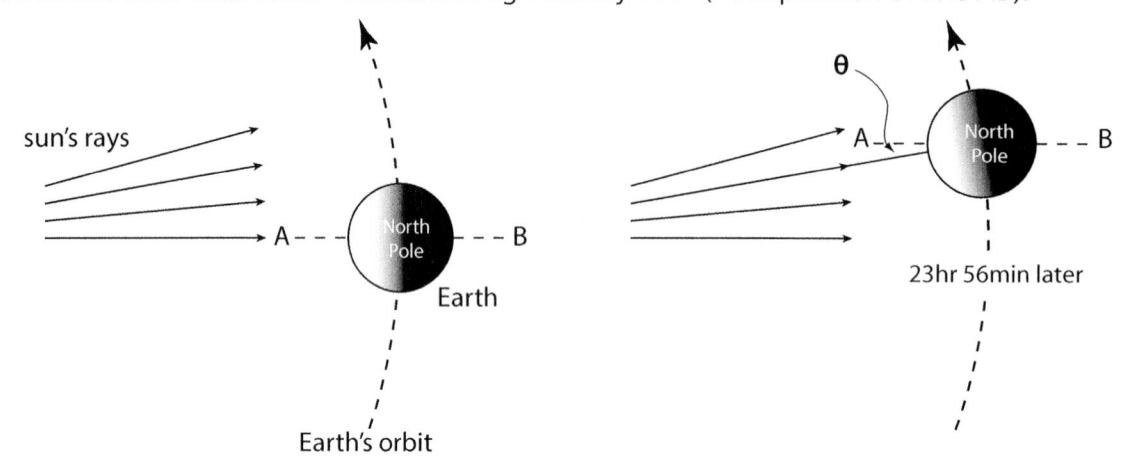

   (a) Explain why it isn't yet midday at that same location.

   (b) The time between the Sun reaching its highest point in the sky one day to its highest point in the sky the next day is **exactly** 24hrs. Why is the hour defined this way?

   (c) What time interval does the Earth take to rotate through angle 'θ'?

   (d) Viewed from the Sun, what angle does the Earth move through in 1 day?

12. (a) If the Earth is a rigid body, what can you conclude about the angular velocity of all points on the surface?

   (b) Calculate the angular velocity (in rad s^{-1}) of a point on the Earth's surface if its period is 23h 56min.

   (c) The Earth orbits the Sun in 365.242 days. Calculate the angular velocity (in rad s^{-1}) of the Earth about the Sun.

13. A certain Blu-ray disc player reads information from a disc by a system known as constant linear velocity (CLV). A point on the disc under the read head **always** has a speed of 4.917m/s, no matter where the read head is above the disc surface.

   (a) The disc spins at 1957rpm when the read head is near the inner rim. Convert this into radians per second.

   (b) Near the outer rim, the disc spins at 810rpm. Calculate the distance of the read head from the centre of the disc.

Unit 1 Equations of Motion

1. Two small spheres move in circular paths as shown below. A timer is started when they are at the 3 o'clock position and their positions are labelled for the first 7 seconds of the motion.

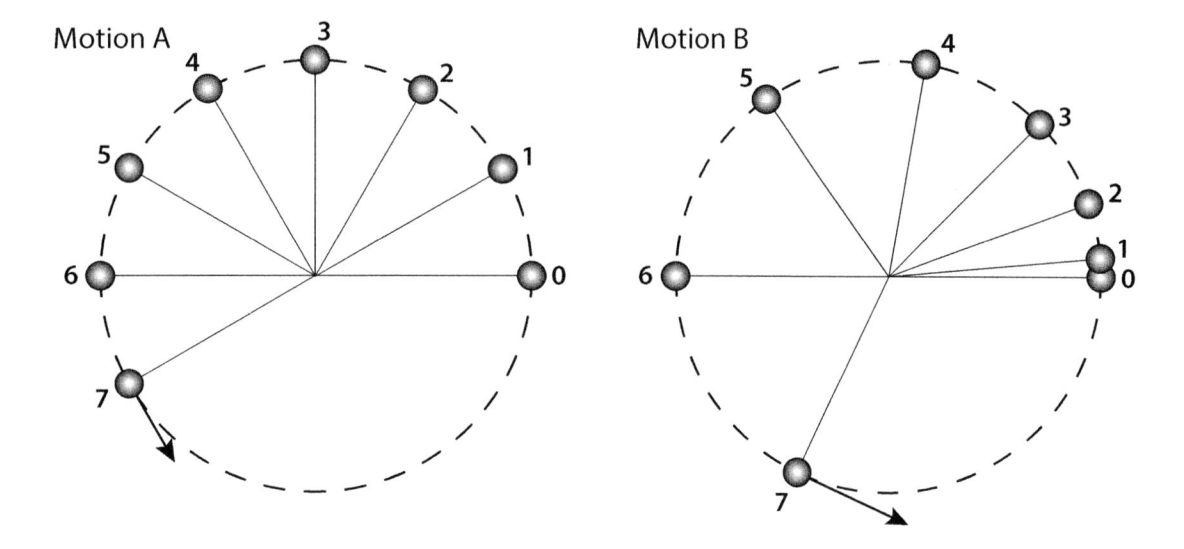

   (a) Describe the motion of the sphere in diagram (A).

   (b) Is the sphere in diagram (A) subjected to a force? If yes, in what direction is it acting?

   (c) Would you need any additional forces to make the sphere in diagram (A) follow the same motion as the sphere in diagram (B)? If yes, in what direction would they act?

   (d) Label these statements as True or False?

   (i) The sphere in diagram (A) moves at constant speed.

   (ii) The sphere in diagram (A) moves with constant velocity.

   (iii) The sphere in diagram (A) is accelerating.

   (iv) There is a force on both spheres acting towards the centre of the circle.

   (v) The centripetal force in diagram (A) is of constant magnitude.

   (vi) The centripetal force in diagram (B) is of constant magnitude.

   (vii) The sphere in diagram (A) has a component of acceleration in the direction of the tangent.

   (viii) The sphere in diagram (B) has a component of acceleration in the direction of the tangent.

   (e) Calculate the angular velocity 'ω' in diagram (A).

   (f) If diagram (B) shows constant angular acceleration, and the position at 6 seconds is at 180°, what is the angle at 3s? How does the angle at 4s compare with the angle at 2s?

2. (a) In each example, use the equation $v = u + at$ to calculate the final velocity 'v':

   (i) accelerating uniformly at 3m s^{-2} for 5s from an initial velocity of 20m s^{-1}.

   (ii) accelerating uniformly at -1.5m s^{-2} for 18s from an initial velocity of 90m s^{-1}.

   (b) In each example, use the equation $\omega = \omega_o + \alpha t$ to calculate the final angular velocity 'ω':

   (i) angular acceleration of 3rad s^{-2} for 5s from an initial angular velocity of 20rad s^{-1}

   (ii) angular acceleration of -1.5rad s^{-2} for 18s from an initial angular velocity of 90rad s^{-1}

(c) The examples in (a) and (b) are very similar. To what do you change 'metres' in (a), to get (b)?

(d) Velocity is the rate of change of displacement with time and is measured in metres per second. Why does the term 'angular velocity' mean?

3. (a) In each example, use the equation $s = ut + \frac{1}{2}at^2$ to calculate the displacement 's':

    (i) accelerating uniformly at 4m s⁻² for 6s from an initial velocity of 30m s⁻¹.

    (ii) accelerating uniformly at -0.5m s⁻² for 45s from an initial velocity of 80m s⁻¹.

(b) In each example, use the equation $\theta = \omega_o t + \frac{1}{2}\alpha t^2$ to calculate the angular displacement 'θ':

    (i) angular acceleration of 4rad s⁻² for 6s from an initial angular velocity of 30rad s⁻¹.

    (ii) angular acceleration of -0.5rad s⁻² for 45s from an initial angular velocity of 80rad s⁻¹.

4. The table below brings out the close connection between motion in a straight line and rotational motion. Complete the table.

Linear Motion			Rotational Motion		
Quantity	Symbol	Units	Quantity	Symbol	Units
time	t	s	time		
displacement					
			initial angular velocity		
final velocity					
acceleration					

5. (a) Here are two different equations for average velocity: $\bar{v} = \frac{s}{t}$ $\bar{v} = \frac{v+u}{2}$

Describe any restrictions on the type of motion for each equation.

(b) Here are two different equations for average angular velocity: $\bar{\omega} = \frac{\theta}{t}$ $\bar{\omega} = \frac{\omega + \omega_o}{2}$

Describe any restrictions on the type of motion for each equation.

6. A rigid, thin rod is spun anticlockwise about one end at a constant rate as shown below:

(a) Calculate the angular velocity of the mid-point 'A' if the angular velocity of point 'B' is π/2 rad s⁻¹

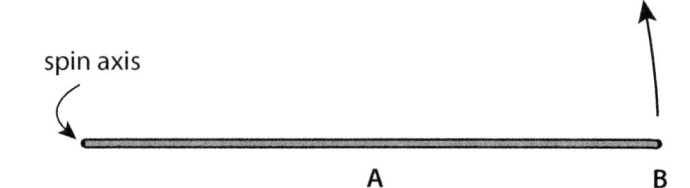

(b) How many complete turns would point 'A' make in 1 minute?

(c) The speed of point 'B' is 25cm s⁻¹. What is the speed of point 'A'?

(d) Calculate the length of the rod.

7. A particle moves in a circle with constant angular acceleration 'α'. Over a time of 20 s it had an average angular velocity of 6π rad s⁻¹.

(a) Calculate its angular velocity after 20 s if its initial angular velocity was 2π rad s⁻¹.

(b) Use the equation $\bar{\omega} = \frac{\theta}{t}$ to calculate its angular displacement 'θ' after 20s.

(c) Use the equation $\omega = \omega_o + \alpha t$ to work out the angular acceleration 'α'.

(d) Use the equation $\omega^2 = \omega_o^2 + 2\alpha\theta$ to calculate the angular displacement 'θ'. Does it agree with your answer to part (b)?

(e) How many turns has it made after 10s?

8. This graph describes the motion of an object moving in a circle:

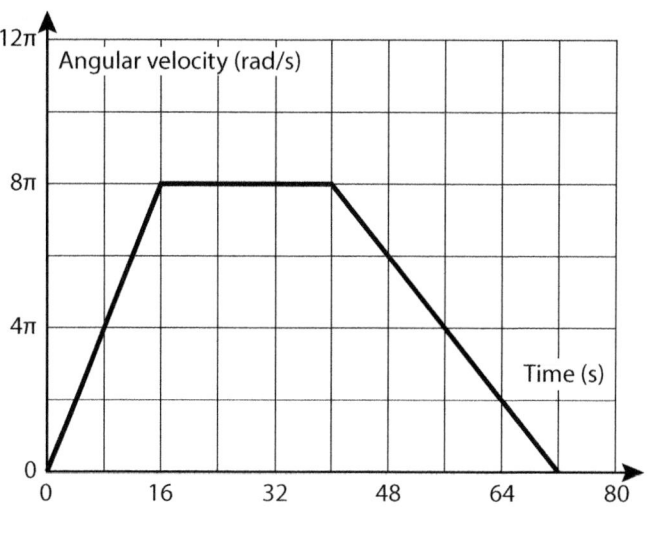

    (a) How many turns does it make between 16s and 40s?

    (b) Calculate the angular acceleration for each of the three stages of the motion.

    (c) What does the area under the graph give?

    (d) Calculate the total angular displacement.

    (e) Calculate the average angular velocity. Explain why you can't work it out by considering each of the three separate stages and taking an average of them.

9. Calculate the angular acceleration of an object which goes from an initial angular velocity of 5π rad s^{-1} to a final angular velocity of 16 rad s^{-1} in 37s.

10. A particle goes through an angular displacement of 2π radians in a time of 6s.

    (a) Calculate its average angular velocity.

    (b) What assumption do you make if you claim that the final angular velocity is $2\pi/3$ rad s^{-1}?

11. The rate of change of angular displacement of an object is constant at $\pi/3$ rad s^{-1}. Write down an expression for the angular displacement as a function of time. Assume that $\theta = 0$ at $t = 0$.

12. (a) What do $\dfrac{d\omega}{dt}$ and $\dfrac{d^2\theta}{dt^2}$ represent?

    (b) What units are they both measured in?

    (c) If they were both zero, how would you describe the motion?

    (d) Starting from the equation $\dfrac{d\omega}{dt} = 5$, use integration to derive an expression for the angular velocity as a function of time. Do not assume it starts from rest.

13. This graph describes the **speed** of a particle undergoing constant angular acceleration in a circle.

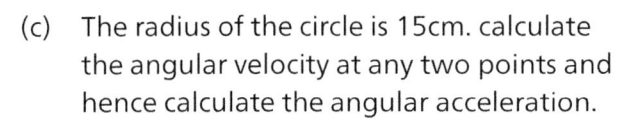

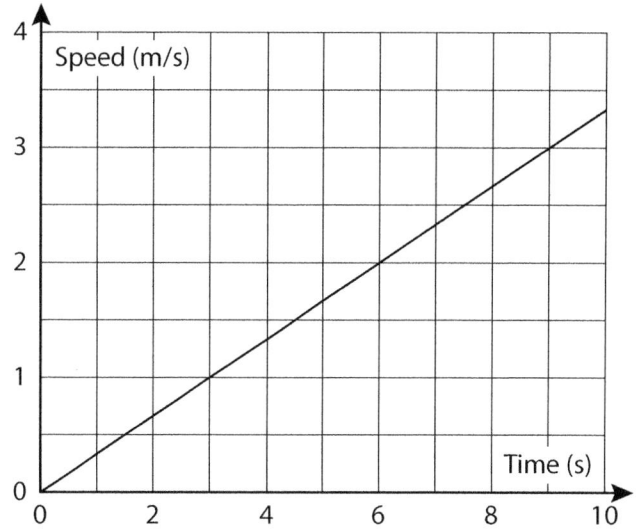

    (a) Treating it as a normal speed-time graph, calculate the acceleration.

    (b) Remembering that it moves in a circle, what is the full name of this acceleration. Write down its symbol and its units.

    (c) The radius of the circle is 15cm. calculate the angular velocity at any two points and hence calculate the angular acceleration.

    (d) If you multiply the radius (r) by the angular acceleration (α), what do you obtain?

14. A particle moving in a circle of radius 4.2m accelerates from a speed of 1.5m s^{-1} to a speed of 2.75m s^{-1} in a time of 18s.

    (a) Calculate its angular acceleration (α).

    (b) At what time has it completed one full turn?

15. An object moves in a circle of radius 0.3m with an angular acceleration of 0.2π rad s^{-2}.

    (a) After 10s its angular velocity was 3π rad s^{-1}. Calculate its initial angular velocity.

    (b) Calculate the speed of the object in metres per second at **time 15s**.

16. This is a question on non-uniform angular acceleration. The particle moves in a circle of radius 25cm under the action of a force producing an angular acceleration of $\alpha = 0.15t - 0.8$. The particle starts from rest at the origin.

    (a) Derive an expression for the angular velocity as a function of time.

    (b) Derive an expression for the angular displacement as a function of time.

    (c) Calculate the angular displacement after a time of 15s.

    (d) At what time does the particle return to the origin for the first time?

    (e) Calculate its velocity when it returned to the origin.

Unit 1 Centripetal Forces

1. (a) If an object moves in a straight line at constant speed, is it accelerating?

    (b) If an object moves in a curve at constant speed, is it accelerating?

    (c) If an object moves in a straight line with increasing speed, is it accelerating?

    (d) If an object moves in a curve with increasing speed, is it accelerating?

    (e) Which one of the above is closest to a description of the Earth around the Sun?

2. A 2kg mass is subjected to a force which is always at right-angles to its velocity. Six examples are shown below:

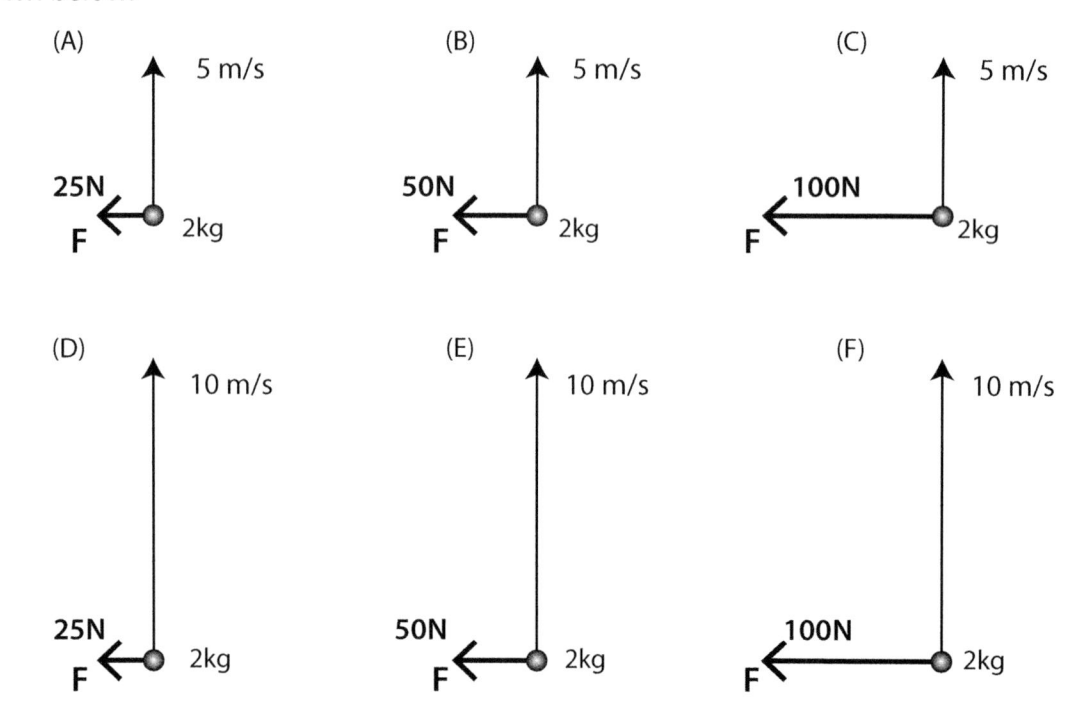

   (A) 5 m/s, 25N F, 2kg
   (B) 5 m/s, 50N F, 2kg
   (C) 5 m/s, 100N F, 2kg
   (D) 10 m/s, 25N F, 2kg
   (E) 10 m/s, 50N F, 2kg
   (F) 10 m/s, 100N F, 2kg

   (a) For each example above, use the expression $F = ma = m\dfrac{v^2}{r}$ to calculate the radius of the circle which the mass will follow.

   (b) What happens to the radius of the circle if the speed is doubled and all else remains constant.

   (c) What name is given to a force which is always at right-angles to the velocity?

3. A car of mass 1200kg follows the horizontal curve of a road of radius 50m at a speed of 20m s⁻¹.

   (a) One of the forces acting on the car is due to gravity. What information in the sentence above tells you that there is **another** force present? In which direction does this force point?

   (b) Calculate the size of the force and comment upon its origin.

4. A 5kg point mass moves in a horizontal circle of radius 3.5m with a speed of 8m/s. Calculate the force required.

5. Explain why a centripetal force on an object does not increase the speed of the object.

6. A centripetal force of 2.75kN keeps an object of mass 60kg moving in a circle of radius 4.5m. What must be the speed of the object if there aren't any other forces involved?

7. A small 25g mass sits on the surface of a 30cm vinyl disc from the record collection of an old rocker. The disc is on a turntable with an angular velocity of 33⅓rpm. The mass is 8cm from the centre.

   (a) Calculate the minimum force of friction required to prevent the mass sliding off the surface.

   (b) In a psychedelic haze, the old rocker reached over and nudged the control on the turntable to 45rpm. The force of friction wasn't sufficient to keep the point mass (it was his 'joint') fixed to the turntable. Describe what he saw!

8. An electron travels at a speed of 1/137th of the speed of light in the lowest orbit of the hydrogen atom of radius 0.529nm.

   (a) Calculate the centripetal force on the electron.

   (b) What is the origin of this centripetal force?

9. A particle moves in a circular path of radius 75cm with a constant speed of 15cm s⁻¹. Calculate the acceleration of the particle in (m s⁻²) and state its direction.

10. A car moves from 'A' to 'N' along a twisty road **at a constant speed** in a series of bends as shown:

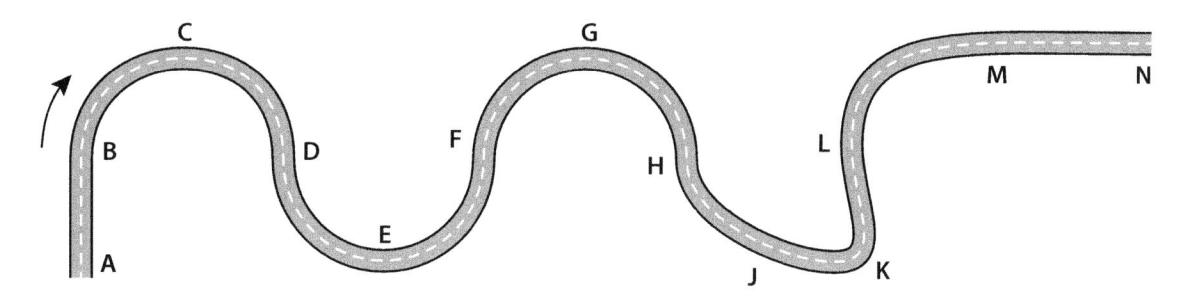

    (a) If you were a passenger in the car, on which sections of the journey would your body move to the left of the seat?

    (b) Along which sections/points does your body **not** move to the left or to the right?

    (c) Which sections/places have no centripetal force acting on the car?

    (d) Why does your body not move towards the front or the back of the car?

    (e) Which part requires the greatest centripetal force on the car? Explain your answer.

    (f) If the speed of the car had been doubled, what effect would this have on the centripetal force?

11. Calculate the centripetal force required to maintain a 450kg mass in a circle of radius 75m at a constant speed of 12m s⁻¹?

12. A car moves at a constant height around a circular banked track with a radius of 25m at a constant speed of 8.37m s⁻¹.

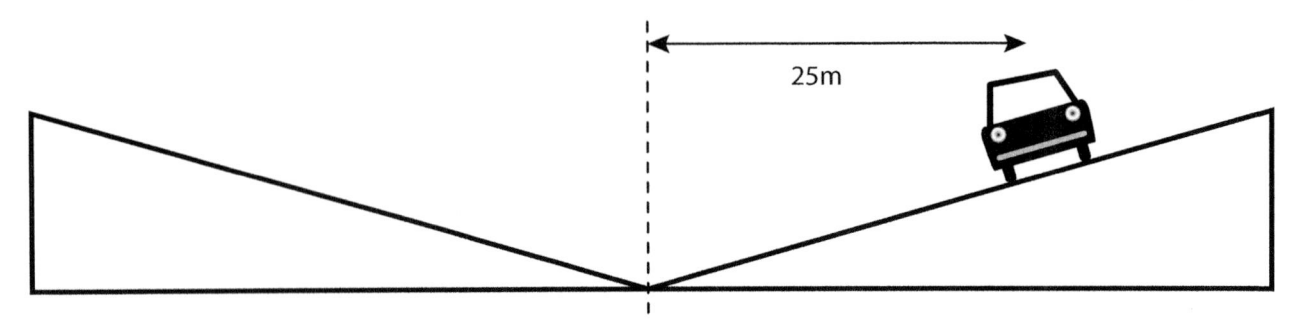

    (a) Why is the distance measured horizontally to the spin axis rather than along the surface of the track?
    (b) To which part of the car should you measure the distance?
    (c) Calculate the centripetal acceleration of the car.
    (d) If there is no friction between the car and the surface, what provides the centripetal force?
    (e) The car has a mass of 1150kg. Calculate the centripetal force on the car.
    (f) The ground under the car applies a force on the car (the 'normal reaction') at right angles to the slope. What is the horizontal component of the normal reaction force in newtons? In which direction does this component of force point?

13. A stone tied to a length of string is spun in a **vertical** circle as shown.

    (a) Ignoring friction, two forces act on the stone; gravity and the string tension. The force of gravity stays constant in magnitude and direction. At which position is the force due to the string tension at its greatest?
    (b) At which position is the string tension at its smallest?
    (c) Does the stone move with constant speed?
    (d) Suppose the string tension drops to zero at the top. What force must provide the centripetal force required to maintain circular motion?
    (e) Calculate the weight of the stone if its mass was 0.15kg.
    (f) The circle has radius 0.38m. Calculate the minimum speed of the stone at the top required to maintain circular motion.

14. A centrifuge spins in a horizontal plane at a frequency of 15Hz. The object on the inside of the wall is at a distance of 0.2m from the centre.

    (a) Calculate the speed at which the mass is moving.
    (b) If the object has a mass of 0.35kg, calculate the force exerted by the wall on the object.
    (c) In which direction does this force point? What effect would it have on the force if the drum spun in the other direction?
    (d) The power is switched off to the motor. Calculate the average angular acceleration if it came to a stop in 40s.

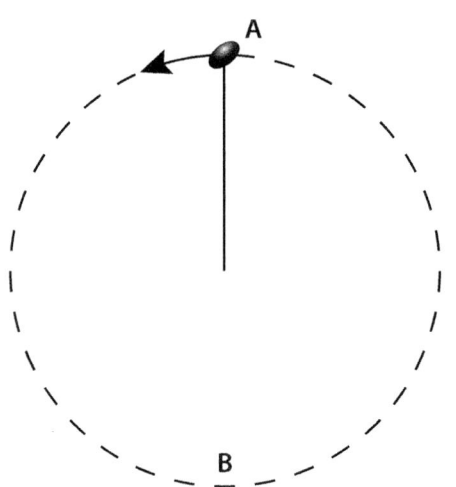

15. This diagram shows the forces on a car on a banked track. The car moves in a circle of constant horizontal height at a constant speed. There is no friction between the wheels and the road surface. The two forces are shown by solid lines and the components of the normal reaction are shown by dotted lines.

    (a) Why is the vertical component 'V' equal in size to the weight?

    (b) Which force provides the centripetal force on the car?

    (c) Write down / derive expressions for the components 'H' and 'V'.

    (d) Use your answer for 'H' above, to derive an expression for the speed of the car moving in a circle of radius 'r'.

    (e) If you suddenly double the mass of the car and maintain the same radius, what effect will this have on the speed of the car?

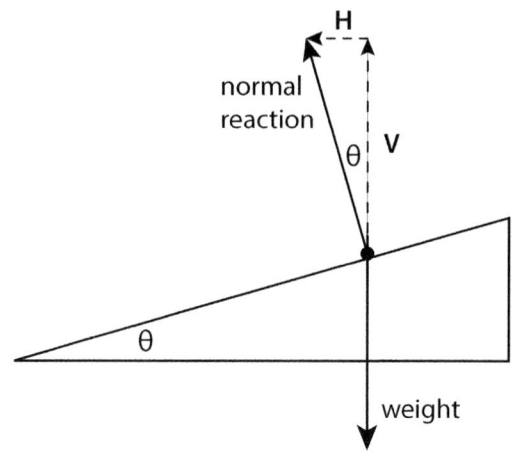

Unit 1 Moment of Inertia

1. Newton's 2nd Law $F = ma$, gives the relation between the force applied to a mass 'm' and its **linear** acceleration. Suppose the object had a size and a shape. Explain why you would apply the force through the object's centre of mass rather than just apply it anywhere.

2. The moment of inertia 'I' of a point mass 'm' about an axis of spin at a distance 'r' is mr^2.

    (a) Describe the effect on the moment of inertia if the distance 'r' was doubled.

    (b) The moment of inertia was doubled but the distance to the spin axis stayed constant. What must have happened?

3. A small sphere (ignore its size) of mass 'm' can be fixed at various positions like 'P', 'Q' or 'R', on a thin rod of negligible mass. The system is spun about the left end of the rod as shown below.

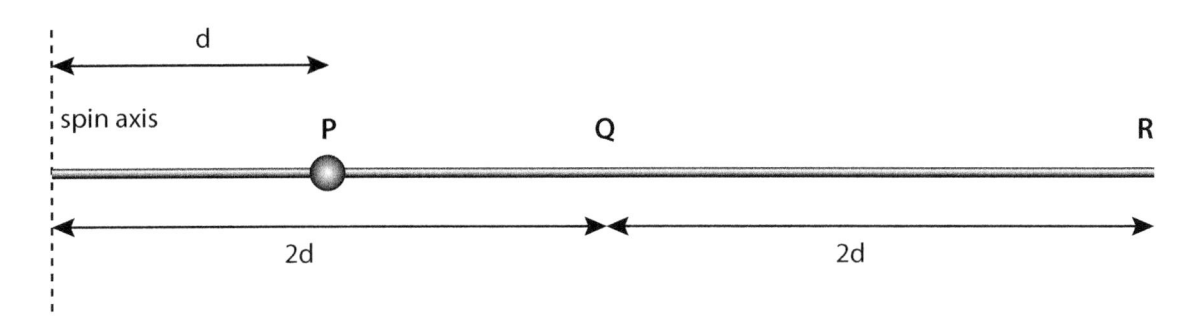

    (a) Suppose you want to make it as hard as possible to spin the system. At which position would you place the small sphere?

    (b) If the moment of inertia at position 'Q' is 16 kgm^2, what is the moment of inertia at positions 'P' and 'R'? Remember that the thin rod has negligible mass.

    (c) Calculate the moment of inertia if the mass is at the midpoint between 'Q' and 'R'.

    (d) Where should the sphere be placed to give the system a moment of inertia of 9 kgm^2.

    (e) Which of these changes would have the most effect on the moment of inertia: a 10% increase in the mass 'm' or a 5% increase in the distance 'r'?

    (f) Where should the mass be placed to minimise the moment of inertia?

15

4. Common shapes in moment of inertia problems are the thin rod, hoop and solid disc. The equation $I = kmr^2$ is used to calculate the moment of inertia. The constant 'k' depends on the shape, and the distance 'r' is one of the dimensions of the shape. Calculate the moment of inertia in the examples below. In all cases, the spin axis is about the centre and points in a direction normal to the plane of the object:

   (a) A thin rod of mass 6kg. and length 18cm.

   (b) A hoop of mass 400g. and diameter 150cm.

   (c) A solid disc of mass 2.45kg. and radius 12cm.

5. Use the moment of inertia formulas $I = mr^2$, $I = \frac{2}{5}mr^2$ to calculate:

   (a) The moment of inertia of the Earth about the Sun.

   (b) The moment of inertia of the Earth spinning on its own axis.

6. A thin rod has a length of 8cm. It is to be melted and cast in the shape of a disc with the same moment of inertia. The spin axis is to be about the centre in both cases.

   (a) Calculate the radius of the disc.

   (b) Starting with the thin rod, into what shape would you mould it to maximise its moment of inertia?

7. The moment of inertia of a solid cylinder of radius 15cm is 4.3kgm².

   (a) Calculate its mass.

   (b) The cylinder is made of pure copper of density 8900kgm⁻³. Calculate its height.

8. A University halls of residence has a washing machine with a drum in the shape of a hollow cylinder. Its radius is 25cm and its mass is 1.2kg.

   (a) Calculate its moment of inertia.

   After 6 months, a student decided to wash his denims. When dry they had a mass of 800g. During the spin, his denims were splattered across the inside of the drum and they dried out a lot. When finished, the moment of inertia of the system had dropped to 0.16kgm².

   (b) Calculate the mass of water in his denims when he removed them from the washing machine?

   (c) Why did the moment of inertia of the system gradually decrease during the spin?

9. The moment of inertia of a thin hoop of radius 'r' is 6kgm². Another hoop of twice the radius is placed concentrically with the first one. Calculate the **total** moment of inertia of the **system** if both hoops are made of the same material and have the same cross section.

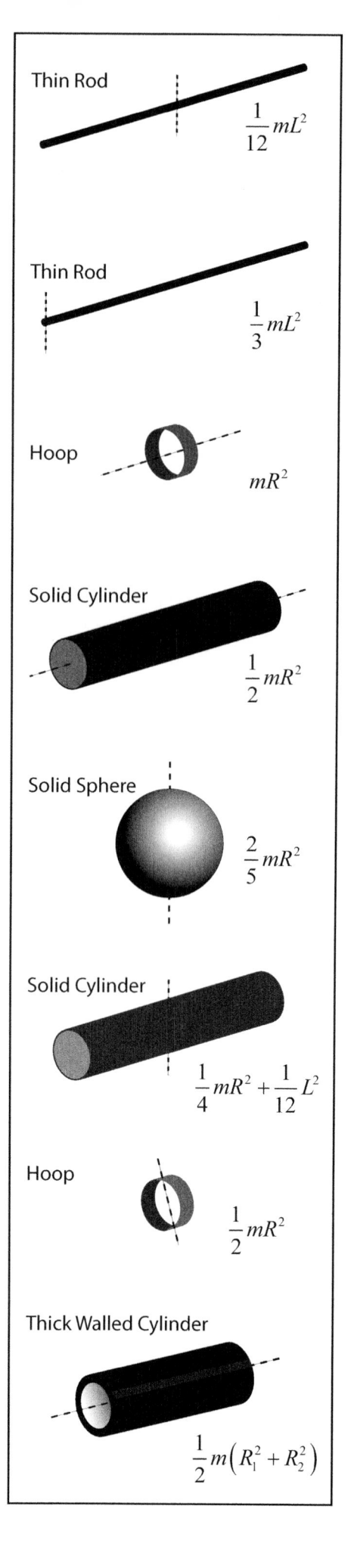

Thin Rod — $\frac{1}{12}mL^2$

Thin Rod — $\frac{1}{3}mL^2$

Hoop — mR^2

Solid Cylinder — $\frac{1}{2}mR^2$

Solid Sphere — $\frac{2}{5}mR^2$

Solid Cylinder — $\frac{1}{4}mR^2 + \frac{1}{12}L^2$

Hoop — $\frac{1}{2}mR^2$

Thick Walled Cylinder — $\frac{1}{2}m(R_1^2 + R_2^2)$

10. The diagram below shows objects moving about the centres of four circles of the same radius. Each system has the same **total** mass, with the largest mass on the left diagram being 12kg.

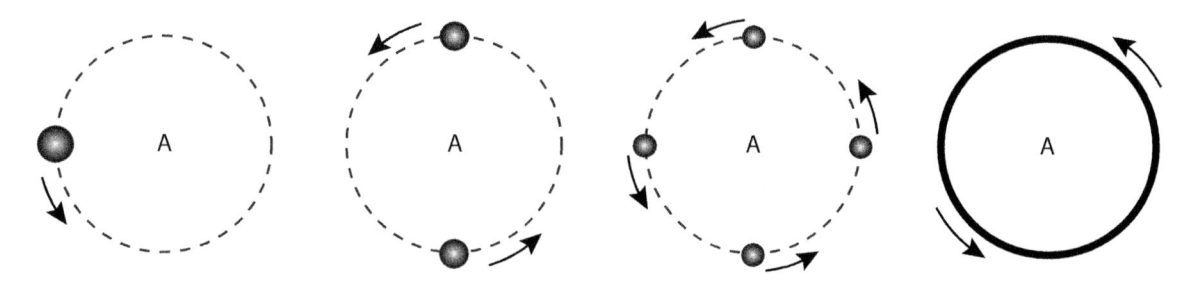

    (a) Why can the same formula for the moment of inertia be used in all four situations?

    (b) The formula is pretty accurate for all four diagrams, but explain why the formula becomes more and more accurate as you go from the left diagram to the right diagram.

    (c) The moment of inertia of any of them is 40kgm². Calculate the radius of the circle.

11. Model the human body of an ice skater using a combination of simple shapes like rods and cylinders. Research or estimate the masses and sizes of your approximations. Use your data to calculate the ratio of the moment of inertia of the skater with arms fully out, to the moment of inertia with arms fully in.

Unit 1 Torque

1. (a) What are the usual units for force and for torque?

    (b) The famous physicist Richard Feynman believed that you didn't really understand anything unless you could explain it to a regular in a bar. Okay, you're in the bar and she wants you to explain the difference between force and torque. What do you say to her?

2. A force 'F' is applied tangentially to the rim of a disc.

    (a) What does it mean by 'tangentially'?

    (b) Calculate the torque applied to the disc if the force was 4N and the radius of the disc was 18cm.

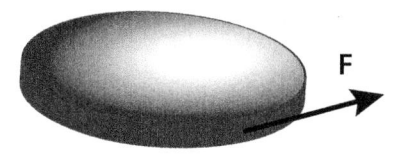

    (c) You can change the direction of the force so that no torque is applied to the disc. What two directions will do this?

    (d) So far I have not mentioned the position of the spin axis. Where did you assume it to be?

    (e) If the spin axis is through the centre and pointing at right angles to the plane of the disc, describe how you could apply a pair of forces to produce no torque.

3. Calculate the torque applied in each example below:

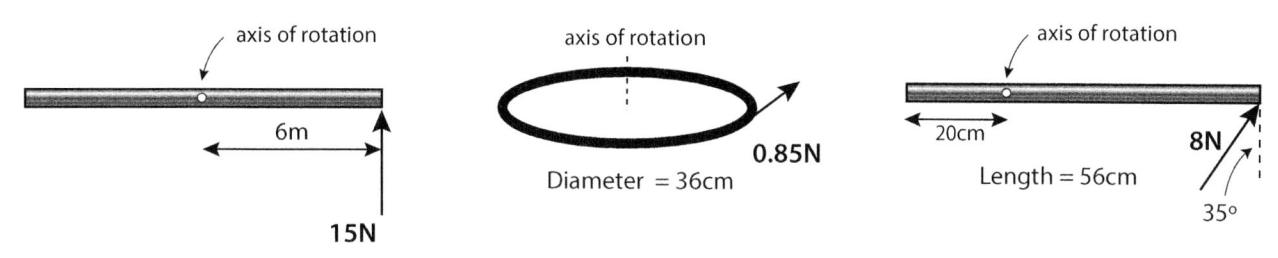

4. A torque of 1.6Nm is applied to a thin rod of length 40cm. The rod is to spin about one of its ends. What force (give the size and the direction) would you apply to the **other end** of the rod to achieve the required torque? Explain why there are in fact an infinite number of answers.

5. Calculate the resultant torque applied to the rod below. The ruler scale marks are 10cm apart. State in which direction the rod will turn.

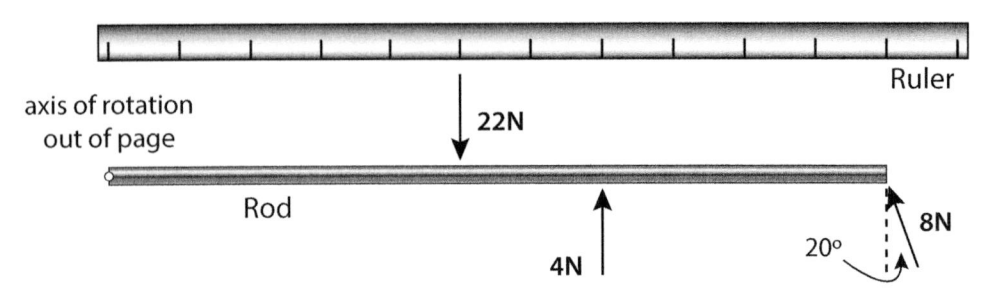

   axis of rotation out of page — 22N — Rod — 4N — 20° — 8N — Ruler

6. *"Give me a place to stand on, and I will move the Earth"*. Famously spoken by Archimedes as he imagined placing a long lever under planet Earth and lifting it up.

   (a) Okay. Place the south pole of the Earth on one end of a 'long' lever. Place your pivot exactly one Earth radius from that same end. Estimate how long the lever would be so that an average person could lift up the Earth. (You can make any whacky assumptions you like!)

   (b) Did you take g = 9.8N/kg in your calculation for part (a)? Explain why this is incorrect.

   (c) Given the possibility of a fixed pivot point, explain why a midge could have done it, and explore the complications!

7. The definition of torque uses the vector cross product: $\mathbf{T} = \mathbf{r} \wedge \mathbf{F} = |r||F|\sin\theta$ where 'θ' is the angle between the position vector r and the applied force F. (Alternative notation is: $\mathbf{T} = \mathbf{r} \times \mathbf{F}$)

   (a) What angle gives the maximum torque and what angle gives zero torque?

   (b) Calculate the angle which gives half of the maximum torque.

   (c) A cross product gives an answer which is a vector (unlike a dot product). Which direction do you think the torque will point?

Unit 1 Moment of Inertia and Torque

1. A torque (T) applied to a body of moment of inertia 'I' will produce an angular acceleration 'α' given by: $T = I\alpha$. Write down the units for each of these three quantities.

2. To use the above equation, you usually have to do separate calculations for the torque and the moment of inertia. Suppose a force of 6N is applied tangentially to one end of a thin rod of mass 0.25kg and length 30cm (diagram on right). The rod spins about its centre.

   (a) Calculate the torque applied to the rod.

   (b) Calculate the moment of inertia of the rod.

   (c) Use the equation to calculate the angular acceleration of the rod.

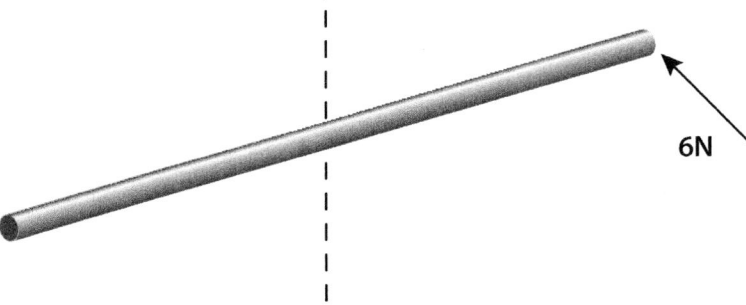

3. From rest, a thin rod of length 40cm has an angular acceleration (α) of 0.16 rad s^{-2} about its centre. Use the equations of motion to calculate:

   (a) Its angular velocity (ω) after 20 s.

   (b) Its angular displacement (θ) after 20 s.

   (c) At what time the speed (v) of its end is 0.4 m s^{-1}.

4. A disc of radius 12cm and mass 0.74kg spins about its centre with an angular velocity of 4π rad s^{-1}.

   (a) Calculate the moment of inertia of the disc.

   (b) Does the moment of inertia of the disc increase or decrease as the angular velocity increases?

   (c) The disc was brought to rest in a time of 18 seconds by applying a constant force to the rim. Calculate the size of this force assuming it was applied at a tangent to the rim.

5. A constant force of 0.5N is applied tangentially at the rim of a 28cm diameter disc. The disc has a mass of 750g.

   (a) Calculate the torque applied to the disc.

   (b) Work out the moment of inertia then use this to calculate the angular acceleration.

   (c) Starting at rest, how much time would it take to rotate 50 times?

6. What force (applied tangentially to one end) is required to accelerate a 40cm long rod of mass 350g from rest to an angular velocity of 500 rpm in 30s if it spins about the other end?

7. A solid drum in the shape of a cylinder has a mass of 240kg and a radius of 30cm. A string attached to a weight is wrapped around the drum causing the drum to rotate about its centre as shown.

   (a) How long would it take for the drum to make 3 complete turns from rest? Take the tension in the string to be equal to the weight of the 50g mass.

   (b) What hanging mass would produce an angular velocity of 4π rad s^{-1} in a time of 5 minutes from rest?

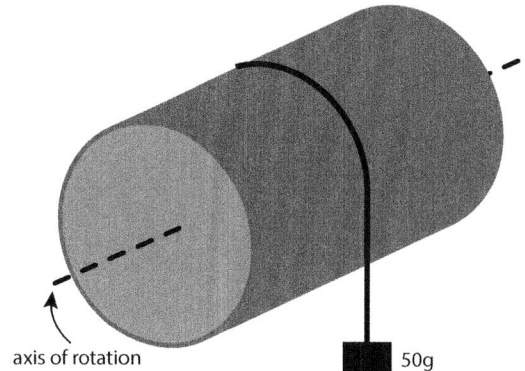

8. A metal loop formed in the shape of a rectangle has a mass of 300g. One metre length of the loop has a mass of 1.2kg and one long side has a mass of 90g.

   (a) Calculate the lengths and masses of each side.

   (b) Calculate the moment of inertia of the loop (spin axis as shown through centre)

   (c) The loop is spun to an angular velocity of 8π rad s^{-1} then released. What is the frictional torque if it comes to rest in 24s?

Unit 1 Rotational Kinetic Energy

1. An object is spinning but its centre of mass isn't going anywhere. Write down an equation for the (rotational) kinetic energy of the object in terms of its moment of inertia and angular velocity.

2. A solid disc spins about its centre as shown opposite.

   (a) Its mass is 4.5kg, it has a radius of 15cm, and it spins with an angular velocity of 18π rad s^{-1}. Calculate the rotational kinetic energy of the disc.

   (b) What effect would it have on the rotational kinetic energy if the radius was doubled and the mass stayed the same?

   (c) The disc in part (a) is sliced in half across a diameter and one part is thrown away. What effect woiuld this have on your answer? The spin axis stays in the same place as before.

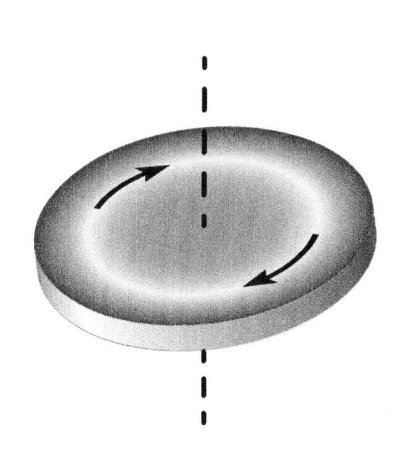

3. Calculate the rotational kinetic energy of each object in the table: (spin axis about centre)

Object	Mass	Size	Angular velocity	Rot. Kin. Energy
Thin Rod	250g	length 45cm	3 revs per second	
Hoop	1.7kg	diameter 6cm	25π rad s⁻¹	
Solid Cylinder	3.2kg	radius 2.8cm	4000rpm	
Sphere	6 × 10²⁴kg	radius 6378km	1 rev per day	

Can you identify the last object?

4. A flat disc of mass 600g and radius 5cm has an angular velocity of 12π rad s⁻¹.

    (a) Calculate its rotational kinetic energy.

    (b) How much **additional** energy is needed (all converted into kinetic energy of rotation) to increase its angular velocity to 20π rad s⁻¹?

5. A thick-walled hollow cylinder of mass 0.85kg has an inner radius of 15cm and an outer radius of 18cm. Its centre of mass is at rest and the cylinder spins about an axis through its centre. Calculate its angular velocity if its total kinetic energy is 3.8J. (See Box on page 16 for the moment of inertia).

6. Calculate the time taken for 5 complete turns if a thin rod of mass 150g and length 18cm is spun at a constant rate about one of its ends and has a rotational kinetic energy of 0.03J.

7. Electrical energy can be converted into kinetic energy by storing it in a flywheel as rotational kinetic energy. The flywheel is made of steel (density = 7800kg m⁻³). It has length 50cm and radius 20cm. Starting from rest it is spun up to an angular velocity of 25 revolutions per second.

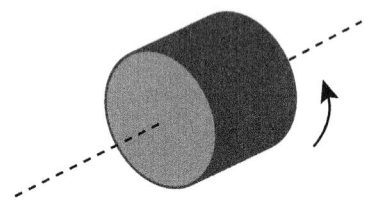

    (a) Calculate the rotational kinetic energy of the flywheel.

    (b) The electrical supply used to spin up the flywheel was 230volts at a current of 6amps. Calculate the time required to reach its final angular velocity (assume no friction and no energy loss).

    (c) Reducing the friction in the system is important. An experiment to determine the frictional torque is performed by switching off the electrical supply and timing how long it takes to come to rest. Calculate the frictional torque if it took 25minutes 18seconds to come to rest.

8. The total kinetic energy of an object is the scalar sum of its translational $E_{Trans} = \frac{1}{2}mv^2$ and rotational $E_{Rot} = \frac{1}{2}I\omega^2$ parts. Calculate the **total** kinetic energy of a cylinder rotating with a period of 0.2s and moving in a straight line with velocity 4m/s. Its mass is 350g and its radius is 2.5cm.

9. A solid cylinder of mass 3.2kg and radius 4cm is released at rest from the top of an inclined plane. It rolls down the plane to position 'A' without slipping. The centre of mass of the cylinder drops through a vertical height 'h' of 16cm.

    (a) Conservation of energy gives the equation:

    $mgh = \frac{1}{2}mv^2 + \frac{1}{2}I\omega^2$. Use the equation $v = \omega r$
    and the formula for the moment of inertia 'I'
    to derive the expression for the velocity $v = \sqrt{\frac{4}{3}gh}$.

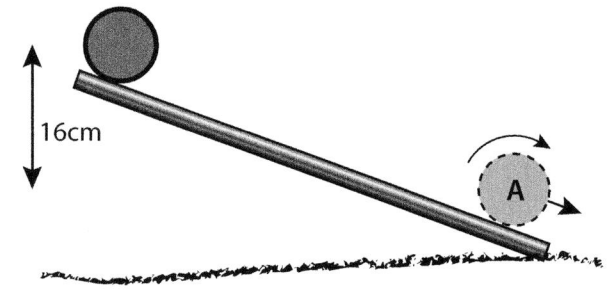

(b) Explain why the answer for the velocity in part (a) is less than the velocity of an object dropped vertically (where $v = \sqrt{2gh}$).

(c) In practice, two other forms of energy would be produced. Which one prevents the cylinder from slipping down the plane?

(d) Describe how you could experimentally test your prediction $v = \sqrt{\frac{4}{3}gh}$.

Unit 1 Angular Momentum

1. Fill in the spaces in this paragraph:

   In linear mechanics, _____ is the rate of change of momentum. Momentum is _____ in a collision if there are no external forces acting on the system. In a similar way, torque is the _____ and will be conserved in interactions where there are no _____. In linear motion, the momentum 'p' is mv. For rotational motion, mass is replaced by the _____ and velocity is replaced by the _____, so the expression for angular momentum 'L' is _____.

2. Two equations are often used to calculate angular momentum: (i) $L = I\omega$ (ii) $L = mvr$

   (a) Which one of these two equations will work for any shape and so is the best one to use?

   (b) In what circumstances can you use the other one?

   (c) What is $\frac{dL}{dt}$ in words and what special name is it given?

3. When you give an answer for the angular momentum you should specify the axis of rotation it is measured with respect to. Here is a snapshot of a point particle 'P' moving in a straight line between two axes of rotation 'A' and 'B' (axes point out of the page). It has a mass of 5kg and a speed of 4m s⁻¹.

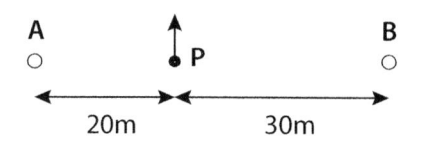

   (a) Calculate the angular momentum with respect to axis 'A' and the angular momentum with respect to axis 'B'.

   (b) Give another example of a 'relative' quantity where the answer depends on what you measure it with respect to.

4. The minute hand of a wonky old watch has a mass of 18g and a length of 3cm.

   (a) Calculate what its angular velocity should be (if it was accurate).

   (b) Its measured angular momentum was 9.39 x 10⁻⁹ kgm² s⁻¹. Starting at 12 noon what time, to the nearest second, will it indicate after one hour (of real time) has passed?

5. Calculate the angular momentum of these objects about each axis:

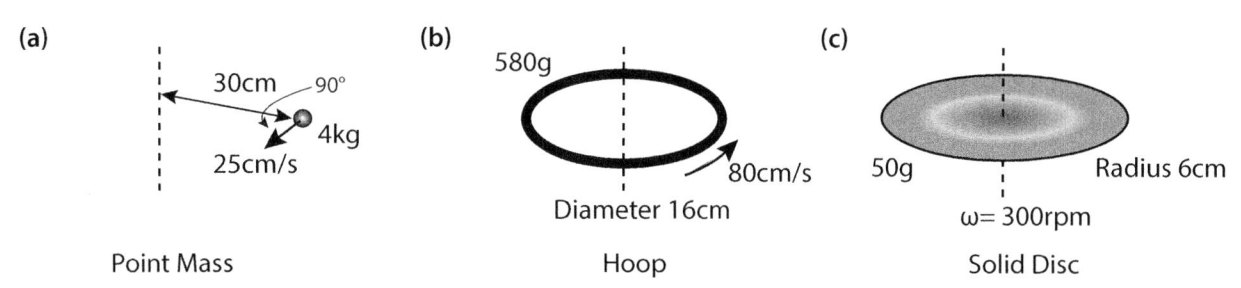

   (a) 30cm, 90°, 4kg, 25cm/s — Point Mass

   (b) 580g, 80cm/s, Diameter 16cm — Hoop

   (c) 50g, Radius 6cm, ω = 300rpm — Solid Disc

6. A common task for the astronauts on the Space Shuttle was to carry out repairs. Suppose they had the simple task of tightening a bolt with a spanner on the outside of the Shuttle. Explain why this isn't as simple as you might think, and suggest a solution.

21

7. A disc of radius 30cm. and mass 250g. rotates with an angular velocity of 45rpm. A 50g point mass is dropped vertically and caught in a light cup on the rim of the disc (physicists call it a 'collision').

    (a) Calculate the total angular momentum before the collision.

    (b) Use the conservation of angular momentum to calculate the final angular velocity (in rpm).

    (c) Calculate the total kinetic energy before and after the 'collision'. Comment on the result.

    (d) In practice, what form(s) of energy would be produced when the point mass makes contact with the disc?

8. Explain why a spinning ice skater increases her angular velocity when she brings her arms closer to her body. State any assumptions.

9. The maverick physicist Wolfgang Pauli placed a rotating flywheel in the suitcase of an unsuspecting colleague without telling him. What would his hapless colleague notice when he tried to turn a corner?

10. In linear mechanics, impulse (FΔt) is defined as the change in momentum.

    (a) Recalling how linear quantities have a correspondence with angular quantities, what combination would be defined as the change in angular momentum?

    Use it to solve the next problem.

    (b) A thin rod of mass 1.5kg and length 0.6m is spinning about an axis through its centre with an angular velocity of 2π rad s^{-1}. A constant torque of magnitude 0.03Nm is then applied for 5s. What will be the final angular velocity? Why are there two possible answers?

11. Physics cartoons are quite rare, and for good reason. Physics can be fun, but usually not funny.

    This cartoon was actually quite funny, in a postmodern sort of way, until I removed the last bit of text. But is what she claims true?

    Will it slow the Earth's rotation, and what happens when she stops? Will it give her more time to do what she wants, or is she just plain wrong?

Unit 1 Gravitation

1. $F = G\dfrac{Mm}{r^2}$ is the gravitational force of attraction between two masses 'M' and 'm', a distance 'r' apart. Use values from the data page at the back of this book to calculate:

    (a) The force between point masses of 60kg. and 70kg. which are 50cm. apart.

    (b) The force between planet Earth and the Moon.

    (c) The gravitational force between a proton and an electron in a hydrogen atom.

2. Two identical point masses 20km apart have a gravitational force of attraction of 5000N. Calculate the mass of one of them.

3. If you worked out $F = G\dfrac{Mm}{r^2}$ with 'M' the mass of planet Earth, 'm' your mass and 'r' the radius of the Earth, what would be the answer in words?

4. The Earth travels around the Sun in a circle (really an ellipse). The centripetal force responsible for this is $F = \dfrac{mv^2}{r} = m\omega^2 r$ and is supplied by the force of gravity: $F = G\dfrac{Mm}{r^2}$.

   (a) Derive Kepler's 3rd Law $T^2 = \left(\dfrac{4\pi^2}{GM}\right)r^3$ from these two equations.

   (b) If a new planet was discovered in our Solar System at a distance of 4 times the Earth's distance to the sun, what would be its period?

   (c) Through a telescope, you observe one of the moons of Jupiter. You measure the time for one orbit and its distance from the centre of Jupiter. Using Kepler's 3rd Law, what can you deduce about Jupiter.

5. The table below shows data on the eight planets of our Solar System.

Planet	Mercury	Venus	Earth	Mars	Jupiter	Saturn	Uranus	Neptune
Period 'T'	0.24	0.62	1.0	1.88	11.86	29.46	84.01	164.79
Distance from Sun 'r'	0.3871	0.7233	1.0	1.524	5.203	9.539	19.19	30.06
T²/r³								

   (a) What must be the units for the period 'T' and for the distance 'r'? Explain your reasoning.

   (b) Calculate and complete the last row. Deduce a conclusion from your result.

   (c) Evaluate T²/r³ for the Earth **in S.I. units** then use Kepler's 3rd Law to calculate the mass of the Sun.

6. The gravitational field strength on Earth is 9.8Nkg⁻¹. Use the equation $g = \dfrac{GM}{r^2}$ to calculate the gravitational field strength at the surface of these planets (refer to the data page at the front).

Planet	Mercury	Mars	Jupiter	Neptune
Mass (kg)				
Radius (m)				
'g' (m/s²)				

7. If you move around in a gravitational field, it's useful to be able to calculate the energy required. This is where the gravitational potential $V = -\dfrac{GM}{r}$ comes in. This example shows its usefulness.

   (a) Calculate the gravitational potential at a distance of 2 x 10⁷m from the centre of the Earth.

   (b) Calculate the gravitational potential at a distance of 5 x 10⁷m from the centre of the Earth.

   (c) Subtract answer (a) from answer (b) (the 'gravitational potential **difference**').

   (d) To calculate the energy required to move a 4kg mass from 2 x 10⁷m to 5 x 10⁷m from the Earth, just multiply the gravitational potential difference by 4kg. Calculate it.

8. Calculate the energy required to lift a 25kg mass from the surface of the Earth to a distance of 1.7 x 10⁷m from the centre of the Earth. Use the same procedure from Q(7).

9. (a) In what circumstances can you use the formula $E = mgh$ as a quick and accurate alternative to the procedure in Q's (7) and (8)?

   (b) Show that the difference in gravitational potential energy $\left(-\dfrac{GMm}{r_2}\right) - \left(-\dfrac{GMm}{r_1}\right)$ between two places at distances r_1 and r_2 ($>r_1$) from the centre of the Earth, reduces to mgh where the height 'h' is expressed as $h = (r_2 - r_1)$ and is small compared with distances r_1 or r_2.

10. Gravitational potential is a scalar quantity. Calculate the gravitational potential at point 'P' due to the two masses M_1 and M_2.

    $M_1 = 5 \times 10^{20}$ kg

    $M_2 = 1.4 \times 10^{21}$ kg

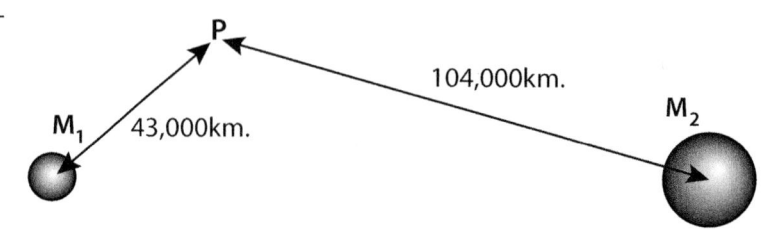

11. The formula for the gravitational potential $V = -\dfrac{GM}{r}$ depends upon the distance 'r' from the centre of the mass 'M'.

    (a) What is the name of the surface where all points on it have the same gravitational potential?

    (b) What shape would it be for a point mass?

    (c) Referring to the diagram, explain why it takes the same energy to go from 'B' to 'A' as it does to go from 'C' to 'A'.

12. (a) Where is gravitational potential 'V' usually chosen to be zero?

    (b) What is the definition of the gravitational potential at a point 'P' due to a point mass 'M'?

    (c) Distinguish between gravitational potential and gravitational potential energy.

13. Thrown with enough speed, a mass 'm' will escape from a planet (mass 'M' and radius 'r'). The expression for this is: $v = \sqrt{\dfrac{2GM}{r}}$ and is called the Escape Velocity.

    (a) The mass which is thrown isn't in the equation. What does this imply?

    (b) Calculate the escape velocity from the surface of planet Earth.

14. Two planets have the same radius. The escape velocity from the surface of one planet is four times the escape velocity from the other. How do the masses of the planets compare with each other?

15. Show that the escape velocity can also be expressed as $v = \sqrt{2gr}$ where 'g' is the gravitational field strength at distance 'r' from the centre of the mass.

16. A spherical asteroid has a radius of 8km and an average density of 5200kg m⁻³.

    (a) Calculate its mass.

    (b) Show by calculation whether or not a rock launched at 15m s⁻¹ will escape the asteroid.

    (c) Derive the expression $v_{esc} = \sqrt{\dfrac{8\pi\rho Gr^2}{3}}$ for the escape velocity where 'ρ' is the density.

    (d) Use this equation to calculate the radius of an asteroid (of density 5200kg m⁻³) which you could escape from by pushing yourself upwards (estimate your own launch velocity).

17. An artificial satellite orbits the Earth with a radius of 6.85×10^7 m.

  (a) Equate the gravitational force with the centripetal force to calculate the period of the satellite.

  (b) Calculate the speed of the satellite in orbit.

  (c) The satellite has a mass of 1500kg. Calculate its kinetic energy.

  (d) Determine the relationship between the kinetic energy of the satellite and the work done by external forces in bringing the satellite from infinity to that point in its orbit (at rest).

18. The graph below shows a plot of the gravitational potential due to two masses, against distance, along a straight line going through the centre of each mass.

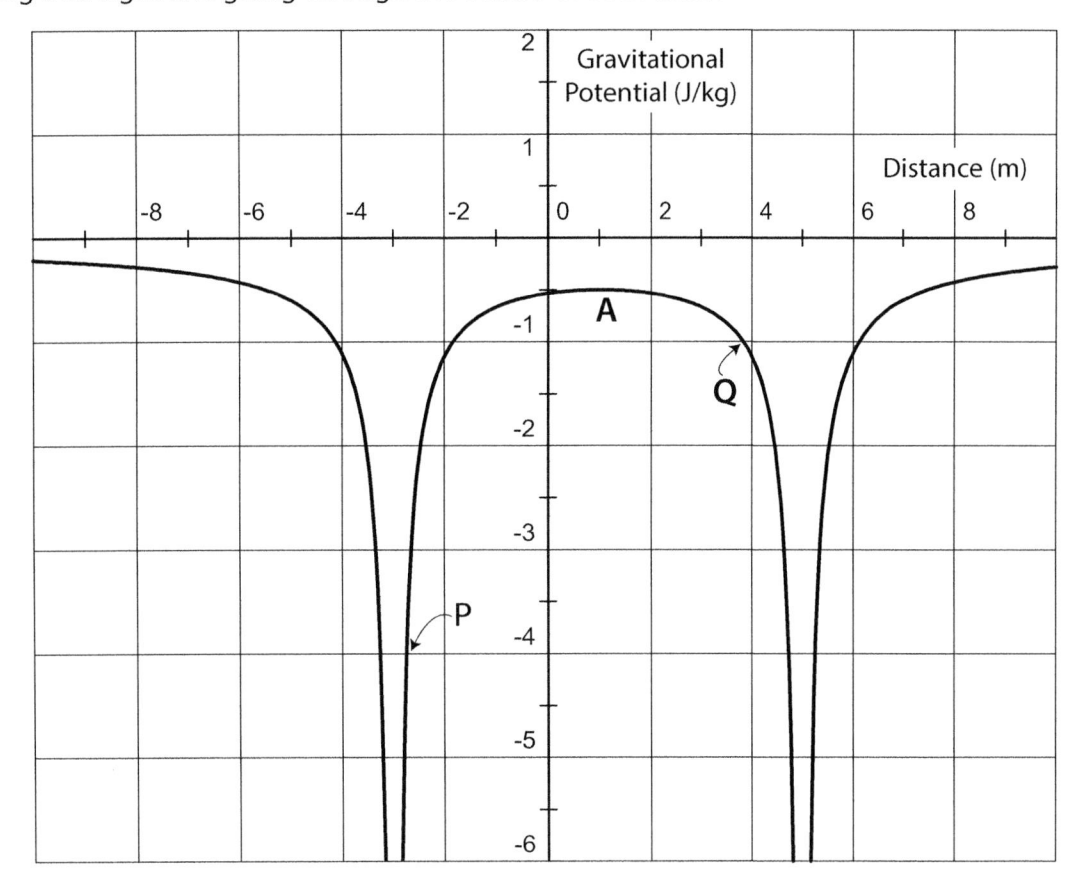

  (a) How far apart are the two masses?

  (b) Write down the gravitational potential at points 'P' and 'Q'.

  (c) Estimate the position and the gravitational potential of point 'A' (the turning point).

  (d) A journey is planned from 'P' to 'Q'. Is this possible without passing through a point with a gravitational potential at least as high as at 'A'?

  (e) A 5kg mass is to be moved from point 'P' to point 'Q'. Usually you would take the gravitational potential difference and multiply it by the mass to calculate the energy required. Explain with the aid of calculations, why this situation is more complicated.

  (f) Tricky question. Can you locate the turning point 'A' between the Earth and the Moon (neglecting all other bodies)?

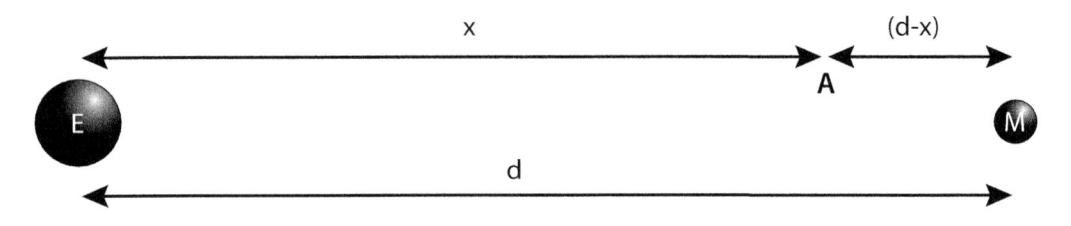

19. The escape velocity from the surface of a particular planet is 4180m s⁻¹. Explain whether you have to launch the projectile **vertically** at 4180m s⁻¹ or if you can you launch it at that speed at any angle? Consider the cases of planets with or without atmospheres.

20. Many different sports have been invented and developed on planet Earth. From skiing to darts, from golf to badminton, from rock climbing to football. They all take place in an environment where the gravitational field strength is about 10Nkg⁻¹. Now imagine a planet where 'g' is less (like 3Nkg⁻¹), or much more (like 25Nkg⁻¹). What difference would it make to these sports? Would new sports become possible? Explore the possibilities, backing up your argument with any appropriate relationships or calculations.

Unit 1 Space & Time

1. BS Bob tries to impress his friend Walter with a number of statements on Relativity. But Walter is good at physics. How should he reply to each of BS Bob's assertions below?

    (a) An inertial reference frame is one which resists motion.

    (b) Nothing can go faster than the speed of light.

    (c) Relativity says that space and time are the same thing.

    (d) A lightyear is the time taken for light to orbit the Sun at the distance of planet Earth.

    (e) An inertial observer shouldn't calculate accelerations; you need General Relativity for that.

    (f) Special Relativity is called 'special' because it only applies to observers making measurements in special frames of reference (ones moving at constant velocity).

2. A scientist observes the motion of a fast moving object and plots the readings of position 'x' at time 't' on a spacetime diagram. His diagram is one in which the motion of a pulse of light in a vacuum is shown by a straight line at 45° to the horizontal (space) axis.

    (a) Describe the units chosen on both axes.

    (b) The motion of the fast moving object was plotted as a straight line at an angle of 20° to the vertical (time) axis. Calculate its speed.

    (c) Which area of the diagram cannot contain any data points and for what reason.

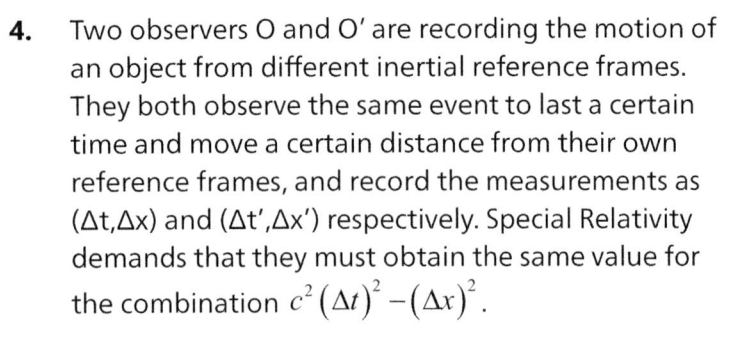

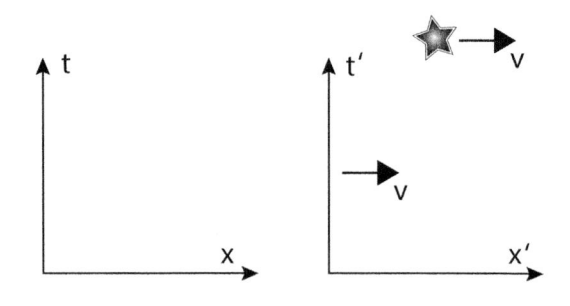

3. Spacetime diagrams are used to plot 'geodesics' and 'worldlines'. Describe what these are, pointing out the difference between them.

4. Two observers O and O' are recording the motion of an object from different inertial reference frames. They both observe the same event to last a certain time and move a certain distance from their own reference frames, and record the measurements as (Δt,Δx) and (Δt',Δx') respectively. Special Relativity demands that they must obtain the same value for the combination $c^2(\Delta t)^2 - (\Delta x)^2$.

    (a) Observer O recorded the event to last for a time of Δt = 5.2s and for its distance from him to increase by Δx = 1.3×10⁹m. The other observer O' was travelling at the same velocity as the object. Calculate the time he recorded for its duration Δt'.

    (b) Calculate the speed of observer O relative to the object.

5. There are two ways of defining the concept of weight. One way is the reading on the scales (like you standing on them), and the other is to get the mass and use the equation W = mg. Explain the differences in these two definitions in these situations:

    (a) An astronaut in the International Space Station.   (b) You waiting for a bus in Princes St.

6. Here are the rules for constructing the grid on a sheet of graph paper:

    1. lines which cross other lines do so at 90°
    2. lines are equally spaced apart

    (a) What assumption must you include for this procedure to produce the expected, familiar grid?

    (b) Which rule has to be dropped for the procedure to be carried out on the surface of a sphere?

7. In 1919, an expedition was sent out under the leadership of Sir Arthur Eddington to measure the effect of the Sun on the observed positions of background stars. The diagram below left shows the configuration of stars near the Sun during the measurements.

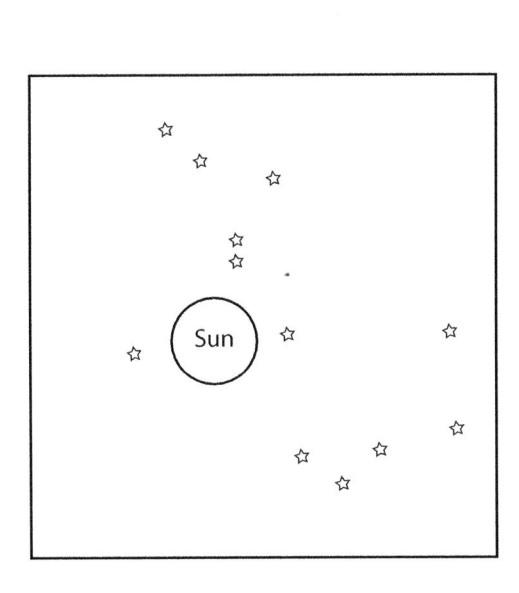

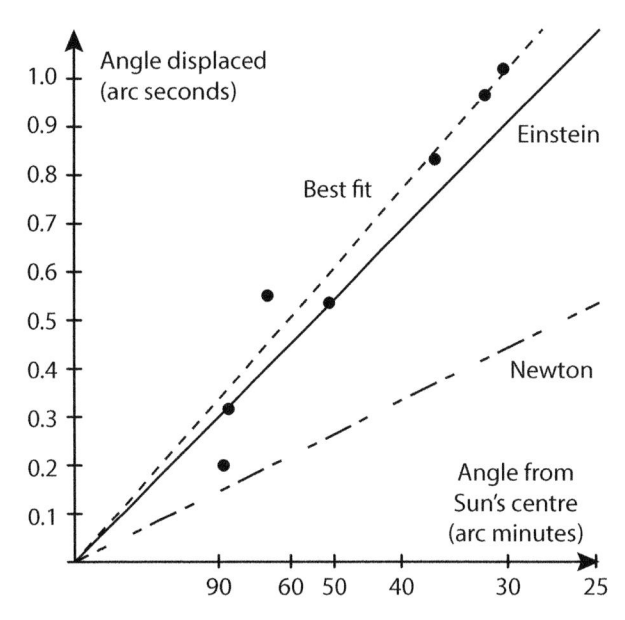

    (a) What effect was the expedition trying to confirm/refute?

    (b) Describe how the positions of the stars were affected by the Sun.

    (c) The Sun is very bright and you can't see stars in the sky during daytime. Describe how you could measure the shift in their positions.

    (d) The results of the expedition produced the results shown on the graph above right. Draw a conclusion from the graph and speculate on why they drew the 'x' axis reversed with a non-linear scale.

8. (a) What is an Einstein Ring and how is it formed?

    (b) The Einstein Ring FOR_J0332-3557 shown below, subtends an angular radius from Earth of 1.48 arc-seconds. Calculate the diameter of the Ring at the distance of the lensing galaxy if its redshift indicates a distance of 7 billion lightyears. State any assumptions.

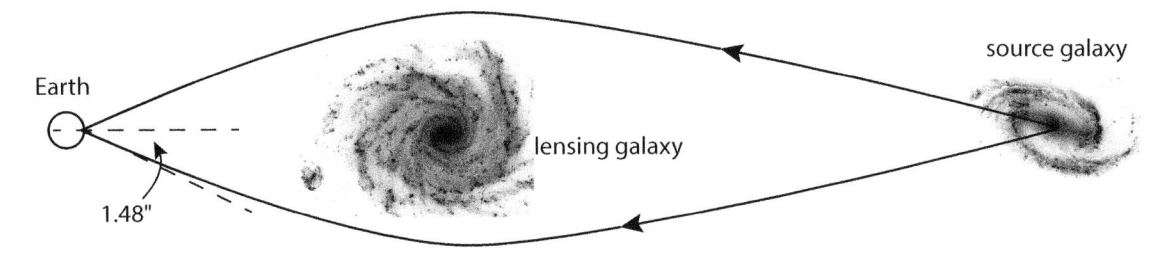

9. (a) Describe what is meant by 'precession' of the orbit of a planet.

    (b) As viewed from distant stars, the major axis of the orbit of planet Mercury precesses by 0.1595 degrees per century. How much time does it take for Mercury's orbit to return to its original orientation with respect to the distant stars?

    (c) How many orbits does Mercury make around the Sun in returning to its original orientation?

10. A pulsar is a neutron star rotating with a high angular velocity. One particular pulsar has a diameter of 12km and flashes with a frequency of 44Hz. By calculation, show whether any part of its surface moves at 'relativistic speeds'.

11. A ray of monochromatic light of wavelength 656nm is emitted from the surface of a star of mass $2.7M_{Sun}$ and radius $0.8R_{Sun}$.

    (a) Calculate the gravitational potential of a point on the surface of the star.

    (b) Explain what is meant by gravitational red shift.

    (c) Light emitted from the star with frequency 'f' changes by an amount Δf given by: $\Delta f = -f \dfrac{\Delta \varphi}{c^2}$

    due to the gravitational red shift. The quantity Δφ is the gravitational potential difference between the emission and detection points, and 'c' is the speed of light in a vacuum. Calculate the change in frequency, and hence the **change in wavelength**, of the light from the star when the ray is at 'infinity'.

12. Fill in the missing words and phrases in this passage:

    The beginning of the Universe is known as the _____ and occurred _____ billion years ago. Since then, _____ has been expanding and the _____ of the universe has been decreasing as matter gets more spread out. Einstein's _____ Theory of Relativity describes physics as viewed from inertial _____ of reference. One of its assumptions is that the _____ of light is _____. In 1915, he published his _____ Theory of Relativity which concerns _____ fields. A central assumption is the _____ Principle which compares the force of _____ with the effect of being accelerated. An expedition was sent out in 1919 to measure the _____ of starlight during a solar _____. The results _____ Einstein's theories. Another test was the _____ of the orbit of planet _____. This is where the _____ of the elliptical orbit changes position with respect to the _____. The effect is _____ and _____ to measure, but the results _____ his theories. Einstein died in the year _____.

13. The Global Positioning System uses a number of satellites with a period of 12 hours.

    (a) Use Kepler's 3RD Law to calculate the radius of the satellite's orbit around the Earth.

    (b) Calculate the minimum and maximum times for a signal travelling at the speed of light to go from a satellite to the surface (refer to the diagram).

    (c) Describe why the effects of Special Relativity and General Relativity have to be taken into account in locating receivers on Earth.

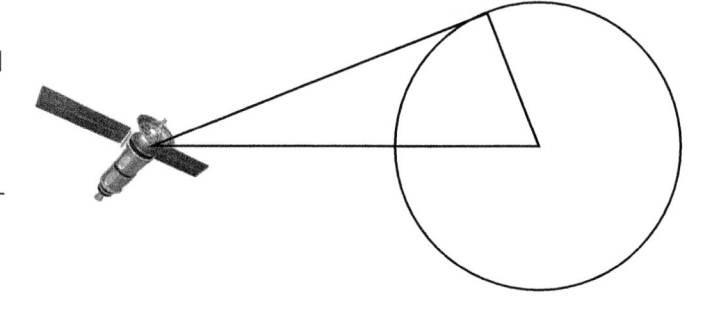

    (d) Describe how the effects of Special and General Relativity would be affected if the satellites were in geostationary orbit.

14. The bending of light by the Sun is correctly predicted by the General Theory of Relativity. This problem shows how Newtonian physics would attempt an explanation. Just like the Earth, the Sun has a gravitational field strength 'g'. Suppose that light, like everything else, accelerated in this gravitational field with acceleration 'g' towards the centre of the Sun. Let's keep the maths simple. Assume that the pulse of light is only accelerated between the dotted lines 'A' to 'B'. Also assume that the acceleration is not towards the Sun's centre, but always downwards towards the bottom of this page (so it's like a projectile problem on Earth). We can work out the bending angle 'θ'.

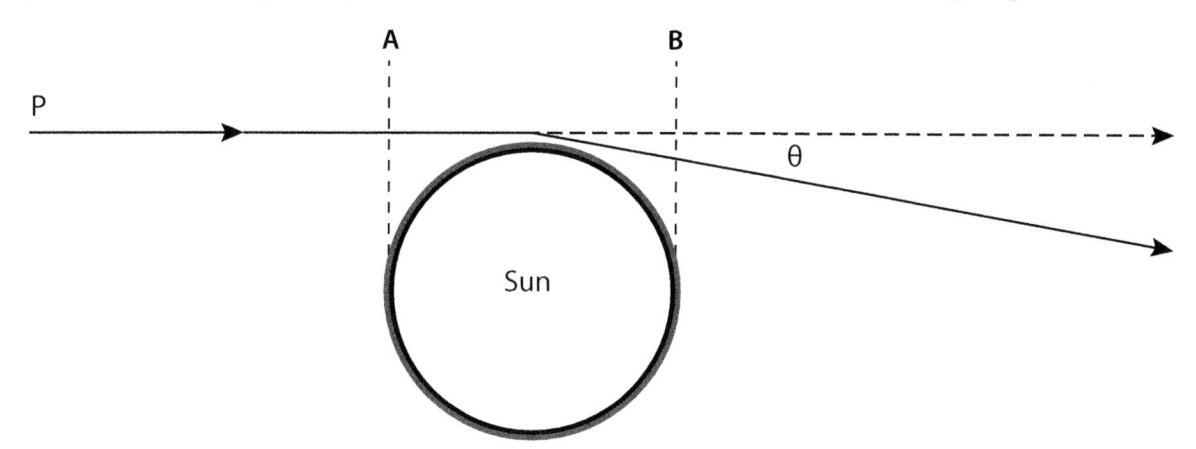

    (a) At the speed of light, calculate the time taken for the light pulse to travel between the dotted lines 'A' to 'B'.

    (b) Calculate the gravitational field strength 'g' at the surface of the Sun.

    (c) Calculate the vertical component of the velocity when it passes the dotted line 'B'.

    (d) Use the horizontal and vertical components of the velocity to calculate the angle 'θ'.

    (e) The correct (measured) value is 1.75 arc-seconds (=0.000486 degrees). Comment on the accuracy of your result and on your assumptions.

15. The idea of a 'Black Hole' was first proposed by John Michell in 1784 (he called it a 'dark star'), using concepts from Newtonian physics. The total energy (that's kinetic plus potential energy) is conserved when an object of mass 'm' comes from infinity towards an object of mass 'M'.

    (a) Expressed in symbols, the conservation of total energy is: $0+0 = \frac{1}{2}mv^2 + \left(-\frac{GMm}{r}\right)$

    What do the zeroes on the left hand side represent?

    (b) Use the equation to derive an expression for the velocity at any distance 'r' from the mass 'M'.

    (c) At what distance does the velocity become equal to the speed of light? What name is given to this distance when its also the radius of a star?

    (d) Calculate this radius for a star of mass $4M_{Sun}$.

16. The centre of our Galaxy contains a Black Hole of mass 4.1×10^6 M_{Sun}. Calculate its radius and compare your answer to the scale of our Solar System.

17. A spherical Black Hole of radius 'r' and mass 'M' has an average density of $\rho = M/V$.

    (a) Deduce the relationship between the Black Hole radius and its density.

    (b) The average density of the universe is about 10^{-26} kg m^{-3} and its radius is 1.3×10^{26} m. Show by calculation if the universe is itself a Black Hole!

18. If interstellar travel becomes possible, describe how future spacecraft can detect and avoid collision with Black Holes in their path.

Unit 1 Stellar Physics

1. Let's start with some astronomy. Fill in the missing words.

   Our _____ is the nearest star and was created about _____ years ago. It's light takes about __ minutes to reach Earth. The energy it produces comes from _____ reactions deep within its _____ . Stars come in many sizes and colours. Hotter stars are _____ in colour. They burn their fuel at a _____ rate and so are_____ lived. Stars known as ____ giants, are cooler and can have a_____ as large as the orbit of Planet Mars. When their supply of fuel is_____, they _____ down over a long period of _____ and are known as red_____. If the mass is _____ enough, the force of _____ can collapse the star into a very _____ state called a _____ _____. With some stars, the force of gravity is so great that it ends its existence as a_____ _____ where not even _____ can escape.

   Our _____ contains over 100 billion stars and is in the shape of a disc about_____ lightyears in diameter. On average, a _____ explosion is seen once every 100 years by humans on Earth. This is where a star explodes and emits large quantities of_____ and _____. The brightest one in recorded history was in the year 1006AD with a_____ of -7.5. Fortunately for us, the ____ will not suffer the same fate.

2. The electromagnetic radiation from the Sun hits the top of Earth's atmosphere with a distribution of wavelengths close to that of a black body spectrum. The maximum power output is at a wavelength of about 525nm. Calculate the energy of a single photon of that wavelength.

3. At the distance of the Earth from the Sun, an area of 1m² held facing the Sun above the atmosphere would receive a power of 1380Watts from all wavelengths. Calculate the total power output of the Sun. The distance from Sun to Earth is 1.49×10^{11}m and the surface area of a sphere is $4\pi r^2$.

4. Mars is further away from the Sun than the Earth. Calculate the power received on a 1m² area held up on Mars and facing the Sun. Assume the atmosphere on Mars is negligible.

5. (a) Use the Stefan-Boltzmann Law to calculate the energy emitted per second from a 1m² surface of each of these stars in the table below. State any assumptions you make.

Star name	Antares	Wolf 359	Tau Ceti	Xi Persei
Surface temperature (K)	3400	2800	5340	35000
Power emitted per square metre (Wm⁻²)				

   (b) Explain why stars with a higher temperature have shorter lifespans.

6. Calculate the surface area of the Sun.

7. The star Rigel in the constellation of Orion has a radius of 74R_{Sun} and a temperature of 12130K.

   (a) Calculate its total surface area.

   (b) Use the Stefan-Boltzmann Law to calculate its power output per square metre. State any assumptions.

   (c) Calculate its luminosity.

   (d) What effect would it have on the luminosity if Rigel was at twice the distance from Earth?

8. The 'apparent brightness' of a star as viewed by an observer is given by $b = \dfrac{L}{4\pi r^2}$, where 'L' is the luminosity and 'r' is its distance from the observer.

   (a) Of the three quantities in the expression, which of these is a property of the star and which of these are observer dependent?

   (b) What units is 'apparent brightness' measured in?

   (c) In words, express the relationship between the apparent brightness and the distance of the observer. State any assumptions you've made and comment on their validity in normal circumstances.

   (c) Calculate the apparent brightness 'b' of the Sun as viewed from Earth.

9. Planet Jupiter is 5.20 A.U. from the Sun. Calculate the luminosity and the apparent brightness of the Sun as viewed from Jupiter.

10. Alcyone is the brightest star in an open cluster known as the Pleiades. It has a surface temperature of 12750K and a radius of $8.2 R_{Sun}$.

    (a) Calculate its luminosity.

    (b) Alcyone is at a distance of 370 lightyears from Earth. Calculate its apparent brightness as seen from Earth.

    (c) How far **towards** Alcyone would we have to travel in a spaceship before its apparent brightness doubled?

11. Astronomers use a system known as 'absolute magnitude' and 'apparent magnitude' to describe the brightness of the stars in the sky (that's 'brightness' with its common meaning).

    (a) The absolute magnitude is always measured at a standard distance. What is that distance?

    (b) At what distance will the absolute and apparent magnitudes be the same?

    (c) The luminosity of a star includes radiation emitted by all wavelengths, visible and non-visible. The apparent brightness 'b' is related to the luminosity. State two reasons why amateur astronomers would prefer the magnitude system rather than the apparent brightness system.

12. The brightnesses of stars spans a very wide range, so the magnitude system isn't a linear scale ie. a star of magnitude 6 isn't twice as bright as one of magnitude 3. It was chosen to be a power law, such that two stars with a difference in magnitude of 5, have a brightness ratio of one hundred. Calculate the brightness ratio if two stars differ in magnitude by 10.

13. Absolute magnitude M_{ABS} and apparent magnitude M_{APP} are related by: $M_{ABS} = M_{APP} + 5 - 5\log_{10} d$, where a star of apparent magnitude M_{APP} is observed from a distance of 'd' parsecs.

    (a) Calculate the absolute magnitude of a star viewed from Earth with an apparent magnitude of 8.2 if it is at a distance of 15 parsecs.

    (b) What would be the magnitude of the Sun seen from a distance of 32.6 lightyears if its magnitude from Earth is -26.7?

14. Remind me why stars with higher surface temperatures have shorter lifetimes.

15. The Hertzsprung-Russell diagram is used to classify stars and indicate their development:

    (a) What quantities would be plotted on the 'x' and 'y' axes?

    (b) Describe the main features of the distribution of stars on the plot.

    (c) Outline the progression on the Hertzsprung-Russell diagram, of an average star as it ages.

16. (a) The highly ionised atoms in the outer layers of a star, and the particles in the core move around with high speed. What source provides the energy to do this?

    (b) Our Sun is currently losing mass at a rate of 4.26×10^9 kg per second. Use Einstein's equation to calculate the energy radiated into space. What did we call this quantity in previous questions?

    (c) What happens to a star once its energy source is exhausted?

17. Before any stars started to form, the Big Bang produced about 32 protons for every 4 neutrons.

    (a) How many helium-4 nuclei can be made from that number of particles?

    (b) How many protons are left over?

    (c) Before the formation of stars, what would have been the ratio of the mass of hydrogen to helium in the universe?

    (d) What happens to this ratio in the cores of stars?

18. The basic proton-proton reaction in stars is:

    $$^1_1H + ^1_1H \rightarrow ^2_1H + e^+ + \nu_e$$

    (a) Identify the three particles on the right hand side of the equation.

    (b) This table shows the mass of each particle:

^1_1H	^2_1H	e^+	ν_e
1.67262×10^{-27}	3.34358×10^{-27}	9.1094×10^{-31}	≈ 0

    Use Einstein's equation to calculate the energy released per reaction. Give your answer in joules and also in MeV.

    (c) The e^+ particle then takes part in this reaction:

    $$e^+ + e^- \rightarrow 2\gamma$$

    Identify the other two particles.

    (d) The e^+ and the γ have different histories after the reactions. Briefly describe their stories.

19. (a) The helium nucleus ^4_2He is a essential ingredient on the way to creating heavier elements. Describe how it is built from the lighter elements through nuclear reactions.

    (b) Describe the process by which the carbon isotope $^{12}_6C$ is produced through nuclear reactions.

20. (a) How many different types of neutrino are there and what are they called?

    (b) The Sun only produces one of these types yet detectors on Earth have detected two of the types of neutrino from the Sun. Describe what has happened and what astrophysics problem this solved.

21. (a) Planet Earth contains many elements, some much heavier than those created in the Sun. Describe how the heavier elements like copper and lead ended up on our planet.

    (b) Why did the first stars not contain any of the heaviest elements like lead? Describe what effect this had on these early stars

22. Describe how the mass of a star determines its ultimate fate, either as a brown dwarf, a white dwarf, a neutron star or as a Black Hole.

Unit 2 Quantum Theory

Where units have not been given for a quantity, assume that they are in S.I. units.

1. Wise people regard problems as opportunities............ Fill in the missing words:

   Classical physics assumes that ____ is flat and that time has no _____ and will continue on to _____. There are no restrictions on the _____ of physical quantities. These assumptions give _____ results for many applications of physics, like f____ in bridges or the cooling in a kitchen _____. By the end of the _____ century, problems became apparent.

   The problem was the _____ of radiation from an ideal radiator called a _____. Classical Theory could not _____ the correct emission for _____ wavelengths. This is known as the _____ _____. The physicist Max _____ tried a new approach and assumed that the objects emitting the _____ could only have _____ energy values. This was the birth of _____ Theory.

2. (a) Sketch the shape of the radiation spectrum emitted by a black-body. Plot the intensity on the y-axis and the wavelength along the x-axis.

   (b) The position of the peak is given by Wien's Displacement Law:

   $$\lambda_{Max} T = 2.9 \times 10^{-3} \, \text{m K}$$

   Calculate the wavelength of the most intense radiation emitted if the black-body is at a temperature of 5800K.

   (c) The Sun has a surface temperature of roughly 5800K. Your answer to part (b) above, should be in the green region of the electromagnetic spectrum. Explain why the Sun isn't green.

   (d) Explain the meaning of the term 'black-body' (and we need more than just 'black').

3. Calculate the energy of a photon of wavelength 1200nm.

4. The graph below shows the electromagnetic radiation which hits the top of Earth's atmosphere and the em. radiation which reaches ground level. A perfect black-body spectrum for a radiator at a temperature of 5800K is superimposed for comparison. The y-axis shows the power per square metre collected over a range of wavelengths of 1μm. For example, if a power of 12Watts (=0.012kW) had been collected on a 1m² surface between wavelengths 560nm to 570nm (a range of 0.01μm), a point would be plotted at (0.565μm, 1.2kW m⁻² μm⁻¹).

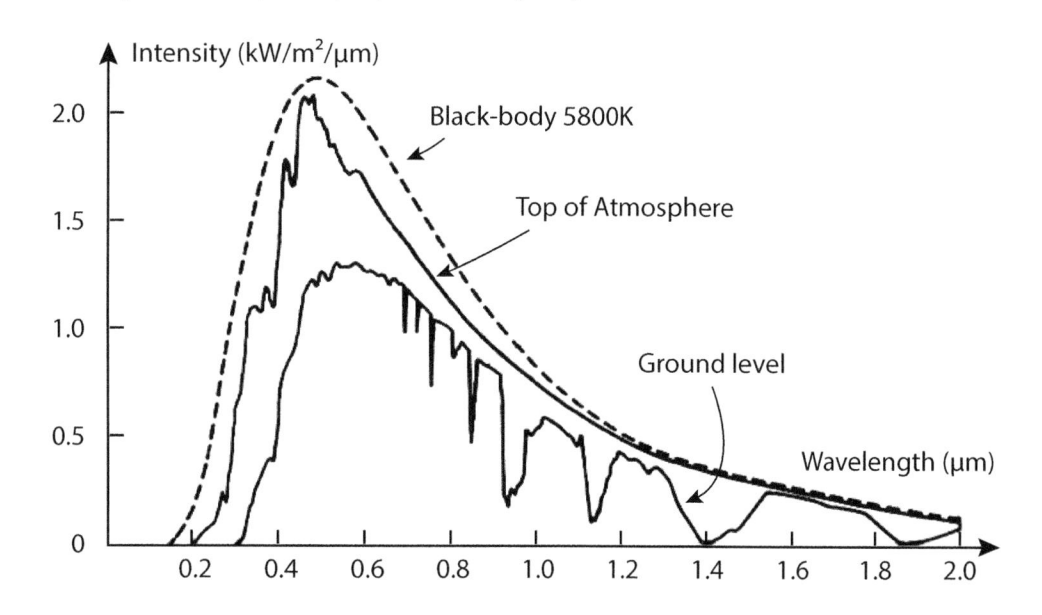

(a) Why was a temperature of 5800K the appropriate one for comparison?

(b) What would the area under a section of graph represent?

(c) Why do you think the graph of the electromagnetic radiation reaching ground level is much more 'spikey' than the one for the top of the atmosphere?

(d) Compare the positions of the peaks for the top of the atmosphere and for ground level. What difference (if any) would the human eye notice?

(e) What difference does the atmosphere make to us humans on ground level for:

   (i) the ultraviolet region

   (ii) the visible region

   (iii) the infrared region

(f) Consider the area under the solid (top of the atmosphere) line. Deform it into a rectangle then estimate its area in W/m². Compare your answer to Q3 on page 30.

(g) From the graph, estimate the power received on a one square meter surface held facing the Sun at ground level on a day with clear blue sky, between the wavelengths 1200nm to 1205nm.

5. (a) Our lives are controlled by Classical Physics. Explain why Quantum Physics doesn't make itself obvious in everyday life.

   (b) If you wanted everyday life to be a quantum experience, what physical parameter would you tweak?

6. In 1916, R.A. Millikan performed an experiment on what's known as the 'Photoelectric Effect'. Describe its contribution to the development of Quantum Theory and why it was important to Albert Einstein.

7. The photoelectric effect occurs where photons collide with a surface and eject electrons. In the diagram, the UV photons enter an evacuated tube through a quartz window at one end.

   (a) Why is the glass tube evacuated?

   (b) The monochromatic photons have a wavelength of 380nm. Use $E = hf$ to calculate the energy in units of eV, for a single photon.

   (c) The photons strike the zinc plate and eject electrons. These electrons are collected by plate 'P' and a current is set up in the circuit. Explain how you could adjust the supply voltage at the bottom of the diagram, to obtain a zero reading on the ammeter.

   (d) A voltage of 0.22volts stops the current flowing. Calculate the speed of an electron as it leaves the zinc plate.

   (e) Use Einstein's Photoelectric equation: $hf = W_o + \frac{1}{2}mv^2$ to calculate the work function (W_o) for zinc.

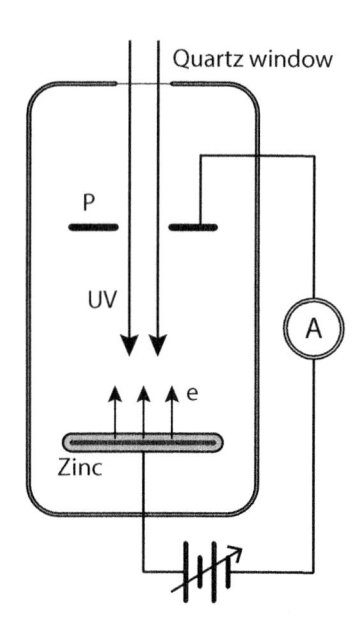

8. Classical Physics and Quantum Physics make different predictions for the photoelectric effect. A certain amount of energy must be given to an electron to knock it out from the zinc metal.

   (a) From the viewpoint of Quantum Theory, what physical variable of the radiation would be changed to eject an electron from the zinc? Describe what Quantum Theory predicts.

   (b) According to Classical Theory, what aspect of the radiation would you change to eject an electron from the zinc? Describe what Classical Theory predicts.

9. An electron travelling at a speed of 8.6×10^5 m/s enters a uniform electric field and is brought to rest. Calculate the potential difference required.

10. Refer to the diagram in question 7. Each electron is ejected from the zinc with a kinetic energy E_K. The variable voltage supply is adjusted until no current registers on the ammeter. The voltage required was V_s.

   (a) Rewrite the equation $hf = W_o + \frac{1}{2}mv^2$ so that it contains the voltage V_s (it's called the stopping potential) and the charge on the electron 'e'.

   This is a plot of frequency 'f' against stopping potential V_s: Notice the location of the origin.

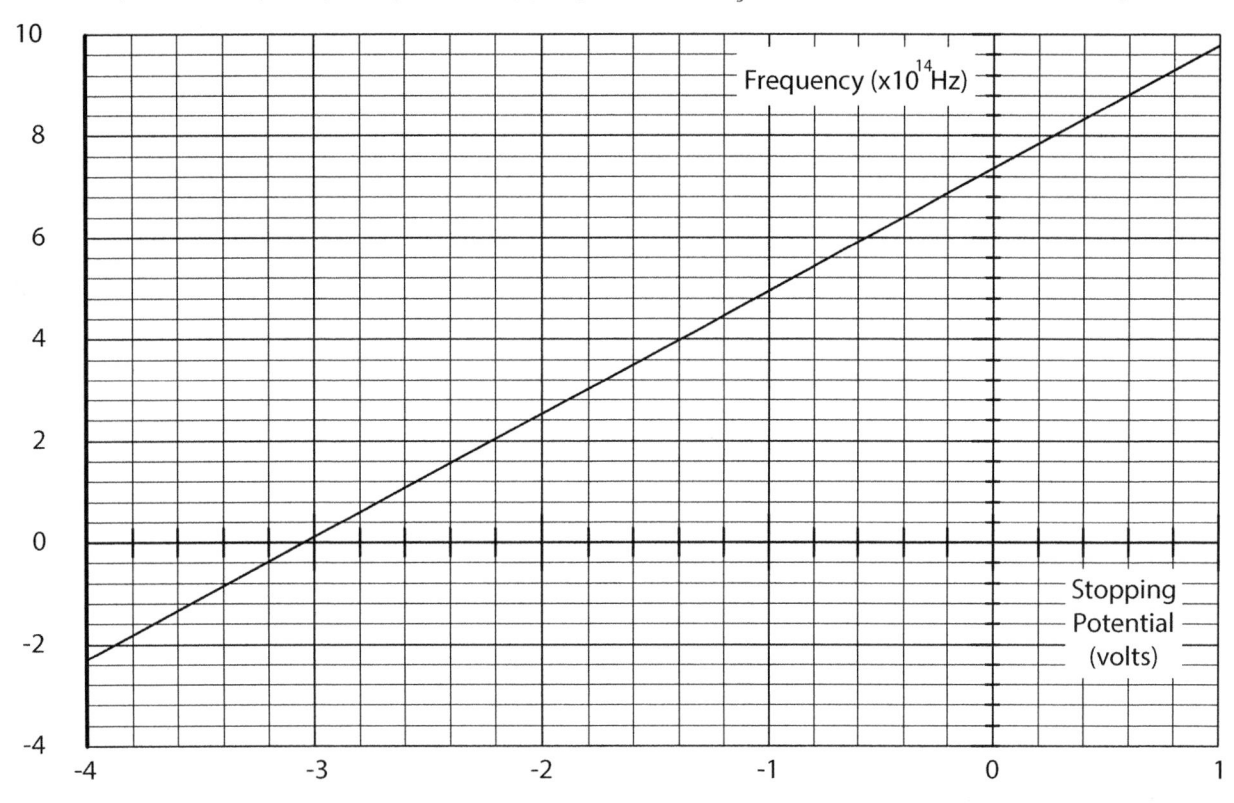

   (b) From your answer to part (a) above, show that the gradient of the graph is $\frac{e}{h}$ and that the intercept on the y-axis is $\frac{W_o}{h}$.

   (c) Measure the gradient and intercept of the graph line.

   (d) When Millikan performed this experiment in 1916, the charge on the electron was know to be 1.6×10^{-19}C. Use your values from part (c) to determine the value of the Work Function for zinc, and also Planck's constant.

   (e) From the graph, a stopping potential of 0volts corresponds to a frequency of 7.4×10^{14}Hz. Describe the physics of this point.

11. Let's go back a bit in time. You don't know what we now know about atoms. Comment on each of these statements:

   (a) As far as electric charge is concerned, the whole universe is neutral so atoms must be neutral.

   (b) Everything is made of atoms/molecules.

   (c) If people are made of atoms, some atoms must contain 'animate' components.

   (d) Human thoughts aren't made of atoms.

   (e) Solids feel solid, so atoms of solids must be solid. Atoms of liquids must be liquid.

   (f) Atoms don't exist; it's just a model of what's really there.

12. A diagram of the Böhr model of the hydrogen atom is shown on the right.

    (a) Describe the main features of the Böhr model.

    (b) What is the mechanism for the emission of a photon of light?

    (c) How is the energy of the emitted photon calculated?

    (d) How did the model accomodate the spectroscopic series of emission lines like the Balmer Series?

    (e) In what ways does the Böhr model of the atom conflict with Classical Physics?

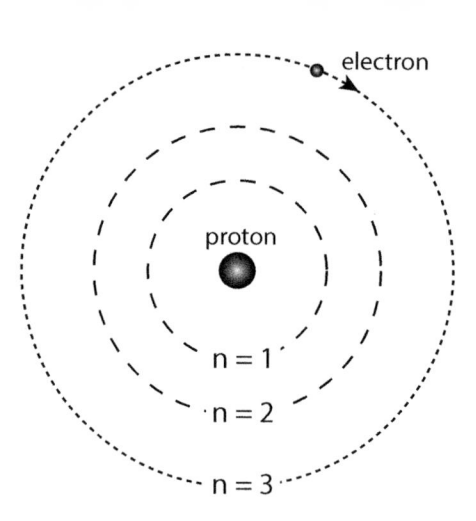

13. Light emitted from the surface of a star will have some of its wavelengths absorbed due to the ionised gases in its photosphere. The stellar spectrum below shows the first four absorption lines from the Balmer Series.

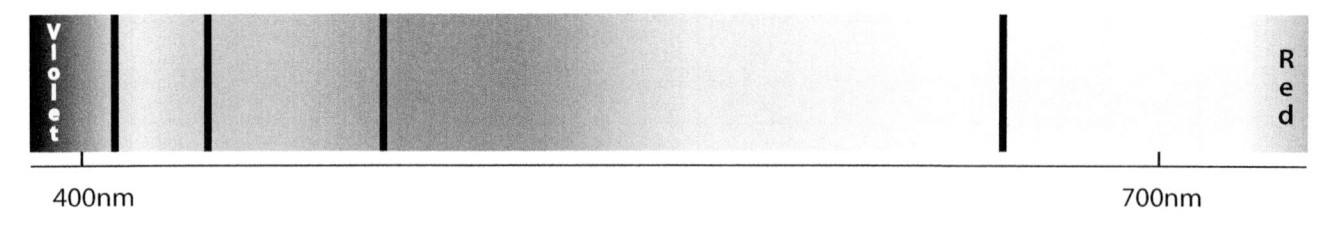

    400nm 700nm

    (a) The line on the right has a wavelength of 656.3nm. This corresponds to the 2 → 3 transition where the light interacts with a hydrogen atom and promotes the electron from the second to the third levels. Use the Balmer equation $\frac{1}{\lambda} = R_H \left(\frac{1}{2^2} - \frac{1}{n^2} \right)$ to calculate the constant R_H.

    (b) Calculate the 2 → 5 transition wavelength then estimate it from the diagram using a ruler.

14. There is only one constant in Quantum Mechanics and that's Planck's constant 'h'. In calculations it's often divided by 2π and this combination $\hbar = \frac{h}{2\pi}$ (it's pronounced 'h-bar') was given a special name: Dirac's constant. Calculate the value of Dirac's constant.

15. The Böhr Model of the atom depicted the electron as a tiny solid particle in a circular orbit. This was modified by de Broglie who introduced wave-particle duality.

    (a) Describe how this changed our picture of the hydrogen atom.

    (b) Illustrate how it works using the quantisation of angular momentum equation $mvr = n\frac{h}{2\pi}$.

16. The de Broglie equation: $p = \frac{h}{\lambda}$ relates the particle properties (momentum) to the wave properties (wavelength) of all objects. Calculate the quantum mechanical wavelength of an electron moving with a momentum of 2.2 x 10⁻²² kg m s⁻¹.

    (de Broglie's full name was Prince Louis-Victor Pierre Raymond de Broglie and he died in 1987.)

17. A neutron has a quantum mechanical wavelength of 3.2 x 10⁻¹¹m. Calculate its momentum.

18. A photon has a frequency of 7.5 x 10¹⁶Hz.

    (a) Use the equation: $c = f\lambda$ to calculate its wavelength.

    (b) Calculate its momentum using the de Broglie equation.

    (c) Use the Planck equation and the de Broglie equation to show that $E = pc$ for a photon.

19. Calculate the speed of a proton which has a quantum mechanical wavelength of 8×10^{-14} m.

20. An electron with a speed of 200 m s^{-1} is directed towards a single slit of width 7×10^{-4} m. Show by calculation whether or not the electron will exhibit diffraction.

21. Open question! Do you think that moving objects like cricket balls have a wavelength?

22. Assuming your answer to Q(21) was yes, answer these:

    (a) What would be the wavelength of the cricket ball (mass 0.16kg) travelling at 50 m s^{-1}?

    (b) What would the value of Planck's constant have to be to give the cricket ball a wavelength of 20cm? What effect would this have on the game of cricket?

23. The orbital angular momentum $L = mvr$ of an electron about the nucleus in the Bohr model of an atom is quantised in multiples of Dirac's constant $\hbar = \dfrac{h}{2\pi}$ according to: $mvr = n\dfrac{h}{2\pi}$

    (a) At what value does the integer 'n' start; is it 0 or 1?

    (b) Calculate the angular momentum of the electron in the n = 2 orbit.

    (c) What would be the momentum of an electron in an orbit of radius 5.3×10^{-11} m with n = 1?

.....waves as particles.....

24. The way to distinguish between competing theories like Classical and Quantum Physics is to compare their predictions.

    (a) What does classical physics predict will happen to the wavelength of a lightwave when it is reflected from a surface or diffracted by an edge or gap?

    (b) What does classical physics predict will happen to the wavelength of a lightwave when it travels from air into glass? What happens when it comes back out into the air?

25. In 1923, A.H.Compton performed an experiment to test the classical predictions posed in question 24 above. He sent a beam of monochromatic X-rays towards a graphite block. He knew the wavelength of the incident beam and measured the wavelength of the beam which emerged. The reflected beam was analysed at various angles – the diagram shows the beam scattered at 90°.

    (a) The graph on the right shows the results from the wavelength analyser. The solid curve is the scattered beam. The dotted curve is superimposed on the graph to show the incident beam. What would you conclude?

    (b) Explain why this is a problem for classical physics.

    (c) Compton derived an expression for the shift in wavelength Δλ as a function of the angle scattered: $\Delta\lambda = \dfrac{h}{m_e c}(1 - \cos\theta)$.

    Calculate the change in wavelength predicted by Quantum Theory when the X-rays are scattered at an angle of 90°. Symbol m_e is the electron mass.

    (d) Explain why this is evidence that waves can exhibit particle properties.

    (e) The expression in part (c) above, doesn't contain any properties of the material (graphite in this case, say, its density). What does this indicate about the basic process?

..... particles as waves.....

26. You've already met the equation $n\lambda = 2d\sin\theta$ in connection with interference and diffraction gratings. Explain why you would not expect to use it in an experiment with particles.

27. In 1927, Davisson and Germer directed a beam of electrons towards a nickel crystal as shown in the diagram.

    (a) If the electrons had behaved like classical objects, that is, as particles, what would you expect them to do when they strike the nickel crystal?

    (b) The detector 'D' could travel along the arc of a circle to detect any scattered electrons. When the energy of each electron was 54eV, a peak occurred at a certain angle. What does the occurrence of a peak suggest about the electrons?

    (c) Davisson and Germer then applied the equation $n\lambda = 2d\sin\theta$ and calculated the 'wavelength of the electron', λ to be 1.65 x 10⁻¹⁰m.

    Check if this is consistent with the de Broglie equation for an electron of energy 54eV. The electron is non-relativistic so use kinetic energy $E_K = \frac{1}{2}mv^2 = \frac{p^2}{2m}$.

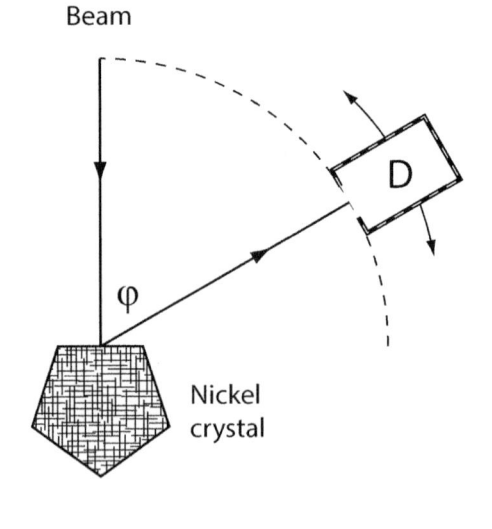

28. While he was Professor of Natural Philosophy at Aberdeen University, George Paget Thomson fired a stream of high speed electrons at thin gold and aluminium foils. The electrons passed through the foil and produced a pattern on a photographic plate as shown opposite.

    (a) What did he deduce about the nature of the electron?

    (b) The electrons were accelerated through a p.d. of 60000V. By calculating their speed, show that these electrons were relativistic.

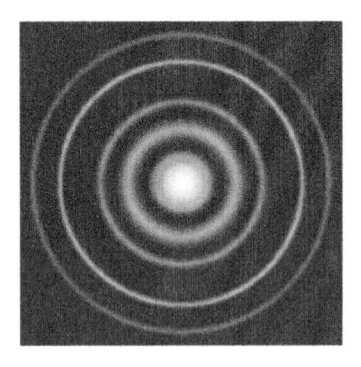

29. Complete the following sentences (bit more ambiguous, so hints given).

    A dice has ___ faces. Throw it a large _____ of times and each face will come up, on _____, a fraction of _____ of the total number of throws. In theory, according to C_____ Physics, you could calculate which face would appear from the traj_____ of the throw and the sur____ on which it la_____.

    On average, a free neutron amongst a large sample of neutrons will last for 15 minutes. In theory, according to Q_____ Physics, it is im_____ to calculate how long an ind_____ neutron will survive before _____ to a proton, _____ and antineutrino.

    Classical Physics is called det_____. The future can be pr_____ to any degree of precision if the _____ conditions are known to a high degree of acc_____. In contrast, _____ Physics cannot predict the outcome of a si_____ event. The best that can be calculated is the _____ of that outcome occuring. It doesn't matter how acc_____ known are the _____ conditions, or how int_____ you are.

30. Heisenberg's Uncertainty Principle sets limitations on how accurately you can measure position and momentum at the same time.

    (a) Write down the equation relating the uncertainties of position Δx and momentum Δp.

    (b) If the uncertainty in position 'Δx' is in metres, and in momentum 'Δp' is in kgm s^{-1}, show that the uncertainty relation gives a product with units J s.

    (c) If the uncertainty in the position of an electron in an atom is $\pm 7 \times 10^{-24}$ kg m s^{-1} calculate the smallest uncertainty you can achieve in a simultaneous measurement of its momentum.

31. A proton is measured to have a speed of $(4.6 \pm 1.8) \times 10^5$ m/s.

    (a) Use the Heisenberg Uncertainty relation to calculate the minimum uncertainty in its position.

    (b) Comment on the size of your answer with relation to the scale of the nucleus.

32. Calculate the uncertainty in the speed of an electron if the uncertainty in its position is equal to the diameter of a hydrogen atom (twice the Böhr radius).

33. (a) Assuming that the Uncertainty Principle can be applied to objects of any size, estimate the minimum uncertainty you could measure in the position of a person walking along the pavement. Take your speed measurement to have an uncertainty of $\pm 10\%$.

    (b) Explain if the mass of the person makes any difference to your answer in part (a).

34. A laser pulse of wavelength 780nm was produced over a time of 24 femtoseconds.

    (a) Use the energy-time uncertainty relation to calculate the minimum uncertainty in the energy of the pulse.

    (b) Calculate the energy of a photon of wavelength 780nm.

    (c) Calculate the shortest and longest wavelengths within the laser pulse.

35. In classical physics, if you take the amplitude of a wave and square it, you get the intensity of the wave. What do you get if you square the amplitude ψ (pronounced 'sigh') of a wave describing a quantum object?

36. Alpha particle emission from a nucleus would be impossible to explain using Classical Physics. The particles are trapped by the nuclear potential well shown in the diagram (a plot of the potential against distance from the centre of the nucleus). It's shown by the solid line in the diagram and is approximated inside the nucleus by a squared-off shape. The radius of the nucleus is r_o.

    (a) Explain why classical physics would not be able to predict the observed alpha particle emission.

    (b) Quantum Mechanics predicts a probability amplitude for a particle shown by the dotted line. Explain how this allows alpha particle emission.

    (c) What name is given to this process?

    (d) What fundamental forces are responsible for the potential inside the nucleus and outside the nucleus.

    (e) Nuclei consist of neutrons and protons. The solid line on the graph shows the potential for a charged proton or an alpha particle. How would the potential differ for a neutron both inside and outside the nucleus?

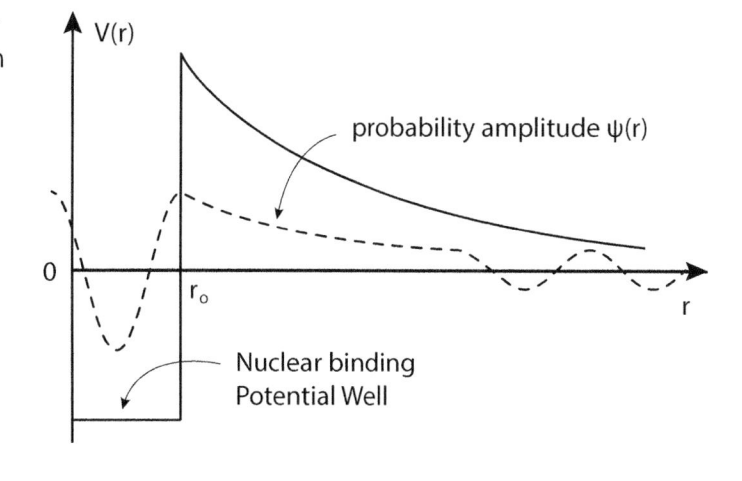

37. In Classical Physics, the double slit experiment of Thomas Young gives an interference pattern and hence is evidence that light is a wave motion.

    (a) Describe an experiment which could test for quantum interference.

    (b) Experiments in 'double slit' quantum interference have been performed.

       (i) Describe the results when firstly one hole is open, then when both holes are open.

       (ii) Describe what happens as the intensity of the incident beam is reduced with two holes.

       (iii) Explain why these results contradict commonsense.

38. Quantum Theory has produced some of the most accurate predictions in physics. The problem is in understanding what's been created. What does Quantum Theory say to us about the nature of the universe? It's fair to say that nobody knows; from Ed Witten and Einstein down to your pet hamster. There are several interpretations of Quantum Theory. Research them then describe the main features of the Copenhagen approach of Böhr, and of the Many-Worlds idea of Everett.

Unit 2 Particles from Space

1. The term 'cosmic ray' was invented before scientists knew what they were dealing with. Explain why the first word is correct but that the second word is inaccurate.

2. Explain the difference between primary cosmic rays and secondary cosmic rays.

3. Why do primary cosmic rays consist of long-lived stable particles whereas secondary cosmic rays consist of short-lived unstable particles?

4. The highest energy recorded for a primary cosmic ray was the 'Oh-my-God' particle detected in 1991 with an energy of 3×10^{20}eV. A golfball has a mass of 40g. Calculate the speed of such a golfball if it had the same kinetic energy as the 'Oh-my-God' particle.

5. The diagram represents a primary cosmic ray proton striking an oxygen nucleus in the upper atmosphere. It produces another nucleus 'X' and a secondary shower of short-lived particles. The possible decay reactions for these particles is shown below for the various pions and other decay products.

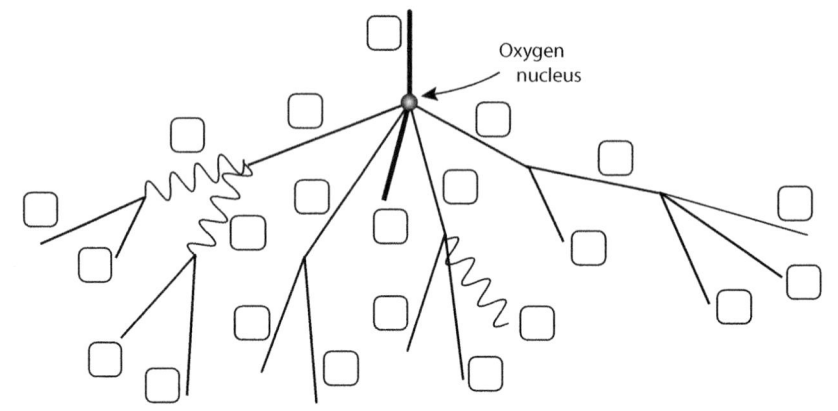

    (a) Identify the particles or rays at the positions of the boxes. A bar above an object denotes an antiparticle.

    Possible particles: X, p, $\pi^+, \pi^-, \mu^+, \mu^-, e^+, e^-, \bar{v}_\mu, v_\mu, \bar{v}_e, v_e, \gamma$

    Reactions: $\pi^+ \rightarrow \mu^+ + v_\mu$ $\quad\quad \pi^- \rightarrow \mu^- + \bar{v}_\mu \quad\quad \pi^0 \rightarrow 2\gamma$

    $\pi^0 \rightarrow e^+ + e^- + \gamma \quad\quad \mu^- \rightarrow e^- + \bar{v}_e + v_\mu \quad\quad \gamma \rightarrow e^+ + e^-$

    (b) Which Conservation Law is obeyed in the list of reactions above?

    (c) Describe what happens to the positrons produced in the secondary shower.

    (d) Gamma rays are part of the electromagnetic spectrum like light rays, are usually stable and do not decay to particles. Do a bit of internet research and find out under what conditions the gamma rays can be persuaded to decay into an electron positron pair.

6. A muon is a sub-atomic particle which decays with a mean lifetime of 2.2μs. It's produced high in the atmosphere as a result of a primary cosmic ray colliding with an oxygen or nitrogen nucleus.

   (a) Calculate the average distance the muon can travel before decaying. Assume it moves at the speed of light in vacuo.

   (b) Muons are produced at least 50km above the Earth's surface. From your answer to part (a), how many muons would you expect to detect on the surface?

   (c) The time dilation effect of Special Relativity predicts that the lifetime of the muon as measured by an observer on the ground, will change according to:

   $$t' = \frac{t}{\sqrt{1 - \frac{v^2}{c^2}}}$$

   The unprimed time, t, is called the 'proper time', that is, the time recorded by a clock riding along with the muon. Calculate the mean lifetime of the muon as measured by the ground observer if the speed of the muon was 0.99995c.

   (d) Calculate the distance travelled by the muon as observed from the ground.

   (e) Explain whether the time dilation effect will alter the muon count on the surface.

7. Primary cosmic rays are composed mainly of protons, alpha particles, other heavy nuclei and electrons. For every 100 primary cosmic rays, how many of each would there be on average?

8. Explain why the cosmic microwave background radiation limits the highest energy of the primary cosmic rays to the order of 10^{20}eV. Google 'GZK cutoff' and refer to the Theory Book p112.

9. Secondary cosmic rays reach the Earth's surface and are detected by an instrument array.

   (a) Explain why an array is required, rather than just a single instrument.

   (b) Water is a major component of one of the detections methods. Explain how this is used to detect the secondary cosmic rays.

10. Complete the following sentences.

    The Sun is our major source of _____. It is in the shape of a _____ of radius _____ m and is at a mean distance from Earth of _____ m. As well as providing us with _____ and _____ energy, it also sends out charged _____. This is known as the _____ _____. It can produce beautiful colours in the night sky known as the _____ _____, but can also cause _____ to communication satellites and _____ power grids. The Sun goes through a _____ with a period of about _____ years. Dark areas on the surface known as _____ become more common for certain periods during the _____ and it is these phenomena which are largely responsible for the effects seen high up in the _____.

    The dark _____ are areas of reduced _____ and are produced by the interplay of the movement of hot volumes of _____ and of the _____ fields due to these moving charges. The _____ fields produced by the Sun can extend out over large _____, as far as _____ and beyond. The Sun's field and the Earth's own field combine around our planet to produce the _____, a region where the _____ particles from the _____ _____ are trapped. These particles move along the _____ lines in _____ and are directed towards the _____ and _____ poles.

41

11. The Sun is more complicated than a simple big hot ball. Label these regions:

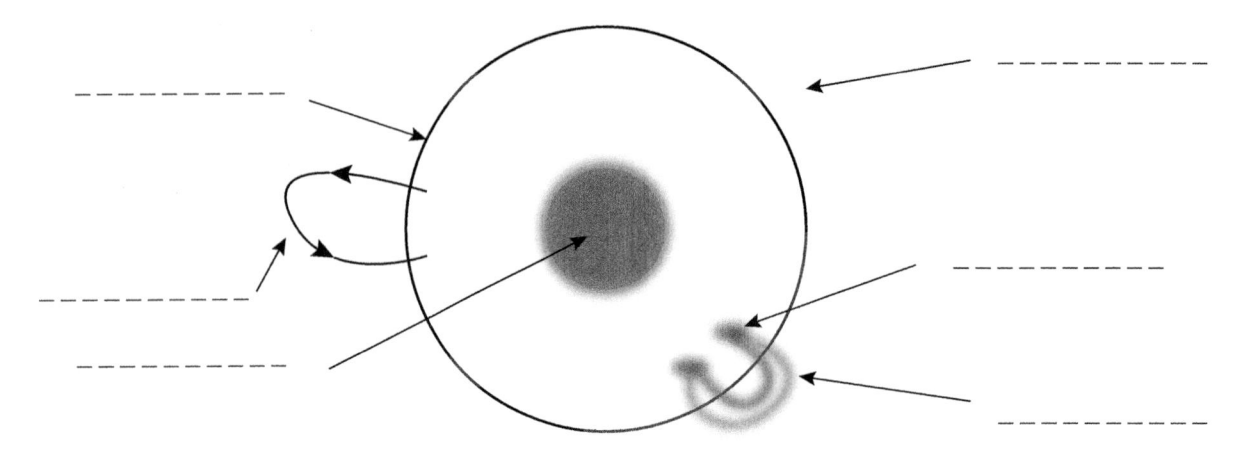

12. (a) Cosmic rays are the particles which reach us from outside the Solar System. Our Sun also emits particles. Describe one difference between the two groups of particles.

    (b) The Sun emits vast numbers of both positively and negatively charged particles. Explain why the Sun remains electrically neutral.

13. (a) A proton emitted from the surface of the Sun takes 3 days to reach planet Earth. Calculate the average speed of the proton.

    (b) Calculate its kinetic energy in joules and also in keV.

14. The Sun's magnetic field reaches throughout the whole solar system. Some planets like Earth have their own magnetic fields; others like Venus have very small fields. Draw a sketch showing the main features of how the magnetic field lines from the Sun and Earth combine around our planet. Use these words to label your sketch: bow shock, magnetosphere, plasmasphere.

15. The Solar Wind (and cosmic rays in general) can produce unwanted side-effects. Take each one of the items below and write a few sentences outlining the problem and how the effects can be mitigated.

    (a) Astronauts in orbit around the Earth.
    (b) Telecommunication equipment and GPS signals.
    (c) Power grids.
    (d) Global weather patterns.

16. (a) The diagram opposite shows a charged particle in a magnetic field. There are five objects/symbols on the drawing. Describe what each one represents.

    (b) One of the oddest parts of magnetism is the direction of the force on the moving electric charge. From the diagram, in which **two** directions does the force **not** act?

    (c) A small sphere is in a magnetic field. Describe three circumstances in which it would **not** experience a force due to the magnetic field.

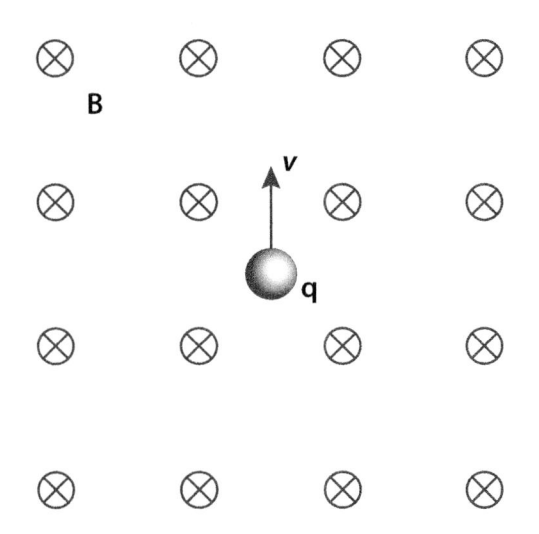

42

17. Trying to work out directions can be tricky at first; which hand, which fingers? The drawing below shows a negatively charged particle moving with velocity 'v' coming **out of** the page. It's immersed within a uniform magnetic field 'B'

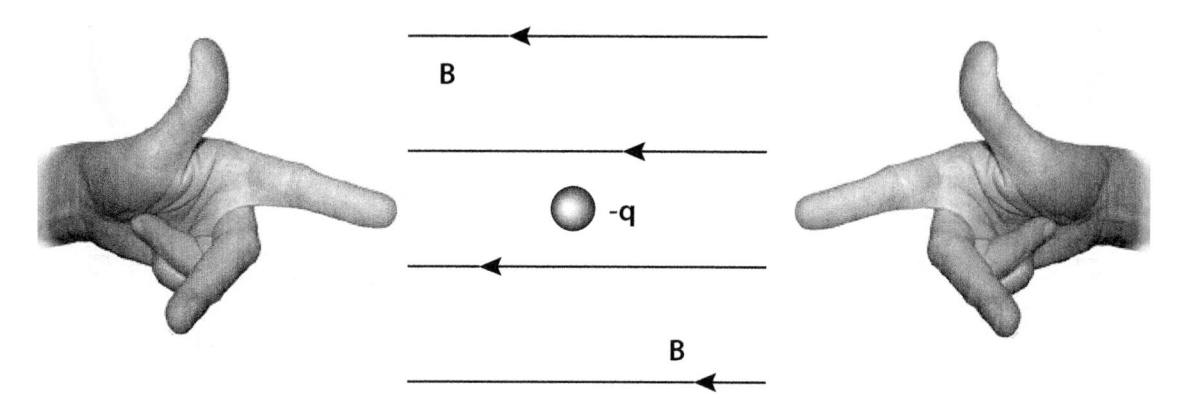

    (a) Imagine these are your hands in front of you. Which one did you choose to determine the direction of the force on the moving, negatively charged particle?

    (b) Describe which fingers do what.

    (c) In which direction does the force act on the particle in the diagram?

18. Calculate the force on these charges (magnitude and direction).

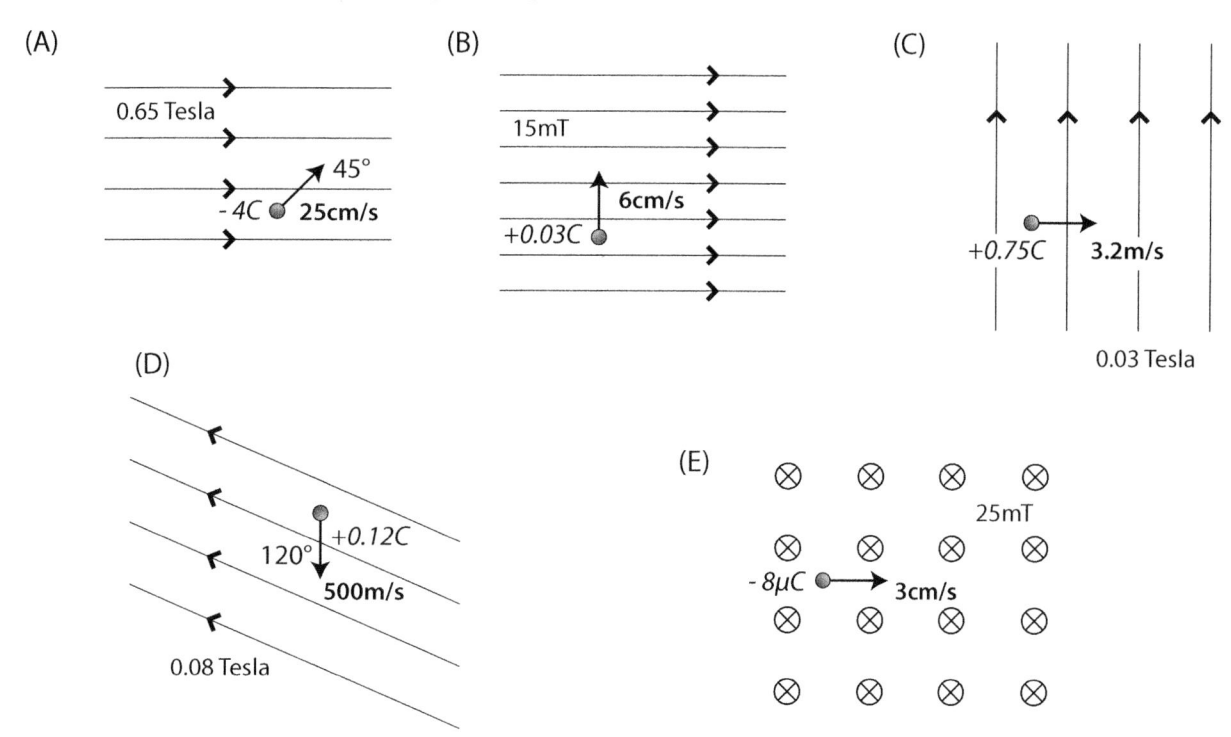

    (A) 0.65 Tesla, −4C, 25cm/s at 45°

    (B) 15mT, +0.03C, 6cm/s

    (C) +0.75C, 3.2m/s, 0.03 Tesla

    (D) +0.12C, 500m/s at 120°, 0.08 Tesla

    (E) −8μC, 3cm/s, 25mT

19. Vectors can be resolved into two components on two dimensional drawings. The left diagram below shows a velocity of 20m/s resolved into horizontal and vertical components.

    (a) Calculate the horizontal and vertical components of the 20m/s velocity.

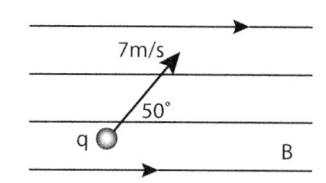

    (b) The right diagram shows a moving electric charge in a uniform magnetic field. Calculate the components of the velocity in the direction of the magnetic field and also at right angles to the magnetic field.

43

20. The two examples below show a particle travelling through a uniform magnetic field. Calculate the component of the velocity in the direction of the magnetic field (think about the signs):

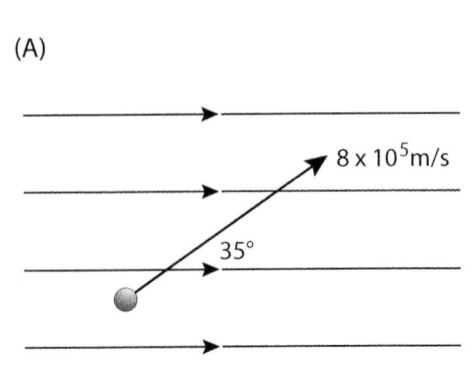

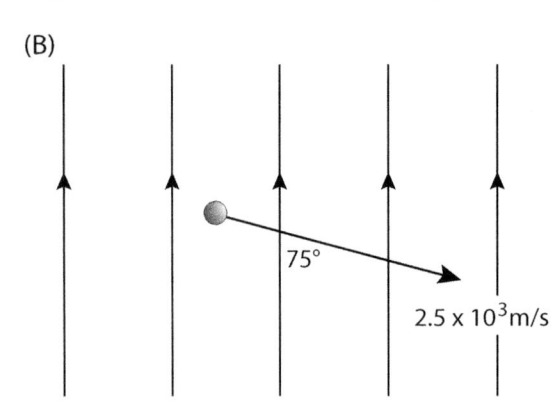

   (A)

   8 x 10⁵ m/s at 35°

   (B)

   2.5 x 10³ m/s at 75°

21. Electric charges can experience a force from both electric and magnetic fields.

    (a) In what direction is the force on an electric charge if it's placed in a uniform electric field?

    (b) In what direction is the force on a moving charge if it's placed in a uniform magnetic field?

    (c) Describe one condition for a force to be present in a magnetic field but not in an electric field.

22. Charged particles in uniform magnetic fields can move in circles, or be drawn-out in spirals. This question derives the equations for circular motion.

    (a) Equate the expression for any centripetal force $F = \dfrac{mv^2}{r}$, with the force on a moving charge in a magnetic field $F = qvB\sin\theta$. Rearrange the equation to derive an expression for the radius of the circular orbit which the charge follows. Assume that the initial velocity is at right angles to the magnetic field.

    (b) Use the equation $v = \omega r$ to obtain an expression for the angular velocity of the orbit.

    (c) Now use $\omega = 2\pi f$ to derive an expression for the frequency 'f' of the orbit.

    (d) Finally, write down the equation for the period (T) of the orbit.

23. A charged particle moves in a circle due to its motion within a uniform magnetic field 'B'.

    (a) Refer to the drawing and use the rule you've been given to determine the polarity of the charge 'q'.

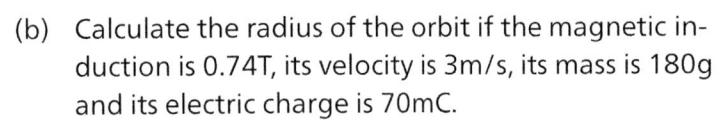

    (b) Calculate the radius of the orbit if the magnetic induction is 0.74T, its velocity is 3m/s, its mass is 180g and its electric charge is 70mC.

    (c) Calculate the angular velocity 'ω' and the angular frequency 'f'.

    (d) Calculate the period 'T' of the orbit.

    (e) Describe the effect on the radius and the period if the speed of the particle is doubled.

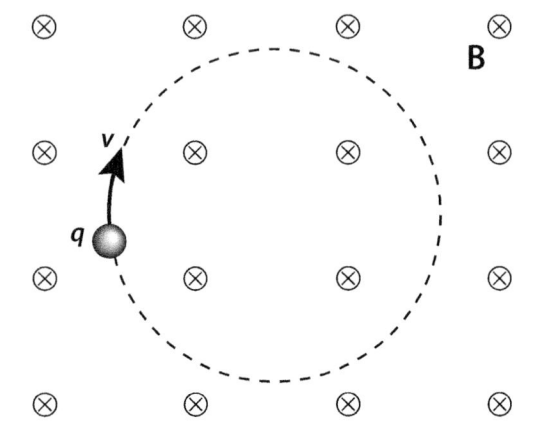

24. An electron with an energy of 1keV travels near the Earth's surface where the magnetic induction is 50μT. Calculate the maximum possible force on the electron and compare this with its weight.

25. In a hydrogen atom, the electrostatic field of the nucleus provides the centripetal force required to make the electron move in a circular orbit. Calculate the magnetic induction 'B' required to make an electron move in an identical orbit. Take the speed of the electron as 2.19 x 10⁶ m/s.

26. An instrument called a spectrometer uses a magnetic field to separate isotopes of an element by their mass. Positively charged ions are accelerated across a potential difference 'V' of 350 volts in an electric field, then enter a region of uniform magnetic field at right angles to it.

    (a) The ions then move along a circular track. What happens to the **speed** of the ions once they enter the magnetic field?

    (b) The ion's speed 'v' is given by: $\frac{1}{2}mv^2 = qV$, where 'V' is the potential difference. Use your expression for the radius of the track, then eliminate the speed from these equations and show that the mass of the ion is given by: $m = \dfrac{qB^2r^2}{2V}$.

    (c) Two sets of singly ionised particles are detected at positions 'P' and 'Q'. Calculate the masses of the two ions if the magnetic induction was 0.12T.

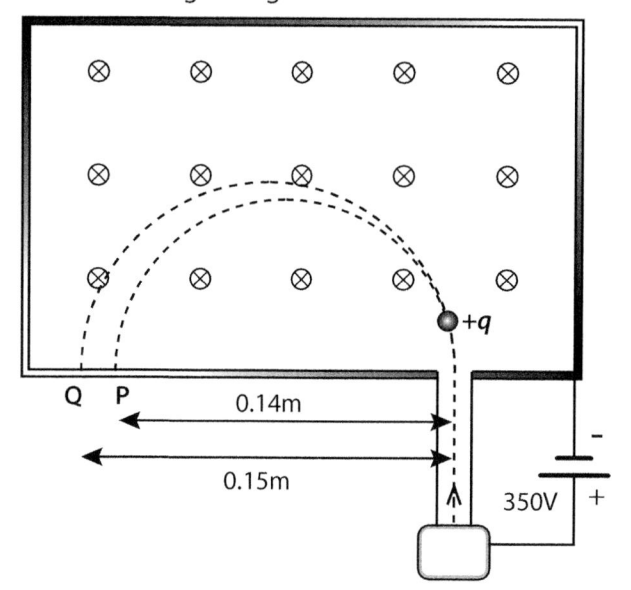

27. The diagram shows a charged particle accelerator called a cyclotron. It is constructed of two halves called 'dees' (shaded and shaped like the letter 'D'). An electric field is applied in the space between the 'dees' using an oscillator. This changes the electric polarity +/- of each 'dee' with frequency 'f'. A uniform magnetic field is applied to the shaded areas.

    (a) The particle track is in the shape of semi-circles or straight sections. Explain how this is achieved using electric and magnetic fields.

    (b) Use letters ABCD to describe what happens to the speed of the particles (they are protons) and explain the reason for the oscillator.

    (c) In which direction is the magnetic field pointing for the beam of charged protons?

    (d) The time to move through a semicircle on either half is $T = \dfrac{1}{2} \times \dfrac{2\pi m}{qB}$. Does this mean that the oscillator frequency has to increase, decrease or stay constant?

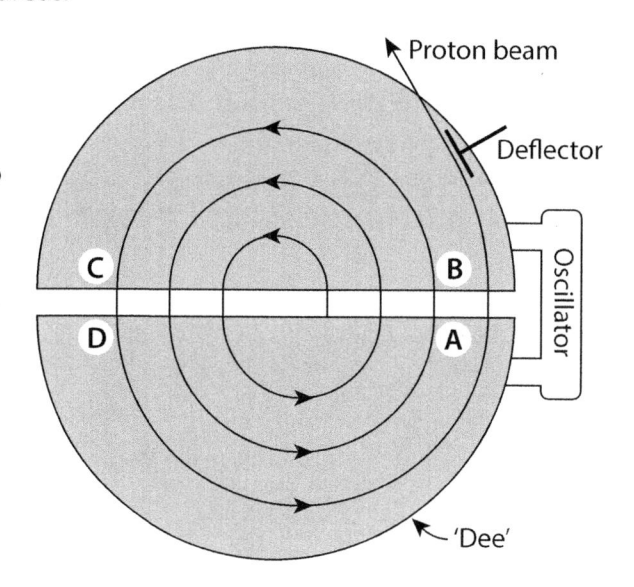

    (e) What is the function of the deflector and what is its polarity for the proton beam?

28. The two diagrams below right show an electron moving in a uniform magnetic field. The left-hand diagram has the electron moving at right angles to a magnetic field of B = 0.28T. The electron will move in a vertical circle relative to the page. The right-hand diagram has the velocity of the electron at an angle to the magnetic field.

    (a) For the left-hand diagram, which way around would the electron go in the vertical circle?

    (b) Calculate the frequency of its orbit.

    (c) In the right-hand diagram, the speed of the electron is 'v'. What would v cos70 represent and what effect does this have on the motion of the electron?

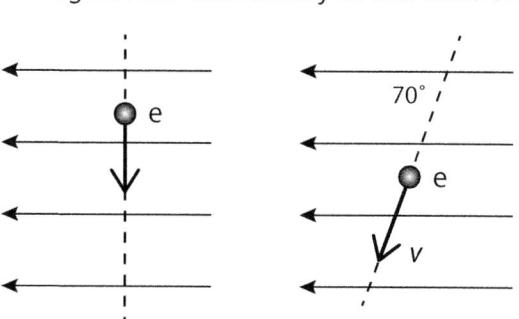

45

29. A cosmic ray carbon-12 nucleus enters a region of uniform magnetic field in outerspace at an angle of 80° to the field as shown below. Its speed is 0.04c and the magnetic field strength is 35μT.

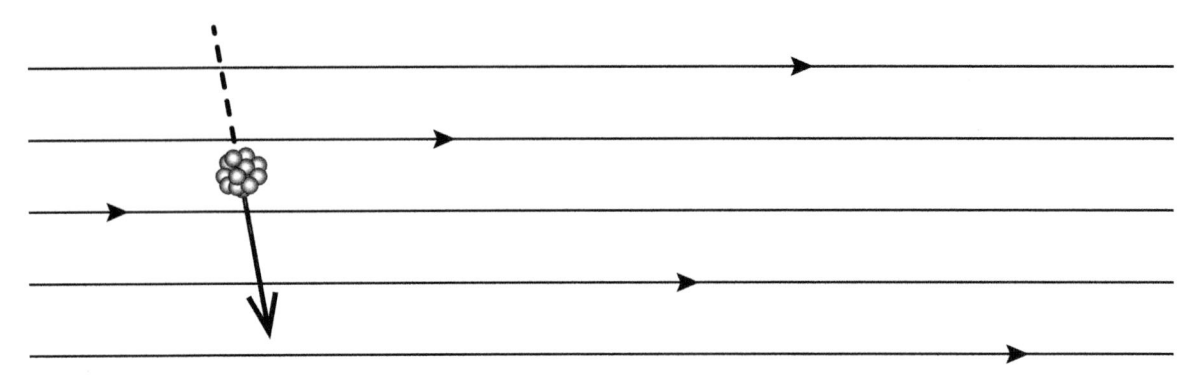

(a) Describe the motion qualitatively.
(b) Calculate the components of the velocity parallel to the field and at right angles to the field.
(c) Use the component of the velocity at right angles to the magnetic field to calculate the radius of the helix. The mass of the nucleus is 2.0×10^{-26} kg.
(d) Calculate the period of the orbit.
(e) How many orbits will the carbon nucleus make for each **kilo**metre of sideways drift?
(f) How far sideways does the nucleus move in one **complete** turn?

30. During the 1960's and 70's sub-atomic particles were detected with bubble chambers. The track of a charged particle through a tank of liquid hydrogen would show up as a stream of bubbles. A magnetic field was applied to separate the decay products of a collision. The example below is of an invisible uncharged neutrino (υ) entering from the bottom of the frame and colliding with one of the protons in the liquid hydrogen. The left half is the actual photograph and the right half is the analysis of the event. Notice the large loop. This is a low energy pion which has looped right back and by coincidence looks like it's returned to the collision site (it's actually just nearer the camera).

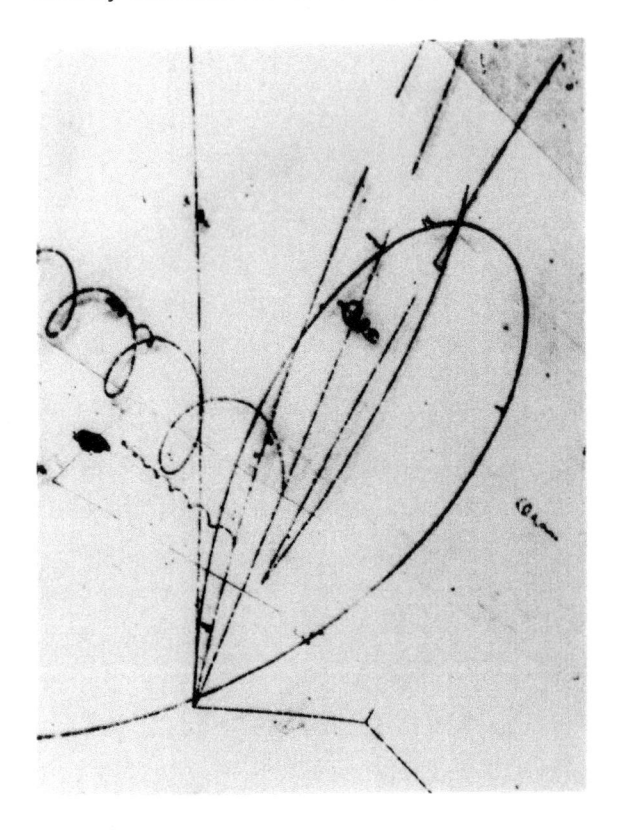

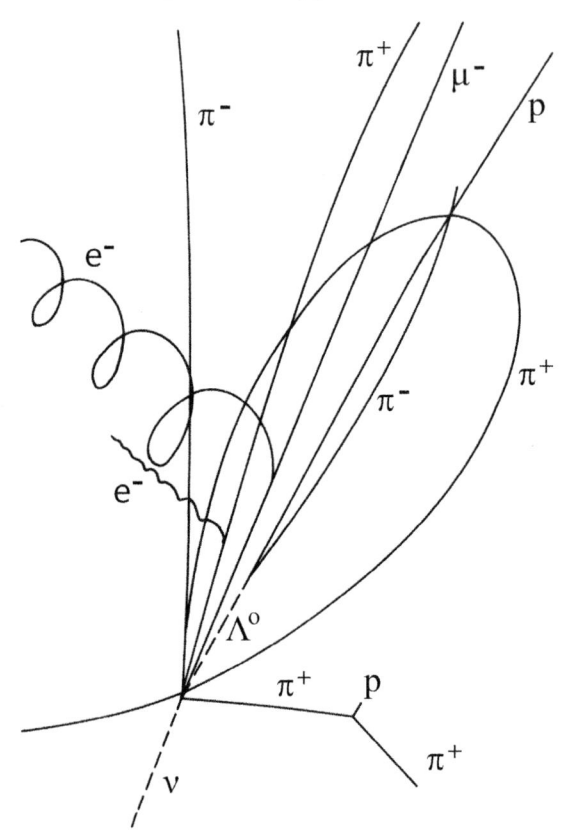

(a) The negatively charged particles bend leftwards and the positive particles bend rightwards (remember that they move in 3 dimensions). In which direction do the magnetic field lines point?

(b) The particle labelled Λ° (called 'Lambda nought') does not leave a track. Why is this?

(c) Suggest a reason why the track of the electron is more tightly coiled than the others.

(d) The six particles produced in the primary collision (μ- π+ π+ π+ π- Λ°) were all sent in a forward direction. What conservation law requires this to happen?

(e) Show that electric charge is also conserved in the collision.

Unit 2 Simple Harmonic Motion

1. Simple Harmonic Motion is a to-and-fro movement about an equilibrium position. The direction of the force is the key.

    (a) Why is a 'restoring' force needed in SHM and in which direction does a restoring force act?

    (b) If the restoring force is zero at x = 0 and doubles when 'x' is doubled, write down an equation which relates the force (F) to the displacement (x).

2. (a) A spring has a spring constant of 4Nm⁻¹. The diagram below shows the restoring force at an extension of +1m. Calculate the other three missing forces beside each arrow (with directions).

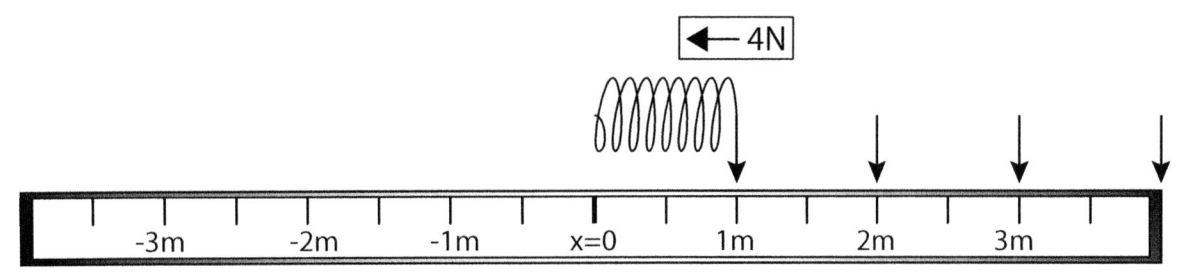

    (b) What difference would it make to your answer for the force if the spring had been extended the other way to -2m instead of +2m?

3. Simple Harmonic Motion isn't just any old restoring force; just one special type. The diagram below shows (any old) restoring forces on a body:

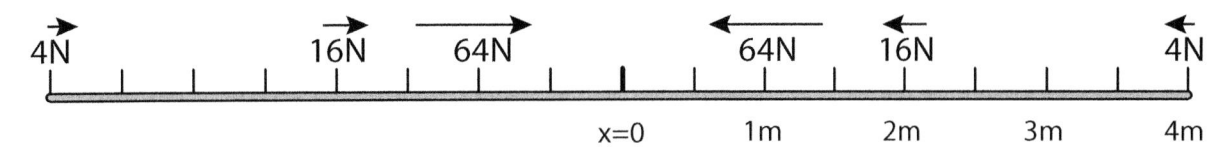

    (a) Explain why this could not be Simple Harmonic Motion.

    (b) The forces are symmetrical about the origin. Write down the relationship between the restoring force and the displacement for the above Harmonic Motion.

4. The equation: $y = A \cos 2\pi f t$ describes the Simple Harmonic Motion of a particle where the oscillations take place along the 'y' direction.

    (a) What does the 'A' stand for?

    (b) How would you obtain the period 'T'?

    (c) What would $\frac{dy}{dt}$ correspond to?

    (d) What would $\frac{d^2y}{dt^2}$ correspond to?

5. The Simple Harmonic Motion of an oscillating mass is described by $y = 5\cos 8\pi t$ (in S.I. units).

    (a) Calculate the amplitude (A), the frequency (f), the period (T) and the angular velocity (ω).

    (b) Calculate $\frac{dy}{dt}$, and use it to write down the maximum speed of the mass.

    (c) At what position does maximum speed occur?

6. Write down an equation for the displacement of an object undergoing simple harmonic motion with an amplitude of 7m and a period of 0.2s.

7. The speed of a mass on the end of a spring is given by $v = -24\sin 30t$ (in S.I. units).

    (a) Integrate the equation to obtain an expression for the displacement 'x'.

    (b) Calculate the amplitude and frequency of the motion.

    (c) What was its position at time t = 0 ?

8. S.H.M. has two solutions: $y = A\cos\omega t$ and $y = A\sin\omega t$. What is the position of the object at t = 0?

9. The restoring force in Simple Harmonic Motion is: $F = -kx = m\frac{d^2x}{dt^2}$

    (a) Substitute the solution $x = A\sin\omega t$ into the last two terms of the above equation and obtain an expression for the angular frequency 'ω'.

    (b) What are the units for the spring constant 'k' ?

    (c) In simple problems involving gravity, the mass often cancels out of an equation and you're left with an expression without an 'm' (remember dropping heavy and light things at the same time from the same height?). With Simple Harmonic Motion, the mass doesn't cancel out. Why does this make SHM useful?

10. The graph on the right shows the displacement of a body undergoing Simple Harmonic Motion as a function of time:

    (a) Calculate the frequency 'f' and the angular frequency 'ω' of the motion.

    (b) Write down an equation expressing the displacement 'y' of the body. Use the information on the axes.

    (c) Calculate the maximum velocity.

    (d) Calculate the spring constant 'k' if the mass is 60g.

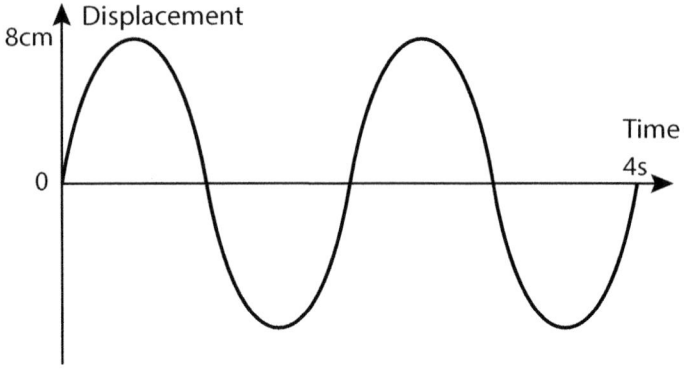

11. Write down the equation for the displacement (y), of a particle undergoing Simple Harmonic Motion if its frequency is 5Hz and it oscillates between two points which are 18cm apart.

12. A point particle undergoes Simple Harmonic Motion described by the equation: $x = 3\sin 200t$. Take all quantities to be in S.I. units and calculate:

    (a) amplitude   (b) frequency   (c) period

    (d) the maximum velocity   (e) maximum kinetic energy if the mass is 50g.

13. The displacement of a small mass is given by the equation: $x = 3\sin 8\pi t$ (in S.I. units)

    (a) Derive expressions for its velocity and acceleration as functions of time.

    (b) How much time is there between the small mass reaching maximum speed on successive occasions?

    (c) Calculate the maximum positive acceleration in m s^{-2}. At what position(s) does this occur?

14. The acceleration of a particle performing SHM is described by: $a = -0.72\pi^2 \sin 6\pi t$ (in S.I. units)

    (a) Read off its maximum positive acceleration and calculate its value in m s^{-2}.

    (b) Calculate its frequency and amplitude.

    (c) Calculate the maximum speed.

15. The displacement and velocity in SHM are given by: $x = A\sin 2\pi ft \quad v = v_o \cos 2\pi ft$. These are expressed as functions of time. Sometimes it's useful to obtain a relationship between the velocity and the displacement (what is its speed at position 'x', rather than at time 't').

    (a) What is the maximum speed v_o in terms of 'A' and 'f'?

    (b) Use the identity: $\sin^2\theta + \cos^2\theta = 1$, to derive the expression: $v = \pm\omega\sqrt{(A^2 - x^2)}$.

16. This question considers the energy of the particle undergoing Simple Harmonic Motion. It involves an interchange between kinetic energy and potential energy.

    (a) Where are the positions of maximum kinetic energy and maximum potential energy?

    (b) What can you say about the total energy of the system if the motion is undamped?

    (c) Use: $v = \pm\omega\sqrt{(A^2 - x^2)}$ to derive an expression for the kinetic energy.

    (d) Write down expressions for the kinetic energy at x = 0 and also at x = A.

    (e) Using the Law of Conservation of Energy, derive expressions for the potential energy at x = 0 and also at x = A?

    (f) Write down an expression for the total energy at any position.

17. The graph opposite shows the kinetic energy and potential energy of a mass 'm' for Simple Harmonic Motion. On the vertical axis, the energy scale is one square equals one joule.

    (a) Write down the amplitude of the motion.

    (b) Which graph (dotted or solid line) shows the kinetic energy plotted against position?

    (c) The total energy is the sum of the potential and kinetic energies. Sketch the graph of total energy on the y-axis, against position along the x-axis. Show values on the energy axis.

    (d) Use the expressions:

    $$E_{Kin} = \frac{1}{2}m\omega^2(A^2 - x^2) \quad E_{Pot} = \frac{1}{2}m\omega^2 x^2$$

    to calculate the displacement where the kinetic and potential energies are equal.

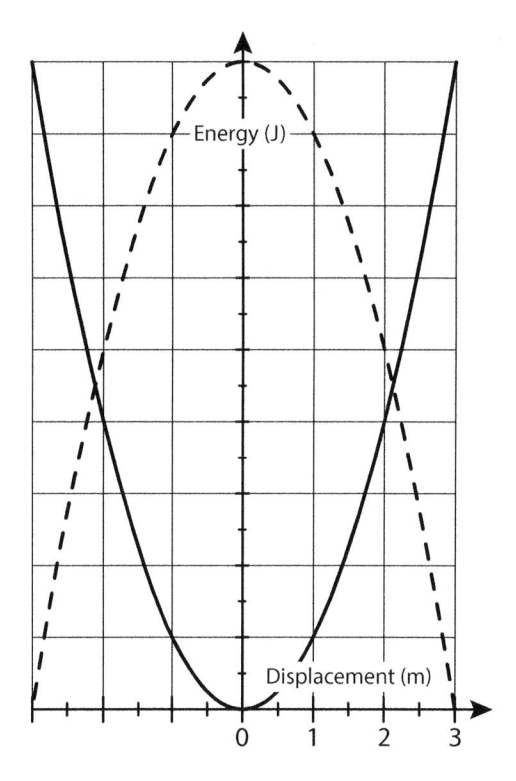

    (e) Calculate the value of the spring constant 'k'.

18. This is a very tricky question with a surprising answer. Suppose an electron is in a region of vacuum and is subjected to an alternating electric field given by: $E = E_0 \sin\omega t$. Will the electron obey Simple Harmonic Motion? It seems like it should, but does it?

    Hint: start from $F = Eq \Rightarrow m\dfrac{d^2x}{dt^2} = qE_o \sin\omega t$, and perform two integrations to obtain the displacement. Be especially careful with the constants of integration.

19. Real systems lose energy and the Simple Harmonic Motion becomes damped; the oscillations decrease. The oscillations of the liquid in a large U-tube are shown in this graph of displacement against time. The displacement 'x' is from the rest position to the liquid level in one of the tubes.

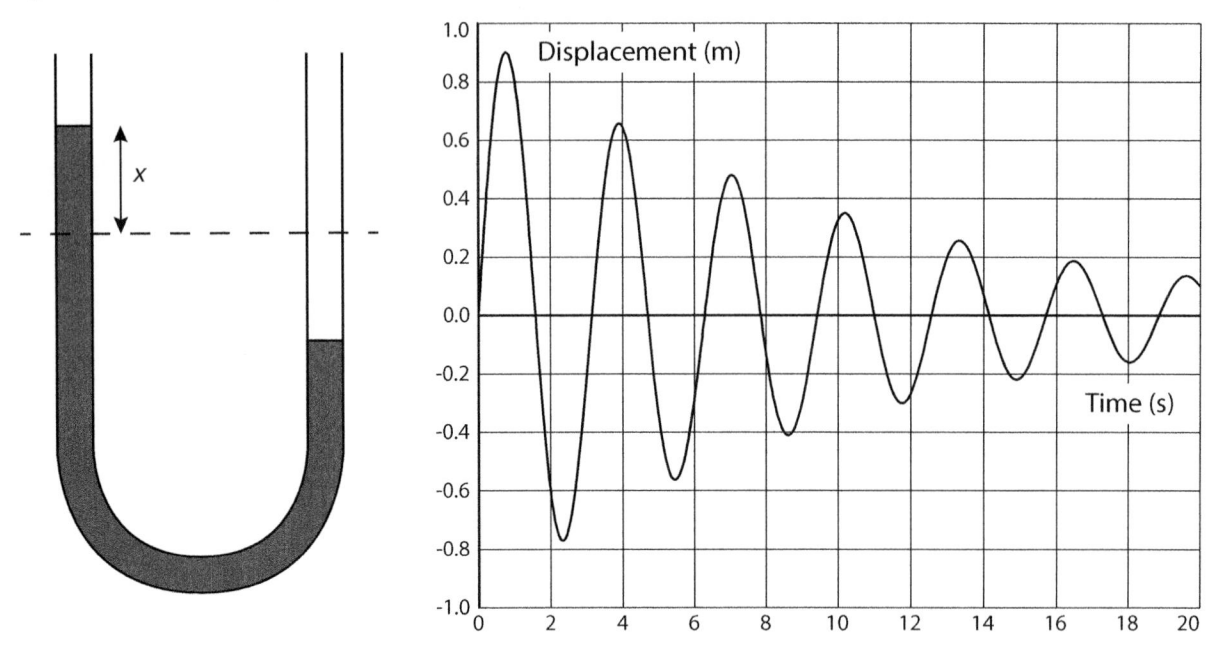

    (a) Where was the liquid level when the clock started?
    (b) The highest level reached by the left hand tube decreases after each oscillation. From the graph, estimate the highest levels reached for the first four peaks.
    (c) Measure the period of the oscillation then calculate the frequency. Does it remain constant?
    (d) The motion of the liquid column is different from that of a point particle (as in all previous examples). In terms of its Simple Harmonic Motion, explore the differences.
    (e) Explain what the decreasing peak means in terms of energy.
    (f) How does the total energy of the system compare at the first two peaks?

20. A point mass swinging on the end of a string in a gravitational field (a simple pendulum) approximates Simple Harmonic Motion.

    (a) What condition must be satisfied for it to be a worthwhile approximation.
    (b) The period of the motion is given by: $T = 2\pi\sqrt{\dfrac{L}{g}}$. Calculate the period of a pendulum of length 1.5m swinging on Earth.
    (c) Calculate the length of a pendulum of period 1s. Explain the drawbacks in using this as a timer.

21. Some clocks go 'tick-tock, tick-tock'. You can build one which counts off the seconds of time with every tick and every tock. It's called a seconds-pendulum.

    (a) A seconds-pendulum can be used as a grandfather clock; ticks on the left, tocks on the right. Calculate the length of the clock pendulum.
    (b) A particular seconds pendulum swings 4° either side of vertical. Calculate the maximum speed of the bottom tip of the pendulum.

22. Estimate the period of a 1m long simple pendulum on the surface of a typical neutron star.

23. The period of a pendulum depends upon the length of the pendulum and the gravitational field strength of the locality. Astronauts at the International Space Station often perform simple experiments. What would happen if they tried the Simple Pendulum. Explain your answer.

Unit 2 Waves

1. Use the equations, $v = f\lambda$ and $f = \dfrac{1}{T}$ to calculate:

    (a) The wavespeed of a wave of frequency 4.5×10^{12} Hz and wavelength 4.0×10^{-5} m.

    (b) The wavelength of a wave of wavespeed 1450 m s^{-1} and frequency 3.2×10^{4} Hz.

    (c) The frequency of a wave of wavespeed 8 m s^{-1} and wavelength 2.5 m.

    (d) The period of a wave of frequency 25Hz.

    (e) The period of a wave of wavespeed 150 m s^{-1} and wavelength 85cm.

2. Describe the difference between transverse and longitudinal waves. Give an example of each.

3. A particle 'P' in a medium is disturbed by a transverse wave. The displacement of the particle can be described by either a cosine or a sine curve as shown below (same scale on both graphs):

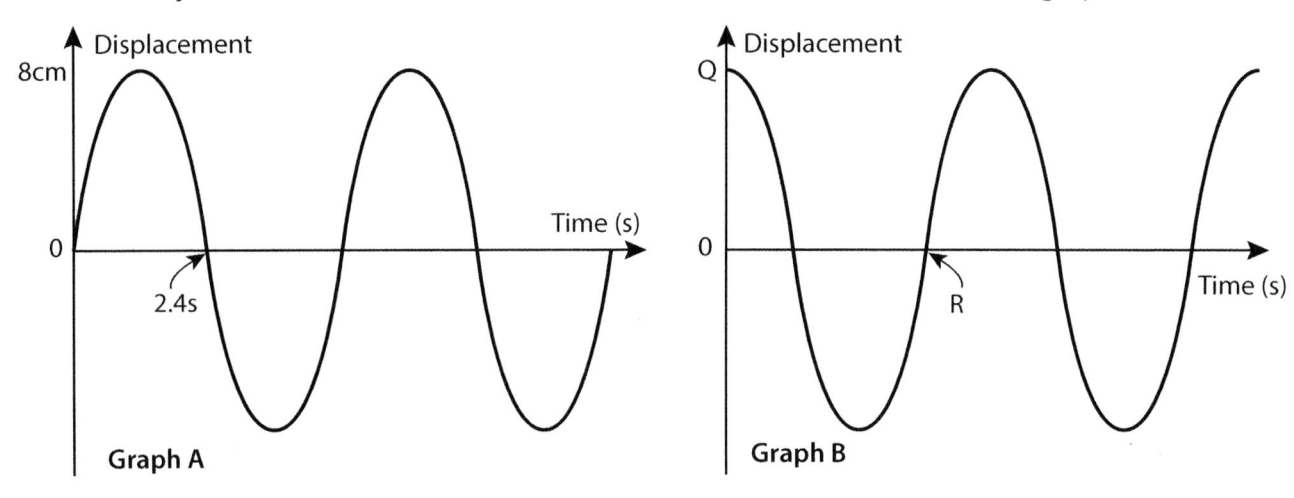

    Graph A

    Graph B

    (a) Which graph is the sine wave?

    (b) Calculate the amplitude, period and frequency of the wave.

    (c) For graph 'A' the clock was started when the displacement of the particle was zero. What was the displacement of the particle when the clock was started in graph 'B'?

    (d) On graph 'B', what time should be labelled at point 'R' ?

    (e) When solving problems in physics involving regular, repeated motion, should it make any difference to experimentally measured quantities if you use a sine or a cosine in the equations?

4. A point particle is disturbed by a passing travelling wave. Its displacement in metres is given by the expression: $y = 4\sin 6\pi t$.

    (a) What will be the particle's amplitude, frequency and period?

    (b) What does the equation: $y = 4\sin(6\pi t \pm 3\pi T)$ represent?

5. Write down the equation for the displacement 'y' of a particle at the origin if:

    (a) The amplitude is 0.03m and the frequency is 12Hz.

    (b) The amplitude is 15cm and the period is 0.25s.

6. Two particles 'P' and 'Q' are vibrating vertically with the same amplitude as shown on the right:

    (a) If the particles always stay side by side, what can you conclude about their frequency?

    (b) Describe what would be seen if the particles had the same frequency but were 180° out of phase.

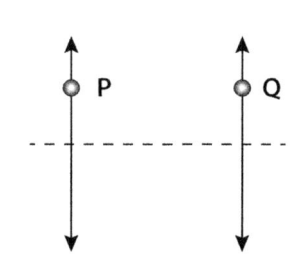

(c) Particles 'A', 'B', 'C', 'D' and 'E' all have the same amplitude and frequency. The diagram below shows a snapshot of their positions when 'A' has zero displacement and is heading upwards.

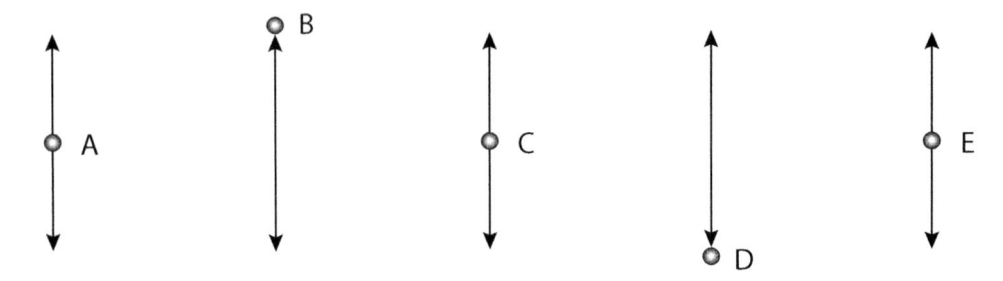

(i) What is the phase difference between neighbouring particles?

(ii) What well-known physics phenomenon would this look like if viewed as a time-lapse sequence?

(iii) Re-draw the diagram showing their positions one quarter of a period later. State in which direction the peak is moving (to the left, or to the right).

7. Re-arrange these phrases to make one complete true sentence:

being slightly out of phase .... **with each particle** .... **Simple Harmonic Motion** .... **under the action of** .... **each vibrating** .... **a line of particles** .... **consists of** .... **A travelling wave** .... **with its neighbour.**

8. The displacement of a particle in a medium with a travelling wave passing through it is given by:
$$y = 0.3\sin 2\pi(50t - 1.25x)$$

(a) What is its amplitude (A), frequency (f), period (T), wavelength (λ) and wavespeed (v)?

(b) Sketch the wave at time t = 0 for one complete wavelength. Show values on both axes.

(c) Sketch the wave at time t = T/4.

(d) What difference would it make if there had been a 'plus' sign instead of a 'minus' sign in the equation for the displacement?

9. A wave of amplitude 4cm has an intensity of 20Wm^{-2}. What would be its intensity if its amplitude was doubled?

10. Use the equation: $I = kA^2$ to calculate the intensity of a wave of amplitude 0.075m where the constant 'k' is 3.5Wm^{-4} for a particular wave.

11. Graph 'A' below left, is a snapshot (solid line) of a wave travelling along a length of string, followed by another snapshot (dotted line) at a later time.

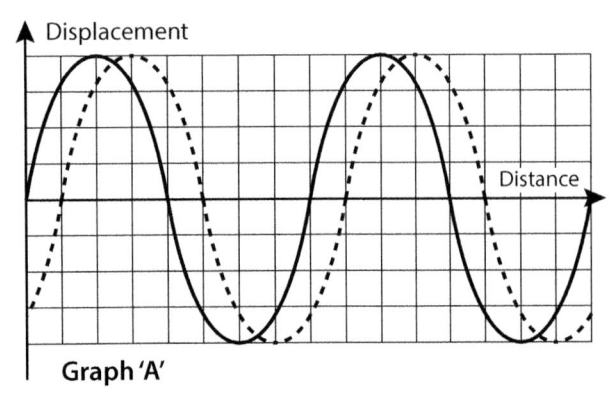

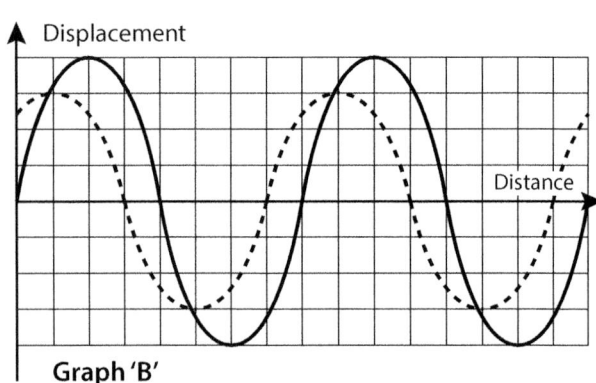

Graph 'A'

Graph 'B'

(a) Calculate the phase difference (in radians and degrees) between the pair of waves in diagram 'A' and repeat for the pair of waves in diagram 'B'.

(b) Calculate the time lapse between the two snapshots in graph 'A' if the frequency is 96Hz.

(c) What must two waves have in common before you can calculate a phase difference between them which stays constant with time?

12. Calculate the amplitude (A), frequency (f), period (T), wavelength (λ) and wavespeed (v) for these travelling waves (assume S.I. units):

(a) $y = 2.4 \sin 2\pi (20t - 5x)$

(b) $y = 0.04 \sin 2\pi (800t + 125x)$

(c) $y = 95 \sin (7t - 0.4x)$

(d) $y = 0.8 \sin \left(\dfrac{x}{6} + \dfrac{t}{40} \right)$

13. Sketch these waves when time t = 0. In all cases λ = 8m and only draw one complete wave.

(a) $y = \sin 2\pi \left(ft + \dfrac{x}{\lambda} \right)$

(b) $y = \sin 2\pi \left(ft - \dfrac{x}{\lambda} \right)$

(c) $y = \sin 2\pi \left(\dfrac{x}{\lambda} + ft \right)$

(d) $y = \sin 2\pi \left(\dfrac{x}{\lambda} - ft \right)$

14. The expression for the displacement in the travelling wave equation usually contains the frequency and the wavelength. Re-write this equation $y = \sin 2\pi \left(ft - \dfrac{x}{\lambda} \right)$ in terms of:

(a) the period 'T' and the wavelength 'λ'

(b) the angular frequency 'ω' and the wavespeed 'v'

15. A standing wave experiment consists of a length of string vibrating between a clampstand and a vibration generator as shown below. The motion of the string is normally very fast and looks blurred. This is what you normally see when viewing the experiment:

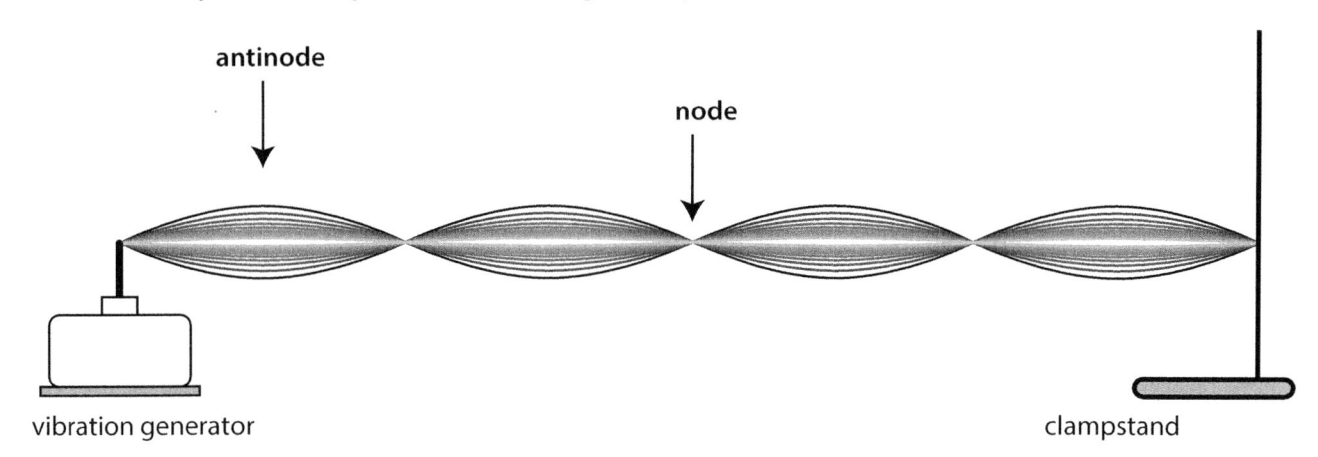

(a) If you could take a snapshot of the string, draw what you would see.

(b) A stationary wave is formed by the interference of two travelling waves. The equation of one of these waves is: $y = \sin 2\pi \left(ft - \dfrac{x}{\lambda} \right)$. Write down the equation of the other wave.

(c) Nodes are formed at regular intervals. What is the wavelength in terms of the positions of these nodes?

(d) If the distance from the vibration generator to the clampstand is 0.72m and the frequency of the generator is set at 18Hz, what is the wavespeed of the waves?

16. Music synthesizers create sounds by adding a number of basic tones with various amplitudes and frequencies. Adding two pure tones together gives this displacement of a loudspeaker cone:

$$y = A_1 \sin 2\pi f_1 t + A_2 \sin 2\pi f_2 t$$

(a) What physics principle has been used in the equation to obtain the resultant displacement?

(b) Here are 4 possible inputs for the amplitude and frequency. Match them to the graphs below:

(i) $A_1 = A_2 \quad f_2 = f_1$

(ii) $A_1 = A_2 \quad f_2 = 2f_1$

(iii) $A_1 = 2A_2 \quad f_2 = f_1$

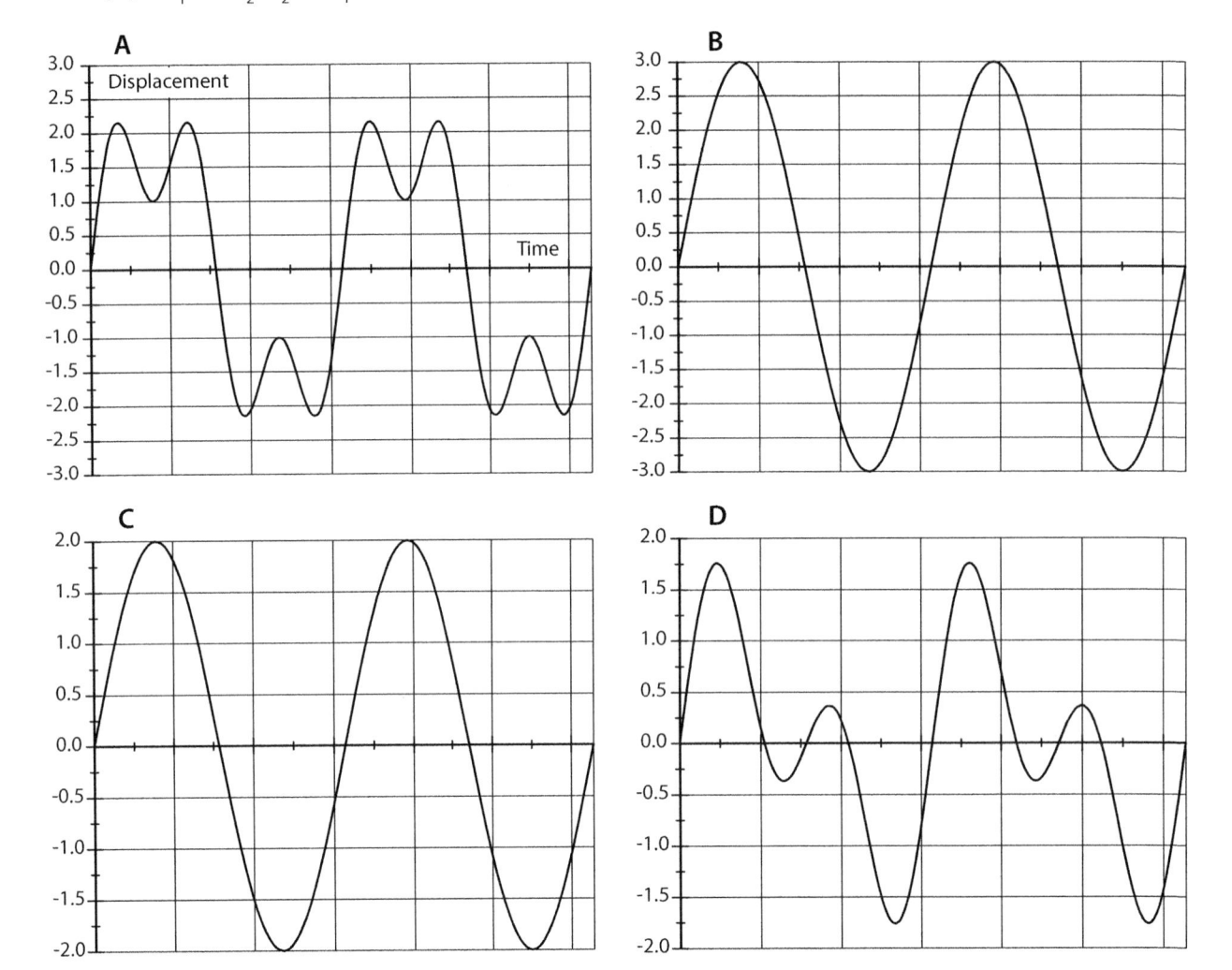

(iv) $A_1 = 2A_2 \quad f_2 = 3f_1$

17. Two microwave generators emitting the same frequency face each other as shown below. A detector, connected to an oscilloscope with its timebase off, can move between the two generators.

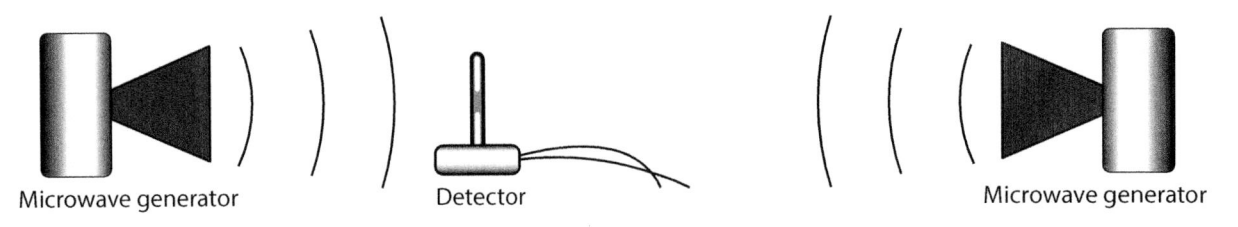

(a) Describe the pattern seen on the oscilloscope as the detector moves between the generators.

(b) Calculate the frequency of the microwaves if the detected nodes are 4cm apart.

Unit 2 Interference by Division of the Amplitude

1. What are the conditions for two beams of light to be coherent?

2. Two waves have amplitudes A_1 and A_2. The intensities (I_1 and I_2), of each wave, are proportional to the amplitude squared: $I_1 \propto A_1^2$ $I_2 \propto A_2^2$

    (a) The two waves are directed towards a point where they meet. Explain why you can't make interference measurements if the two waves have different frequencies.

    (b) What condition must be imposed on the two beams for measurements to be made?

    (c) Given two amplitudes A_1 and A_2, there are two ways of obtaining the resultant intensity: add first then square, or square first then add. Taking $A_1 = 3$ and $A_2 = 5$ with a constant of proportionality of one in both cases, show that these two methods give different results for the resultant intensity.

    (d) You've got two waves and you wish to calculate the resultant intensity. Which of the two methods outlined in part (c) above, is used for two waves which are coherent?

3. If two waves of the same frequency have a phase difference of 45° at a particular instant, what happens to the phase difference as time passes?

4. Light waves can change when passing from one transparent material to another.

    (a) List three ways in which the wave can change.

    (b) Define the Geometric Path Length and the Optical Path Length of a ray.

    (c) Calculate the Geometric Path Length and the Optical Path Length for each light ray below:

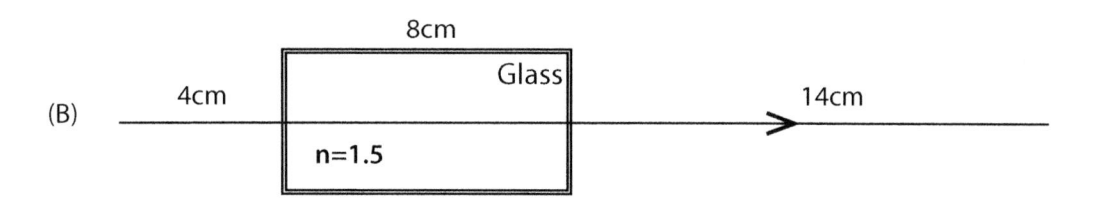

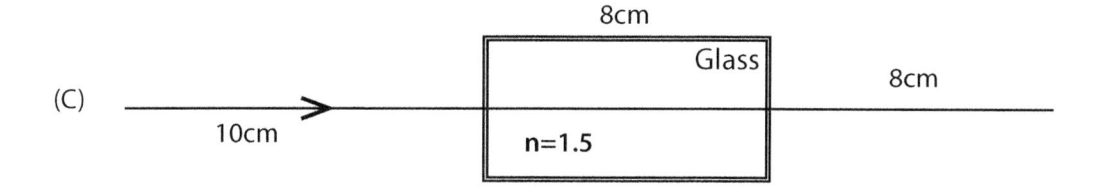

    (A) ———————————————→————————————————————
                              26cm

    (B) ——4cm——[8cm Glass n=1.5]——14cm——→

    (C) ——10cm——→——[8cm Glass n=1.5]——8cm——

5. A wave travelling from left to right passes from air into a transparent block as shown below:

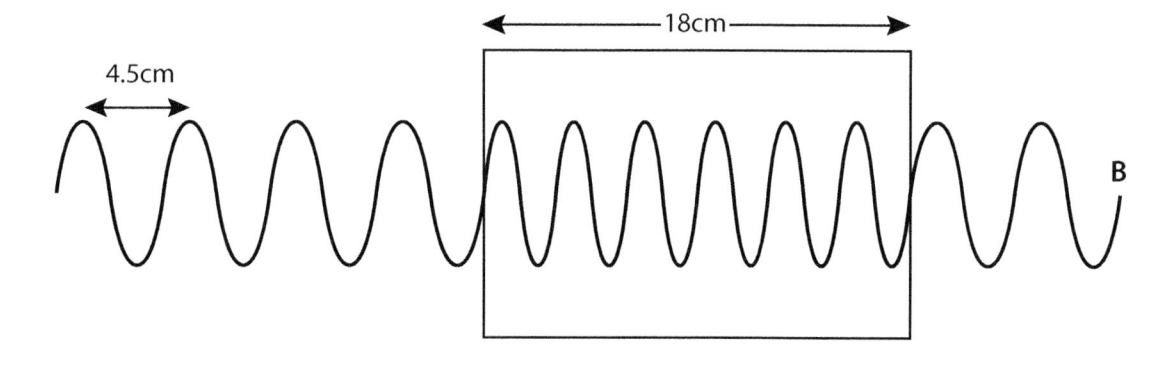

   (4.5cm wavelength in air, 18cm block, point B on right)

(a) Calculate the refractive index of the block.

(b) What change in phase at point 'B' would occur if the block was removed?

(c) The block was replaced by a new block of the same length but greater refractive index. This resulted in the phase at 'B' changing by 180°. Calculate the refractive index of the new block.

6. The diagram on the right shows an electromagnetic wave from 'A' reflecting off the top surface of a block to position 'B'. Its wavelength is 3cm and the block has a refractive index of 1.56.

   (a) Sometimes an additional phase shift of 180° is added on reflection. What is the rule for this?

   (b) What would be the phase difference between position 'A' and position 'B' if the wave is travelling in air and the block is made of glass?

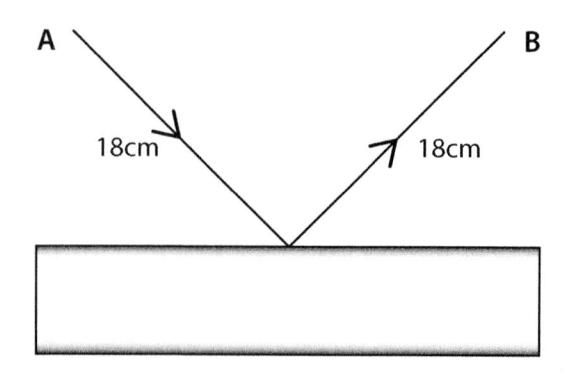

7. Two thin films of the same composition, thickness and refractive index (1.375) are shown in the diagrams below. They sit on top of two different materials with refractive indices 1.26 and 1.52. In both cases, air is above the films and all distances are in centimetres.

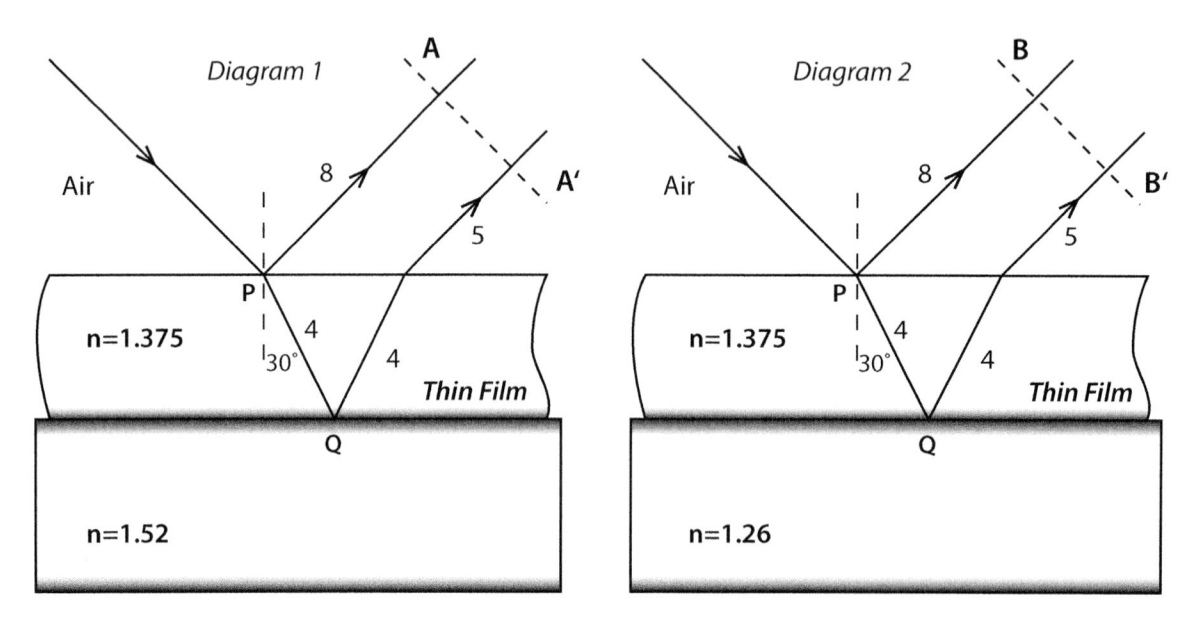

   (a) A ray of wavelength 2cm in air strikes the top surface of diagram 1 at point 'P'. It is split into two separate rays which can be brought together at another position and interfere. What is this type of interference known as?

   (b) Determine the phase difference of the two reflected rays where they cross the line AA'.

   (c) Repeat the calculation for diagram 2 along the line BB'. (There is a difference!)

   (d) In diagram 1, the angle of incidence is now decreased. Show by calculation whether the optical path difference of the two emerging beams would increase or decrease.

8. When a thin film of thickness 't' with refractive index 'n' is coated onto a glass of higher refractive index, destructive interference for normally incident light is given by: $2nt = \frac{1}{2}\lambda$.

   (a) Why is it preferable to use monochromatic light with the thin film? Explain the effect of using white light with a thin film.

   (b) What effect will it have on the thickness of the film required for destructive interference of the reflected light if you increase the refractive index of the **glass**?

9. A thin film of refractive index 1.35 is coated onto glass of refractive index 1.52. What thickness of film will produce destructive interference of the reflected rays for red light at normal incidence?

10. A thin film of thickness 2×10^{-7} m and refractive index 1.25 is coated on top of a material of refractive index 1.17. It is designed to give destructive interference for reflections.

    (a) The thin film has a higher refractive index than the material below it. What difference does this make to the analysis of the physics?

    (b) Calculate the wavelength which will give perfect destructive interference on reflection. Assume normal incidence.

    (c) If the material underneath the thin film had refractive index 1.45 instead of 1.17, what difference would it make and what thickness of film would be required to achieve the same effect as before (destructive interference at the same wavelength from part (b))?

11. (a) Interference is divided into two types. What names are given to them?

    (b) The diagrams below show examples of each type. Identify which is which.

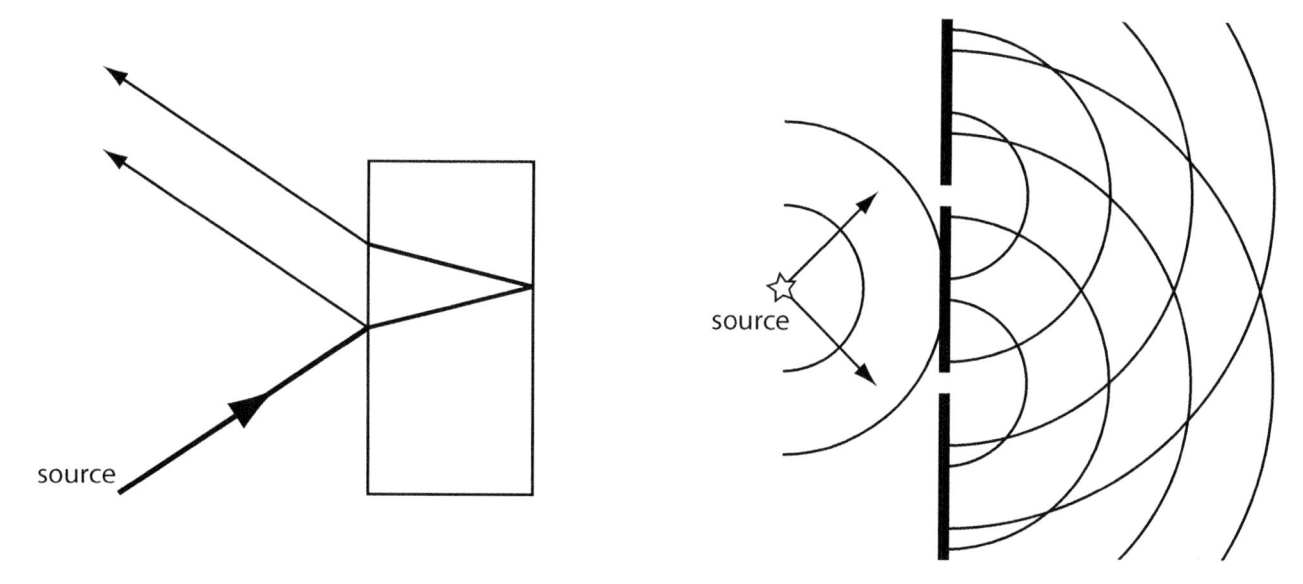

    (c) Sources can be either point sources or extended sources.

        (i) Which one must be used with the right-hand diagram above?

        (ii) Which one can be used with the left-hand diagram above?

        (iii) If a point source wasn't available for use with the experiment in the right-hand diagram, you could still perform the experiment with an extended source, but you would need one additional piece of equipment. What would that be, and how would you use it?

12. Monochromatic light of frequency 5.09×10^{14} Hz travels through a block of calcite of refractive index 1.658. Calculate its period 'T' and its wavelength 'λ' in the calcite.

13. A plano-convex glass lens is placed on top of a flat glass plate as shown in the diagram. Monochromatic light is normally incident upon the top surface and interference occurs on reflection. Fringes are produced due to the air gap between the lens and plate.

    (a) Of the two types of interference, which type is used in this experiment?

    (b) Write down which surfaces give reflections for the interference pattern

    (c) Describe the shape and spacing of the fringes as viewed from above.

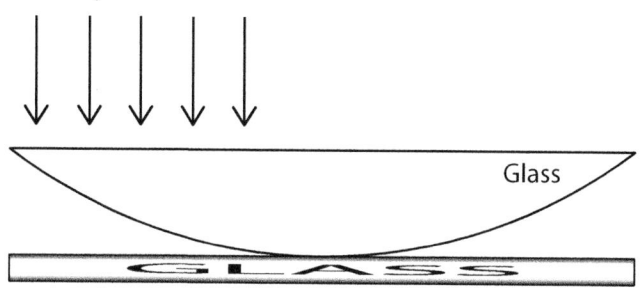

14. Two rectangular glass slides, each 8cm by 2cm, are separated along the short end by a human hair as shown below. The wedge of air between them is used to create an interference pattern viewed by a low powered travelling microscope.

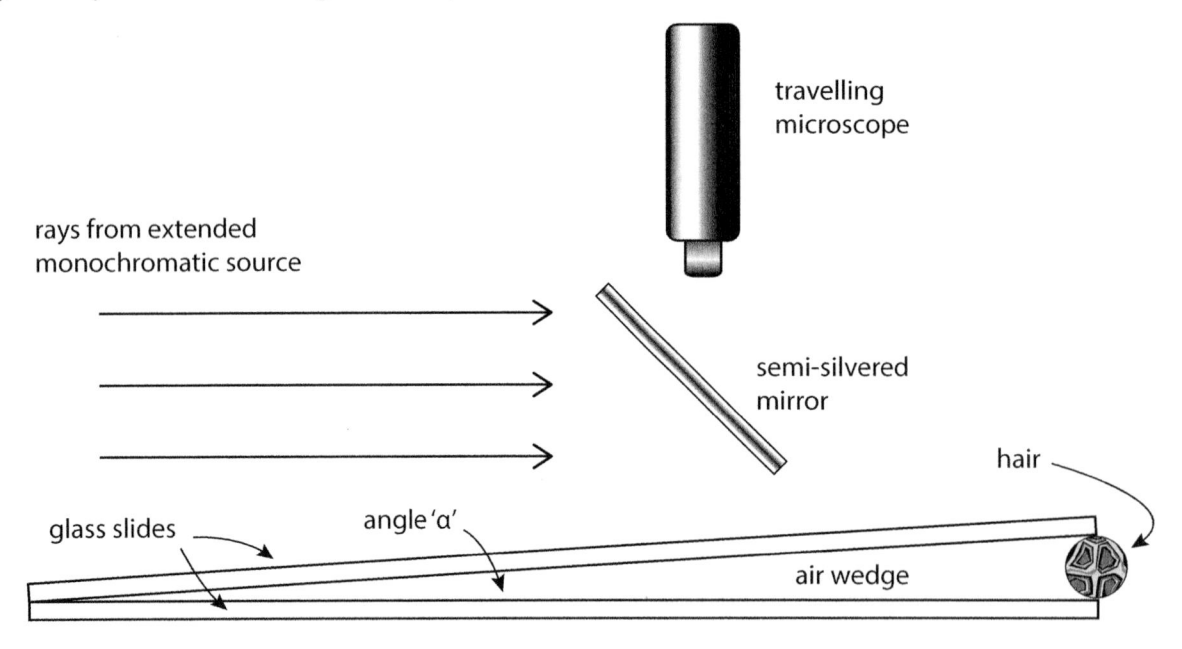

(a) Explain how the use of the semi-silvered mirror enables the light to strike the glass plates normally, while at the same time allowing the interference fringes to be viewed through the microscope.

(b) Straight line fringes are observed in the microscope. Eleven of them are shown below. The travelling microscope is used to measure the fringe spacings:

The distance measured between the end fringes was 4.7mm and the light source used was a monochromatic sodium lamp ($\lambda = 5.89 \times 10^{-7}$m).

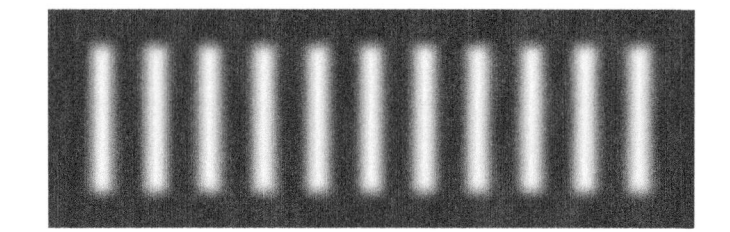

   (i) Calculate the fringe spacing 'd'.

   (ii) Calculate the angle 'α' formed by the two glass slides. Use the equation: $d = \dfrac{\lambda}{2n \tan \alpha}$.

   (iii) Work out the diameter of the hair.

(c) What would be the effect upon the fringe spacing if the air in the wedge was replaced by a gas of higher refractive index?

15. Three transparent blocks with different refractive indices are placed end-to-end as shown below. A ray of light starting at point 'A', passes through the blocks in succession. Calculate the phase difference at point 'B' relative to point 'A'. The wavelength of the ray in air is 3cm.

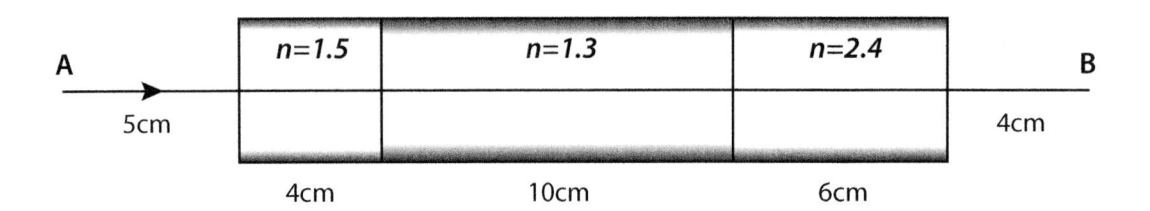

Unit 2 Interference by Division of the Wavefront

1. What type of source is used when viewing interference by division of wavefront?

2. The classic double slit experiment of Thomas Young produces interference by division of the wavefront. The left-hand diagram below, shows wavefronts (a snapshot of a line of crests), and the right-hand diagram shows the same experiment illustrated using rays.

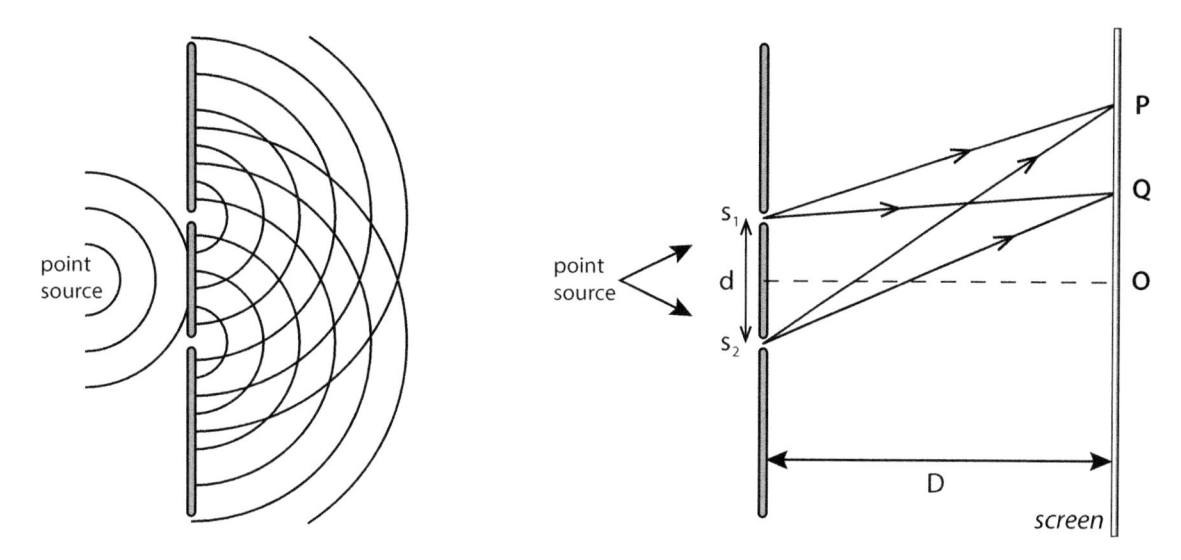

   (a) Use the left-hand diagram to explain why there is always a constant phase difference between the light at the slits S_1 and S_2.

   (b) The right-hand diagram shows the centre (O) and the first two bright fringes (Q and P). What can you deduce about:

   (i) ....the optical path difference at Q due to the two sources S_1 and S_2?

   (ii) ....the optical path difference at P due to the two sources S_1 and S_2?

   (c) Explain why the centre-point 'O' shows a bright fringe on the screen.

   (d) The distance 'x' from point 'O' to the nth bright fringe on the screen is given by: $n\lambda = \dfrac{xd}{D}$, where 'n' is an integer 0, 1, 2, 3.... etc. Derive an expression for the separation Δx of neighbouring fringes.

   (e) In a real experiment the right-hand diagram would not be to scale. How is it different?

3. In a Young's slit experiment, the screen is placed 1.5m away from the double slit. The distance across 20 bright fringe spacings on the screen is measured by ruler to be 65mm.

   (a) Calculate the fringe spacing Δx.

   (b) Calculate the distance between the slits 'd', if the wavelength of the light used was 624nm.

4. Young's slits can be described using these two equations: $\Delta x = \dfrac{\lambda D}{d}$ and $n\lambda = \dfrac{xd}{D}$.

   (a) Describe what each quantity represents in these equations.

   (b) Both equations aren't exactly correct, but they're very accurate for certain layouts of the double slit experiment. What approximation has been made in deriving these equations?

   (c) Why is it easier in practice to use the first equation?

   (d) Describe the procedure for measuring Δx on the screen.

5. The centre fringe (n = 0) in a Young's slit experiment is bright. Counting out from this one, the fifth (n = 5) bright fringe is at a distance of 2.4cm. The slit separation is 0.46mm and the screen is at a distance of 4.09m. Calculate the wavelength of the light used in the experiment.

6. Using red light of wavelength 620nm, the third bright fringe (n = 3) was 1.76cm from the centre bright fringe (n = 0) in a Young's slit experiment.

    (a) What effect would it have on the position of the third fringe if the screen distance was doubled?

    (c) Going back to the original set-up, what would have been adjusted in the experiment to reduce the distance to the third fringe by half, from 1.76cm to 0.88cm?

    (c) From the original set-up, what would be the position of the third bright fringe if blue light of wavelength 440nm was used instead?

7. Young's slit experiment normally uses monochromatic light. In this question we use white light with a spread of wavelengths from 420nm to 630nm. The distance to the screen was 2.4m and the slit separation was 0.15mm.

    (a) Is the centre fringe bright or dark?

    (b) Calculate the distance from the centre fringe to the first bright fringe corresponding to constructive interference at the wavelength of 420nm.

    (c) Repeat part (b) for the 630nm wavelength.

    (d) White light has been used as a source. Explain why the fringes aren't white in colour.

    (e) At which fringe number 'n' does the fringe pattern start to overlap, that is, the red from the 'n' fringe overlaps the blue from the 'n + 1' fringe? What is your answer independent of?

8. Microwaves of wavelength 2.8cm emanate from a point aperture 'P' as shown on the right. A detector is positioned along a line 60cm from a double slit. 'A', 'B' are the first two positions of constructive interference and the double slit separation is 10cm.

    (a) This is like Young's slits experiment using microwaves. How does this one differ from the experiment using lightwaves?

    (b) Calculate the distances BC and AC.

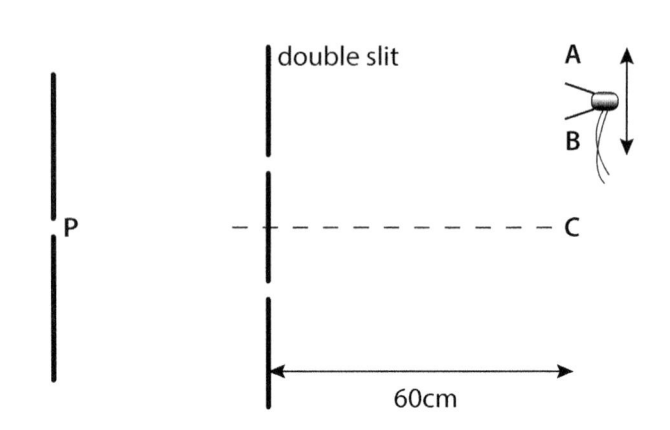

9. Young's experiment used two narrow slits to divide the wavefront and produce interference. The diagram below shows another method, called Fresnel's Biprism. It's a glass block formed from two triangles (actually triangular prisms) back to back with the ends trimmed off. Light rays from a single point source **S** are refracted by the biprism and emerge through the flat side.

    (a) The diagram shows two imaginary objects S_1 and S_2. These are called virtual sources. Explain how they help us understand the physics.

    (b) What does the shaded region signify?

    (c) Where would you place the screen and describe what you would observe on it.

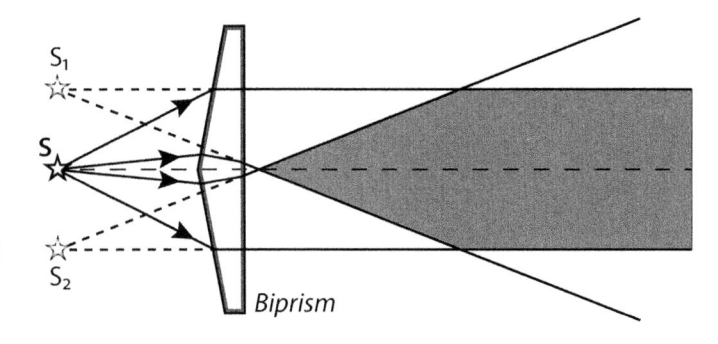

Unit 2 Polarisation

1. In a sound wave, the vibrations of the medium are in line with the direction of the disturbance.

   In a light wave, the vibrations are transverse.

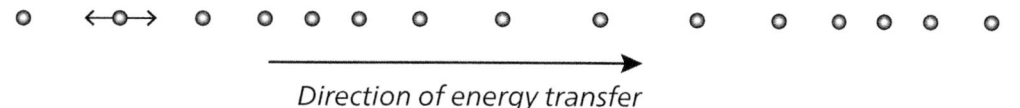

   Direction of energy transfer

   (a) Explain why polarisation isn't possible in a sound wave.

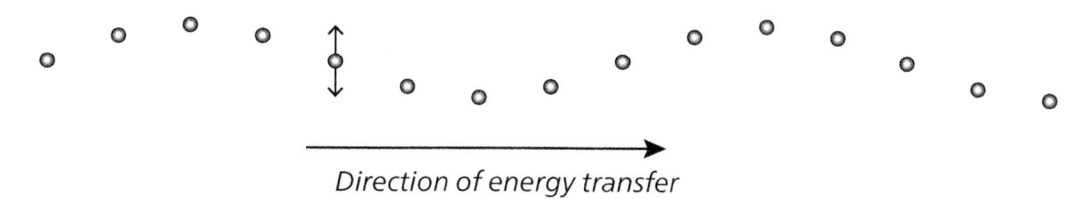

   Direction of energy transfer

   (b) In the sound wave diagram, what would the dots represent if it was travelling through air?

   (c) If the light ray was travelling through a vacuum, what would the dots represent?

2. These diagrams show the transverse vibrations of several light rays coming **towards** you:

   (a) What words are used to describe the beams in diagram 1 and diagram 2?

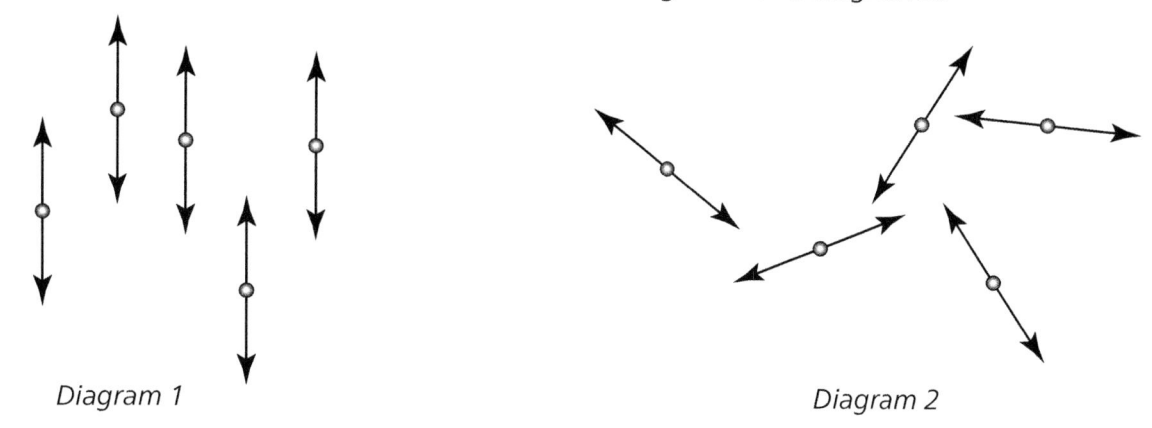

   Diagram 1   Diagram 2

   (b) In the diagrams below, a single arrow is used to show the magnitude of the electric field vector at an instant in time in a set of light rays. We've already covered coherence in the course and now know about polarisation. How would you describe the beams in A, B, C and D?

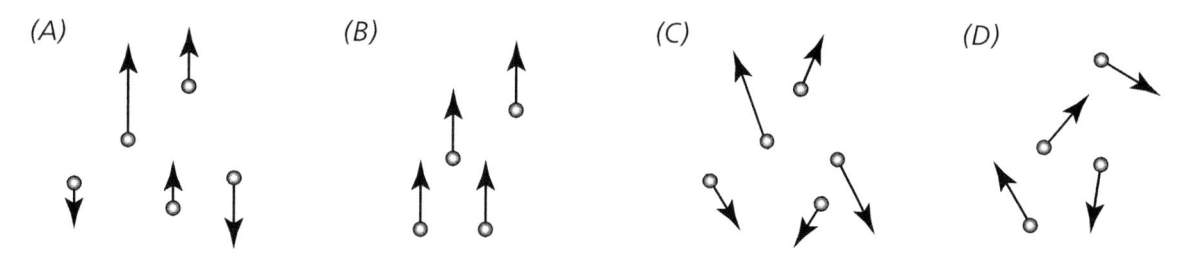

   (A)   (B)   (C)   (D)

   (c) Which of the above would have been emitted by a filament light bulb?

3. A grid of parallel metal bars held in place by two plastic yokes is a piece of equipment used to explain polarisation and is shown on the right. You often hear this 'explanation':

   'A plane polarised microwave can only pass between the metal bars if its plane of polarisation is in line with the gaps'.

   Explain why this sounds plausible, but is in fact, complete garbage.

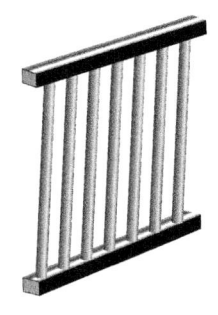

4. A plane polarised wave will pass through a polarising sheet if it's 'lined-up'. Tilt the wave through an angle 'θ' and less of it passes through. If the amplitude of the wave is one unit before it enters the polarising sheet, it will be cosθ when it leaves it.

   (a) What will be its intensity before entering the polarising sheet, and what will be its intensity after leaving the sheet?

   (b) Sketch the graph of $\cos^2\theta$ against θ between 0° and 90°.

   (c) A plane polarised wave has an intensity of 2.75W/m² and enters a polarising sheet at an angle of 20°. Calculate the maximum possible intensity on leaving the sheet.

5. Hold two polarising sheets, one behind the other in line with your eyes, with their polarising directions parallel. Light can pass through both of them.

   (a) Describe what happens to the intensity transmitted as you rotate one of them through 360°.

   (b) Explain whether you must have plane polarised light entering the first sheet or if unpolarised light will produce the same result.

   (c) Using the law with the angles in question 4, what fraction would be transmitted when one of the sheets was rotated by 45°.

6. A source of unpolarised light from direction 'A' is shone on a polarising sheet as shown in the diagram. The intensity at 'A' is 6Wm⁻².

   (a) When the right-hand polarising sheet is held with the **same** orientation as the first sheet, the intensity at 'C' is 0.8Wm⁻². Calculate the intensity at 'B' if the sheets are identical.

   (b) The right hand sheet is now rotated to the position shown in the diagram. Calculate the intensity at 'C' when the sheet is rotated by 40°.

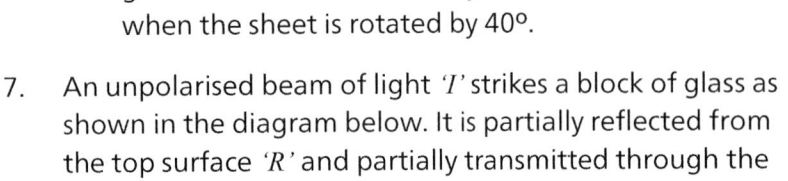

7. An unpolarised beam of light 'I' strikes a block of glass as shown in the diagram below. It is partially reflected from the top surface 'R' and partially transmitted through the glass block 'T'.

   (a) The angle between the reflected and transmitted beams is 90°. Calculate the angle of incidence θ_i if the refractive index of the glass is 1.58.

   (b) Describe the polarisation of the reflected beam 'R'.

   (c) What would be observed if the incident beam was plane polarised in the plane of the diagram?

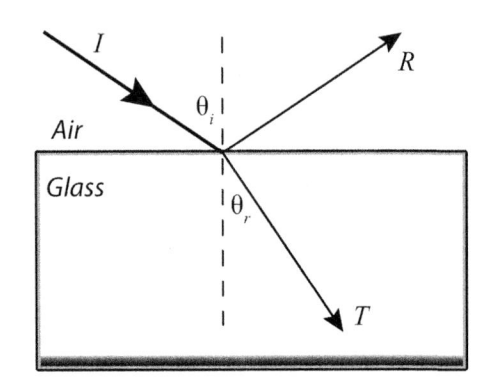

8. Question 7 above had an angle of 90° between reflected and transmitted beams. When this happens, the reflected beam is plane polarised and the angle of incidence is called the Brewster Angle. Calculate the Brewster Angle for:

   (a) Perspex (n = 1.48)   (b) Diamond (n = 2.41)   (c) Glass (n = 1.68)

9. Two polarising sheets are crossed such that no light emerges from the second sheet. Explain why a third polarising sheet placed **between them** can let light through!

Unit 3 Electric Fields

1. Coulomb's Law for the electrostatic force between two point charges Q_1 and Q_2 is: $F = \dfrac{1}{4\pi\varepsilon_o}\dfrac{Q_1Q_2}{r^2}$.

   (a) For rough calculations, what value can you take for $\dfrac{1}{4\pi\varepsilon_o}$?

   (b) What is the full name of the constant ε_o and what are its units?

   (c) The constant of proportionality $\dfrac{1}{4\pi\varepsilon_o}$ is large. Hold your hands one metre apart and face north. What would happen if a +1Coulomb charge was superglued to your left hand and a +1Coulomb charge was superglued to your right hand?

2. Calculate the electrostatic force for the examples below. All charges are point charges.

   (a) 15µC and 12µC charges which are 25cm apart.

   (b) Double the distance of the last question: 15µC and 12µC charges which are 50cm apart.

   (c) 1.6×10^{-19}C and -1.6×10^{-19}C which are 5.3×10^{-11}m apart (aka the hydrogen atom).

   (d) 5000C on the moon and -5000C on the Earth.

3. A charge 'q' in an electric field of electric field strength 'E' experiences a force of $F = Eq$. A charged oildrop of mass 2g, is held stationary in a uniform electric field of 5×10^3NC^{-1}.

   (a) Calculate the weight of the drop.

   (b) The oildrop is held stationary. What two forces are balanced?

   (b) Calculate the charge on the oildrop.

4. A one coulomb electric point charge is fixed 10m vertically above your belly-button. Look-up now; what do you see? Ok, let's pretend it's there. You're also wearing a waist harness containing another electric charge. You feel weightless.

   (a) Explain your weightlessness and support your reasoning with a calculation.

   (b) Someone hands you a bag of potatoes and you take them. What happened next?

   (c) What would happen if the sign of one of the charges was changed?

5. Coulomb's Law mentioned in Q1 is an example of an 'inverse square' Law. What does this mean?

6. Two electrically charged point masses are held on light threads suspended from a common point as shown. Each one has charge '$+q$' and mass 'm'.

   (a) There are three forces on each mass. Sketch and label a force diagram for one of the masses.

   (b) Resolve the force **from the string** on one of the small spheres into horizontal and vertical components. Derive an expression for the horizontal component of the string force on the sphere.

   (c) Calculate the separation of the spheres if the mass of each sphere is 5g, the charge on each sphere is 0.25µC and the angle θ is 20°.

63

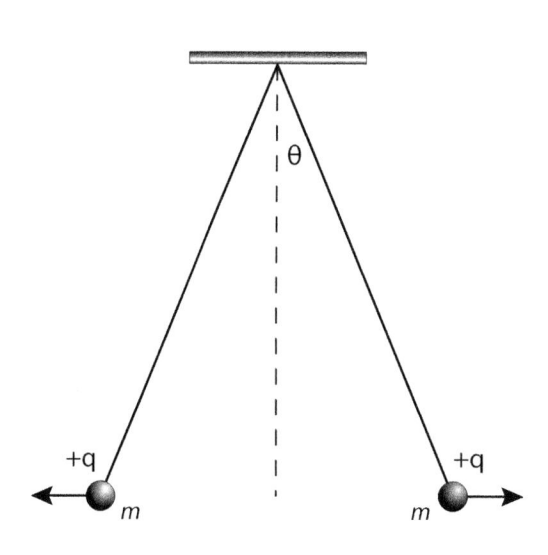

7. Two point electric charges Q and q are separated by a distance of 0.8m. If Q is replaced by a charge of 3Q and q is replaced by a charge of 5q, at what distance would they have to be separated to retain the same electrostatic force of repulsion?

8. If you want to tuck your chair in under a kitchen table you have to hold it with your hand and push it in. You can't just stand there and 'will it' under the table like some Jedi Knight. And yet, an electric charge can make other electric charges move without having to touch them. To explain this effect, scientists came up with a concept. What is this idea called? Does it solve the problem of how it's done, of how it works? Or does it just beg the question? Discuss.

9. An electric field can be illustrated graphically using lines.

    (a) How do you distinguish between the lines around a positive charge from the ones around a negative charge on such a drawing?

    (b) List the rules for drawing electric field lines.

    (c) Sketch the pattern of electric field lines around an electric dipole (a positive and a negative charge separated by distance).

10. This diagram shows some of the electric field lines in the region of space surrounding a distorted charged conductor 'P'.

    (a) What is the sign of the charge on 'P'?

    (b) Why does the electric charge reside at the surface?

    (c) A test charge +q is placed as shown. Why doesn't it modify the pattern of field lines?

    (d) Describe how you define the electric field strength where the test charge is placed.

    (e) Is the electric field uniform? How can you tell?

    (f) Calculate the electric field strength at the position of the test charge if the test charge is +0.02 coulombs and it experiences a force of 180N.

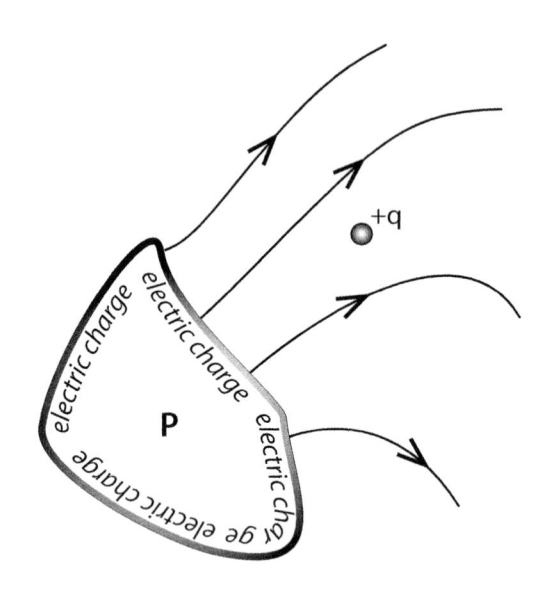

11. Electrostatic and gravitational forces are examples of inverse square laws. What other things do they have in common and what are the differences?

12. The electric field lines due to a point positive electric charge 'Q' give the pattern shown below in the surrounding space.

    (a) What name is given to this pattern?

    (b) Is the strength of the electric field uniform over any region of this space? Justify your answer.

    (c) At a distance 'r' from the point charge Q, write down an expression for the electric field at that point.

    (d) What happens to the size of the electric field strength if you double the distance from a point charge?

    (e) What effect will doubling the charge 'Q' have on the electric field strength at any point outside it?

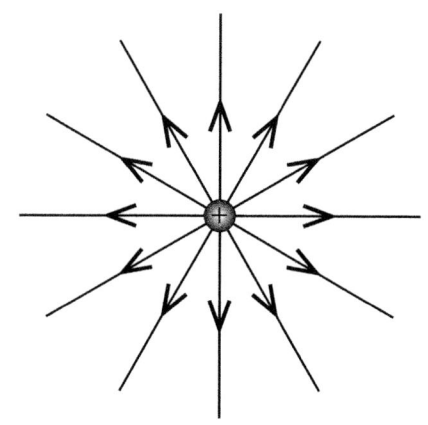

13. Charged parallel plates are the simplest way to produce a uniform electric field.

    (a) Use the equation $F = qE$ to calculate the electric field strength between the parallel plates in the diagram. The charge 'q' is 0.2C.

    (b) Using the information on the diagram, calculate the electric field strength between the plates using an alternative method? Check that it gives the same answer as part (a).

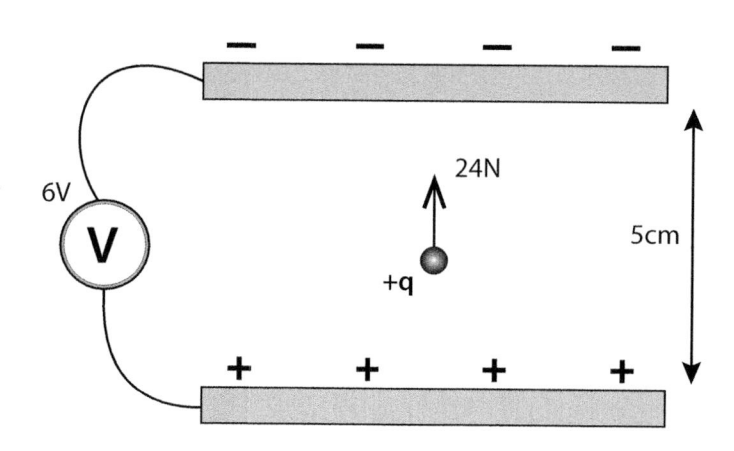

14. Use the equation $E = \dfrac{1}{4\pi\varepsilon_o}\dfrac{Q}{r^2}$ to calculate the electric field strength at a distance of 25m from a point charge of 4 x 10⁻³C.

15. This question is about the different shapes of electric fields.

    (a) A group of electric charges give rise to an electric field strength of 600N C⁻¹ at a distance of 3m in any direction from a reference position. At a distance of 6m in any direction from the same position, the electric field strength is still 600N C⁻¹. What can you deduce about the shape of the electric field?

    (b) From the reference point, the electric field strength at 3m was still 600N C⁻¹ but was now 150N C⁻¹ at a distance of 6m in any direction. What could you deduce about the shape of the electric field this time? Where must the reference position have been in this case?

16. The diagram below shows two point electric charges Q_1 and Q_2 separated by a distance of 28m. Use the Principle of Superposition to calculate the electric field strengths at points 'A', 'B' and 'C' due to the two charges. The charges are $Q_1 = +5 \times 10^{-4}$C and $Q_2 = +5 \times 10^{-4}$C.

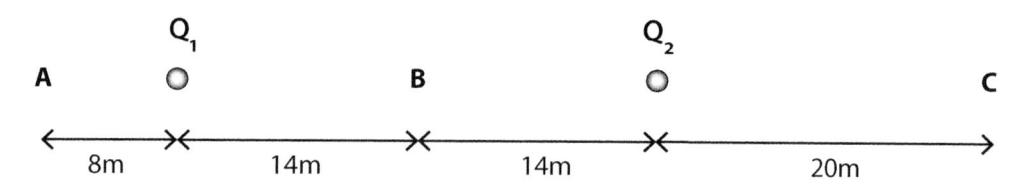

17. Four small spheres are laid out in the shape of a square as shown in the diagram. The length of a side is 30cm and all the spheres are charged positively of magnitude 2 x 10⁻⁴C.

    (a) What effect does the size of the sphere have on any calculations of the electric field strengths at positions 'A' and 'B'?

    (b) Calculate the electric field strength at the mid-point 'A' of the left side.

    (c) Calculate the electric field strength at the centre of the square 'B'.

    (d) What would be the electric field strength at 'B' if Q_4 had been negative?

    (e) What configuration of pluses and minuses would produce an electric field at position 'B' where its direction was pointing towards 12 o'clock?

18. An electron enters the region between charged parallel plates with a speed of 1.68 × 10⁷ms⁻¹ at the mid-point as shown in the diagram.

    (a) Describe the shape of the electric field between the plates.

    (b) Calculate the time to traverse the region between the plates.

    (c) Calculate the electric field strength between the plates.

    (d) Locate the position of the electron as it leaves the plates.

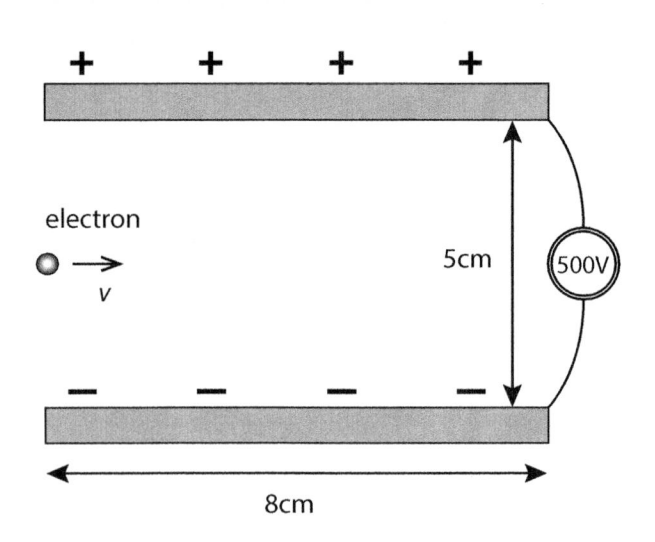

Unit 3 Electrostatic Potential

1. A point electric charge 'Q' creates an electric field as shown in the diagram opposite.

    (a) What sign has the charge and how can you tell?

    (b) The magnitude of 'Q' is: 4 × 10⁻⁵C and the distance to point 'A' is 28cm from 'Q'.

    Use $|E| = \dfrac{1}{4\pi\varepsilon_o}\dfrac{Q}{r^2}$ $V = \dfrac{1}{4\pi\varepsilon_o}\dfrac{Q}{r}$

    to calculate the electric field strength and the electrostatic potential at point 'A'.

    (c) What difference would it make to your answers to part (b) if the sign of 'Q' was reversed?

    (d) What other positions for point 'A' would give the same electrostatic potential?

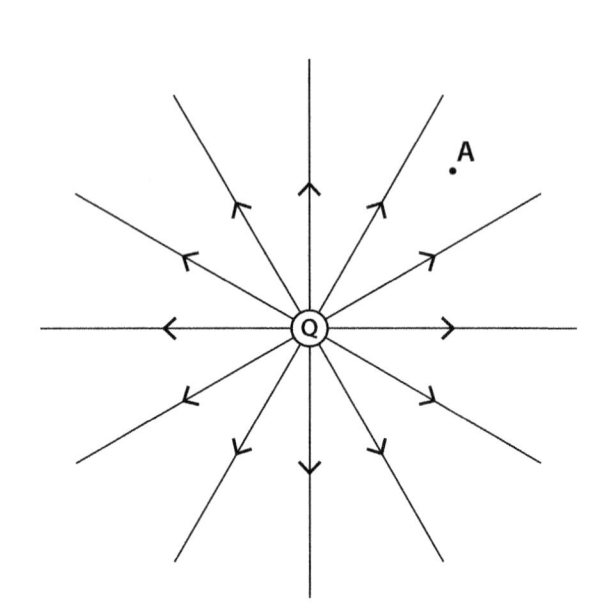

2. Electrostatic potential is a scalar. Why does this make calculations easier?

3. The electrostatic potential is helpful in calculating the energy required to move a charged object from one position to another in an electric field.

    (a) What are the units for electrostatic potential (V) and energy (E)?

    (b) Calculate the potential difference between any two points 'A' and 'B' due to a point charge 'Q' where 'A' is 40m from 'Q' and 'B' is 60m from 'Q'. Charge 'Q' is : +8 × 10⁻⁴C.

    (c) How much energy is required to move a charge 'q' of +3μC from 'B' to 'A'?

4. Electric field lines for a non-uniform field are as shown on the diagram (the solid lines):

    (a) Identify the areas with the strongest and weakest electric field strengths.

    (b) The dotted line on the diagram cuts the electric field lines at 90°. What is it called and what is its significance?

    (c) Should the dotted line have an arrow?

    (d) How much work would be done in moving an electric charge along the dotted line?

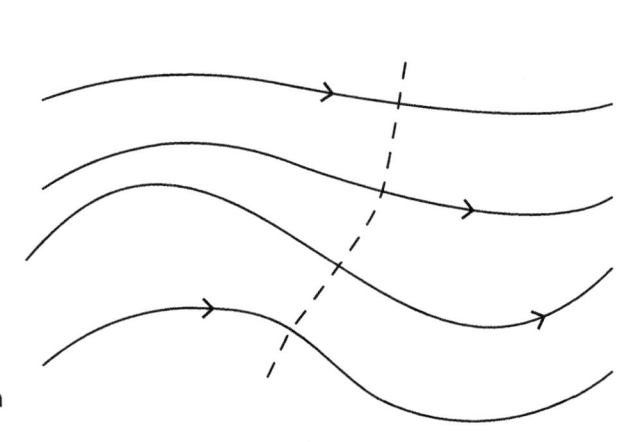

66

5. What shape is the equipotential surface outside a point charge? Why is this?

6. Two smooth solid metal conducting shapes 'A' and 'B' have the same quantity of electric charge.

   (a) Make a rough sketch of the shapes then label the regions just outside the surface with either 'H' for high, 'M' for medium and 'L' for low electric field strength.

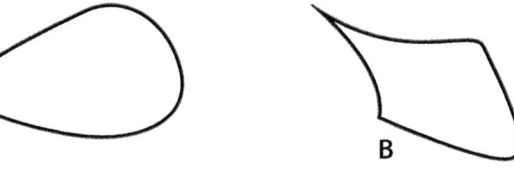

   (b) The surface of each shape is at an electrostatic potential of 350volts. What is the electric field strength and the potential **inside** each shape?

7. (a) The solid copper sphere in the diagram below has a positive electric charge of 2μC. Calculate the electrostatic potential at the grid points along the line AB. The grid spacing is 0.2m.

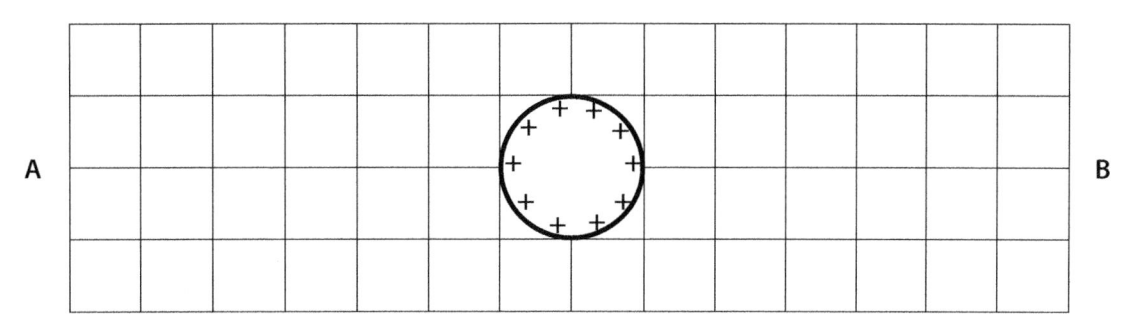

   (b) Sketch the graph of electrostatic potential against distance between 'A' and 'B' from -1.4m to +1.4m.

   (c) Sketch the graph if the charge was the same magnitude but negative.

8. Two electric charges, $Q_1 = +6\mu C$ and $Q_2 = -4\mu C$ are placed 80cm apart. Locate any positions where the electrostatic potential is zero. Assume that they are point charges.

9. Four charges are placed on a square as shown. The length of the diagonal is in units of metres.

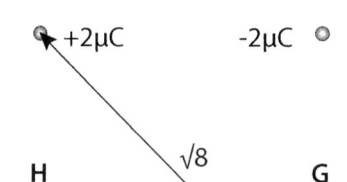

   (a) Calculate the potential at mid-points 'G' and 'H'.

   (b) Calculate the work done in moving a +5μC charge 'q' from 'G' to 'H'.

   (c) Unlike the electrostatic potential 'V', the electric field strength 'E' is a vector. In which direction does the electric field vector point at the centre of the square?

10. A D.C. supply maintains a constant potential difference across a pair of parallel plates as shown on the diagram. The voltmeter measures a potential difference of 80volts.

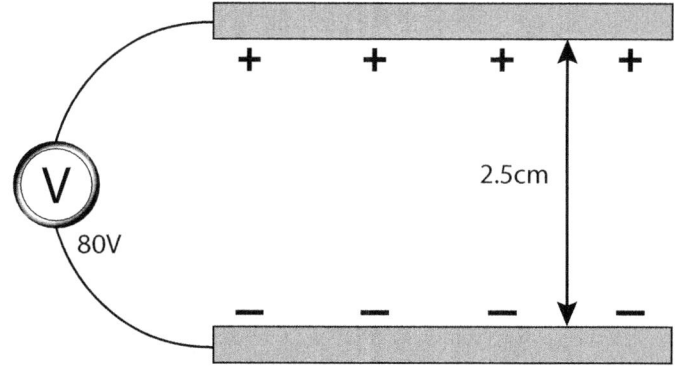

    (a) What word describes the electric field pattern between the plates?

    (b) Describe the pattern of equipotential lines between the plates.

    (c) Taking the zero of electrostatic potential at the bottom plate, locate and draw the line at 48volts constant electrostatic potential.

67

11. Planet Earth is spherical in shape. Suppose, like the ancients thought, it was flat like a 2-dimensional plane. You could walk any distance across its surface and still see the land receeding off to infinity in all directions. Suppose the surface of such a world was uniformly charged; every square metre of surface had the same electric charge. Describe the electric field pattern above this charged infinite plane sheet.

12. How far away from a +5µC point charge is an equipotential surface of +3kV?

13. The diagram shows a 2-dimensional slice through the space around a charged, metal sphere. The sphere has charge of Q =+3µC and the grid spacing is 5metres.

    (a) What do the dotted lines represent?

    (b) Calculate the electrostatic potential at the surfaces 'a', 'b' and 'c'.

    (c) Calculate the potential at the surface of the metal sphere (radius 2.5m).

    (d) What is the electric field strength and potential inside the sphere?

    (e) At what angle do the electric field lines cut the equipotential surfaces?

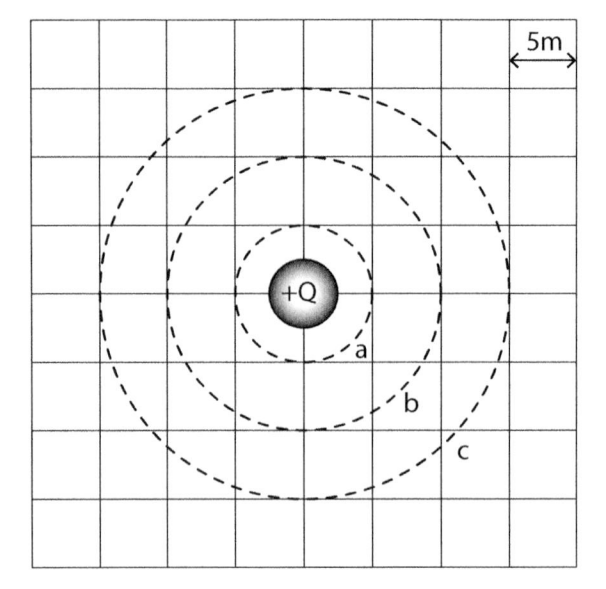

14. Two point charges 'q' and 'Q' an infinite distance apart, are 'knackered'. They have no (potential) energy. Give them (potential) energy by pushing them together until they are a distance r apart.

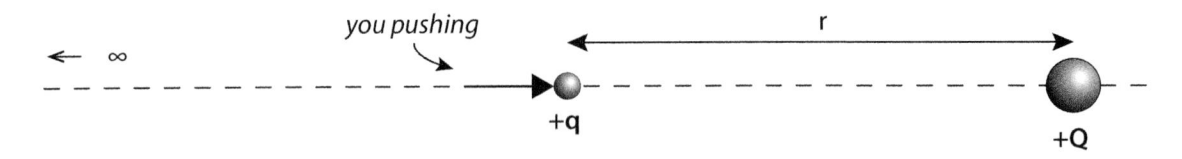

    They take the energy you've put in and store it in the joint electric field. For the system above, you had to push to the right. Work done is calculated from force and distance.

    (a) Explain why you have to use $\int_{\infty}^{r} F dr$ rather than Fr in calculating the Work Done.

    The integral contains the variable 'r' which goes **out** from charge 'Q' but you are pushing in the opposite direction so we put a negative sign in front of the integral: $-\int_{\infty}^{r} F dr$

    (b) Use the expression for the force of repulsion of two point electric charges, substitute it into the integral and calculate the work done by you in bringing the two charges from infinity to a distance r apart.

    (c) Use your answer to part (b) above to calculate the potential energy of a system of charges comprising q =+4µC and Q =+28µC at a separation of 50cm.

15. Two points in space, 'A' and 'B' are within a uniform electric field of 350volts per metre.

    (a) Calculate the potential difference between these two points if they are 20cm apart.

    (b) A point charge of 80µC was placed at position 'A'. Calculate the magnitude of the force on the charge.

16. The diagram shows charged parallel plates with a separation of 12cm, placed within a vacuum. They have an electric field strength of 150Vm⁻¹ between them.

    (a) Calculate the potential difference of the battery supplying the plates.

    (b) An electron pops out of the cathode. Describe the motion of the electron as it moves towards the anode

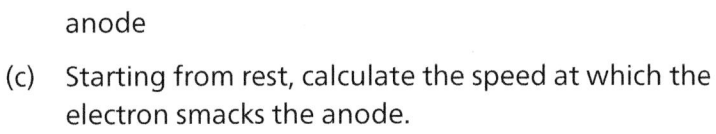

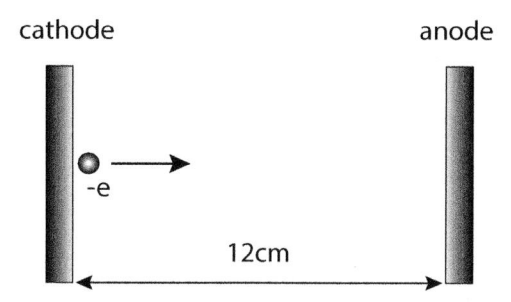

    (c) Starting from rest, calculate the speed at which the electron smacks the anode.

17. An evacuated tube contains charged parallel plates as shown below. An electron enters at point 'A' along the mid-point line with a constant velocity v. The plates are d = 6cm apart, 15cm long and the point 'C' is 2cm up from the mid-point line.

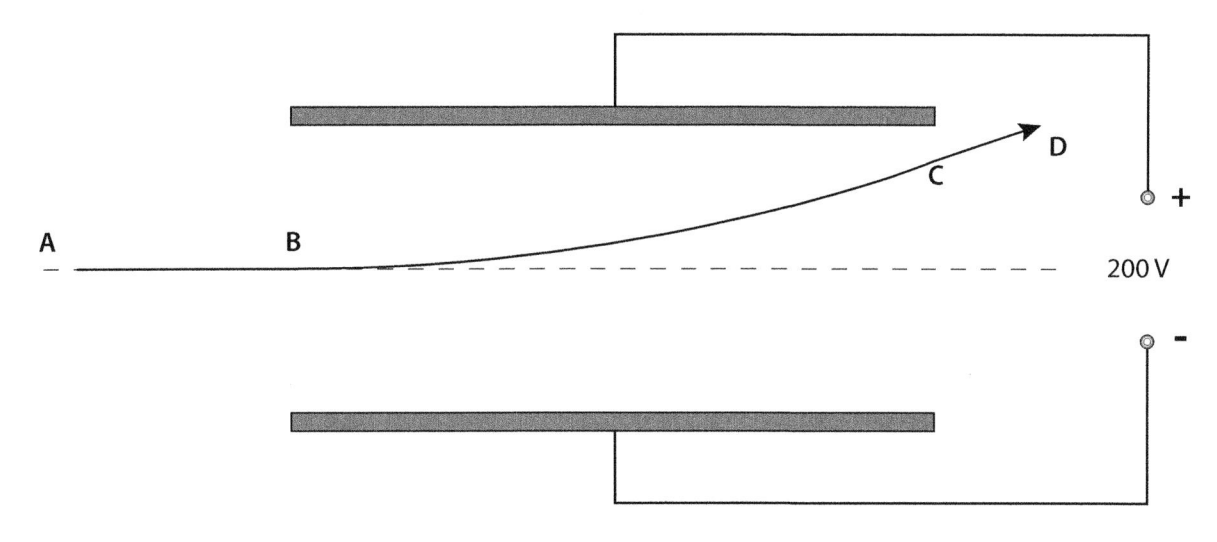

    (a) Describe, with reasons, the motions of the trajectories 'AB', 'BC' and 'CD'.

    (b) The trajectory BC is described by the equation: $y = \left(\dfrac{Vq}{2mv^2d}\right)x^2$ where the origin of the (x,y) co-ordinate system is at 'B'. Graphing y as a function of x gives a certain shape of graph. What is this shape called in mathematics?

    (c) Calculate the (x,y) co-ordinates of point 'C'.

    (d) Use the equation in part (b) to calculate the initial speed v of the electron.

    (e) Where would point 'C' move to if the initial speed of the electron was doubled?

18. (a) The accepted SI unit for energy is the *joule*. Particle physicists use a different unit based on the behaviour of an electron in an electric field. What is this unit called, how is it defined, and how is it related to the *joule*?

    (b) A cricket ball of mass 0.4kg was bowled at a speed of 50mph. A particle physicist calculated the answer for the kinetic energy of the ball in joules. This was the sensible unit to use in the circumstances, but he decided to convert the answer into his more familiar unit. What is his final answer?

    (c) The particle physicist was dreaming about comparing cricket balls with cosmic rays at the time and this explained his late conversion. Describe the connection! (See the Theory Book p111).

    (d) Why is this other unit the preferred unit of energy in semiconductor physics?

19. R.A.Millikan performed a famous experiment with charged oil drops as illustrated in the diagram.

    (a) How did Millikan charge the oil drops?

    (b) How did he keep the oil drop stationary?

    (c) The observed oil drop has a density of 860kg m⁻³ and diameter of 1.2 x 10⁻⁶m. Calculate the mass of the oil drop.

    (d) He brought the drop to rest with an electric field strength between the plates of 5280 Vm⁻¹. Calculate the electric charge on the drop.

    (e) Millikan repeated the experiment many times and reached a famous conclusion. What was his conclusion?

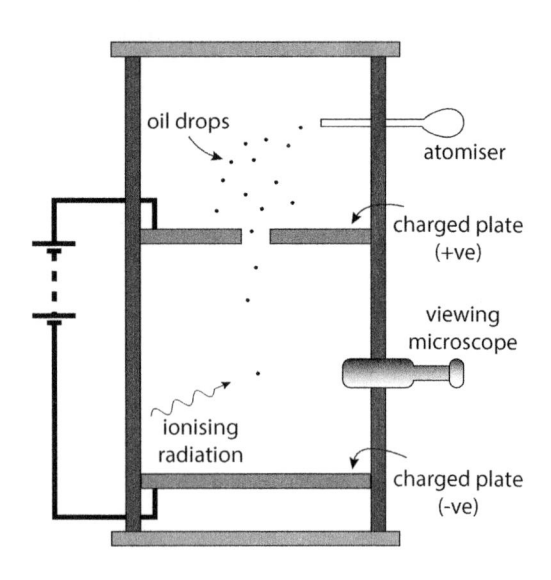

20. Charged parallel plates are held at a potential difference of 27500 volts and have a separation of 8cm. The three main types of ionising radiation, alpha, beta and gamma are travelling between them in the direction shown. All three start from the midpoint between the plates with the alpha and beta particles starting with an initial speed of 1.2 × 10⁶m/s.

    (a) Calculate the electric field strength between the plates.

    (b) Describe with calculations, the motions of the three particles. Give as much information as possible, including times of notable events, any distances, and speeds of impact.

    (c) The potential difference across the plates was adjusted until the beta particle came to rest just as it reached the cathode. Calculate the new potential difference.

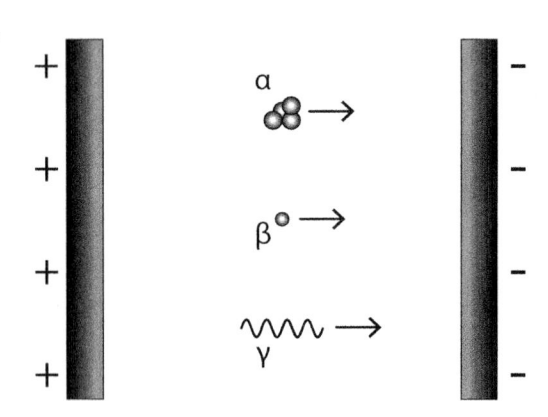

21. An alpha particle is travelling directly towards a magnesium nucleus as shown in the diagram below. When very far away from the nucleus, its speed is 7.2 × 10⁵m/s.

    (a) Why is it important to specify where the particle was at the quoted speed?

    (b) Calculate the kinetic energy of the alpha particle.

    (c) The alpha particle slows down and comes to a momentary stop at the position of closest approach. What has happened to the kinetic energy of the alpha particle?

    (d) Use the equation for the electrostatic potential energy of a system of two charges to calculate the distance (r) of closest approach. Magnesium has 12 protons in its nucleus.

    (e) What assumptions did you make in your calculations?

Unit 3 Magnetic Fields

1. Electricity and Magnetism used to be thought of as separate areas of scientific study. Which Scottish scientist revealed the close connection between them, and which eventually led to the idea of Grand Unified Theories of particle physics?

2. An observer watches an electrically charged object moving with a velocity 'v'. He measures the electric field at a point as it passes.

   (a) What other field can he also measure?

   (b) What difference would it make if the electric charge stopped moving?

   (c) Since this effect depends upon the velocity of the charge relative to the observer, what theory of Physics would you suspect is responsible?

3. (a) The equation $F = qE$ is used to define the electric field strength 'E' from the force on a charge 'q'. Why doesn't a similar approach work when trying to define 'magnetic field strength'?

   (b) What is the proper term for 'magnetic field strength' and what is its symbol?

4. (a) Describe how to use the fingers of your right hand to work out the direction of the force on a wire carrying a current of electrons in a magnetic field.

   (b) How could you adapt the above rule to calculate the direction of the force on a beam of protons or alpha particles in a vacuum?

5. The equation $F = BIL \sin \theta$ is used to calculate the force 'F' on a wire of length 'L' passing a current 'I' in a magnetic field 'B'.

   (a) Use the equation to calculate the forces on the wires in the diagrams below and use the right-hand rule to work out the direction in which the force acts on the wire. Each wire is of length 1 metre.

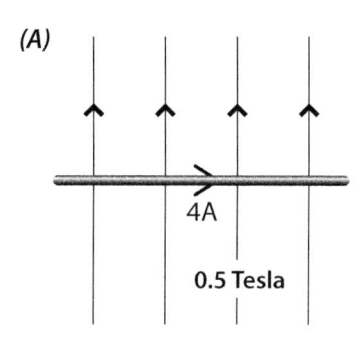

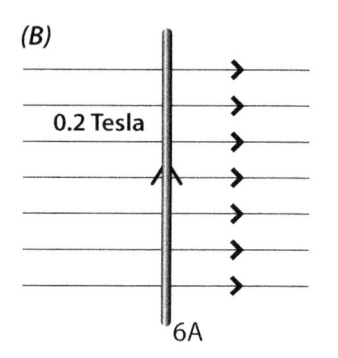

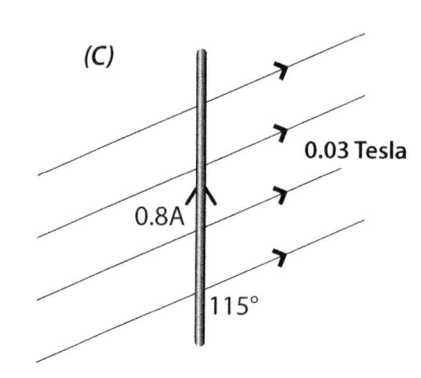

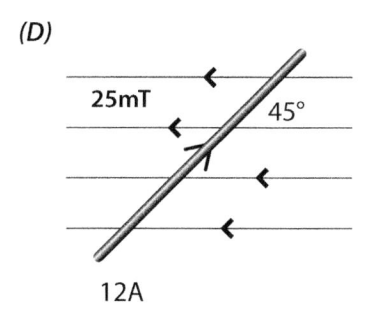

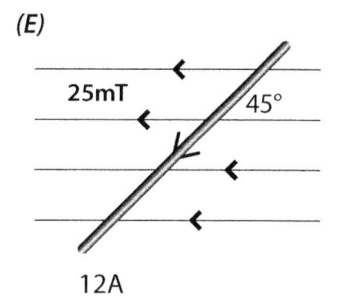

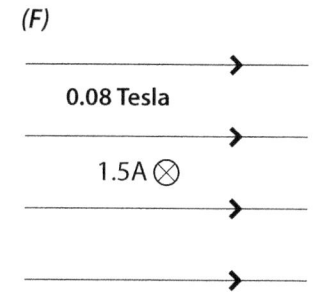

   (A) 4A, 0.5 Tesla

   (B) 0.2 Tesla, 6A

   (C) 0.03 Tesla, 0.8A, 115°

   (D) 25mT, 45°, 12A

   (E) 25mT, 45°, 12A

   (F) 0.08 Tesla, 1.5A

   (b) In each case above, the current is travelling through a metal wire. Is the force acting on the wire or is the force acting on the moving electric charges in the wire. Is the wire necessary?

6. A current carrying wire is formed into the shape of a rectangle to form the basis of an electric motor spinning about an axis PQ:

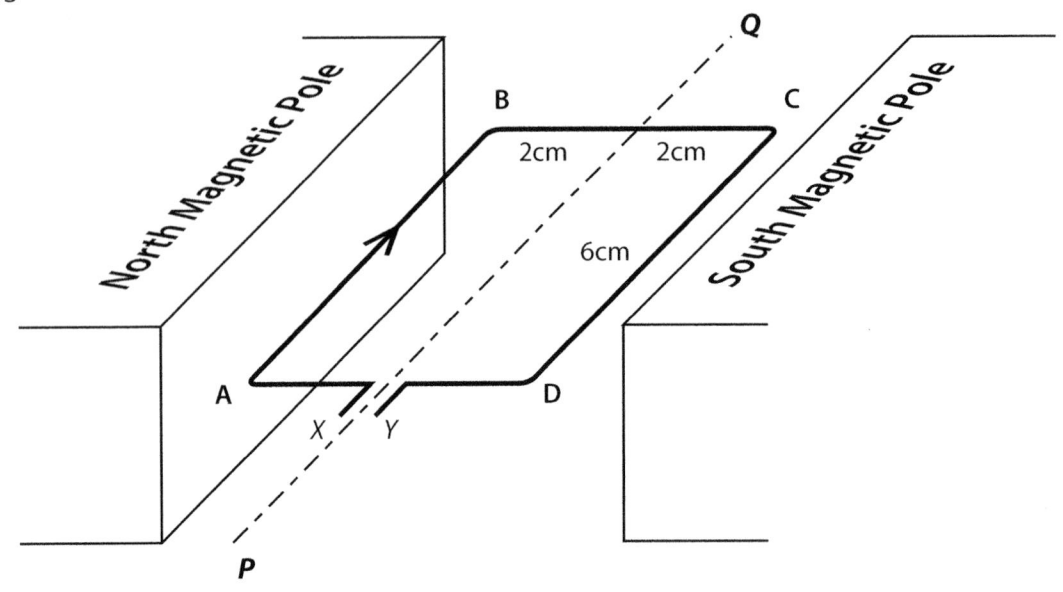

(a) In which direction do the magnetic field lines point?

(b) A DC battery is connected to the ends of the wire at 'XY' through an arrangement known as a commutator. From the direction of current flow shown on the diagram, which end is connected to the positive side of the battery?

(c) Use the right-hand rule to describe the direction of the force on sections AB, BC, CD and AD of the wire (in the position shown in the diagram).

(d) The loop experiences a torque due to the current in the magnetic field. Explain why there is a position of the loop where the torque is zero. What is this position?

(e) A one metre length of the wire has mass 9g. Calculate the Moment of Inertia of the loop.

(f) Use $F = BIl\sin\theta$ and $T = rF$ to calculate the torque and angular acceleration on the loop at the position shown. The current is 0.25A and the magnetic induction B = 0.15T.

7. Most magnets are long-boxy-shapes with their poles at the ends. The magnets in the diagram opposite are different. They have their poles on the sides of them! A pair of them sit on a top-pan balance with opposite poles facing each other. A current carrying wire is positioned between them. This wire is formed into straight sections as shown. It doesn't touch the balance and is held in a fixed position by a clamp above it (not shown). The reading on the balance is 483.03g when no current is flowing through the wire and 485.64g when a current of 8A flows in the wire. Each of the 3 sections of wire is 4cm long.

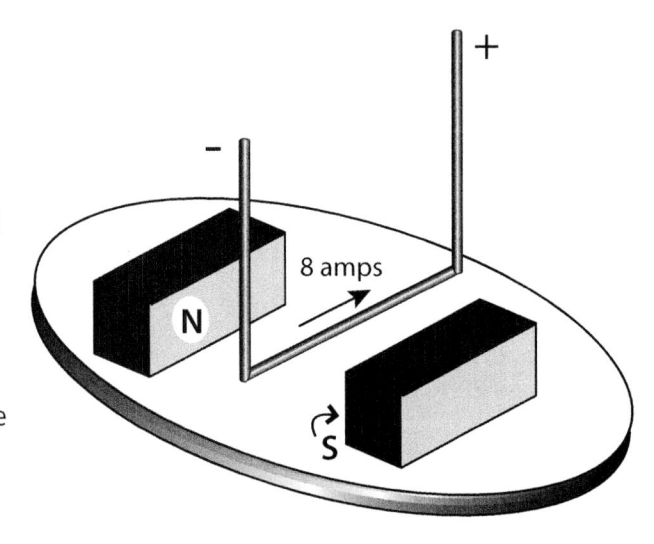

(a) Why is this particular type of magnet used rather than the poles-at-the-ends type?.

(b) Explain why only the middle section of the wire contributes to the change in reading on the balance when the current flows.

(c) Calculate the magnetic induction due to the permanent magnets.

8. (a) The diagram on the right shows a current carrying wire at an angle to a magnetic field. Use $F = BIl\sin\theta$ and the Right-Hand Rule to calculate the force (magnitude and direction) on each metre length of wire.

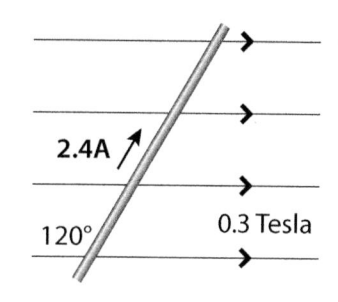

    (b) What difference would it make if you reversed the current direction **or** the direction of the magnetic field?

9. An electron has a charge of -1.6 x 10⁻¹⁹C.

    (a) How many electrons are needed to make up a charge of -4C?

    (b) What current flows if 28 coulombs of charge passes a point in 1 minute?

10. A proton beam is directed towards a uniform magnetic field as shown in the diagram:

    (a) In which direction will the protons be deflected when they enter the magnetic field?

    (b) If the proton beam is 'continuous' and makes a current of 6mA, calculate the force on a 1 metre length of the beam.

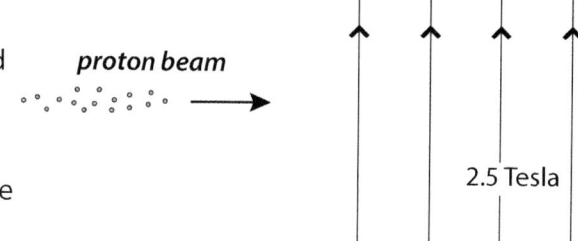

11. The diagram shows a current 'I' in a straight wire creating a magnetic field around it.

    (a) The current consists of electrons moving in the direction as shown. Use the Left-Hand grip rule to determine the direction of the arrows on the magnetic field lines.

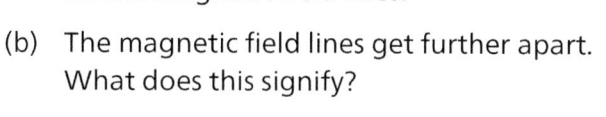

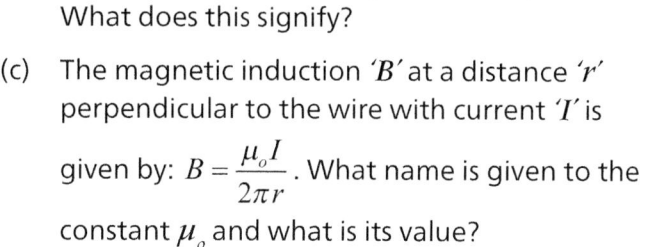

    (b) The magnetic field lines get further apart. What does this signify?

    (c) The magnetic induction 'B' at a distance 'r' perpendicular to the wire with current 'I' is given by: $B = \dfrac{\mu_o I}{2\pi r}$. What name is given to the constant μ_o and what is its value?

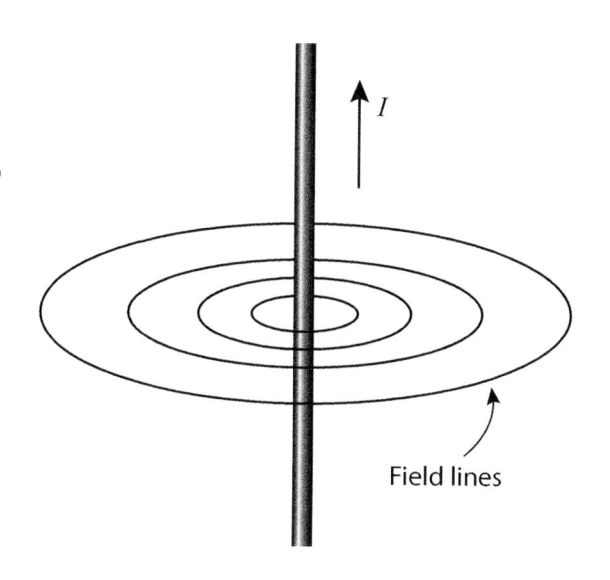

    (d) Calculate the magnetic induction at a distance of 0.1m from a wire with a current of 2A.

12. (a) A straight piece of copper wire carries a current of 0.75A. How far away from it would you have to go to get a magnetic induction of 6µT?

    (b) What would be the magnetic induction at twice the distance?

    (c) The combination $\dfrac{\mu_o}{2\pi}$ often occurs in calculations. Calculate (or just write down) its value.

13. The power cables in a house are usually wired in a ring mains arrangement. The cable below has two current carrying conductors and an earth wire. Explain why this arrangement produces only a weak magnetic field around it even for relatively large currents.

14. Calculate the magnetic induction 'B' at a distance of 20m from a wire carrying a current of 3A.

15. Over the UK, the Earth's magnetic field varies from 48μT in the south to 50μT in the north.

    (a) What is the maximum possible magnetic force on a 1 metre length of wire with a 2A current?

    (b) What else does the force depend upon?

16. The Earth's magnetic field is similar to the field produced by a bar magnet (it's called a 'dipole field'). It's shown on the diagram opposite. The geographic north (the arctic) and south (the antarctic) poles are marked.

    (a) What do you notice about the direction of the arrows on the field lines?

    (b) What does this suggest about the magnetic polarity of the north geographic pole?

    (c) Explain why it's difficult to take a compass reading near the poles.

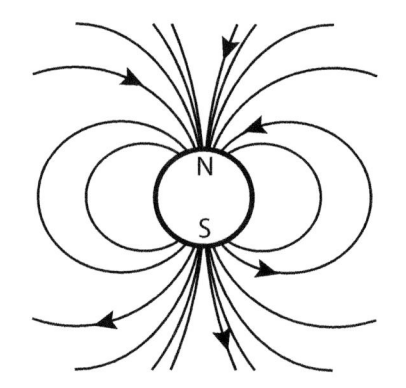

17. Overhead transmission lines operate at voltages of up to 400kV and can carry currents up to several hundred amps. The charges produce electric fields and the currents produce magnetic fields. Some people claim that these magnetic fields can be detrimental to health. In response, the electricity suppliers publish graphs like the one opposite. On the horizontal scale, the zero metres point is vertically under the cable. Real transmission lines carry 6 pairs of cables (3 pairs each side) and the currents are deliberately placed out of phase on opposite sides to reduce the magnetic field.

    Do a calculation of the magnetic field strength 'B' directly under a single cable with a current of 250A at a height of 10m above the ground. Compare your answer with the Earths own magnetic field.

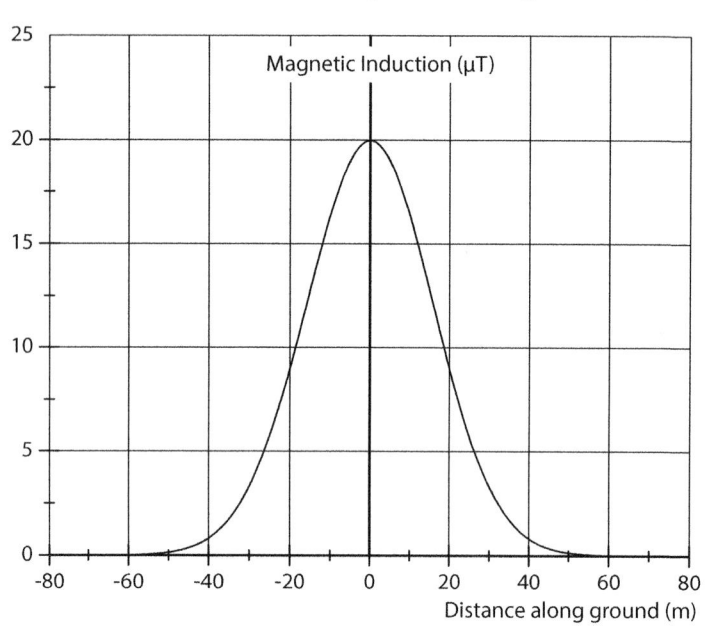

18. Two parallel wires 'A' and 'B' carry currents I_1 and I_2 as shown in the diagram below.

    (a) Consider the magnetic field due only to the current I_1 in wire 'A'. Use the left-hand grip rule to work out the direction of the magnetic field lines at points 'P' and 'Q'.

    (b) Wire 'B' with current I_2 is now moved over to point 'Q'. What effect would the magnetic field due to 'A' have on the current in wire 'B'?

    (c) What difference would it make if the current in wire 'B' was reversed?

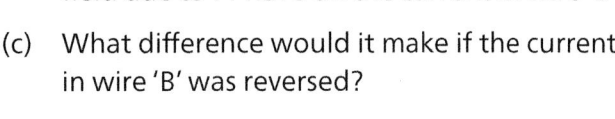

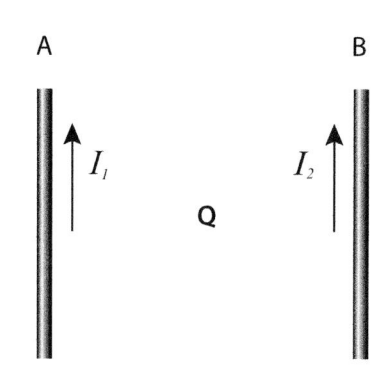

    (d) Calculate the force on a 1metre length of wire 'A' if the current in wire 'A' is 2.5A, the current in wire 'B' is 1.5A and the wires are 8cm apart.

19. Two parallel wires carry currents of 3A and 5A in the same direction. Both wires are 25cm long and are 15cm apart. Calculate the force on each wire and describe its direction.

20. Two samples of a semiconductor are placed within a magnetic field whose direction is **into** the page (circled crosses). Sample 'A' on the left has 'holes' moving downwards and sample 'B' on the right has electrons moving upwards.

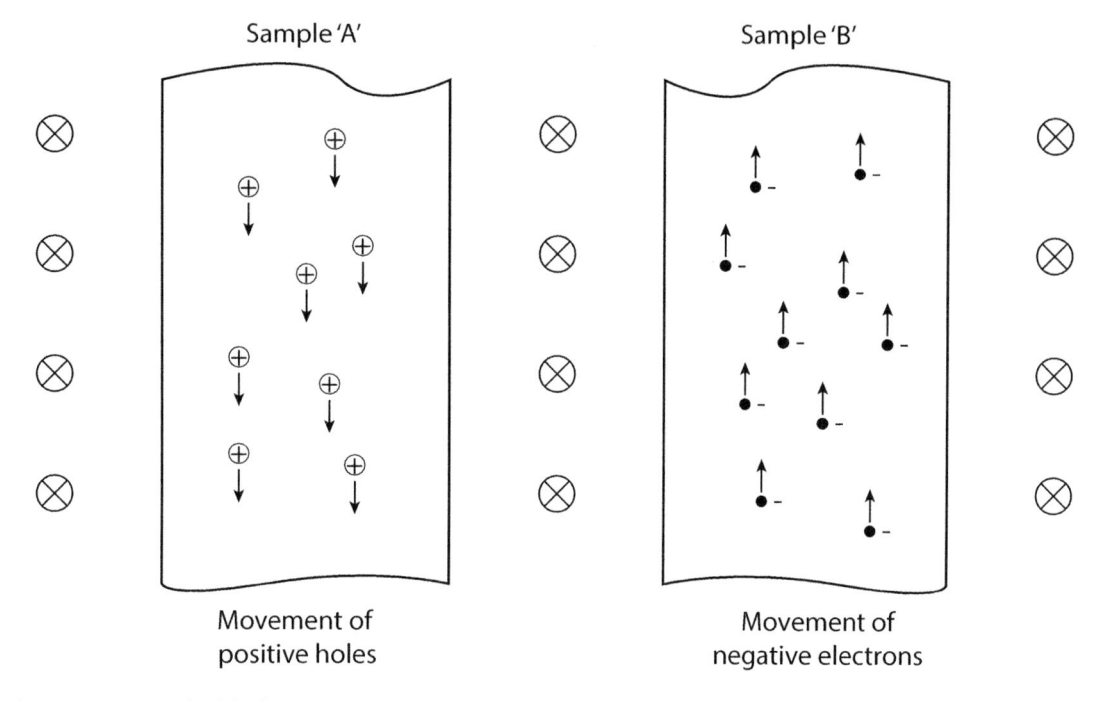

Sample 'A' — Movement of positive holes

Sample 'B' — Movement of negative electrons

   (a) The magnetic field also permeates the semiconductor. In which direction does the magnetic field deflect the holes and in which direction does it deflect the electrons?

   (b) Electric charge will build up on the sides of each sample due to this deflection. This maintains a voltage (the Hall voltage) across the sides of each sample. Will the polarity (which side is plus and which is minus), be the same for each sample? Describe the polarity for each sample.

21. A uniform magnetic field can be created by passing a direct current through a coil of wire. The field inside the coil is almost constant within its volume and can be varied by increasing or decreasing the current through the wire. This arrangement is used to investigate the magnetic properties of a sample of iron by placing it inside the coil.

   (a) The term *'magnetic domain'* is used in ferromagnetism. Explain what is meant by a domain in the sample of iron.

   (b) Describe what happens to the magnetic properties of the iron sample as the current is increased in the coil.

   (c) The current is now switched off. Is the sample magnetically changed from its initial state? Explain.

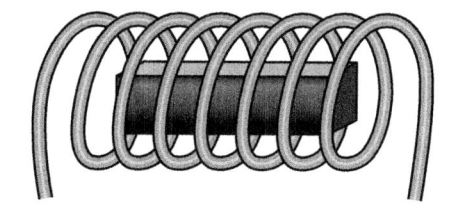

22. (a) Name three metals from the periodic table which exhibit ferromagnetism.

   (b) Increasing the temperature of a ferromagnet can alter its magnetic properties. Describe what happens as you increase the temperature, and explain the significance of the Curie temperature T_c.

23. (a) Explain the difference between a 'soft' magnetic material and a 'hard' magnetic material.

   (b) Give examples of the applications of 'soft' and 'hard' magnetic materials.

Unit 3 Capacitors

1. Remember capacitors from 5th year? Try this. A 64µF capacitor has a potential difference of 12volts across it. Calculate the charge stored on each plate.

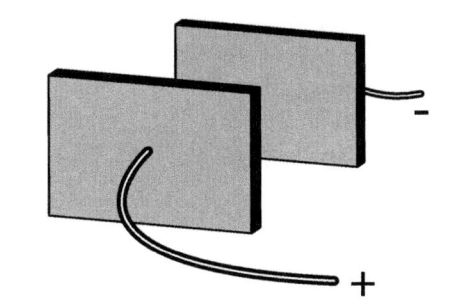

2. And this. Calculate the energy stored in a 2000µF capacitor when the potential difference of 240volts is across its plates.

3. Let's not forget graphs. This one shows the charging of a 5000µF capacitor through a resistance of 2kΩ. The y-axis is the voltage across the capacitor.

    (a) What was the p.d. of the charging battery?

    (b) Describe how you could:

    (i) make the charging happen more quickly.

    (ii) slow down the charging.

    (c) Calculate the initial current just as the charging started.

    (d) Sketch the graph of voltage-time but this time for the voltage across the resistor.

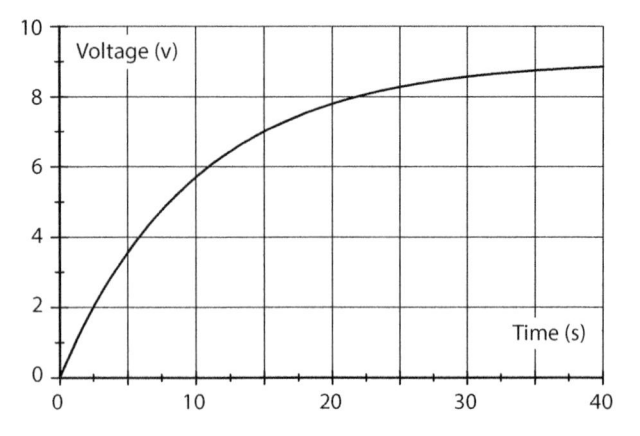

4. One common use of a capacitor is in a circuit like the one in the diagram using an NPN transistor.

    (a) What is the circuit designed to do?

    (b) Explain how it works in terms of the voltages at various points in the circuit.

    (c) Describe how the circuit can have a degree of adjustability.

    (d) What is the function of the resistor R_2?

    (e) How could you modify the circuit to control the operation of a more powerful lamp? You can replace or add new components.

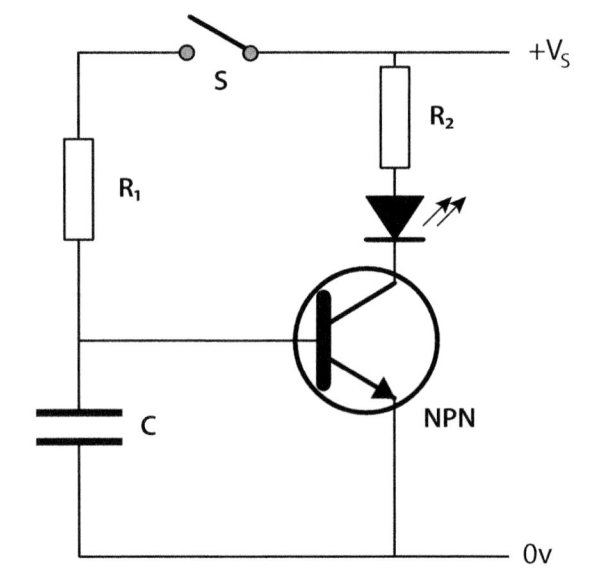

5. In a circuit containing a resistor and capacitor, the combination CR is known as the time constant.

    (a) What units is CR measured in?

    (b) Calculate the time constant for these combinations:

    (i) Capacitance of 2F with a resistance of 8Ω.

    (ii) Capacitance of 32µF with a resistance of 15kΩ.

    (iii) Capacitance of 80nF with a resistance of 22MΩ.

6. A 12volt supply is used to charge a capacitor 'C' through a resistor 'R'. The potential difference across the capacitor is given by the equation: $V_C = V_S\left(1 - e^{-\frac{t}{CR}}\right)$. Calculate the potential difference across the capacitor at a time equal to the time constant.

7. The graph of the potential difference across a 47μF capacitor charging as a function of time is shown opposite.

   (a) What was the supply voltage?

   (b) The time constant is the time taken to reach a certain fraction of the supply voltage. That fraction is $\left(1-\dfrac{1}{e}\right)$. Estimate the time constant from the graph.

   (c) The capacitor charged through a resistor. Calculate its resistance.

   (d) The supply voltage was changed to one of 9 volts. What effect would this have on the time constant. Justify your answer.

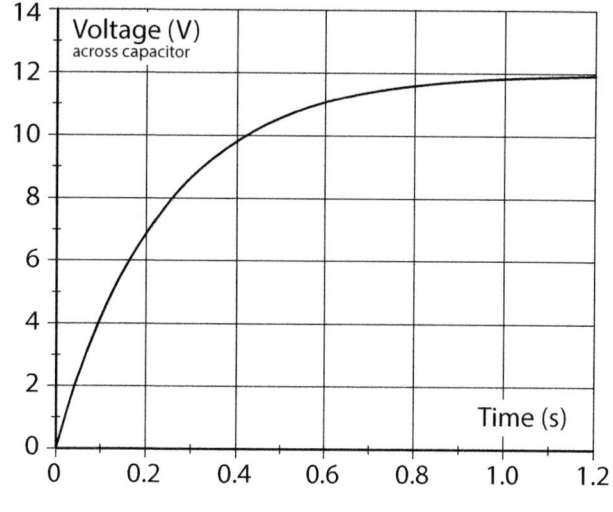

8. The circuit below left produced the graph below right.

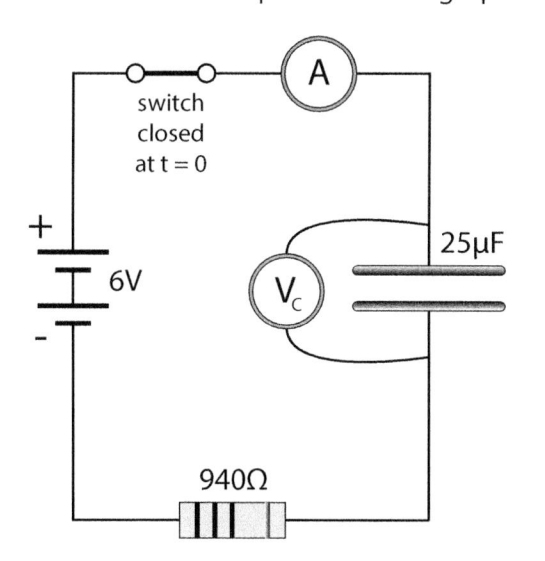

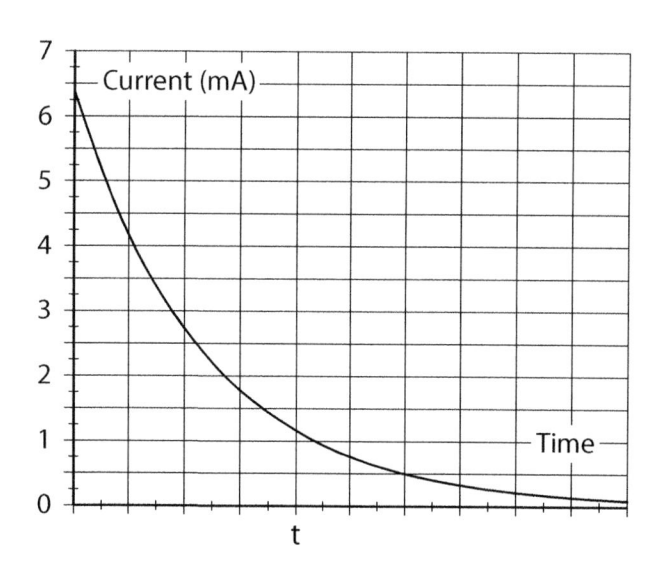

   (a) Is this a charging or a discharging circuit when the switch is closed?

   (b) The initial value of the current from the graph is a bit over 6mA. Use the values on the circuit to calculate the initial current more accurately.

   (c) The current 'I' as a function of time is given by the equation: $I = I_o e^{-\frac{t}{CR}}$. Calculate the value of the time constant and hence evaluate time 't' on the time axis. The ticks on the time axis are at 'sensible' values.

9. A capacitor and resistor are connected to a d.c. supply as shown in the circuit below.

   (a) Describe the purpose of the circuit. Include the operation of the switch in your description.

   (b) There are two time constants in the circuit, one for switch position S_1 and another for switch position S_2. Calculate the time constants for both switch positions.

   (c) The switch is set to position S_1, held there for several seconds, then moved over to position S_2. Calculate the initial current when the switch reaches S_2.

   (d) By what time would you claim the capacitor has 'discharged'?

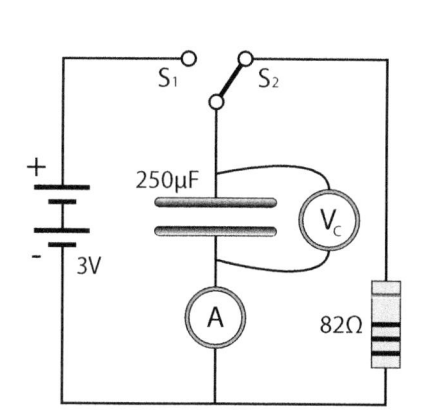

10. A company made a d.c. power supply which had a capacitor internally connected across its output terminals.

   (a) An unwary user switched off the supply but still got a shock on touching the terminals. Explain how this happened.

   (b) A safety level is set by the company at 20volts. Which of the two situations below becomes 'safest' soonest on discharge. The potential difference across a discharging capacitor is given by $V_C = V_S e^{-\frac{t}{CR}}$.

   (i) A supply of 50volts with a 2700µF capacitor discharging through a resistance of 680Ω.

   (ii) A 400µF capacitor discharging through a resistance of 5kΩ resistance with the output voltage positioned at 40volts.

11. A 10,000µF capacitor is fully charged using a d.c. supply. It's stored energy is used to project a golfball of mass 45g vertically into the air. Calculate the voltage of the supply required so that the golfball can reach the top of Ben Nevis.

12. The circuit diagram on the right has a power supply called a square wave supply. Its output voltage spends an equal time at either zero volts or 5 volts, with no in-between values. It changes at a regular frequency, taking 0.02s for a complete cycle, giving a frequency of 50Hz. The switch is also special. It vibrates between positions S_1 and S_2 in step with the supply.

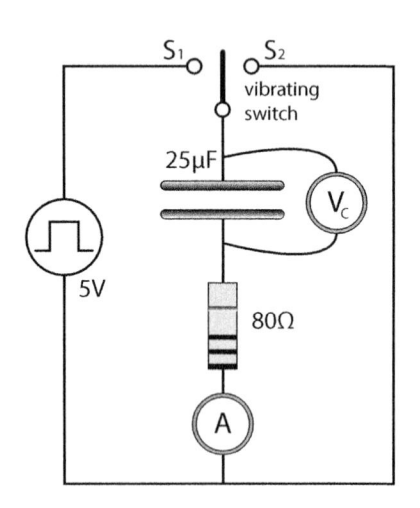

   (a) Describe how the circuit could be operated to show charging and discharging of the capacitor.

   (b) Explain why the time constants for charging and discharging are the same. Calculate its value.

   The voltage across the capacitor was recorded as a function of time and is shown on the graph below.

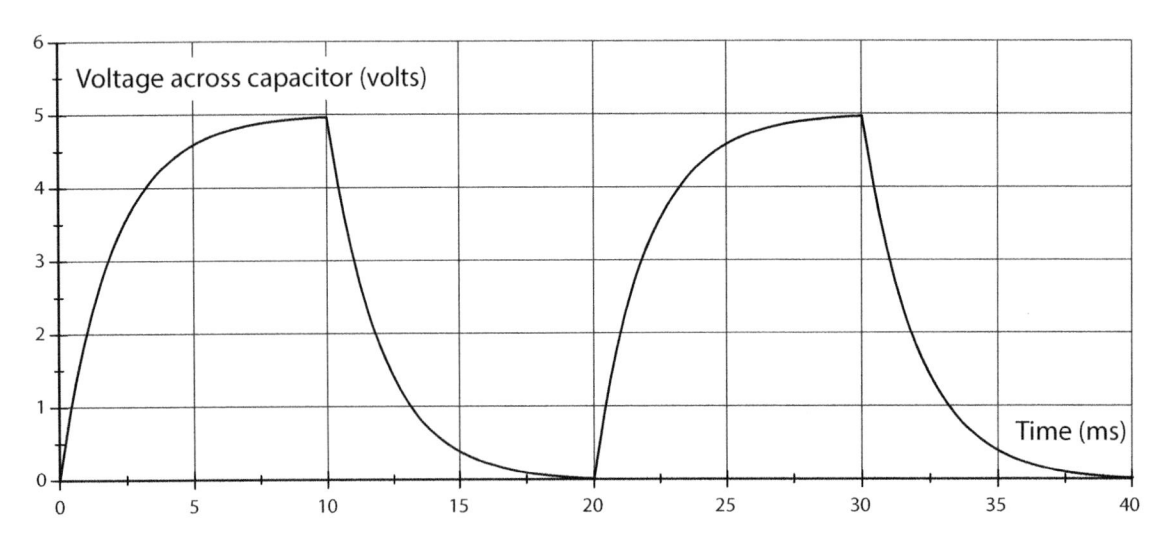

   (c) Describe the physics of the circuit at times of 0s, 10ms and 20ms.

   (d) In terms of the time constant, how much time elapsed during charging?

   (e) Use the expression for the voltage across the capacitor as a function of time $V_C = V_S\left(1 - e^{-\frac{t}{CR}}\right)$, to calculate the voltage reached when discharge is about to begin.

   (f) The resistor is now removed. What effect would this have on the shape of the graph?

13. An automatic hand dryer is to be installed in the public toilet of a department store. The design-spec calls for the device to be touch-free, switch on when the user places their hands in position, and switch off after 20 seconds or when the hands have been withdrawn from the dryer.

    (a) Describe how electromagnetic radiation and capacitors could be used to implement these requirements.

    (b) Suggest suitable values of the components for the time delay system.

14. Capacitors can be connected to a.c. supplies. The potential difference across the plates is continually changing, and current is flowing onto/off of the plates. The ratio of the potential difference across the plates to the current flowing in the circuit is known as the capacitive reactance.

    (a) What is the symbol for capacitive reactance and what is its unit?

    (b) Calculate the capacitive reactance of these circuits in each case below:

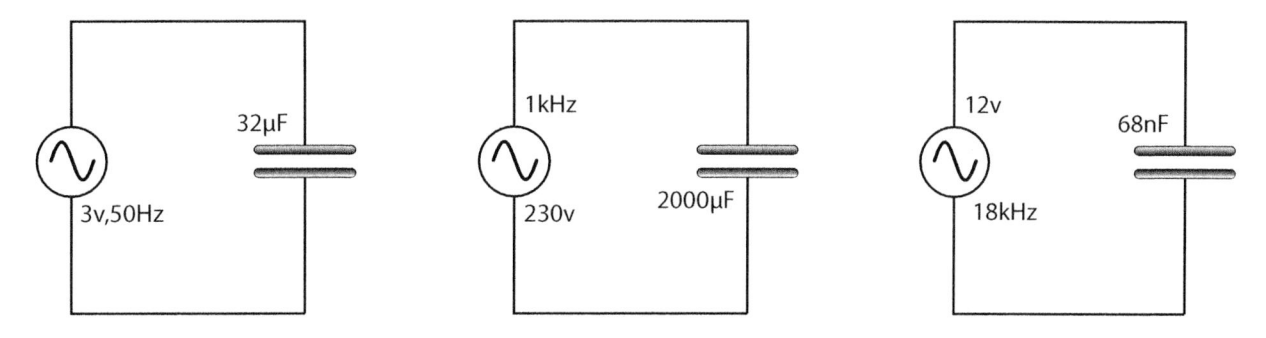

    [Circuit 1: 3v, 50Hz supply with 32μF capacitor]
    [Circuit 2: 230v, 1kHz supply with 2000μF capacitor]
    [Circuit 3: 12v, 18kHz supply with 68nF capacitor]

    (c) The circuit diagrams above also give the supply voltage. This is the r.m.s. value. In each case, calculate the r.m.s. current flowing in the circuit.

15. The circuit on the right shows a capacitor connected to an a.c. supply. The current is recorded with an ammeter, and the supply can have its frequency set to any value over a wide range.

    (a) The frequency is increased from an initial value of 20Hz, but a careful watch is kept on the voltmeter reading to ensure that the supply voltage stays at a constant r.m.s. value. What effect does this have on the ammeter reading?

    (b) In determining the dependence of the current on the frequency, why is it important to keep the supply (r.m.s. or peak) voltage constant?

    (c) The frequency is now held at a constant value of 3volts r.m.s. and the ammeter reads 15mA. Calculate the capacitive reactance.

    (d) The capacitor has a capacitance of 8μF. Calculate the frequency of the supply set at 3volts rms.

16. Connect a 400μF capacitor to a 12volt r.m.s. alternating current supply and set the frequency to 50Hz.

    (a) Calculate the r.m.s. current in the circuit.

    (b) The capacitance is reduced to 200μF. Calculate the new current.

    (c) Reset things back to their initial values. This time you double the supply voltage to 24volts. What is the new current reading?

    (d) Okay! Back again to initial readings. Halve the supply voltage, halve the frequency and halve the capacitance. New current reading please!

17. We now add in a resistor to make a CR series circuit. We still have a variable frequency a.c. supply.

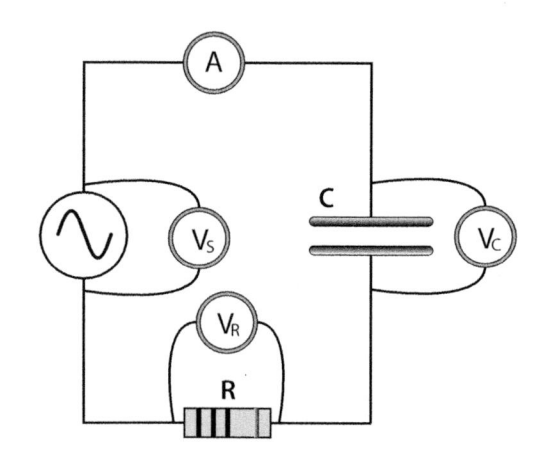

    (a) Why do we require separate voltmeters across the supply, resistor and the capacitor?

    (b) What quantity is constant in all parts of the circuit except between the capacitor plates?

    (c) The circuit is set-up using centre-zero voltmeters. These are old fashioned meters with an analogue pointer which can swing either side of zero depending on the polarity of the component. The frequency of the supply is set to a low value of 0.5Hz. What would you discover as you watch all three voltmeter pointers at the same time?

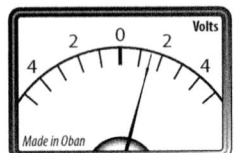

    (d) Replace the classic voltmeters with modern digital ones which read r.m.s. values, and increase the frequency of the supply to 100Hz. The three voltmeter readings you now obtain are related by Pythagoras Theorem. Write down that relationship.

18. A resistor of resistance 'R' and a capacitor of capacitance 'C' are connected to an a.c. supply in series (like the diagram in Q17 above). Voltmeters are connected across each component and give the following readings: across the resistor V_{rms} = 1.25volts, across the capacitor V_{rms} = 2.6volts.

    (a) Use the relationship $V_S^2 = V_R^2 + V_C^2$ to calculate the r.m.s. value of the supply voltage.

    (b) The supply frequency is 1.8kHz and the capacitance of the capacitor is 4μF. Calculate the capacitive reactance of the capacitor.

    (c) Calculate:

       (i) the r.m.s. current in the circuit.

       (ii) the resistance of the resistor.

19. A capacitor is connected to an a.c. supply. The voltage across the capacitor and the current in the circuit are out of phase. This is illustrated in the graph opposite (assume standard S.I.units).

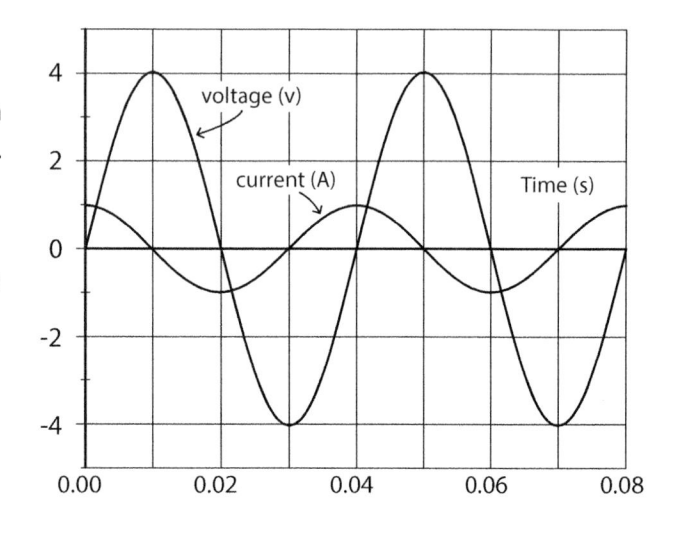

    (a) Refer to the current peak at a time of 0.04s and the subsequent voltage peak. What is the phase difference between the current and the voltage?

    (b) Which quantity reaches its peak first, the voltage or the current?

    (c) Calculate the capacitive reactance of the capacitor.

    (d) Deduce the frequency of the supply and hence calculate the capacitance of the capacitor.

20. Capacitors have an insulator between two conducting plates. Current cannot flow inside the capacitor between the plates. Whether it's connected to an a.c. or a d.c. supply, the current only flows in the wires connected to the capacitor. Explain why the current flowing in the wires of a sinewave a.c. circuit is 90° ahead of the potential difference across the capacitor plates.

21. The diagram on the right shows the relationship between the potential differences across the components in a CR series circuit powered by a sinewave a.c. supply of r.m.s. voltage V_S. The r.m.s. readings noted were: V_C = 2.5volts, V_S = 5volts.

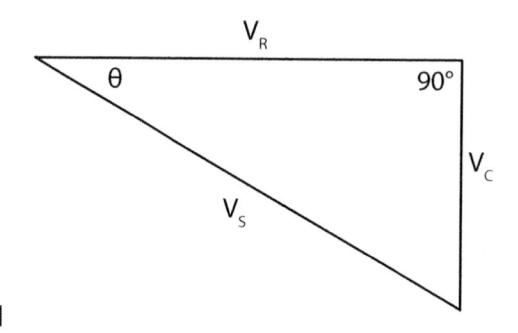

    (a) Calculate the phase angle 'θ' between the p.d. across the resistor and the p.d. of the supply.

    (b) The current in the circuit was also measured and found to be 3.8mA. Calculate the resistance of the resistor.

    (c) Calculate the reactance of the capacitor.

    (d) The supply frequency was 484Hz. Calculate the capacitance 'C' of the capacitor.

    (e) The impedance 'Z' of the circuit is defined as $Z = \dfrac{V_S}{I}$. Calculate the impedance of the circuit, then use your results to show numerically that $Z^2 = R^2 + X_C^2$.

22. The impedance of a CR series circuit is plotted against frequency in the graph below.

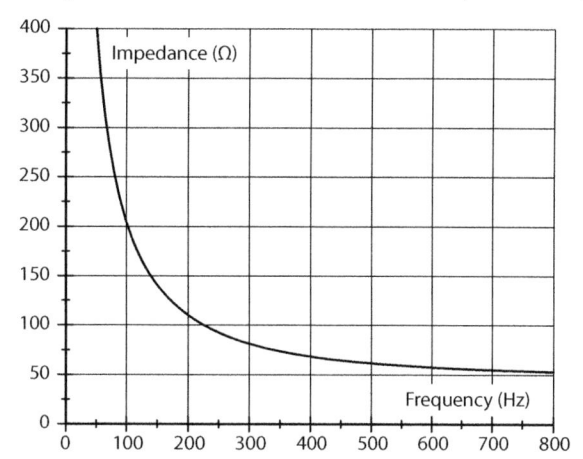

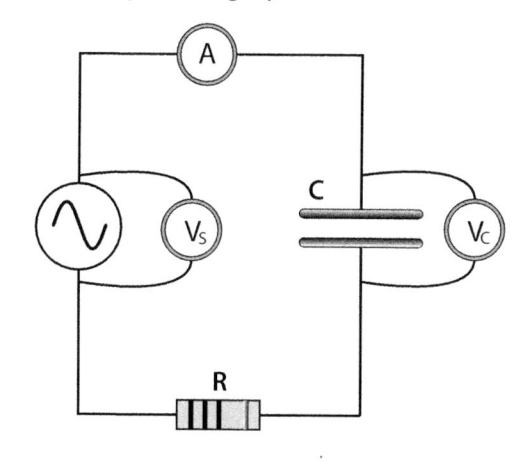

    (a) Describe the behaviour of the resistance of the resistor and the reactance of the capacitor as the frequency is increased.

    (b) Explain why the graph approaches a fixed impedance when the frequency is increased greatly.

    (c) Let's make this a bit trickier (no lead-in). Calculate / estimate the value of the capacitance.

23. The circuit below is used as a low pass filter circuit in audio applications. The graph shows the ratio of output to input voltages as a function of frequency.

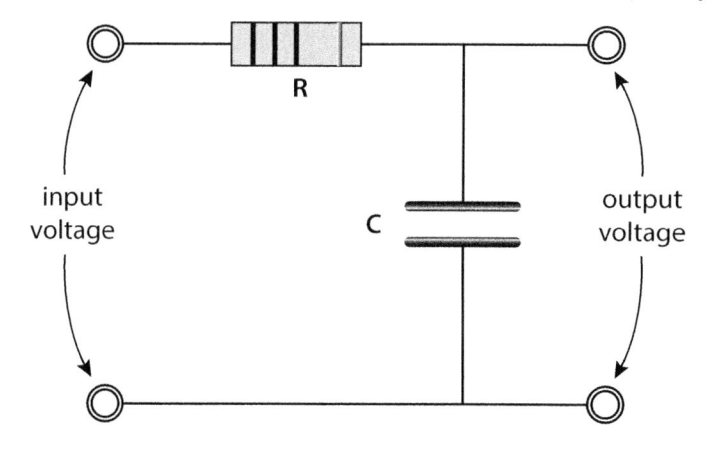

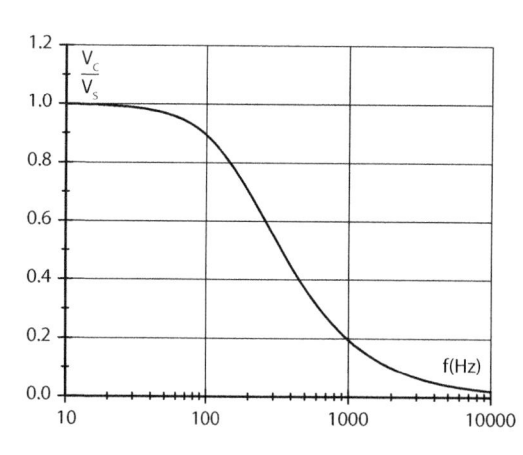

    (a) Describe what an mp3 track would sound like if played through the above filter.

    (b) What difference would it make to the graph if the output was taken across the resistor?

81

Unit 3 Inductors

This section involves circuits and batteries, so we start with a gentle warm-up.

1. Calculate the current through a 220Ω resistor driven by a 12V dc battery.

2. A current of 1.26A flows through a resistor. The power output of the resistor is 3.1W.

    (a) Calculate the potential difference across the resistor?

    (b) The energy from the battery goes into the resistor. In what form does it appear?

3. Calculate the current through each resistor in the three circuits below:

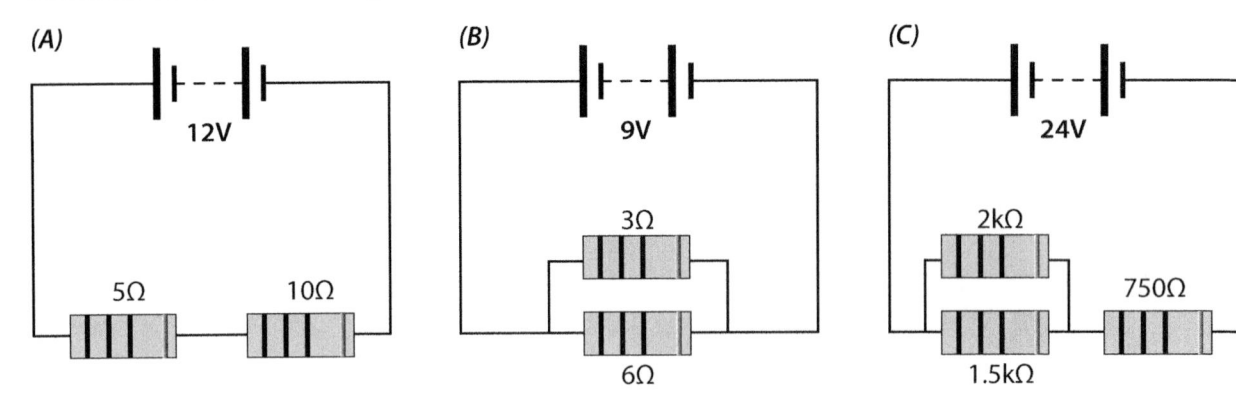

    (A) 12V, 5Ω, 10Ω

    (B) 9V, 3Ω, 6Ω

    (C) 24V, 2kΩ, 750Ω, 1.5kΩ

4. (a) Calculate the current flowing in the circuit shown below left. Note that the right hand cell is the 'wrong way around'.

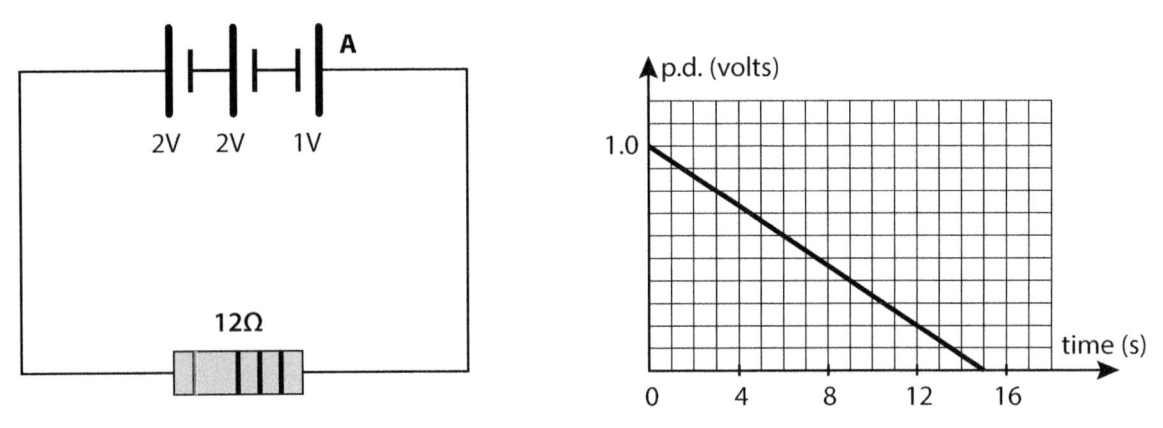

    Cells: 2V, 2V, 1V (A); resistor 12Ω

    (b) The cell labelled 'A' in the above diagram develops a fault and its potential difference starts to reduce uniformly to zero as shown by the graph on the right.

    Calculate the current flowing in the circuit at times: 3s, 6s, 9s, 12s and 15s.

5. The current in a circuit starts off at 2A and increases uniformly at a rate of 0.05A per second (A s⁻¹) Calculate the current after 30s.

6. (a) Current increases uniformly in a circuit from 0.25A to 0.70A in a time of 5s. Calculate the rate of change of current $\frac{dI}{dt}$ in amps per second.

    (b) What must be happening to the emf of the circuit during this time?

    (c) If the circuit resistance was 6Ω, calculate the emf of the supply at the start and also at the end of the experiment.

7. The current in a circuit is given by the expression: $I = 3e^{-0.4t}$. Calculate the rate of change of current at a time of 5s.

82

8. A coil of wire, a switch and a 6Ω resistor were connected in series to a dc supply of emf 12V. The table below shows readings of current and time for the first 18s after the switch was closed:

Time (s)	0	2	4	6	8	10	12	14	16	18
Current (A)	0	0.66	1.10	1.40	1.60	1.73	1.82	1.88	1.92	1.95

(a) Go get some graph paper and plot a graph of current (y-axis) against time. Draw a smooth curve through the points.

(b) At what value will the current eventually level off?

(c) What is the value of $\frac{dI}{dt}$ when: (i) the current levels off, and (ii) it's at its maximum value?

(d) What is the voltage across the coil at time t = 0s and also when the current levels off?

(e) Calculate the potential difference across the resistor and the potential difference across the coil, at time t = 2s.

9. The expression for the back emf across a coil is: $emf = -L\frac{dI}{dt}$. Use it to calculate:

(a) The back emf across a 3H coil when the current is changing at a rate of 1.6As⁻¹.

(b) The rate of change of current when a back emf of 4.5volts is across a 60mH coil.

(c) The inductance of a coil if a rate of change of current of 6.4 As⁻¹ gives an emf of 2.5volts.

10. The Ohm, Farad and Henry are defined using these equations: $V = IR \quad Q = CV \quad emf = -L\frac{dI}{dt}$.

With current in amps, voltage in volts, charge in coulombs and time in seconds, derive the basic units for these combinations:

(a) CR (b) L/R (c) LC

11. A 3Ω resistor, a switch and a coil of wire are connected in series to a 6V dc supply. The switch is closed and the current is monitored as a function of time.

(a) What steady value of current is eventually reached?

(b) What difference would it make to this steady value for the current if:

(i) the resistance is doubled.

(ii) the inductance of the coil is doubled

12. A neon bulb requires about 70volts to make it light. Describe how you could make it flash **once** using a 1.5V cell and a suitable inductor. Why can't it be lit continuously with this method?

13. Michael Faraday liked the concept of 'magnetic flux' 'ϕ'. You calculate the flux through a loop of wire carrying a current, by multiplying the magnetic induction 'B' by the area 'A' of the coil (the vector Dot Product to be exact). Calculate the magnetic flux through these three current loops:

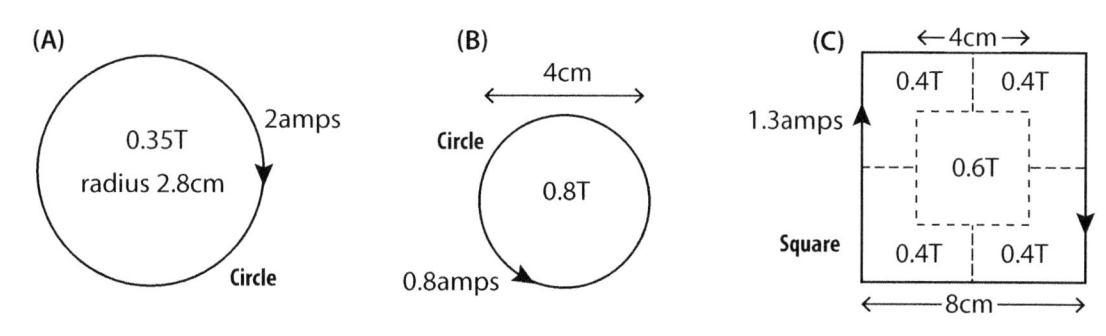

(A) Circle, 0.35T, radius 2.8cm, 2amps

(B) Circle, 4cm, 0.8T, 0.8amps

(C) Square, 4cm × 8cm, 0.4T, 0.4T, 0.6T, 0.4T, 0.4T, 1.3amps

83

14. An inductor, resistor and switch were connected in series to a 12V dc supply. The switch was closed and readings of current and time were recorded then plotted on the graph below (the solid line).

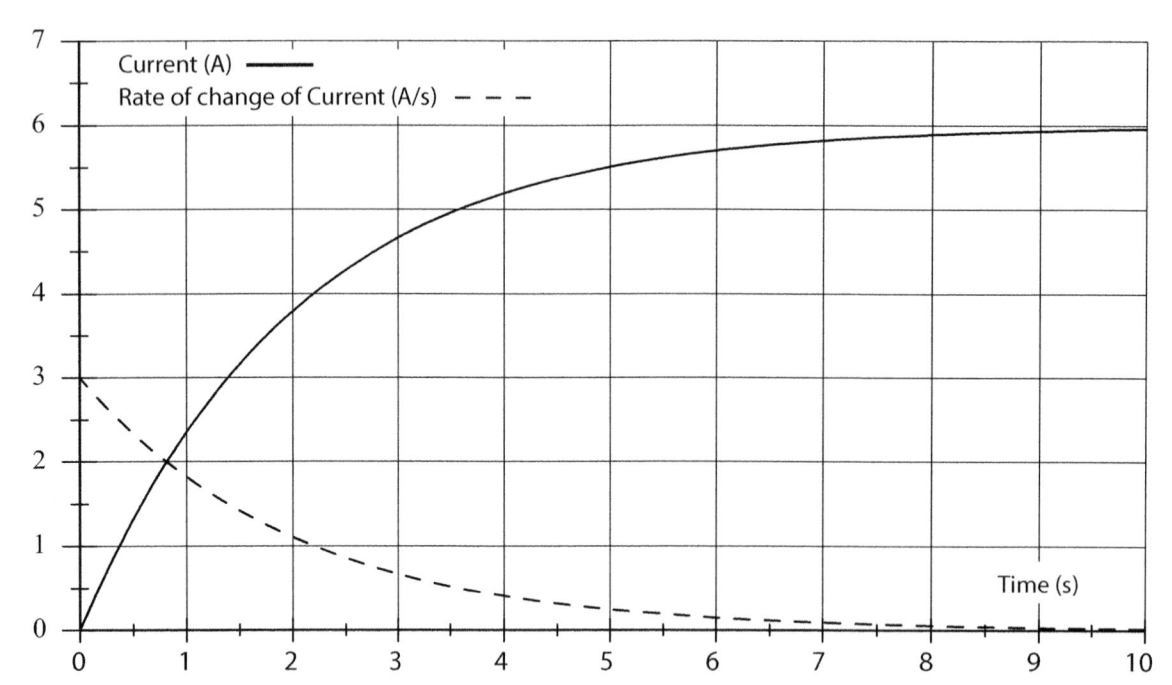

(a) The current levels off at 6amps. Calculate the resistance 'R' of the circuit at that time.

The graph also plots the rate of change of current $\frac{dI}{dt}$ (the dotted line).

(b) Calculate the emf (in volts) across the inductor at time t = 0. Take care with the sign.

(c) Use the equation $emf = -L\frac{dI}{dt}$ with the dotted line, to calculate the inductance 'L'.

(d) At time t = 2s, read off values from the two graphs and calculate the emf across the coil and the p.d. across the resistor. Check that the sum of the emfs from the coil and battery add up to the p.d. which drives the current through the resistor.

15. An LR series circuit was set up with a d.c. supply and readings of current against time plotted from the moment of switch-on. One of the components was then replaced with another of the same type but different value, and the experiment repeated. Both sets of results are shown on the graph opposite:

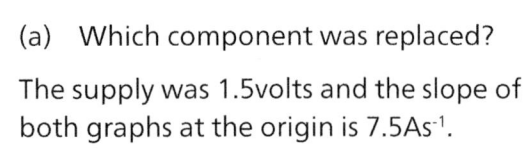

(a) Which component was replaced?

The supply was 1.5volts and the slope of both graphs at the origin is 7.5As⁻¹.

(b) Calculate the resistance and inductance values used in both experiments.

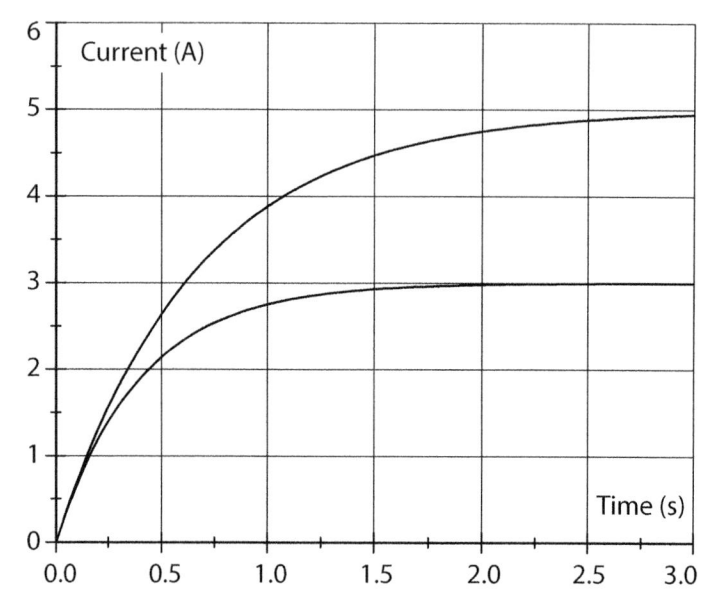

16. Calculate the energy stored in the magnetic field of these inductors:

(a) A 0.25H inductor with a steady current of 3.6A.

(b) A 75mH inductor with a current of 1.5A.

(c) When the current in a 6H inductor is 2.15A.

17. An inductor of inductance 0.8H has an energy of 0.28J stored within its magnetic field. Calculate the current flowing in the inductor.

18. An inductor stores an energy of 65mJ when a current of 0.92A is flowing through it. Calculate the inductance of the inductor.

19. When the switch is closed in a circuit with an inductor, the battery has to do work to build up the current.

    (a) Where does the energy from the battery go to?

    (b) Calculate the energy transferred from the battery to the inductor if its inductance is 0.4H and a steady current of 2.7A is flowing.

    (c) Describe any differences between the energy transfer process from a battery to a coil and the energy transferred from a battery to a resistor.

    Real inductors have resistance due to the material of the coil (usually copper).

    (d) What other form of energy will be produced in a real inductor regardless of whether the current is steady or changing.

20. In a circuit with an inductor, why does 'switching off' produce a greater back emf across an inductor than 'switching on'?

21. Refer to the circuit on the right.

    (a) Describe the intended operation of the circuit at switch positions 'A' and 'B'.

    (b) The switch was set to position 'A' and left there for several minutes. It was then moved to position 'B' and the current recorded on the ammeter at regular time intervals. Sketch the graph of current (on y-axis) against time from the moment the switch is set to position 'B'.

    (c) Describe two ways of slowing-down the decay of the current in part (b).

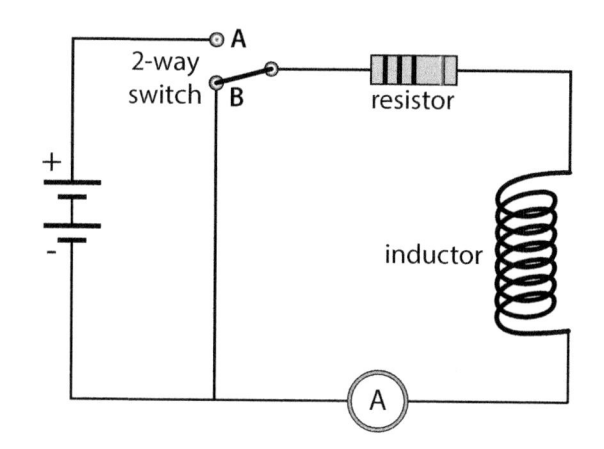

22. A transformer can be considered to be two coils 'side by side'. Suppose it is of the 'step up' type.

    (a) What does 'step up' mean for a transformer?

    (b) How is the voltage across the secondary coil related to the voltage across the primary coil?

    Suppose the current to the primary coil of the transformer is switched off suddenly.

    (c) Explain why a large voltage is briefly observed across the secondary coil.

    (d) Give an example of a common device which uses this process.

23. An ac supply is labelled '**6V rms, 50Hz**'. Calculate:

    (a) The peak voltage.

    (b) The time between successive voltage peaks of the **same** polarity.

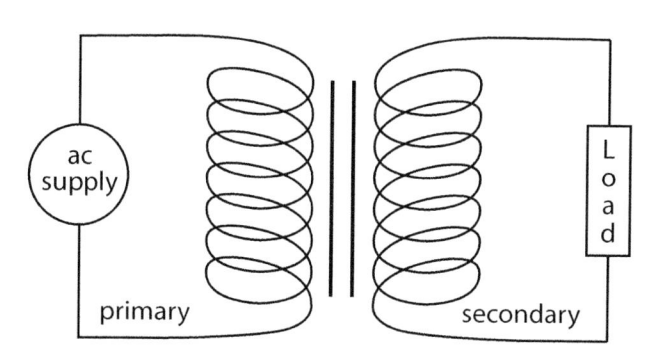

24. A variable frequency a.c. supply was connected to a coil as shown in the circuit below. Current readings at a number of frequencies were taken and recorded in the table. The output voltage of the supply was kept constant at 6volts r.m.s.

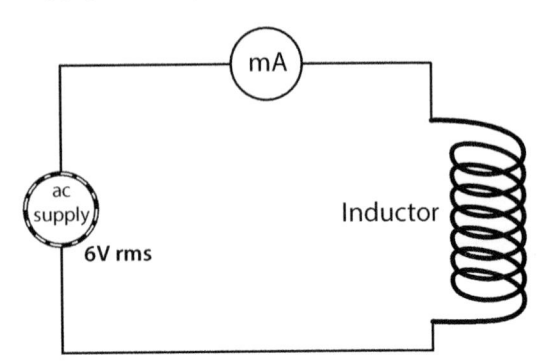

Frequency (Hz)	Current (mA)
100	238
200	119
500	48
800	30
1000	24
1200	20
1500	16
1800	13

(a) Acquire a sheet of graph paper and draw the graph of current (y-axis) against frequency.

(b) Does it become easier or more difficult to pass current from the a.c. supply as the frequency increases?

(c) What can you conclude about the 'resistance' of the inductor to alternating current as the frequency increases? ('Resistance' here should be called 'reactance').

(d) The reactance of an inductor is given by: $X_L = \dfrac{V}{I} = 2\pi f L$.

   (i) Take one data pair and calculate the inductance of the inductor.

   (ii) Describe how you can calculate the inductance of the coil from the slope of the graph.

25. An ac supply of negligible internal resistance is connected to three components in parallel: a resistor, a capacitor and an inductor. Identical bulbs are placed in series with each component.

   (a) Describe what happens to the brightness of each bulb as the frequency of the supply is increased from low to high (the voltage output stays constant).

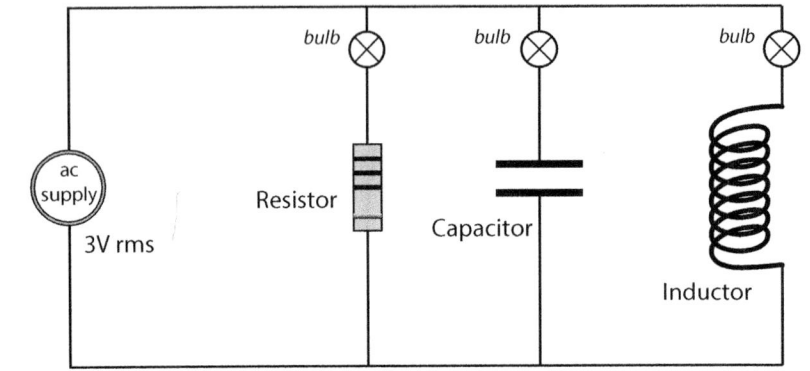

   (b) In what circumstances will an inductor 'choke' an ac current?

   (c) In what circumstances will a capacitor 'block' an ac current?

26. Calculate the inductive reactance 'X_L' of the inductor 'L' for each of these cases:

   (a) A 50Hz a.c. supply connected to a 0.35H inductor.

   (b) A current of 120mA flows through the inductor when the p.d. across it is 4volts.

   (c) A frequency of 1.75kHz with an 8mH inductance.

27. The behaviour of a capacitor to changes in frequency is the opposite to the behaviour of an inductor. Describe how these components could be connected in a circuit to:

   (a) **block** a current in a circuit over a narrow range of frequencies.

   (b) **allow** a current to flow in a circuit over a narrow range of frequencies.

28. Copy and complete the table:

Component	Value	Setting 1 Frequency (Hz)	Setting 1 V/I (Ω)	Setting 2 Frequency (Hz)	Setting 2 V/I (Ω)
Resistor	15Ω	20		800	
Capacitor	32μF	20		800	
Inductor	60mH	20		800	

29. Complicated circuits can contain resistors, capacitors and inductors at the same time. When connected all in series to an a.c. supply of frequency 'f', the ratio of the supply voltage 'V' to the current 'I' delivered by the supply 'V/I' is called the impedance 'Z' and is given by: $Z = \sqrt{R^2 + (X_L - X_C)^2}$.

   (a) Calculate the impedance of such a circuit at a frequency of 50Hz if the resistance is 10Ω, the capacitance is 80μF and the inductance is 20mH.

   (b) Calculate the impedance if the reactances of the inductor and capacitor are equal.

   (c) What can you state about the magnitude of the impedance when the reactances of the inductor and capacitor are equal?

   (d) At what frequency would you set the supply to make $X_L = X_C$?

   (e) At the frequency calculated in part (d), is the current at its maximum or minimum?

Unit 3 Electromagnetic Radiation

1. (a) Electricity and magnetism used to be thought of as two separate areas of physics. Which scientist showed that they could be unified under one theory, *electromagnetism*?

   (b) Electricity contains the constant ε_o, and magnetism the constant μ_o. State the full names of these constants and write down the expression which links them with the speed of light 'c'.

   (c) Visible rays are part of the electromagnetic spectrum. Explain why its called 'electromagnetic'.

2. The permeability of free space μ_o can be measured using apparatus known as a current balance. Two parallel bars pass equal currents in the opposite direction. The bottom bar is fixed in position and the top bar is repelled upwards. A small mass is used to balance this upwards force.

   (a) The force is calculated using the expression:
   $F = \dfrac{\mu_o I_1 I_2 l}{2\pi r}$. An experiment using a current of 9.5A restored balance with a mass of 60mg. The bars were 25cm long and separated by a distance of 0.8cm. Calculate the value for the permeability of free space.

   (b) The magnetic induction 'B' due to one of the bars at a distance of 0.8cm is $B = \dfrac{\mu_o I}{2\pi r}$. The horizontal component of the Earth's magnetic field over the UK is about 17μT. Calculate whether or not you have to be concerned with the Earth's field in the experiment.

Unit 4   Units & Uncertainties

1. Metres, centimetres, miles, lightyears, inches and millimetres all have something in common. They are all used to measure distances. They have what is called *'Dimensions'* of Length [L] and each one is an example of a *'Unit'*.

    (a) Give three examples of units with the dimensions of time [T].

    (b) Give three examples of units with the dimensions of mass [M].

    (c) The dimensions of speed are [LT^{-1}]. Give three examples of units for speed.

    (d) The Universal Constant of Gravitation 'G' is contained in the equation $F = \dfrac{GMm}{r^2}$. Derive its dimensions and express the answer using the square bracket notation.

2. A result is given as 45 ± 5. Does this mean the answer **must be** between 40 and 50? Explain.

3. Calculate the **percentage** uncertainty for each example:

    (a) 2.4 ± 0.3 V   (b) 35.2 ± 0.2 N   (c) (1.8 ± 0.2) x 10^3 J

    (d) 47.28 ± 0.01 kg   (e) 0.038 ± 0.002 K   (f) 9.17 ± 2.4 W

4. A tricky experiment requires a current reading taken with an ammeter. It's rerun many times, with the results displayed on this histogram:

    (a) The readings are only at 0.15A, 0.2A, 0.25A, 0.3A and 0.35A. There's nothing in-between.

    What does this tell you about the ammeter?

    (b) How many readings were taken?

    (c) Your boss orders you to express the answer in the form (answer ± uncertainty). What would you give them?

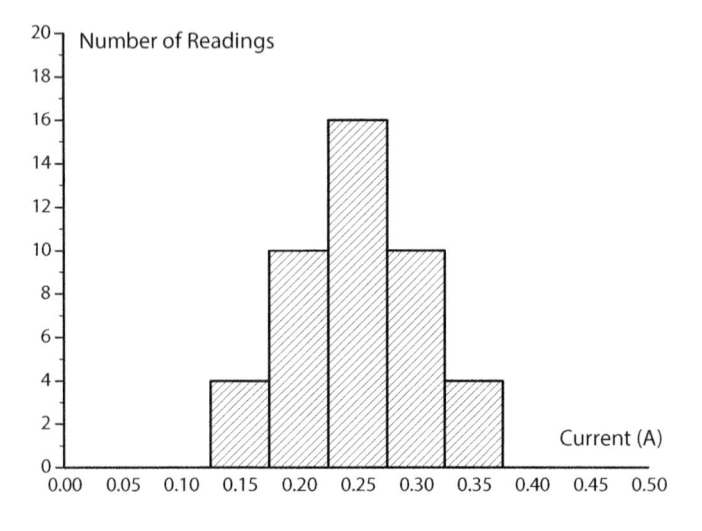

5. Six results from various experiments are shown below. Calculate the fractional uncertainty in each case, expressing the answer as a decimal. The first one is done for you.

    (a) 5.2 ± 1.2 W is 0.23   (b) 13.8 ± 0.1 J   (c) 0.263 ± 0.005

    (d) (2.96 ±0.04) x 10^8 m s^{-1} (e) 729.2 ±0.1 g   (f) 1.37 ±0.02 V

6. An experiment in the Amazon gave the following results:

    1.4 , 1.4 , 1.45 , 1.42 , 1.46 , 1.38 , 1.43 , 1.42 , 1.45 , 1.39 , 1.40 , 1.43 , 1.38 , 1.42 , 1.40

    (a) Calculate the mean and random uncertainty for the dataset.

    (b) Write the result in the form (answer ± uncertainty).

7. (a) Convert these numbers to standard form:

    (i) 62,540   (ii) 0.00027   (iii) 2.5   (iv) 0.94

    (b) Convert these numbers to decimal form:

    (i) 4.9 x 10^2 (ii) 16 x 10^3 (iii) 0.03 x 10^6 (iv) 82.1 x 10^{-1}

8. The equation $V = IR$ is used to calculate the potential difference across a resistor. The data for the current and resistance are: $I = 3.15 \pm 0.10$ A $R = 47 \pm 5\,\Omega$

    (a) Calculate the fractional uncertainty in each reading.

    (b) Use your judgement. Can you ignore one of the uncertainties? If so, which one and why?

    (c) Describe the rough rule for comparing fractional uncertainties.

    (d) Calculate the voltage and express your answer in the form (answer ± uncertainty).

9. An experiment to measure the force on an object uses Newton's 2nd Law. The mass and acceleration were measured to be: $m = 3.28 \pm 0.02$ kg $a = 0.925 \pm 0.007$ m s^{-2}.

    (a) Use the data to calculate the largest possible answer.

    (b) Repeat the calculation for the smallest possible answer.

    (c) Use your answers from (a) and (b) to express the result for the force in the form (force ± uncertainty).

    (d) Calculate the fractional uncertainty for each reading.

    (e) In any pair of readings, you are unlikely to get **both** at their maximum uncertainty. Pythagoras Theorem can be used with the fractional uncertainties to obtain a more realistic answer. Use it to calculate the force and (**yet again**) express your answer in the form (answer ± uncertainty).

10. A whole class of third year pupils take readings of current and voltage in a circuit. The same resistor is used each time then passed on to the next pupil to measure. The measurements from each pupil are shown in the table and plotted on the graph.

Current (A)	Voltage (V)
3.59	5.22
3.59	5.24
3.59	5.20
3.61	5.21
3.61	5.23
3.61	5.18
3.62	5.25
3.62	5.26
3.63	5.24
3.63	5.20
3.63	5.18
3.63	5.22
3.64	5.24
3.64	5.22
3.64	5.20
3.64	5.16
3.65	5.27
3.65	5.19
3.65	5.21
3.65	5.25
3.66	5.23
3.66	5.18
3.67	5.20
3.67	5.25
3.68	5.23
3.68	5.19
3.68	5.22
3.69	5.20

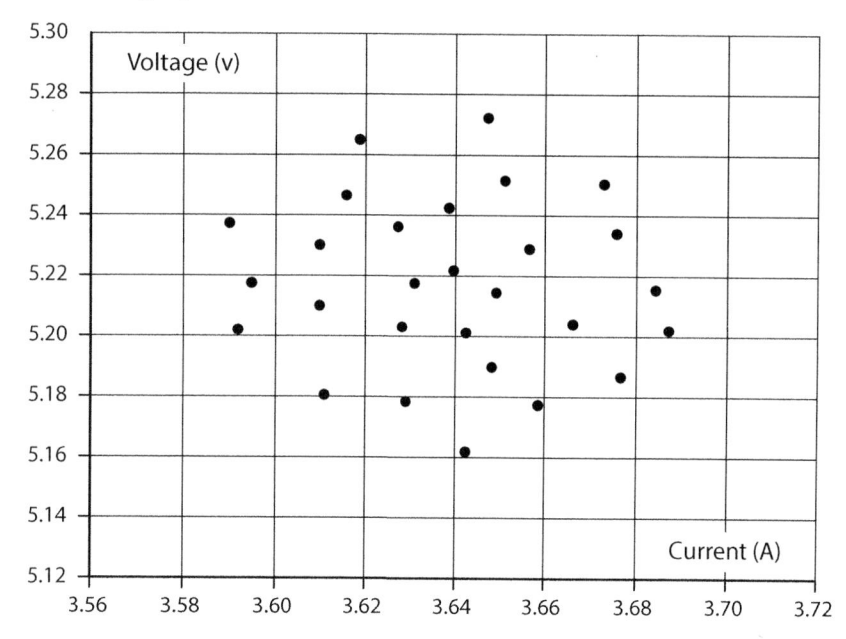

(a) From the table, calculate the mean value for the current and also for the voltage.

(b) Locate this value on the above graph. What do you notice about its position?

(c) How many pupils were in the class? Suppose the class size had been much larger, like 500 pupils! Describe what the overall pattern of dots would now look like on the graph.

89

11. A ball of mass (362 ± 5)g is travelling with a speed of (1.46 ± 0.04)m s⁻¹. Use the 'root sum of squares method' with fractional errors to calculate the kinetic energy of the ball (with the uncertainty!).

12. The gravitational potential energy of an object is calculated from its mass, the height above ground and the gravitational field strength: $E_p = mgh$. The mass was measured to be 29 ± 2 kg and g was taken to be (9.8 ± 0.1)Nkg⁻¹. The result for the potential energy was E_p = (99.5 ± 9)J. What must have been the height measurement (with its uncertainty)?

13. The table below shows the most common prefixes and their values.

Name	pico	nano	micro	milli	kilo	mega	giga	tera
Prefix	p	n	μ	m	k	M	G	T
Value	1 x 10⁻¹²	1 x 10⁻⁹	1 x 10⁻⁶	1 x 10⁻³	1 x 10³	1 x 10⁶	1 x 10⁹	1 x 10¹²

Use the table to express the quantities (a) to (h) below with the appropriate prefix.

(a) 4 x 10⁻⁹A (b) 7 x 10⁻³m (c) 2.8 x 10⁻¹¹J (d) 4.98 x 10⁻⁸kg

(e) 3.2 x 10¹³W (f) 1.61 x 10¹⁰K (g) 7.0 x 10⁻⁷s (h) 2.93 x 10⁵V

Which one of the basic S.I. units in the examples (a) to (h) above, is the 'odd one out'?

14. The number 72.67 is given to two decimal places and four significant figures. State how many decimal places and how many significant figures are given in the examples below:

(a) 14.2 (b) 395.28 (c) 0.275 (d) 0.00048

15. The solution to the Böhr model of the hydrogen atom predicts a radius of $r = \dfrac{\varepsilon_o h^2}{\pi m_e e^2}$. Use the data on the inside back cover to calculate the radius of the hydrogen atom:

16. During an experiment, a stopwatch recorded a series of times shown on the histogram below.

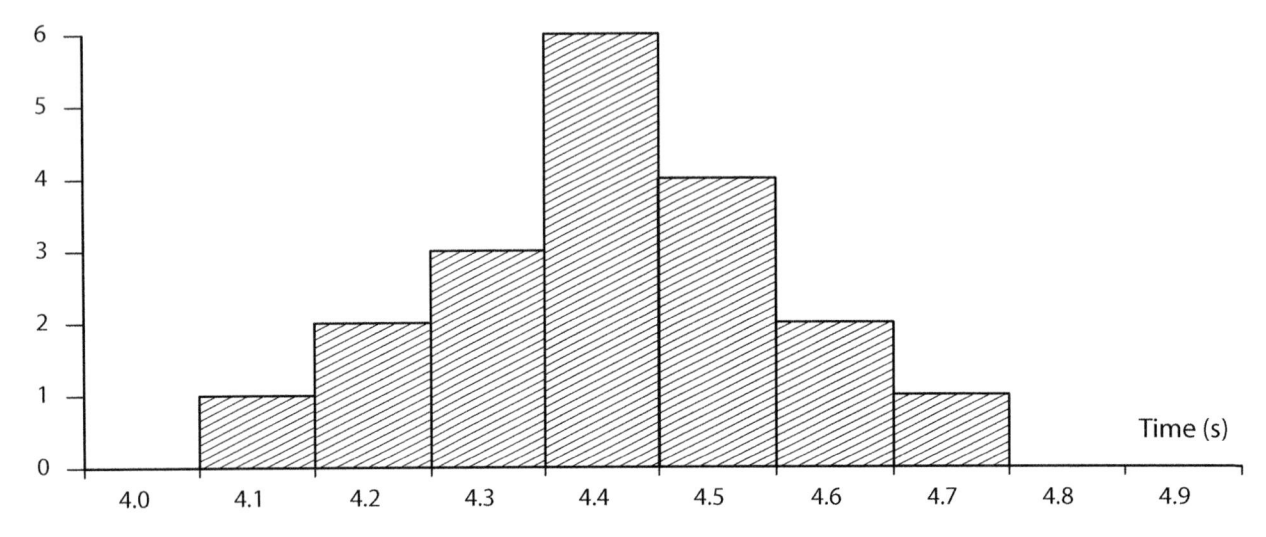

(a) How many readings were taken?

(b) Calculate the mean and random uncertainty.

The digital stopwatch displayed its results to one decimal place. The manufacturer claimed it to be accurate to ±0.05s.

(c) What is this type of uncertainty called?

(d) Is there a Reading Uncertainty?

(e) Use the mean as your main value to calculate the percentage uncertainty for each of the three types of uncertainty and combine them to give a final result in the form (value ± uncertainty).

17. A scientific result is written in the form (6.24 ± 0.08)km. The ± 0.08 part is called the **absolute** uncertainty. You can use Pythagoras Theorem with absolute uncertainties for expressions involving additions and subtractions, like this: $z = x \pm y \Rightarrow (\Delta z)^2 = (\Delta x)^2 + (\Delta y)^2$.

    Use this method to calculate the results, (answer ± uncertainty), for these:

    (a) $P = (3.1 \pm 0.2) + (4.5 \pm 0.1)$ (b) $F = (15 \pm 0.5) - (9.5 \pm 0.5)$

    (c) $V = (0.37 \pm 0.08) - (1.16 \pm 0.22)$ (d) $T = (8.3 \pm 0.4) + (2.9 \pm 0.2) - (5.1 \pm 0.3)$

18. Calculate the fractional and percentage uncertainty for each of these examples:

    (a) 26 ± 4 (b) 91.5 ± 0.3 (c) 7.0 x 10⁻⁷ ± 3 x 10⁻⁸ s (d) 0.68 ± 0.04

19. The period of a pendulum is a common measurement at Advanced Higher. The analysis often calls for the uncertainties in the period 'T' and its square 'T²'. The period measured in an experiment was T = 2.7 ± 0.2 s. Calculate the fractional uncertainties $\frac{\Delta(T)}{T}$ and $\frac{\Delta(T^2)}{T^2}$.

20. Here are three examples involving equations with multiplication and powers. Use Pythagoras Theorem (aka, root-sum-of-squares) and fractional uncertainties to calculate the best answer in the form (value ± uncertainty).

    (a) $V = IR$ $R = 275 \pm 20\,\Omega$ $I = 0.18 \pm 0.01\,A$

    (b) $E_p = mgh$ $m = 4.45 \pm 0.02\,kg$ $g = 9.81 \pm 0.01\,ms^{-2}$ $h = 17.62 \pm 0.01\,m$

    (c) $E_k = \frac{1}{2}mv^2$ $m = 1.53 \pm 0.01\,kg$ $v = 0.82 \pm 0.03\,ms^{-1}$

21. An experiment was performed to determine the mass of a model car using Newton's 2ND Law. The results were recorded in the table below and graphed as shown.

F (N)	a (m/s²)
3.2	0.32
3.755	0.39
4.25	0.5
4.745	0.61
5.3	0.7
5.555	0.79
6.005	0.89
6.65	0.99
6.83	1.1
7.31	1.18
7.92	1.32
8.3	1.4
8.92	1.49

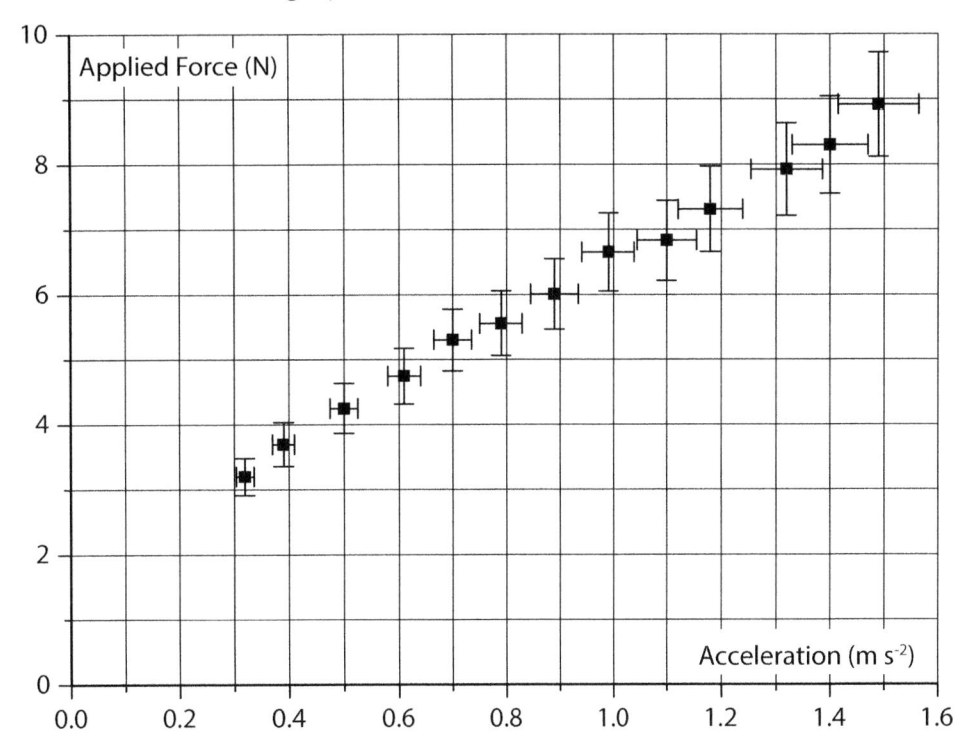

    (a) What name is given to those little spidery things around the data points on the graph?

    (b) From the **table**, calculate the mean of the acceleration and the mean of the force. This gives the (x,y) co-ordinates of the centroid. The best-fit line must pass through the centroid. Mark it on the graph and draw in your best-fit line with a ruler.

91

(c) Use the slope and intercept of the graph to determine the mass of the model car and the friction in the experiment.

22. An engineer uses a metre stick to measure the distance between two scratch marks on a stainless steel rod. The manufacturer of the metre stick claims it is accurate to ' ± 0.1% + ½ smallest division'.

    (a) What is this type of uncertainty called?

    The engineer lines up the end of the metre stick at the first scratch mark, then takes a reading at the other scratch mark. He estimates his uncertainty as '±½ smallest division' for each reading.

    (b) What is this second type of uncertainty called?

    (c) If his result was 835mm, what would his uncertainty have been?

23. A steel sphere is dropped from an electromagnetic catch at the top of a clampstand. It falls through a vertical distance then hits and opens a trap. The release of the ball to the opening of the trap door is timed electronically. The experiment was repeated 9 times and each time the result was the same, 0.86s.

    (a) What type of error is absent in these results? Explain why it is absent.

    (b) The manufacturer claimed an accuracy for the timer of '± 0.5% + ½ smallest division'. What would the result be in the form 'answer ± uncertainty' ?

    (c) Would repeating the experiment many more times improve the accuracy of the result? Explain your answer.

24. A group of 10 pupils time a sprinter in a 100m race. Their times were:

    10.8, 10.6, 10.8, 10.9, 10.7, 10.9, 10.3, 10.7, 10.8, 10.8   (all in seconds)

    (a) Calculate the mean and random uncertainty.

    (b) Would the result be more accurate if more pupils had been involved?

    (c) The 10 pupils asked the sprinter to repeat his run. Would this improve the result? Explain.

    (d) Looking at the data, what could you do to improve the accuracy of the result? If you can improve it, recalculate the mean and random uncertainty.

25. Random uncertainty is calculated by taking the smallest reading away from the largest reading then dividing by the number of readings.

    (a) Explain whether this would give a reliable estimate for only two or three readings.

    (b) As you take more and more readings, what happens to the size of the random uncertainty?

    (c) Would the result be reliable if one of the readings was suspect (as in Q24, above)?

26. A mean result of 1.87A from several measurements in a circuit was subject to a calibration uncertainty of '± 1% + ½ smallest division' , a reading uncertainty (it's from an analogue meter) of '± ½ smallest division' and a random uncertainty of '± 0.02A'.

    Calculate the **absolute** uncertainties for all three types in amps (that's the kind of uncertainty with just the ΔI), then use the 'root sum of squares' method (Pythagoras Theorem) to compute the combined uncertainty.

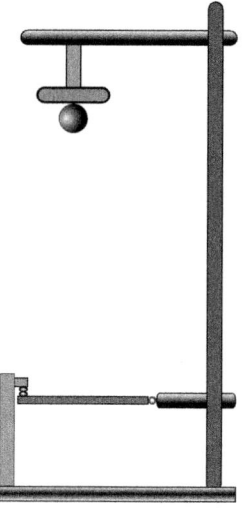

27. This is a problem considering only calibration uncertainty. On two digital meters measuring voltage and current in a particular experiment, the calibration uncertainties were stated to be '±4%'. Used in a circuit to measure the resistance of a resistor, they gave the table and graph below.

Voltage (volts)	Current (amps)
1.87 ± 0.07	0.046 ± 0.002
4.01	0.11
6.08	0.15
8.07	0.21
10.4	0.25
12.0	0.31
14.3	0.35
16.0	0.40
18.3	0.45
20.1	0.50

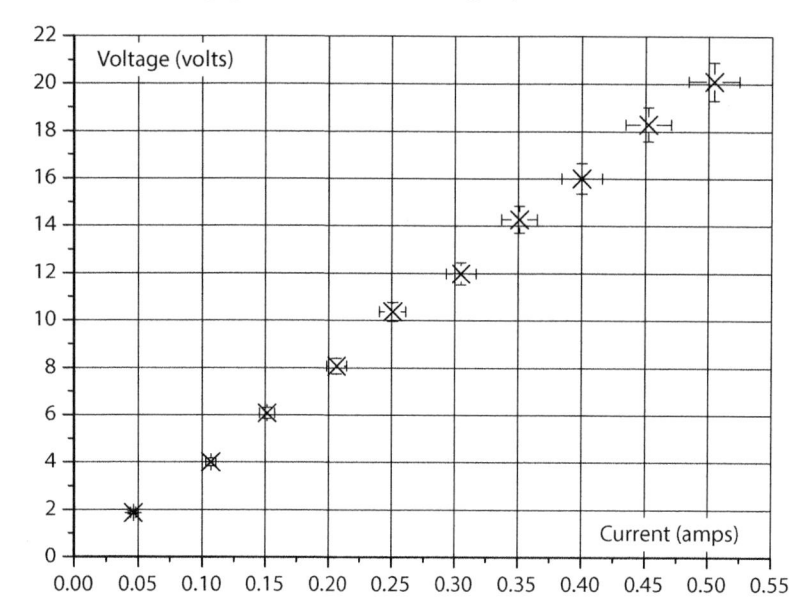

(a) Copy and complete the table showing the calibration uncertainties.

(b) On the graph, why do the error bars get progressively wider?

(c) Draw the best-fit straight line and calculate the resistance.

(d) Why does the increasing width of the error bars make it easier to draw the steepest and shallowest lines?

(e) Calculate the steepest and shallowest slopes, then express the result for the resistance in the form 'answer ± uncertainty'.

28. Use the equation $s = \frac{1}{2}at^2$ to calculate the displacement 's' (and its uncertainty) from these measurements of acceleration and time:

$a = (0.31 \pm 0.02)$m/s² $t = (1.15 \pm 0.05)$s

29. Why is it inappropriate, and also 'bad form', to express a result like this: 6.237 ± 0.2J?

30. Calculate the results for these examples in the form 'answer ± uncertainty'. This is the last question, so they get trickier. Chip away at them.

(a) $V = I^2 R$ $I = (38 \pm 1)$mA $R = 4.7$kΩ ± 10%

(b) $v = u + at$ $u = (27 \pm 2)$m/s $a = (1.5 \pm 0.1)$m/s² $t = (6.0 \pm 0.4)$s

(c) $v^2 = u^2 + 2as$ $u = (12.8 \pm 1.0)$m/s $a = (0.27 \pm 0.02)$m/s² $s = (415 \pm 0.5)$m

Unit 1 Kinematic Relationships.....Answers

1. (a) 4 litres per second (b) 12 litres (c) $V = 4t + 6$
   (d) started with 36 litres and emptied at a rate of 1.2 litres per second (empty after 30s)

2. (a) 40 is the initial speed and 1.5 is the change in speed each second (b) yes

3. (a) rate of change of displacement with time in units of metres per second. (b) 21 m s⁻¹
   (c) It is important since it tells you the initial displacement and you have to add this on to the change (given by the $\frac{ds}{dt}$ bit).

4. (a) 20 is the initial displacement and its unit is metres.
   (b) 0.8 is the rate of change of displacement with time ('velocity') in units of m s⁻¹
   (c) $\frac{ds}{dt} = 0.8$ and its velocity is constant

5. (a) accelerating (b) $\frac{ds}{dt} = 0.4t + 0.8$ $\frac{d^2s}{dt^2} = 0.4$
   (c) 0.2 is half the rate of change of rate of change of displacement (0.2 is half the acceleration)
   0.8 is the initial rate of change of displacement (initial velocity, symbol 'u')
   20 is the initial displacement

6. $s = 1.2t^2 + 5t + 30$

7. Using: $s = ut + \frac{1}{2}at^2$ and substituting the data pairs gives: $96 = 4u + 8a$ $480 = 10u + 50a$
   Solving for 'u' and 'a' gives: u = 8 m s⁻¹ and a = 8 m s⁻²

8. This is just the equation: $v^2 = u^2 + 2as$ in an unfamiliar arrangement: $v = \sqrt{2as + u^2}$
   Match up the terms with: $v = \sqrt{(12s + 225)}$ to give u = 15 and a = 6

9. (a) 3.12 m s⁻² 5.4 m s⁻² (b) $v = 0.03t^2 + 3t$ (no constant term since v=0 at t=0)
   (c) $s = 0.01t^3 + 1.5t^2$ (no constant since s = 0 at t=0) (d) v = 168 m s⁻¹ s = 3040m

10. Wally accelerating: $v = u + at = 0 + 1.5 \times 6 = 9$m/s $s = ut + \frac{1}{2}at^2 = 0 + \frac{1}{2} \times 1.5 \times 6^2 = 27$m
    Wally at constant speed: $s = ut = 9 \times (t - 6)$ Total distance: $s_{Tot} = 27 + 9(t - 6)$
    Willy accelerating: $v = u + at = 0 + 1.75 \times 8 = 14$m/s $s = ut + \frac{1}{2}at^2 = 0 + \frac{1}{2} \times 1.75 \times 8^2 = 56$m
    Willy at constant speed: $s = ut = 14 \times (t - 38)$ Total distance: $s_{Tot} = 56 + 14(t - 38)$
    Distances must be same at catch-up time: $56 + 14(t - 38) = 27 + 9(t - 6)$ ⇒ t = 89.8s
    Distance at catch-up from Wally or Willy: $27 + 9(89.8 - 6) = 56 + 14(89.8 - 38) = 781.2$m

11. 'A': v = 10m/s $a = (15 - (-5))/4 = 5$m/s² $s = \frac{1}{2} \times 1 \times (-5) + \frac{1}{2} \times 2 \times 10 = 7.5$m
    'B' v = 15m/s a = 0m/s² $s = \frac{1}{2} \times 1 \times (-5) + \frac{1}{2} \times 3 \times 15 + 6 \times 15 = 97.5$m
    'C' v = −7.5m/s $a = (-15 - 15)/16 = -1.875$m/s²
    $s = \frac{1}{2} \times 1 \times (-5) + \frac{1}{2} \times 3 \times 15 + 8 \times 15 + \frac{1}{2} \times 8 \times 15 + \frac{1}{2} \times 4 \times (-7.5) = 185$m

12. Non-uniform Accⁿ. $v = \int a\,dt = \int(3t + 5)dt = \frac{3}{2}t^2 + 5t$ $s = \int v\,dt = \int\left(\frac{3}{2}t^2 + 5t\right)dt = \frac{1}{2}t^3 + \frac{5}{2}t^2$
    $s = \frac{1}{2} \times 12^3 + \frac{5}{2} \times 12^2 = 864 + 360 = 1224$m $v = \frac{3}{2} \times 12^2 + 5 \times 12 = 276$m/s

Uniform decell^n. $v = u + at$ $\Rightarrow$ $0 = 276 + a \times 8$ $\Rightarrow$ $a = -34.5 \text{m/s}^2$

$$s = ut + \tfrac{1}{2}at^2 = 276 \times 8 + \tfrac{1}{2}(-34.5) \times 8^2 = 2208 - 1104 = 1104 \text{m}$$

Total distance travelled is: $1224 + 1104 = 2328\text{m}$

13. Convert parsecs into metres: $3.22 \times 3.26 \times 9.46 \times 10^{15} = 9.94 \times 10^{16}\text{m}$

    Convert miles per hour into m/s: $150,000\text{mph} = 150,000 \times 1609 / 3600 = 67,000\text{m/s}$

    Velocity of Epsilon Eridani relative to spaceship: $67,000 - 15,500 = 51,500\text{m/s}$

    Time taken: $t = \dfrac{9.94 \times 10^{16}}{51,500} = 1.93 \times 10^{12}\text{s} = \dfrac{1.93 \times 10^{12}}{365.25 \times 24 \times 60 \times 60} = 61,200 \text{years} \Rightarrow \text{AD63200}$

14. (a) 'A' and 'C' (both 0.5m) (b) Slope of displacement/time graph is the velocity and graph 'A' has the steepest slope at t = 2s.

    (c) Here's one way. For **'A'** the data pairs are (0,0), (1,0.5), (2,4). As the time doubles (1s to 2s), the displacement is multiplied by 8 (from 0.5m to 4m). That suggests a cubic equation so $s \propto t^3$ $\Rightarrow$ $s = kt^3$ $\Rightarrow$ $4 = k \times 2^3$ $\Rightarrow$ $k = 0.5$ $\Rightarrow$ $s = 0.5t^3$. For **'B'** the data pairs are (0,0), (2,1), (4,4). As the time doubles (2s to 4s), the displacement is multiplied by 4 (from 1m to 4m). That suggests a quadratic so: $s \propto t^2$ $\Rightarrow$ $s = kt^2$ $\Rightarrow$ $1 = k \times 2^2$ $\Rightarrow$ $k = 0.25$ $\Rightarrow$ $s = 0.25t^2$. For **'C'** it's a straight line through the origin so $s \propto t$ $\Rightarrow$ $s = kt$ $\Rightarrow$ $1 = k \times 2$ $\Rightarrow$ $s = 0.5t$

    (d) 'A' $s = 0.5t^3$ $\dfrac{ds}{dt} = 1.5t^2$ $\dfrac{d^2s}{dt^2} = 3t$ 'B' $s = 0.25t^2$ $\dfrac{ds}{dt} = 0.5t$ $\dfrac{d^2s}{dt^2} = 0.5$

    'C' $s = 0.5t$ $\dfrac{ds}{dt} = 0.5$ $\dfrac{d^2s}{dt^2} = 0$

Unit 1 Motion in a Circle.....Answers

1. (a) 2π (b) 4π (c) 2n (d) 60 is a property of the human mind, π is a property of a circle.

2. 2π radians = 6.283 radians is 360 degrees.

   So 1 radian is 360/6.283 = 57.3° (angle on diagram looks about this size)

3. (a) 180° (b) 90° (c) 45° (d) 60° (e) 270°

4. (a) 2 (b) 2½ (c) ½ (d) ⅛ (e) 1.5 × 10⁸

5. (a) 120° = 2π/3 radians

   (b) 'A' must catch up 2π/3 radians in 4 seconds so it must be catching up 2π/12 each second on 'B'. So 'A' is going at (2π/12 + π/12) = π/4 radians per second.

   (c) For 'A'; covering 2π radians at π/4 radians per second takes 8 s.

   For 'B'; covering 2π radians at π/12 radians per second takes 24 s.

   (d) 'A' takes 4 seconds to catch 'B' at a rate of π/4 radians per second so it goes through an angle of π radians. It will be at the opposite side of the circle from where it starts.

   (e) 'B' would be stationary and 'A' would be turning anticlockwise at a rate of π/6 rad s⁻¹.

   (f) Observer (vertically above circle) is turning at a rate of π/2 radians per second anticlockwise. The time taken for 'A' to catch 'B' remains unchanged at 4s.

6. π/6 radians is $\tfrac{1}{12}$th of a complete circle of 12 hours. So π/6 radians is one hour. 1 o'clock.

7. π or 3π or 5π etc. Many answers since a wave is a shape which repeats itself.

8. 360° at 15 degrees per second takes 24 seconds.

9. (a) 0.7742 revs per minute is 0.7742 ÷ 60 = 0.0129 turns each second. So takes 1/0.0129 = 77.5s

   (b) 122.5 seconds

10. (a) $f = \dfrac{1}{T} = 716.4\,Hz$ 716.4 turns per second is $716.4 \times 2\pi \Rightarrow \omega = 4501\,rad\,s^{-1}$

    (b) Circumference of equator = $2\pi r = 2\pi \times 16 \times 10^3 = 1.005 \times 10^5$ metres

    Period = 0.00139595482 seconds $v = \dfrac{s}{t} = \dfrac{1.005 \times 10^5}{0.00139595482} = 7.20 \times 10^7\,m\,s^{-1} = 0.24c$

11. (a) The dotted line 'AB' is no longer pointing towards the sun. It still has to rotate through the small angle 'θ'.

    (b) So that the sun reaches its highest point in the sky at the same clock time each day. This keeps daylight between morning and evening, and night-time between evening and morning. People like the routine of getting up at the same time in the morning when it's getting light.

    (c) From the second diagram (drawn at 23hr 56min later), it must take 4minutes.

    (d) It moves through a complete orbit (360º) in 1 year (just over 365 days) so it moves through an angle of just under 1 degree (0.986º) each day.

12. (a) All points on the surface (and under it) have the same angular velocity since they all take the same time to make one orbit.

    (b) 360º in 23hr 56min is 0.004178 degrees per second (=7.29 x 10^{-5} rad s^{-1}).

    (c) 360º in 365.242 days is 2π radians in 365.242×60×60×24 secs, which gives 1.99 x 10^{-7} rad s^{-1}.

13. (a) 1957rpm = 1957 × 2π ÷ 60 = 205.2 rads s^{-1}.

    (b) 810rpm = 84.82 rads s^{-1} $v = \omega r \Rightarrow r = \dfrac{v}{\omega} = \dfrac{4.917}{84.82} = 0.058\,m$

Unit 1 Equations of Motion.......Answers

1. (a) Constant angular velocity. (b) Yes. Towards the centre. (c) Yes. Along the tangent.
   (d) (i) T (ii) F (iii) T (iv) T (v) T (vi) T (vii) F (viii) T
   (e) 6s to reach 180º is π/6 rad s^{-1}.
   (f) Starting at rest with constant 'α', angular displacement is proportional to the square of the time, so at half the time, it will be one quarter of 180º = 45º

   Angle at 4s is four times bigger (80º compared with 20º).

2. (a) (i) 35m s^{-1} (ii) 63m s^{-1} (b) (i) 35rad s^{-1} (ii) 63rad s^{-1} (c) radians
   (d) Rate of change of angular displacement with respect to time (rad s^{-1})

3. (a) (i) 252m (ii) 3093.75m (b) (i) 252rad (ii) 3093.75rad

4.

Linear Motion			Rotational Motion		
Quantity	Symbol	Units	Quantity	Symbol	Units
time	t	s	time	t	s
displacement	s	m	angular displacement	θ	rad
initial velocity	u	m s^{-1}	initial angular velocity	ω$_o$	rad s^{-1}
final velocity	v	m s^{-1}	final angular velocity	ω	rad s^{-1}
acceleration	a	m s^{-2}	angular acceleration	α	rad s^{-2}

5. (a) $\bar{v} = \dfrac{v+u}{2}$ is for **constant** acceleration (b) $\bar{\omega} = \dfrac{\omega + \omega_o}{2}$ is for **constant** angular acceleration

6. (a) $\pi/2$ rad s^{-1} (b) 15   (c) 12.5cm s^{-1} (d) $v = r\omega \Rightarrow r = 15.9$cm

7. (a) Use $\bar{\omega} = \dfrac{\omega + \omega_o}{2}$ to get $\omega = 10\pi$ rad s^{-1} (b) 120π radians
    (c) $\omega = \omega_o + \alpha t$ gives $\alpha = 0.4\pi$ rad s^{-2}
    (d) $\omega^2 = \omega_o^2 + 2\alpha\theta \Rightarrow \theta = \dfrac{\omega^2 - \omega_o^2}{2\alpha} = \dfrac{(10\pi)^2 - (2\pi)^2}{2 \times 0.4\pi} = 120\pi$ radians   Yes!!!
    (e) $\theta = \omega_o t + \tfrac{1}{2}\alpha t^2 = 2\pi \times 10 + \tfrac{1}{2} \times 0.4\pi \times 10^2 = 40\pi$ rad. This is 20 turns.

8. (a) 8π rad s^{-1} is 4 turns per second, so for 24s this gives 96 turns.
    (b) Using $\alpha = \dfrac{\omega - \omega_o}{t}$ gives $\dfrac{8\pi - 0}{16}$, $\dfrac{8\pi - 8\pi}{24}$, $\dfrac{0 - 8\pi}{32} \Rightarrow \pi/2$, 0, $-\pi/4$ (all rad s^{-2})
    (c) angular displacement   (d) Areas: $\dfrac{1}{2} \times 16 \times 8\pi + 24 \times 8\pi + \dfrac{1}{2} \times 32 \times 8\pi = 384\pi$ radians
    (e) Use $\bar{\omega} = \theta/t$ to get $5\tfrac{1}{3}\pi$ rad s^{-1}. The contribution from each part is 'weighted' by the time for each part. If you add up and divide by three, you assume each section has equal 'weight'.

9. $\alpha = \dfrac{\omega - \omega_o}{t} = \dfrac{16 - 5\pi}{37} = 0.00789$ rad s^{-2} 10. (a) $\omega = \pi/3$ rad s^{-1} (b) constant 'α'   11. $\theta = \dfrac{\pi}{3} t$

12. (a) both represent angular acceleration   (b) rad s^{-2} (c) constant angular velocity
    (d) $\dfrac{d\omega}{dt} = 5 \Rightarrow \int d\omega = \int 5 dt \Rightarrow [\omega - \omega_o] = 5[t - 0] \Rightarrow \omega = \omega_o + 5t$

13. (a) At 6s, speed is 2m s^{-1}. From rest this is an acceleration of 0.333m s^{-2}.
    (b) Tangential acceleration, symbol: a_t, units: m s^{-2}
    (c) At origin $\omega = 0$ and at 6s $\omega = \dfrac{v}{r} = \dfrac{2}{0.15} = 13.3$ rad s^{-1} hence: $\alpha = \dfrac{\omega - \omega_o}{t} = \dfrac{13.3 - 0}{6} = 2.22$ rad s^{-2}
    (d) the tangential acceleration $a_t = r\alpha$

14. (a) $a_t = \dfrac{(2.75 - 1.5)}{18} = 0.0694$ m s^{-2} $a_t = r\alpha \Rightarrow \alpha = 0.0165$ rad s^{-2}
    (b) $\omega_o = \dfrac{v}{r} = \dfrac{1.5}{4.2} = 0.357$ rad s^{-1} $\theta = \omega_o t + \tfrac{1}{2}\alpha t^2 = 0.357t + \tfrac{1}{2} \times 0.0165 t^2$
    Now put $\theta = 2\pi$ and solve the quadratic equation. This gives t = 13.4s. Can you interpret the other solution at -56.7s? (It's because the particle was not just accelerating after time zero).

15. (a) $\omega = \omega_o + \alpha t \Rightarrow \omega_o = 3\pi - 0.2\pi \times 10 = \pi$ rad s^{-1}
    (b) At 15s, $\omega = \omega_o + \alpha t = \pi + 0.2\pi \times 15 = 4\pi$ rad s^{-1}. Then use $v = r\omega$ to get $1.2\pi = 3.77$m s^{-1}

16. (a) $\alpha = \dfrac{d\omega}{dt} \Rightarrow \omega = \int \alpha\, dt = \int (0.15t - 0.8) dt = 0.075t^2 - 0.8t$
    (b) $\omega = \dfrac{d\theta}{dt} \Rightarrow \theta = \int \omega\, dt = \int (0.075t^2 - 0.8t) dt = 0.025t^3 - 0.4t^2$
    (c) $\theta = 0.025t^3 - 0.4t^2 = 0.025 \times 15^3 - 0.4 \times 15^2 = -5.625$ rad
    (d) With $\theta = 2\pi$, from part (b) we obtain $2\pi = 0.025t^3 - 0.4t^2$. Solve graphically to get t = 16.88s.
    (e) $\omega = 0.075t^2 - 0.8t = 0.075 \times 16.88^2 - 0.8 \times 16.88 = 7.87$ rad s^{-1} $\Rightarrow v = wr = 7.87 \times 0.25 = 1.97$ m/s

Unit 1 Centripetal Forces.......Answers

1. (a) No (b) Yes (c) Yes (d) Yes (e) b

2. (a) A 2m B 1m C 0.5m D 8m E 4m F 2m (b) Radius is x4 bigger (c) centripetal force

3. (a) 'Car follows a horizontal curve'. Force is at right angles to its velocity.

   (b) $F = \dfrac{mv^2}{r} = \dfrac{1200 \times 20^2}{50} = 9600\text{N}$. Force is due to friction.

4. $F = \dfrac{mv^2}{r} = \dfrac{5 \times 8^2}{3.5} = 91.4\text{N}$

5. An increase in speed requires a component of the force along the direction of travel. A force at right angles is the only direction where there is no component along the direction of travel.

6. $F = \dfrac{mv^2}{r} \Rightarrow v = \sqrt{\dfrac{rF}{m}} = \sqrt{\dfrac{4.5 \times 2750}{60}} = 14.36\text{m/s}$

7. (a) $\omega = 33\tfrac{1}{3}\text{rpm} = 33\tfrac{1}{3} \times 2\pi \div 60 = 3.49\text{rad/s}$ $F_{Fr} = F_{cent} = \dfrac{mv^2}{r} = mr\omega^2 = 0.025 \times 0.08 \times 3.49^2 = 0.024\text{N}$

   (b) He witnessed his joint move in an outward spiral across the surface.

8. (a) $F = \dfrac{mv^2}{r} = \dfrac{9.109 \times 10^{-31} \times \left(\tfrac{1}{137} \times 3 \times 10^8\right)^2}{0.529 \times 10^{-9}} = 8.25 \times 10^{-9}\text{N}$

   (b) Electrostatic force of attraction between the positive proton and the negative electron.

9. $a = \dfrac{v^2}{r} = \dfrac{0.15^2}{0.75} = 0.03\,\text{m s}^{-2}$ towards the centre of the circle.

10. (a) B → C, C → D, F → G, G → H, L → M, (wherever the car takes a right hand bend).

    (b) A → B, K → L, M → N, and points D, F and H   (c) same as answer to part (b)

    (d) Car has constant speed. There is no acceleration in the direction of the car's velocity and hence no force on the car or its occupants in that direction.

    (e) Point 'K'. The centripetal force is inversely proportional to the radius of the curve and point 'K' has the smallest radius of curvature. The mass and speed of the car remain constant.

    (f) It would be x4 greater since the centripetal force is proportional to the square of the speed.

11. $F = \dfrac{mv^2}{r} = \dfrac{450 \times 12^2}{75} = 864\text{N}$

12. (a) the car moves in a circle of that radius   (b) the centre of mass

    (c) $a = \dfrac{v^2}{r} = \dfrac{8.37^2}{25} = 2.80\,\text{m s}^{-2}$ (d) the horizontal component of the normal reaction

    (e) $F = ma = 1150 \times 2.80 = 3220\text{N}$ (f) 3220N Horizontally towards the spin axis

13. (a) B (b) A (c) no (d) the gravitational force (e) $W = mg = 0.15 \times 9.8 = 1.47\text{N}$

    (f) $F = \dfrac{mv^2}{r} \Rightarrow v = \sqrt{\dfrac{rF}{m}} = \sqrt{\dfrac{0.38 \times 1.47}{0.15}} = 1.93\,\text{m s}^{-1}$

    Note: if W = F at the top of the arc, then $F = \dfrac{mv^2}{r} = W = mg \Rightarrow g = \dfrac{v^2}{r} \Rightarrow v = \sqrt{gr}$.

    Thus the minimum speed is independent of the mass. Since the centripetal force at the top is provided by gravity, the centripetal acceleration must be 'g'. (The gravitational force and the centripetal force point in the same direction, straight down).

14. (a) $v = \omega r = 2\pi f r = 2\pi \times 15 \times 0.2 = 18.85\,\text{m s}^{-1}$

    (b) $F = \dfrac{mv^2}{r} = \dfrac{0.35 \times 18.85^2}{0.2} = 622\text{N}$ (ignore gravity since it spins horizontally)

(c) towards the centre of the drum / no difference.

(d) $\alpha = \dfrac{\omega - \omega_o}{t} = \dfrac{0 - 2\pi \times 15}{40} = -2.36\,\text{rad s}^{-2}$

15. (a) because the car doesn't accelerate vertically (b) H, the horizontal component

    (c) $V = mg$ $H = V\tan\theta = mg\tan\theta$

    (d) $H = mg\tan\theta = \dfrac{mv^2}{r} \Rightarrow v^2 = gr\tan\theta \Rightarrow v = \sqrt{gr\tan\theta}$

    (e) the expression for the speed does not contain the mass, so doubling it makes no difference.

Unit 1 Moment of Inertia......Answers

1. To make sure you don't rotate the object. All the energy goes into translational motion.

2. (a) Moment of inertia is ×4   (b) The mass must have doubled.

3. (a) R   (b) 4 kgm² at P and 64 kgm² at R

   (c) At 'Q' $I = m(2d)^2 = 16\,\text{kg m}^2$ Midpoint 3d so, $I = m(3d)^2 = m\left(\dfrac{3}{2} \times 2d\right)^2 = \dfrac{9}{4} \times 16\,\text{kg m}^2 = 36\,\text{kg m}^2$

   (d) $I = m(2d)^2 = 16\,\text{kg m}^2$, so at position 'x', $I = m(x)^2 = 9\,\text{kg m}^2$. Divide one equation by the other to get: $\dfrac{m(x)^2}{m(2d)^2} = \dfrac{9}{16}$. Solving gives x = 1½d from spin axis (midway between 'P' and 'Q'.

   (e) The change in distance (try it with some numbers).   (f) At the spin axis.

4. (a) $I = \dfrac{1}{12}mL^2 = \dfrac{1}{12} \times 6 \times 0.18^2 = 0.0162\,\text{kg m}^2$ (b) $I = mr^2 = 0.4 \times 0.75^2 = 0.225\,\text{kg m}^2$

   (c) $I = \dfrac{1}{2}mr^2 = \dfrac{1}{2} \times 2.45 \times 0.12^2 = 0.01764\,\text{kg m}^2$

5. (a) $I = mr^2 = 5.976 \times 10^{24} \times (1.496 \times 10^{11})^2 = 1.34 \times 10^{47}\,\text{kg m}^2$

   (b) $I = \dfrac{2}{5}mr^2 = 0.4 \times 5.976 \times 10^{24} \times (6.378 \times 10^6)^2 = 9.72 \times 10^{37}\,\text{kg m}^2$

6. (a) Equate the moments of inertia: $I = \dfrac{1}{12}mL^2 = \dfrac{1}{2}mr^2$. Cancel the m's, use L=8cm, to get r = 3.27cm

   (b) Get the mass as far away from the spin axis as possible (shape it like a dumbbell).

7. (a) $I = \dfrac{1}{2}mr^2 \Rightarrow 4.3 = \dfrac{1}{2} \times m \times 0.15^2 \Rightarrow m = 382\,\text{kg}$

   (b) $\rho = \dfrac{m}{V} \Rightarrow V = \dfrac{m}{\rho} = \dfrac{382}{8900} = 0.0429\,\text{m}^3 = \pi r^2 h \Rightarrow h = 0.607\,\text{m}$

8. (a) $I = mr^2 = 1.2 \times 0.25^2 = 0.075\,\text{kg m}^2$

   (b) Mass of drum and denims all at same distance from spin axis,

   So, $I = mr^2 = 0.16 = m \times 0.25^2 \Rightarrow m = 2.56\,\text{kg}$. This is the mass of damp denims plus the drum.

   Hence, mass of water is: 2.56 (the total) – 1.2 (the drum) – 0.8 (dry denims) = 0.56kg.

   (c) Wet denims gradually drying out and losing mass.

9. Circumference is 2πr so twice the radius has twice the length and twice the mass. Moment of inertia of inner hoop is $I = mr^2$ (which equals 6kgm²), so outer hoop is $I = (2m)(2r)^2 = 8mr^2$. The total moment of inertia is $9mr^2$, which is 54kgm².

10. (a) All masses are at the same distance from the spin axis, (so can use $I = mr^2$ for them all)

   (b) The masses have a size, so parts of it are at different distances from the spin axis. Since $I \propto r^2$ further away parts have more effect. This effect is biggest with the left hand diagram.

   (c) For the left hand diagram: $I = mr^2 \Rightarrow r = \sqrt{\dfrac{I}{m}} = \sqrt{\dfrac{40}{12}} = 1.83\,\text{m}$

11. Refer to the companion Theory Book page 45. Take human body as a cylinder with two rods for arms. Each arm is about 6.5% of the total body mass (internet research). For a 50kg skater this gives 3.5kg for an arm and 43kg for the rest of the body. Take body cylinder 30cm thick, a radius of 15cm.

   With arms sticking straight out: $I_{before} = 2 \times \dfrac{1}{3} m_{arm} l_{arm}^2 + \dfrac{1}{2} m_{body} r_{body}^2 = 1.31 + 0.48 = 1.79\,\text{kg m}^2$.

   With arms in: $I_{after} = \dfrac{1}{2} m_{body} r_{body}^2 = \dfrac{1}{2} \times 50 \times 0.15^2 = 0.56\,\text{kg m}^2$. This is a ratio of 3.2 to 1. Where do the largest uncertainties arise? Being a square relationship, the radius estimates have to be good!

Unit 1 Torque......Answers

1. (a) Newtons (N) for force and Newton-metres (Nm) for torque.

   (b) The answer isn't 'enrol in physics classes and drink up'. The answer is ' if I push you in the stomach you'll go backwards, but if I push you on the shoulder you'll spin around on your bar stool. The first one's a force, the second one's a torque'. Beat that!

2. (a) 'along the tangent', though a better definition is 'at right angles to the radius vector'.

   (b) $T = rF = 4 \times 0.18 = 0.72\,\text{Nm}$ (c) towards or away from, the centre of the disc.

   (d) (Probably) through the centre at right angles to the plane of the disc.

   (e) Apply equal forces at opposite ends of a diameter pointing in **same** direction.

3. (a) $T = rF = 15 \times 6 = 90\,\text{Nm}$

   (b) $T = rF = 0.18 \times 0.85 = 0.153\,\text{Nm}$

   (c) $F_\perp = 8 \cos 35° = 6.55\,\text{N}$ $T = rF = 0.36 \times 6.55 = 2.36\,\text{Nm}$

   Note: this answer uses the cosine of the angle to calculate the component of the force along the tangent. If you wish to form good habits at an early age, then use $T = rF \sin\theta$, where 'θ' is the angle between the force and the radial vector. This would give $T = rF \sin\theta = 0.36 \times 8 \sin 55°$

4. $T = rF \Rightarrow F = \dfrac{T}{r} = \dfrac{1.6}{0.4} = 4\,\text{N}$ at right angles to both the spin axis and the rod. The angle at which the force is applied can be changed by the finest amount eg. $4\sqrt{2}$ N at 45° would apply the same torque. Applying the force at right angles gives maximum torque for minimum force.

5. From the ruler, the forces are applied at positions of 0.5m, 0.7m and 1.1m from spin axis.

   Clockwise torque: $T = rF = 0.5 \times 22 = 11\,\text{Nm}$. Anticlockwise torques: $0.7 \times 4 + 1.1 \times 8 \cos 20° = 11.07\,\text{Nm}$

   Result is a torque of 0.07Nm anticlockwise.

6. (a) Mass of Earth is 6×10^{24}kg so 'weight' is 5.88×10^{25}N. The radius of the Earth is 6.38×10^6m so the torque to be applied is $T = rF = 6.38 \times 10^6 \times 5.88 \times 10^{25} = 3.75 \times 10^{32}\,\text{Nm}$. An average person could lift a new-size bag of cement, which is 25kg. This is a weight of about 250N, which you apply to the other end of the rod: $3.75 \times 10^{32} = rF = r \times 250 \Rightarrow r = 1.5 \times 10^{30}\,\text{m}$. That's a distance over 10,000 times larger than the 'radius' of the universe.

   (b) Yes, I did! The Earth is weightless since it's in freefall about the Sun. Think of an astronaut in a spacecraft orbiting the Earth. He doesn't need much force to 'lift' a pencil hanging in the space inside.

(c) A weightless Earth on one end requires anything greater than zero force on the other end to move it. That's taking mass as 'gravitational mass'. What about the Earth's 'inertial mass', the one used in Newton's 2nd Law? Moving a body from 'rest' requires a change in speed and by the Second Law, this requires a force. However, you can make the acceleration as small as you wish by taking a very long time to apply your infinitesimal force. Just remember to point the lever towards the Sun so that the Earth doesn't go closer to it as it moves. Which brings in the slight arc as the Earth lifts which alters its distance from the Sun and hence bring 'gravitational mass' back into it. Anything else.....?

7. (a) $\sin\theta = \pm 1 \Rightarrow \theta = 90°, 270°$ for maximum torque and $\sin\theta = 0 \Rightarrow \theta = 0°, 180°$ for minimum torque.

   (b) $\sin\theta = \frac{1}{2} \Rightarrow \theta = 30°$. A common example of this would be the electric motor with parallel sided magnetic pole pieces. Note that the angle is the one between the force 'F' (produced by the field and current) and the outwards pointing radial direction (dotted line on diagram).

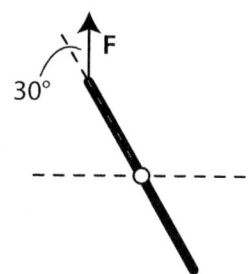

   (c) This answer seems weird; it points at right angles to both the radial direction and the force (like the z-axis in an xyz Cartesian co-ordinate system).

Unit 1 Moment of Inertia and Torque......Answers

1. Torque in units of N m   Moment of Inertia in kg m²   Angular acceleration in rad s⁻²

2. (a) $T = rF = 0.15 \times 6 = 0.9\,\text{Nm}$ (b) $I = \frac{1}{12}mL^2 = \frac{1}{12} \times 0.25 \times 0.3^2 = 0.001875\,\text{kg m}^2$

   (c) $\alpha = \frac{T}{I} = \frac{0.9}{0.001875} = 480\,\text{rad s}^{-2}$

3. (a) $\omega = \omega_o + \alpha t = 0 + 0.16 \times 20 = 3.2\,\text{rad s}^{-1}$

   (b) $\theta = \omega_o t + \frac{1}{2}\alpha t^2 = 0 + \frac{1}{2} \times 0.16 \times 20^2 = 32\,\text{rad}$ or use: $\overline{\omega} = \frac{\theta}{t} \Rightarrow \theta = \overline{\omega}t = 1.6 \times 20 = 32\,\text{rad}$

   (c) $v = \omega r \Rightarrow \omega = \frac{v}{r} = \frac{0.4}{0.2} = 2\,\text{rad s}^{-1}$ $\omega = \omega_o + \alpha t \Rightarrow t = \frac{(\omega - \omega_o)}{\alpha} = \frac{2}{0.16} = 12.5\,\text{s}$

4. (a) $I = \frac{1}{2}mr^2 = \frac{1}{2} \times 0.74 \times 0.12^2 = 0.005328\,\text{kg m}^2$

   (b) Neither. It is independent of the angular velocity just as mass is independent of linear velocity.

   (c) This question combines kinematics with dynamics. The link between them is the angular acceleration, so calculate 'α' first: $\alpha = \frac{(\omega - \omega_o)}{t} = \frac{0 - 4\pi}{18} = -0.698\,\text{rad s}^{-2}$, then use it for the torque:

   $T = I\alpha = 0.005328 \times (-0.698) = -0.00372\,\text{Nm}$ $F = \frac{T}{r} = \frac{-0.00372}{0.12} = -0.031\,\text{N}$ $|F| = 0.031\,\text{N}$

5. (a) $T = rF = 0.14 \times 0.5 = 0.07\,\text{Nm}$

   (b) $I = \frac{1}{2}mr^2 = \frac{1}{2} \times 0.75 \times 0.14^2 = 0.00735\,\text{kg m}^2$ $\alpha = \frac{T}{I} = \frac{0.07}{0.00735} = 9.52\,\text{rad s}^{-2}$

   (c) 50 turns = 50×2π = 100π radians. $\theta = \omega_o t + \frac{1}{2}\alpha t^2 = \frac{1}{2}\alpha t^2 \Rightarrow t = \sqrt{\frac{2\theta}{\alpha}} = \sqrt{\frac{2 \times 100\pi}{9.52}} = 8.12\,\text{s}$

6. $\omega = 500\,\text{rpm} = 500 \times \frac{2\pi}{60} = 52.36\,\text{rad s}^{-1}$ $\alpha = \frac{(\omega - \omega_o)}{t} = \frac{52.36 - 0}{30} = 1.745\,\text{rad s}^{-2}$

   $I = \frac{1}{3}mL^2 = \frac{1}{3} \times 0.35 \times 0.4^2 = 0.0187\,\text{kg m}^2$ $T = I\alpha = 0.0187 \times 1.745 = 0.0326\,\text{Nm}$

   $F = \frac{T}{r} = \frac{0.0326}{0.4} = 0.0814\,\text{N}$

7. (a) $T = rF = 0.3 \times (0.05 \times 9.8) = 0.147 \, \text{Nm}$ $\qquad I = \frac{1}{2}mr^2 = \frac{1}{2} \times 240 \times 0.3^2 = 10.8 \, \text{kg m}^2$

$$\alpha = \frac{T}{I} = \frac{0.147}{10.8} = 0.0136 \, \text{rad s}^{-2} \qquad \theta = \omega_o t + \frac{1}{2}\alpha t^2 = \frac{1}{2}\alpha t^2 \Rightarrow t = \sqrt{\frac{2\theta}{\alpha}} = \sqrt{\frac{2 \times 6\pi}{0.0136}} = 52.6 \, \text{s}$$

It's easy to assume that the force on the rim is equal to the weight of the hanging mass, but it's not. The force on the rim is the tension in the string. For hanging masses much less than the mass of the drum (like this example), the force on the rim is almost equal to the weight– see the Advanced Higher Physics Theory Book pages 40/41 for the general case.

(b) $\alpha = \dfrac{(\omega - \omega_o)}{t} = \dfrac{4\pi - 0}{300} = 0.0419 \, \text{rad s}^{-2} \qquad T = I\alpha = 10.8 \times 0.0419 = 0.453 \, \text{Nm}$

$F = \dfrac{T}{r} = \dfrac{0.453}{0.3} = 1.5 \, \text{N} \qquad m = \dfrac{W}{g} = \dfrac{1.5}{9.8} = 0.154 \, \text{kg}$ (still much less than 240kg)

8. (a) long side: 7.5cm and 90g   short side: 5cm and 60g

(b) $I_{total} = m_l r^2 + m_l r^2 + \frac{1}{12} m_s r^2 + \frac{1}{12} m_s r^2 = 2 \times 0.09 \times 0.025^2 + \frac{1}{6} \times 0.06 \times 0.05^2 = 0.0001375 \, \text{kg m}^2$

(c) $\alpha = \dfrac{(\omega - \omega_o)}{t} = \dfrac{0 - 8\pi}{24} = -1.047 \, \text{rad s}^{-2} \qquad T = I\alpha = 0.0001375 \times (-1.047) = -0.000144 \, \text{Nm}$

Unit 1 Rotational Kinetic Energy......Answers

1. $E_k = \frac{1}{2}I\omega^2$

2. (a) $I = \dfrac{1}{2}mr^2 = \dfrac{1}{2} \times 4.5 \times 0.15^2 = 0.0506 \, \text{kg m}^2 \Rightarrow E_{Rot} = \dfrac{1}{2}I\omega^2 = \dfrac{1}{2} \times 0.0506 \times (18\pi)^2 = 80.9 \, \text{J}$

(b) Radius doubled means that moment of inertia is quadrupled, so kinetic energy is quadrupled.

(c) Moment of inertia is halved, so kinetic energy is halved.

3. a $E_{Rot} = \dfrac{1}{2}I\omega^2 = \dfrac{1}{2} \times \left(\dfrac{1}{12} \times 0.25 \times 0.45^2\right) \times (6\pi)^2 = 0.75 \, \text{J}$

b $E_{Rot} = \dfrac{1}{2}I\omega^2 = \dfrac{1}{2} \times (1.7 \times 0.03^2) \times (25\pi)^2 = 4.72 \, \text{J}$

c $E_{Rot} = \dfrac{1}{2}I\omega^2 = \dfrac{1}{2} \times \left(\dfrac{1}{2} \times 3.2 \times 0.028^2\right) \times \left(\dfrac{4000 \times 2\pi}{60}\right)^2 = 110 \, \text{J}$

d $E_{Rot} = \dfrac{1}{2}I\omega^2 = \dfrac{1}{2} \times \left(\dfrac{2}{5} \times 6 \times 10^{24} \times (6.378 \times 10^6)^2\right) \times \left(\dfrac{2\pi}{24 \times 60 \times 60}\right)^2 = 2.58 \times 10^{29} \, \text{J}$ Planet Earth

4. (a) $E_{Rot} = \dfrac{1}{2}I\omega^2 = \dfrac{1}{2} \times \left(\dfrac{1}{2} \times 0.6 \times 0.05^2\right) \times (12\pi)^2 = 0.533 \, \text{J}$

(b) $E_{Rot} = \dfrac{1}{2}I\omega^2 = \dfrac{1}{2} \times \left(\dfrac{1}{2} \times 0.6 \times 0.05^2\right) \times (20\pi)^2 = 1.48 \, \text{J} \Rightarrow$ additional 0.95J

5. The energy is all rotational: $I = \dfrac{1}{2}m(R_1^2 + R_2^2) = \dfrac{1}{2} \times 0.85 \times (0.18^2 + 0.15^2) = 0.0233 \, \text{kg m}^2$

$E_{Rot} = \dfrac{1}{2}I\omega^2 \Rightarrow \omega = \sqrt{\dfrac{2 E_{Rot}}{I}} = \sqrt{\dfrac{2 \times 3.8}{0.0233}} = 18.05 \, \text{rad s}^{-1}$

6. $I = \dfrac{1}{3}mr^2 = \dfrac{1}{3} \times 0.15 \times 0.18^2 = 0.00162 \, \text{kg m}^2 \Rightarrow \omega = \sqrt{\dfrac{2 E_{Rot}}{I}} = \sqrt{\dfrac{2 \times 0.03}{0.00162}} = 6.086 \, \text{rad s}^{-1}$

$\theta = \omega_o t + \dfrac{1}{2}\alpha t^2 \underset{(\alpha=0)}{=} \omega_o t \Rightarrow t = \dfrac{\theta}{\omega_o} = \dfrac{5 \times 2\pi}{6.086} = 5.16 \, \text{s}$

7. (a) Calculate the mass: $m = \rho V = 7800 \times (\pi r^2 h) = 7800 \times \pi \times 0.2^2 \times 0.5 = 490\text{kg}$

Then the kinetic energy: $E_{Rot} = \frac{1}{2}I\omega^2 = \frac{1}{2} \times \left(\frac{1}{2} \times 490 \times 0.2^2\right) \times (25 \times 2\pi)^2 = 1.21 \times 10^5 \text{J}$

(b) $P = VI = 230 \times 6 = 1380\text{W}$ $P = \frac{E}{t} \Rightarrow t = \frac{E}{P} = \frac{1.21 \times 10^5}{1380} = 87.7\text{s}$

(c) $\alpha = \frac{\omega - \omega_o}{t} = \frac{0 - 50\pi}{1518} = -0.103 \text{rad s}^{-2}$ $T = I\alpha = \left(\frac{1}{2} \times 490 \times 0.2^2\right) \times (-0.103) = -1.01\text{Nm}$

8. $E_{Trans} = \frac{1}{2} \times 0.35 \times 4^2 = 2.8\text{J}$ $E_{Rot} = \frac{1}{2} \times \left(\frac{1}{2} \times 0.35 \times 0.025^2\right) \times \left(\frac{2\pi}{0.2}\right)^2 = 0.054\text{J}$ $\Rightarrow$ $E_{Tot} = 2.854\text{J}$

9. (a) $mgh = \frac{1}{2}mv^2 + \frac{1}{2}I\omega^2$ $\Rightarrow$ $\frac{1}{2}mv^2 + \frac{1}{2}\left(\frac{1}{2}mr^2\right)\left(\frac{v}{r}\right)^2$ $\Rightarrow$ $\frac{1}{2}mv^2 + \frac{1}{4}mv^2 = \frac{3}{4}mv^2$

cancel the m's: $gh = \frac{3}{4}v^2$ $\Rightarrow$ $v = \sqrt{\frac{4}{3}gh}$.

(b) When it's vertically dropped, all of the potential energy goes into translational kinetic energy. When it rolls down the slope, some of the potential energy goes into rotating the object. From (a) above, the rotational kinetic energy is half the translational ($\frac{1}{4}mv^2$ compared with $\frac{1}{2}mv^2$).

(c) Heat and Sound energy. Friction (producing heat) prevents the cylinder slipping (and also makes the initial assumption of 'no heat loss' inconsistent).

(d) The two variables are 'v' and 'h' so plot 'v²' against 'h' and look for a straight line graph (of slope 4g/3). Set up a light gate at position 'A' and measure the time for the beam to cut the cylinder (either length-ways or vertically with a polished runway/hole in runway etc). Measure diameter of cylinder using calipers and calculate the speed using v=d/t. Repeat for various starting positions up the runway taking care to measure the correct vertical fall.

Unit 1 Angular Momentum.......Answers

1. In linear mechanics, __FORCE__ is the rate of change of momentum. Momentum is __CONSERVED__ in a collision if there are no external forces acting on the system. In a similar way, torque is the __RATE OF CHANGE OF ANGULAR MOMENTUM__ and will be conserved in interactions where there are no __EXTERNAL TORQUES__. In linear motion, the momentum 'p' is mv. For rotational motion, mass is replaced by the __MOMENT OF INERTIA__ and velocity is replaced by the __ANGULAR VELOCITY__ , so the expression for angular momentum 'L' is __$I\omega$__.

2. (a) $L = I\omega$ works for any shape   (b) $L = mvr$ is only for a point particle.
   (c) 'Rate of change of angular momentum'. Special name is 'torque'.

3. (a) For axis 'A': $L = I\omega = mvr = 5 \times 4 \times 20 = 400 \text{kgm}^2\text{s}^{-1}$

   For axis 'B': $L = I\omega = mvr = 5 \times 4 \times 30 = 600 \text{kgm}^2\text{s}^{-1}$

   (b) **velocity** (you are sitting at your desk at rest which is about 30km s⁻¹ with respect to the sun).
   potential energy (where do you measure your height from?)

   Examples of absolute quantities (same measurement for all observers) are electric charge and mass (the modern approach to Special Relativity doesn't do 'relativistic mass').

4. (a) The minute hand **should** rotate 2π radians in 1 hour: $\omega = \frac{2\pi}{T} = \frac{2\pi}{60 \times 60} = 1.745 \times 10^{-3} \text{rad s}^{-1}$

(b) $I = \frac{1}{3}mL^2 = \frac{1}{3} \times 0.018 \times (0.03)^2 = 5.4 \times 10^{-6} \text{kgm}^2$ $\omega = \frac{L}{I} = \frac{9.39 \times 10^{-9}}{5.4 \times 10^{-6}} = 1.7389 \times 10^{-3} \text{rad s}^{-1}$

After 3600s, the angle is $\theta = \omega t = 1.7389 \times 10^{-3} \times 3600 = 6.26 \text{rad} \Rightarrow 3587\text{s}$

So, after 1 hour, the clock is 13 seconds slow, indicating 12:59:47

5. (a) $L = mvr = 4 \times 0.25 \times 0.3 = 0.3 \text{kgm}^2\text{s}^{-1}$ (b) $L = I\omega = (0.58 \times 0.08^2) \times \left(\frac{0.8}{0.08}\right) = 0.037 \text{kgm}^2\text{s}^{-1}$

(c) $L = I\omega = \left(\frac{1}{2} \times 0.05 \times 0.06^2\right) \times \left(\frac{300 \times 2\pi}{60}\right) = 0.0028 \text{kgm}^2\text{s}^{-1}$

6. You're 'floating' freely out in space with your spanner attached to the bolt. You start to turn it and take up the slack on the threads so everything is okay (you probably didn't notice a very slight body rotation due to the distraction of the beautiful planet down below). You then tighten it. What happens? The torque you applied to the spaceship over a certain time gives it a change in angular momentum. Having a large moment of inertia only results in a small change in its angular velocity. The spaceship applies an equal and opposite torque to you (think Newton's 3RD Law stuff), but having a small moment of inertia, you get a large change in angular velocity. The solution is for your feet to be firmly attached to the spacecraft so that you don't rotate. You could 'sit' on the spacecraft like riding a horse, or try the more exotic magnetic boots.

7. (a) $I\omega_{before} = \frac{1}{2}mr^2\omega = \frac{1}{2} \times 0.25 \times 0.3^2 \times \left(\frac{45 \times 2\pi}{60}\right) = 0.053 \text{kgm}^2\text{s}^{-1}$

(b) $I\omega_{after} = 0.053 \text{kgm}^2\text{s}^{-1} = I\omega_{Disc} + I\omega_{point\,mass} = \frac{1}{2} \times 0.25 \times 0.3^2 \times \omega + 0.05 \times 0.3^2 \times \omega$

$0.053 = 0.01575\omega \Rightarrow \omega = 3.365 \text{rad s}^{-1}$ $(= 32.1 \text{ rpm})$

(c) $E_{Rot} = \frac{1}{2}I\omega^2$ Before: $\frac{1}{2} \times \frac{1}{2} \times 0.25 \times 0.3^2 \times \left(\frac{45 \times 2\pi}{60}\right)^2 = 0.1249 \text{J}$

After: (Disc) $\frac{1}{2} \times \frac{1}{2} \times 0.25 \times 0.3^2 \times (3.365)^2 = 0.0637 \text{J}$

(Mass) $\frac{1}{2} \times 0.05 \times 0.3^2 \times (3.365)^2 = 0.0254 \text{J} \Rightarrow$ Total = 0.0892 J

Kinetic energy is reduced, so it's an inelastic collision. (d) Heat energy and sound energy.

8. Use conservation of angular momentum: $I\omega_{before} = I\omega_{after}$. With her arms outstretched, the moment of inertia is high. As she brings in her arms, her moment of inertia decreases (more of her mass towards the centre) and her angular velocity increases. The effect is quite marked since the moment of inertia depends upon the square of the distance. Assumption is that there are no external torques (which means no friction where her ice skate spins on the ice).

9. His suitcase would continue pointing in the same direction no matter the direction he travelled (think about turning a corner). Pauli was an 'interesting' character. He was a theoretical physicist and had a reputation for breaking equipment by just entering a room (known as the 'Pauli effect'). He featured in the Futurama animation series with "St. Pauli's Exclusion Principle Beer". There are many anecdotes about Pauli, mostly the result of his intellectual honesty rather than any intended rudeness (like his 'terrible rubbish' comment on Einstein's attempt at a Unified Theory in 1927). He visited the psychiatrist Carl Jung (often enough to have 400 of his dreams analysed), after the breakup of his first marriage and subsequent boozing. Also noted for his driving, he would turn around to his passengers and take his hands off the wheel……..you get the idea.

10. (a) Time stays as it is and force becomes torque, so it's Torque x time. (If the torque isn't constant, you would use the integral form $\int T(t)\,dt$.

(b) Change in angular momentum $\Delta L = Tt = 0.03 \times 5 = 0.15 \text{Nms} = 0.15 \text{kgm}^2\text{s}^{-1}$

$L_{Before} = I\omega = \left(\frac{1}{12} \times 1.5 \times 0.6^2\right) \times 2\pi = 0.283 \text{kgm}^2\text{s}^{-1}$

This will change by 0.15 kgm²s⁻¹ but the question doesn't state which direction the torque is applied, so result is: (0.283 ± 0.15) kgm²s⁻¹ $\Rightarrow$ 0.433 kgm²s⁻¹ or 0.133 kgm²s⁻¹.

Using $L = I\omega$ this gives ω = 9.62 rad s⁻¹ and ω = 2.96 rad s⁻¹ respectively.

11. Looking down on the north pole, the planet spins anticlockwise. Hold your right hand with the fingers curled and the thumb pointing upwards. The thumb points along the direction of the angular momentum vector, and your fingers show the rotation. Total angular momentum is conserved. To reduce the time taken for one rotation of the planet requires an angular momentum vector pointing downwards. In the northern hemisphere you would spin clockwise (or anticlockwise in the southern hemisphere). As soon as you stop spinning, you transfer the angular momentum back to the planet. All it does is make you dizzy.

Unit 1 Gravitation......Answers

1. (a) $F = G\dfrac{Mm}{r^2} = \dfrac{6.674 \times 10^{-11} \times 60 \times 70}{0.5^2} = 1.12 \times 10^{-6}$ N

   (b) $F = G\dfrac{Mm}{r^2} = \dfrac{6.674 \times 10^{-11} \times 5.976 \times 10^{24} \times 7.349 \times 10^{22}}{(3.85 \times 10^8)^2} = 1.977 \times 10^{20}$ N

   (c) $F = G\dfrac{Mm}{r^2} = \dfrac{6.674 \times 10^{-11} \times 1.673 \times 10^{-27} \times 9.109 \times 10^{-31}}{(0.529 \times 10^{-10})^2} = 3.63 \times 10^{-47}$ N

2. $5000 = \dfrac{6.674 \times 10^{-11} \times m^2}{(20 \times 10^3)^2} \Rightarrow m = 1.73 \times 10^{11}$ kg

3. Your weight at the surface.

4. (a) $m\omega^2 r = G\dfrac{Mm}{r^2} \Rightarrow \omega^2 r = G\dfrac{M}{r^2} \Rightarrow \omega^2 = G\dfrac{M}{r^3} \quad \omega^2 = \left(\dfrac{2\pi}{T}\right)^2 = G\dfrac{M}{r^3} \Rightarrow T^2 = \left(\dfrac{4\pi^2}{GM}\right)r^3$

   (b) Both planets orbit the same mass so:

   Planet 1 $T_1^2 = \left(\dfrac{4\pi^2}{GM}\right)r_1^3$ \qquad Planet 2 $T_2^2 = \left(\dfrac{4\pi^2}{GM}\right)r_2^3$ \qquad Divide these two equations,

   $\Rightarrow \left(\dfrac{T_2}{T_1}\right)^2 = \left(\dfrac{r_2}{r_1}\right)^3 \quad \left(\dfrac{r_2}{r_1}\right)^3 = 4^3 = 64 \Rightarrow \left(\dfrac{T_2}{T_1}\right)^2 = 64 \quad T_1 = 1 \text{ year} \Rightarrow T_2 = 8 \text{ years}$

   (c) Jupiter's mass

5. (a) The Period is in units of years (since the Earth's period is 1 unit) and the distances are in units of Astronomical Units, the A.U. (since the Earth's distance is 1 unit). That's about 93 million miles in old money.

   (b)

Mercury	Venus	Earth	Mars	Jupiter	Saturn	Uranus	Neptune
0.993	1.016	1.00	0.999	0.999	1.00	0.999	1.00

   $\dfrac{T^2}{r^3} = $ constant $(= 1 \text{ yr}^2 \text{ AU}^{-3})$ for an orbit about our Sun.)

   (c) $\dfrac{T^2}{r^3} = \dfrac{(365.26 \times 24 \times 60 \times 60)^2}{(1.496 \times 10^{11})^3} = 2.975 \times 10^{-19}$ s² m⁻³ $= \dfrac{4\pi^2}{GM_S} \Rightarrow M_S = 1.99 \times 10^{30}$ kg

105

6.

Planet	Mercury	Mars	Jupiter	Neptune
Mass (kg)	3.303×10^{23}	6.421×10^{23}	1.900×10^{27}	1.024×10^{26}
Radius (m)	2.4397×10^6	3.394×10^6	7.1492×10^7	2.4746×10^7
'g' (m/s²)	3.70	3.72	24.8	11.2

7. (a) $V = -\dfrac{GM}{r} = -\dfrac{6.674 \times 10^{-11} \times 5.976 \times 10^{24}}{2 \times 10^7} = -1.99 \times 10^7 \, \text{J kg}^{-1}$ (note the units for 'V')

(b) $V = -7.98 \times 10^6 \, \text{J kg}^{-1}$

(c) $(-7.98 \times 10^6) - (-1.99 \times 10^7) = 1.19 \times 10^7 \, \text{J kg}^{-1}$

Note that the sign depends on which way you subtract them.

The rule is always (final position minus initial position), so in the above example we went from the initial 2×10^7 m out to the final 5×10^7 m (away from Earth).

(d) Energy = 4 kg × 1.19 × 10⁷ J kg⁻¹ = 4.76 × 10⁷ J (note how simple the units are).

8. Gravitational potential at surface $V = -\dfrac{GM}{r} = -\dfrac{6.674 \times 10^{-11} \times 5.976 \times 10^{24}}{6.378 \times 10^6} = -6.25 \times 10^7 \, \text{J kg}^{-1}$

Gravitational potential at 1.7×10^7 m $V = -2.35 \times 10^7 \, \text{J kg}^{-1}$

Grav. Pot. Difference $(-2.35 \times 10^7) - (-6.25 \times 10^7) = 3.9 \times 10^7 \, \text{J kg}^{-1}$

Energy required ('work done') = 3.9 × 10⁷ × 25 = 9.75 × 10⁸ J.

Note how similar this procedure is to Work Done = Vq in electricity.

9. (a) If 'h' is small compared with 'r'.

(b) $\left(-\dfrac{GMm}{r_2}\right) - \left(-\dfrac{GMm}{r_1}\right) = GMm\left[\dfrac{1}{r_1} - \dfrac{1}{r_2}\right] = GMm\left[\dfrac{r_2 - r_1}{r_2 r_1}\right] = \dfrac{GMm}{r_2 r_1}(r_2 - r_1)$

and using $h = (r_2 - r_1)$ and $r^2 = r_2 r_1$ with $g = \dfrac{GM}{r^2}$ gives $E_p = mgh$

10. Since gravitational potential is a scalar, you just add the contributions like ordinary numbers:

Due to M₁: $V = -\dfrac{GM_1}{r} = -\dfrac{6.674 \times 10^{-11} \times 5 \times 10^{20}}{4.3 \times 10^7} = -776 \, \text{J kg}^{-1}$

Due to M₂: $V = -\dfrac{GM_2}{r} = -\dfrac{6.674 \times 10^{-11} \times 1.4 \times 10^{21}}{1.04 \times 10^8} = -898 \, \text{J kg}^{-1}$

Total = (−776) + (−898) = − 1674 J kg⁻¹

11. (a) equipotential surface (b) surface of a sphere

(c) 'B' and 'C' have the same gravitational potential and the energy required depends upon the gravitational potential difference at the start and finish positions – it is path independent.

12. (a) at infinity

(b) The work done **per unit mass** by external forces in moving unit mass from infinity to point 'P' at rest. Note that the parts in bold are missing from the SQA syllabus.

(c) If you miss out the bit in bold in answer (b) above, you get the Gravitational Potential Energy of a 1kg mass at point 'P'. Units are: Grav. Pot. in J kg⁻¹   Grav. Pot. Energy in J

13. (a) The escape velocity is the same for a cricket ball as for a bus (ignoring air resistance).

    (b) $v_{esc} = \sqrt{\dfrac{2GM}{r}} = \sqrt{\dfrac{2 \times 6.674 \times 10^{-11} \times 5.976 \times 10^{24}}{6.378 \times 10^6}} = 11200 \text{ m s}^{-1}$

14. $v_{esc} = \sqrt{\dfrac{2GM}{r}} \Rightarrow v_{esc} \propto \sqrt{M}$ so 'M' must be 16 times bigger to make 'v' 4 times bigger.

15. $v_{esc} = \sqrt{\dfrac{2GM}{r}} = \sqrt{\dfrac{2GMr}{r^2}} = \sqrt{2gr}$ since $g = \dfrac{GM}{r^2}$

16. (a) $\rho = \dfrac{M}{V} \Rightarrow M = \rho V = 5200 \times \dfrac{4}{3}\pi \times 8000^3 = 1.12 \times 10^{16}$ kg

    (b) $v_{esc} = \sqrt{\dfrac{2GM}{r}} = \sqrt{\dfrac{2 \times 6.674 \times 10^{-11} \times 1.12 \times 10^{16}}{8000}} = 13.6 \text{ m s}^{-1}$ it escapes

    (c) $v_{esc} = \sqrt{\dfrac{2GM}{r}} = \sqrt{\dfrac{2G\rho\left(\dfrac{4}{3}\pi r^3\right)}{r}} = \sqrt{\dfrac{8\pi\rho G r^2}{3}}$

    (d) $v_{esc} = \sqrt{\dfrac{8\pi\rho G r^2}{3}} \Rightarrow r = v_{esc}\sqrt{\dfrac{3}{8\pi\rho G}}$ assume a launch speed of 1 m s^{-1}

    $\Rightarrow r = 1 \times \sqrt{\dfrac{3}{8 \times \pi \times 5200 \times 6.674 \times 10^{-11}}} = 586 \text{ m}$ a diameter of over 1 km.

17. (a) as in Q4, $T^2 = \left(\dfrac{4\pi^2}{GM}\right)r^3 \Rightarrow T = 1.78 \times 10^5$ s

    (b) $v = \dfrac{\text{distance}}{\text{time}} = \dfrac{2\pi r}{T} = \dfrac{2\pi \times 6.85 \times 10^7}{1.78 \times 10^5} = 2418 \text{ m s}^{-1}$

    (c) $E_k = \dfrac{1}{2}mv^2 = \dfrac{1}{2} \times 1500 \times 2418^2 = 4.39 \times 10^9$ J

    (d) ...'the work done by external forces in bringing the satellite from infinity to that point in its orbit (at rest)'...   is the gravitational potential **energy** at point 'P'

    $[V_P - V_\infty]m = \left[\left(-\dfrac{GM}{r}\right) - 0\right]m = -\dfrac{GMm}{r} = -\dfrac{6.674 \times 10^{-11} \times 5.976 \times 10^{24} \times 1500}{6.85 \times 10^7} = -8.73 \times 10^9$ J

    This is twice the size of the answer for the kinetic energy in part (c) above, and of opposite sign. This is true in general for a satellite in orbit: $E_K = -\dfrac{1}{2}E_P$ Can you prove it?

18. (a) From x = -3m to x = +5m is 8m apart.   (b) V_P = -4 J kg^{-1} V_Q = -1 J kg^{-1}

    (c) position approx. x = +1m V_A approx. -0.5 J kg^{-1}

    (d) No. The gravitational potential at point 'A' is about -0.5J kg^{-1}. If you take any other route, you always go into a region where the gravitational potential is higher (like -0.4J kg^{-1}). So the route from 'P' to 'Q' through 'A' uses up least energy. See page 62 of the Theory Book for more details of a journey from Earth to the Moon.

    (e) Journey is 'P' to 'A' to 'Q'.

    'P' to 'A' requires: (-0.5-(-4))×5 = 17.5 Joules   'A' to 'Q' requires:(-1-(-0.5))×5 = -2.5 Joules

    You put in 17.5J to get to 'A' and get back 2.5J in going from 'A' to 'Q'. So taking the start and finish point in the calculation gives: (-1-(-4))×5 = 15J , this is the **overall** energy.

    Note: using up chemical energy in going from 'P' to 'A' and then getting back some kinetic energy isn't a good deal (what can you do with the kinetic energy?).

107

(f) $V_A = \left(-\dfrac{GM_E}{x}\right) + \left(-\dfrac{GM_m}{(d-x)}\right) = -GM_E x^{-1} - GM_m(d-x)^{-1}$

To locate the turning point, differentiate with respect to 'x' and put equal to zero: $\dfrac{dV_A}{dx} = 0$

$\dfrac{dV_A}{dx} = \dfrac{GM_E}{x^2} - \dfrac{GM_m}{(d-x)^2} = 0$ cancel the G's and rearrange:

$\dfrac{M_E}{x^2} = \dfrac{M_m}{(d-x)^2} \Rightarrow \dfrac{(d-x)}{x} = \sqrt{\dfrac{M_m}{M_E}} \approx \sqrt{\dfrac{1}{81}} = \dfrac{1}{9}$ solve for 'x' $\Rightarrow x = 0.9d$

Earth to Moon distance 'd' is 385,000km, so turning point is at 'x' = 347,000km from Earth.

19. Assuming no atmosphere, the direction doesn't matter. The escape speed is derived from the conversion of kinetic energy into potential energy. The difference in potential energy between the launch point and infinity doesn't depend upon the path taken, just on the end points. Hence the kinetic energy (and so the launch speed) doesn't depend upon the path taken.

    With an atmosphere, some kinetic energy is converted into heat energy and the amount will depend upon the length of the path through the atmosphere. Low angle launches in an atmosphere will require higher escape speeds.

20. Ball games all involve the physics of projectiles. Ignoring any atmosphere (which you would in a low gravity planet, but not in a high gravity planet) gives the equations from Higher Physics you learned last year. The range is $R = \dfrac{v^2}{g}\sin 2\theta$ and the maximum height achieved is $h = \dfrac{v^2}{2g}\sin^2\theta$. The gravitational field strength is on the denominator of both equations, so the range and maximum height are both inversely proportional to the 'g' value. The dependence on the angle remains unchanged, and both range and maximum height are still proportional to the square of the launch speed.

    For example, golf shots on a **low 'g'** planet with g = 2Nkg^{-1} would have 5 times the range and 5 times the maximum height. This has implications for the size of the golf course and the required accuracy of a drive off the tee! Putting would remain unchanged on a horizontal green. Spectating would change with most people using motorized transport. Football on a **high 'g'** planet would favour players who pass along the ground rather than use high balls etc. Goalkeepers would underhand the ball to the outfield and corners would be unusual. The football pitch could be smaller and there would be fewer players on each team etc etc. Implications for TV coverage?

    Sports requiring running of the participants would be difficult, either tiring under large 'g' forces or falling over under low 'g' gravity.

Unit 1 Space & Time......Answers

1. (a) No, an inertial frame is one ridden by an observer moving at a constant velocity.

    (b) Nothing can go faster than the speed of light in a vacuum. Subatomic particles can go faster than light through water (or any other material with a refractive index greater than one).

    (c) No it doesn't. Newton thought they were entirely different and separate quantities. Relativity involves equations where both space and time measurements depend on the speed of the observer but that doesn't mean they are the same.

    (d) Nice try Bob, but the lightyear isn't a time. It's the distance light travels in a vacuum in 1 year.

    (e) Common myth dude! It's the motion of the observer/his frame that counts, not the motion of the object being observed.

    (f) Well done Bob, you got one correct. Can I suggest a good book.....?

2. (a) At an angle of 45°, the pulse of light must travel 1 unit of distance in 1 unit of time. Usual choice is to take the unit of time as the second. This means 1 unit on the space axis is the distance light travels in 1s, a distance of 300,000,000metres (called the 'lightsecond').

(b) The graph of the motion is shown on the right. The tangent of the angle is the ratio of the distance travelled to the time taken.

$$\tan 20° = 0.364 = \frac{x}{t}$$

With units of seconds and light-seconds, this is the fraction of the speed of light 'c'. Speed is $0.364 \times 3 \times 10^8 = 1.09 \times 10^8$ m/s.

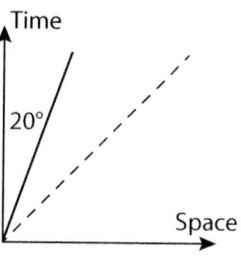

(c) The triangular area under the dotted line. Datapoints there would require the object to travel faster than the speed of light.

3. The worldline is the plot on a spacetime diagram of the motion of an object. This object can be moving any way you like eg a spacecraft with its rocket motors on. A geodesic is the plot on a spacetime diagram of an object moving in freefall. Moving in freefall means no forces except gravity acting on the object (or as Einstein would say, 'no forces at all').

4. (a) For observer O: $c^2(\Delta t)^2 - (\Delta x)^2 = (3 \times 10^8)^2 \times 5.2^2 - (1.3 \times 10^9)^2 = 7.44 \times 10^{17}$

    Observer O' must get the same answer with his particular values. He travels with the object so it stays the same distance from him and $\Delta x = 0$, giving:

    $$7.44 \times 10^{17} = c^2(\Delta t')^2 - (\Delta x')^2 = (3 \times 10^8)^2 \times (\Delta t')^2 - (0)^2 \Rightarrow \Delta t' = 2.87\text{s}$$

    (b) $v = \frac{s}{t} = \frac{1.3 \times 10^9}{5.2} = 2.5 \times 10^8$ m/s

5. (a) If a 70kg astronaut stood on scales in the International Space Station, the reading would be zero. Both the astronaut and the scales are in freefall ('falling' together). His mass remains the same no matter where he goes and the 'g' value at the ISS is about 8.8Nkg⁻¹ so his weight would be $W = mg = 70 \times 8.8 = 616$ N.

    (b) Both definitions give the same answer on Princes St of 686N.

6. (a) The assumption is that the procedure is carried out on a flat plane.

    (b) Rule 2 has to be dropped. Think of the lines of longitude on a map of the Earth. They get further apart as you head towards the equator. Rule 1 still works since lines of latitude and longitude always cross at 90°.

7. (a) The bending of light in a gravitational field predicted by Einstein's General Theory of Relativity.

    (b) When the Sun is in position, the actual positions of the stars are all slightly 'closer' to the Sun. Stars 'closer' to the Sun get displaced more.

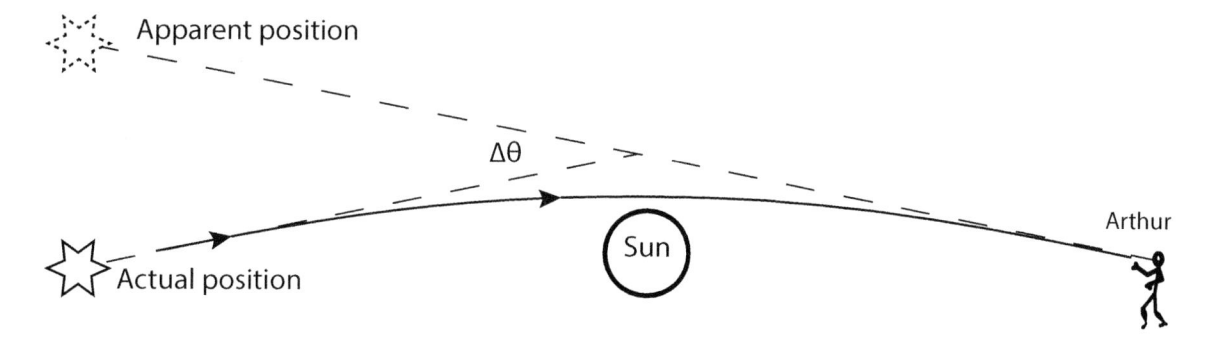

    (c) Wait for a total eclipse of the Sun. Record star positions using photographic plates taken during and after the eclipse. Compare positions back home.

    (d) Einstein's prediction is significantly more accurate than that from Newtonian physics. The 'x' axis is the angle the star is from the Sun as viewed from Earth and so is a measure of the distance sideways from the Sun. The gravitational field strength is proportional to the deflection and decreases in inverse proportion to the distance. Plot the 'x' axis back-to-front with a linear scale (zero on the left at the origin) and it'll fall-off as inverse proportion.

109

8. (a) An Einstein Ring is a circle (or partial circle) of light observed around a distant galaxy. It isn't part of the galaxy but is formed by the bending of light from an even more distant (source) galaxy by the gravitational field of the nearer (lensing) galaxy.

   (b) Angle subtended by whole ring is 2 × 1.48 = 2.96 arc-seconds.

   360 degrees is 2π radians, so 2.96 arc-seconds is $\dfrac{2.96}{60 \times 60 \times 360} \times 2\pi = 1.44 \times 10^{-5}$ rads.

   Distance to lensing galaxy is $7 \times 10^9 \times 9.46 \times 10^{15} = 6.62 \times 10^{25}$ m

   Width of the Einstein Ring at the distance of the lensing galaxy is:

   $$s = r\theta = 6.62 \times 10^{25} \times 1.44 \times 10^{-5} = 9.54 \times 10^{20} \text{ m}$$

   This is about 100,000ly, so is comparable to our own galaxy. Assumption is that spacetime is flat between Earth and the lensing galaxy (to allow use of the formula s = rθ.

9. (a) The orbit of a planet is an ellipse. The major axis of the ellipse points in a certain direction. When the planet completes one orbit around the Sun the direction of the major axis has shifted slightly. The new direction of the major axis still lies on the same plane (to a high degree of accuracy).

   (b) One century shifts the direction of the major axis by 0.1595°. It will take 360/0.1595 centuries to return to its original orientation. This is 225700 years.

   (c) From datasheet, orbital period of Mercury is 87.97 days.

   In 225700 years it will make: $\dfrac{225700 \times 365.25}{87.97} = 937100$ orbits around the Sun.

10. Diameter of 12km is a radius of 6000m. A flash frequency of 44Hz means it's rotating with an angular frequency of ω = 2π × 44 = 276.5 rad s⁻¹. The fastest part of the surface is on the equator where the distance from the spin axis to that point equals the radius, so:

    $$v = \omega r = 276.5 \times 6000 = 1.66 \times 10^6 \text{ m/s}$$

    'Relativistic' speeds are taken to be greater than 10% of the speed of light. The fastest point on the pulsar is 0.55% of 'c', so is non-relativistic.

11. (a) Mass of star is $2.7 M_{Sun} = 2.7 \times 1.99 \times 10^{30} = 5.37 \times 10^{30}$ kg

    Radius of star is $0.8 R_{Sun} = 0.8 \times 6.96 \times 10^8 \text{ m} = 5.57 \times 10^8$ m

    Gravitational potential at surface is: $\varphi = -\dfrac{GM}{R} = -\dfrac{6.67 \times 10^{-11} \times 5.37 \times 10^{30}}{5.57 \times 10^8} = -6.43 \times 10^{11}$ Jkg⁻¹

    (b) Gravitational red shift is the change in frequency of a ray of light due to a change in the gravitational potential between emission and detection points.

    (c) Grav. potential at infinity is zero, so $\Delta\varphi = (\varphi_{inf} - \varphi_{star}) = 0 - (-6.43 \times 10^{11}) = 6.43 \times 10^{11}$ Jkg⁻¹

    Frequency of light is $f = \dfrac{c}{\lambda} = \dfrac{3 \times 10^8}{656 \times 10^{-9}} = 4.57 \times 10^{14}$ Hz

    Change in frequency is $\Delta f = -f \dfrac{\Delta\varphi}{c^2} = -4.57 \times 10^{14} \times \dfrac{6.43 \times 10^{11}}{(3 \times 10^8)^2} = -3.27 \times 10^9$ Hz.

    This is a decrease in frequency, which is an increase in wavelength of:

    $$\lambda = \dfrac{c}{f} = cf^{-1} \Rightarrow \Delta\lambda = -\dfrac{c}{f^2}\Delta f = -\dfrac{3 \times 10^8}{(4.57 \times 10^{14})^2} \times (-3.27 \times 10^9) = 4.7 \times 10^{-12} \text{ m} = 0.0047 \text{nm}$$

    The last line shows the correct method for relating changes in one quantity to changes in another. The Δ's are treated as differentials.

12. The beginning of the Universe is known as the __Big Bang__ and occurred _13.7_ billion years ago. Since then, _space_ has been expanding and the _density_ of the universe has been decreasing as matter gets more spread out. Einstein's _Special_ Theory of Relativity describes physics as viewed from inertial _frames_ of reference. One of its assumptions is that the _speed_ of light is __constant__. In 1915, he published his _General_ Theory of Relativity which concerns _gravitational_ fields. A central assumption is the _Equivalence_ Principle which compares the force of _gravity_ with the effect of being accelerated. An expedition was sent out in 1919 to measure the _deflection_ of starlight during a solar _eclipse_. The results _confirmed_ Einstein's theories. Another test was the _precession_ of the orbit of planet _Mercury_. This is where the _major axis_ of the elliptical orbit changes position with respect to the _distant stars_. The effect is _small_ and _difficult_ to measure, but the results _confirmed_ his theories. Einstein died in the year _1955_.

13. (a) Kepler's 3RD Law is $T^2 = \left(\dfrac{4\pi^2}{GM}\right)r^3$. Rearrange and substitute values from the datapage:

    $r^3 = \left(\dfrac{GM}{4\pi^2}\right)T^2 = \dfrac{6.674 \times 10^{-11} \times 5.96 \times 10^{24}}{4\pi^2} \times (12 \times 60 \times 60)^2 = 1.88 \times 10^{22} \Rightarrow r = 2.66 \times 10^7 \text{ m}$

    (b) Minimum time is for signal to travel the minimum distance which is the answer to part (a) minus the radius of the Earth. This is $2.66 \times 10^7 - 6.37 \times =10^6 = 2.02 \times 10^7$m. At the speed of light, this takes 0.067s.

    Maximum distance is for signal to reach the tangent to the surface. Using Pythagoras Theorem we obtain: $d = \sqrt{(2.66 \times 10^7)^2 - (6.37 \times 10^6)^2} = 2.58 \times 10^7 \text{ m}$. At the speed of light, this takes a time of 0.086s.

    (c) The timer on the fast moving satellite runs at a slower rate than the timers on Earth due to the time dilation effect of Special relativity.

    There is a gravitational potential difference between the surface and the satellite which produces a slower clock rate on Earth due to the distortion of spacetime from General Relativity.

    (d) Geostationary orbit is at a greater distance from the Earth. The Period of 24hrs is twice that of a GPS satellite. It's speed is slower at about 80% of the GPS orbital speed (can show using Kepler's Law) so the effect from Special Relativity is reduced. The gravitational potential difference will be greater so the effect from General Relativity will be enhanced.

14. (a) The radius of the Sun is 6.955×10^8 m. Time taken is: $t = \dfrac{d}{v} = \dfrac{2 \times 6.955 \times 10^8}{3 \times 10^8} = 4.637\text{s}$

    (b) $mg = \dfrac{GMm}{r^2} \Rightarrow g = \dfrac{GM}{r^2} = \dfrac{6.67 \times 10^{-11} \times 1.99 \times 10^{30}}{(6.955 \times 10^8)^2} = 274 \text{Nkg}^{-1} \ (= 274 \text{m/s}^2)$

    (c) $v = u + at = 0 + gt = 274 \times 4.637 = 1270 \text{m/s}$

    (d) $\tan\theta = \dfrac{1270}{3 \times 10^8} = 4.23 \times 10^{-6} \Rightarrow \theta = 0.000243°$

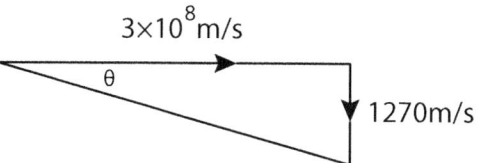

    (e) This is about half the correct value. It's close enough to warrant a proper calculation using calculus. The mathematical assumptions are quite rough and we can expect no better than a factor of 2 accuracy. The physics assumption that everything gets accelerated requires testing back in the lab on Earth. Part (b) assumes that light rays have mass (the small 'm' in the equation). This turns out not to be true. Photons have energy and momentum, but no mass.

15. (a) The zeroes are the kinetic energy and potential energy of mass 'm' at infinity.

    (b) $0+0 = \frac{1}{2}mv^2 + \left(-\frac{GMm}{r}\right) \Rightarrow \frac{1}{2}mv^2 = \frac{GMm}{r} \Rightarrow \frac{1}{2}v^2 = \frac{GM}{r} \Rightarrow v = \sqrt{\frac{2GM}{r}}$

    (c) $v = \sqrt{\frac{2GM}{r}} \Rightarrow v^2 = \frac{2GM}{r} \Rightarrow r = \frac{2GM}{c^2}$ Schwarzschild radius or Event Horizon

    (d) $r = \frac{2GM}{c^2} = \frac{2 \times 6.67 \times 10^{-11} \times 4 \times 1.99 \times 10^{30}}{(3 \times 10^8)^2} = 11800 \, m$

16. $r = \frac{2GM}{c^2} = \frac{2 \times 6.67 \times 10^{-11} \times 4.1 \times 10^6 \times 1.99 \times 10^{30}}{(3 \times 10^8)^2} = 1.21 \times 10^{10} \, m$

    This distance is about one fifth of the radius of Mercury's orbit.

17. (a) $M = \rho V = \rho \times \frac{4}{3}\pi r^3 \quad r = \frac{2GM}{c^2} = \left(\frac{2G}{c^2}\right) \times \rho \times \frac{4}{3}\pi r^3 \Rightarrow r = \sqrt{\frac{3c^2}{8\pi\rho G}} \Rightarrow r \propto \frac{1}{\sqrt{\rho}}$

    (b) $r = \sqrt{\frac{3c^2}{8\pi\rho G}} = \sqrt{\frac{3 \times (3 \times 10^8)^2}{8 \times \pi \times 10^{-26} \times 6.67 \times 10^{-11}}} = 1.27 \times 10^{26} \, m = \frac{1.27 \times 10^{26}}{9.46 \times 10^{15}} = 13.4 \text{ billion lightyears}$

    This is about the radius of the universe, so Yes, the universe is a gigantic Black Hole!

18. Black Holes come is a range of sizes. The distant star background behind a Black Hole will distort the apparent positions of the stars due to the bending of light by a gravitational field, and possibly spread out the light due to the lensing effect. The spacecraft would have to monitor the positions of stars in the direction of travel and look for a particular distortion pattern. At sublight speeds (remember Relativity?), you'd have plenty of time to detect it and avoid collision (unless there are mini-Black Holes out in space….). Better to spend time avoiding ordinary matter like small asteroids, and deflecting sand grain sizes of rock which could puncture the spacecraft.

Unit 1 Stellar Physics……Answers

1. Our _Sun_ is the nearest star and was created about _5 billion_ years ago. It's light takes about _8_ minutes to reach Earth. The energy it produces comes from _nuclear_ reactions deep within its _core_. Stars come in many sizes and colours. Hotter stars are _blue_ in colour. They burn their fuel at a _faster_ rate and so are_short_ lived. Stars known as _red_ giants, are cooler and can have a_diameter_ as large as the orbit of Planet Mars. When their supply of fuel is_exhausted_, they _cool_ down over a long period of _time_ and are known as red_dwarves_. If the mass is _large_ enough, the force of _gravity_ can collapse the star into a very _dense_ state called a _white_ _ dwarf_. With some stars, the force of gravity is so great that it ends its existence as a_black_ _hole_ where not even _light_ can escape.

    Our _galaxy_ contains over 100 billion stars and is in the shape of a disc about_100,000_lightyears in diameter. On average, a _supernova_ explosion is seen once every 100 years by humans on Earth. This is where a star explodes and emits large quantities of_particles_ and _radiation_. The brightest one in recorded history was in the year 1006AD with a_magnitude_ of -7.5. Fortunately for us, the _Sun_ will not suffer the same fate.

2. $E = hf = h\frac{c}{\lambda} = 6.626 \times 10^{-34} \times \frac{3 \times 10^8}{525 \times 10^{-9}} = 3.79 \times 10^{-19}$ Joules $(= 2.36 \, eV)$

3. The surface area of the sphere of radius 1A.U. is: $4\pi r^2 = 4\pi \times (1.49 \times 10^{11})^2 = 2.79 \times 10^{23} \text{ m}^2$.

   Each square metre of that receives 1380 Watts.

   Total power output is $2.79 \times 10^{23} \text{ m}^2 \times 1380 \text{ Wm}^{-2} = 3.85 \times 10^{26} \text{ W}$. This is called the Luminosity.

4. The power received on a square metre (the intensity, or irradiance), is proportional to the inverse square of the distance from the Sun (the Luminosity of the Sun is spread over a larger surface area, and the surface area is proportional to the square of the radius).

   $$\text{Power per square metre} \propto \frac{1}{r^2} \Rightarrow \frac{\text{Power per square metre (Mars)}}{\text{Power per square metre (Earth)}} = \frac{r^2_{Earth}}{r^2_{Mars}} = \frac{(1.49 \times 10^{11})^2}{(2.28 \times 10^{11})^2} = 0.427$$

   Hence, Mars receives $0.427 \times 1380 = 589 \text{ Wm}^{-2}$. (It varies from 493 to 716 in its elliptical orbit.)

5. (a) eg. Antares. Power emitted per square metre: $\sigma T^4 = 5.67 \times 10^{-8} \times 3400^4 = 7.58 \times 10^6 \text{ Wm}^{-2}$

Star name	Antares	Wolf 359	Tau Ceti	Xi Persei
Surface temperature (K)	3400	2800	5340	35000
Power emitted per square metre (Wm⁻²)	7.58×10⁶	3.49×10⁶	4.61×10⁷	8.51×10¹⁰

   Assume that the star's surface is a blackbody and so obeys the Stefan-Boltzmann Law.

   (b) Stars at a higher temperature emit more power so use up their energy supply in less time.

6. Approximating the Sun as a perfect sphere (and it almost is):

   $$A = 4\pi r^2 = 4\pi \times (6.955 \times 10^8)^2 = 6.079 \times 10^{18} \text{ m}^2$$

7. (a) $A = 4\pi r^2 = 4\pi \times (74 \times 6.955 \times 10^8)^2 = 3.33 \times 10^{22} \text{ m}^2$

   (b) $\sigma T^4 = 5.67 \times 10^{-8} \times 12130^4 = 1.23 \times 10^9 \text{ Wm}^{-2}$. Surface emits like a perfect blackbody radiator.

   (c) $L = 1.23 \times 10^9 \text{ Wm}^{-2} \times 3.33 \times 10^{22} \text{ m}^2 = 4.1 \times 10^{31} \text{ W}$

   (d) None, since luminosity isn't a property of the observer. It's a property of the star.

8. (a) The luminosity is a property of the star. The apparent brightness and distance are observer dependent.

   (b) From the formula its W divided by m², to give Wm⁻².

   (c) The apparent brightness is inversely proportional to the square of the distance between source and observer. This assumes a point source, which is highly accurate for all distant stars. Our Sun though has an angular diameter of about half a degree viewed from Earth, so isn't a perfect point to our eyes, but the difference would only introduce a small error.

   (d) From question 3 above, the Sun's luminosity is 3.85×10^{26} W.

   $$b = \frac{L}{4\pi r^2} = \frac{3.85 \times 10^{26}}{4\pi \times (1.49 \times 10^{11})^2} = 1380 \text{ Wm}^{-2}$$

   The apparent brightness is the energy received each second on each square metre of surface from **all** wavelengths as viewed by the observer. Remember that the word 'brightness' also has the common use meaning of perception of the **visible** spectrum by the human eye.

9. The luminosity of the Sun is independent of the observer and is 3.85×10^{26} W.

    There are two methods for calculating the absolute brightness:

    Either use the method as in Q4 which compares values on Jupiter with those on Earth then employs the inverse square law:

    $$\text{Power per square metre} \propto \frac{1}{r^2} \Rightarrow \frac{\text{Power per square metre (Jup.)}}{\text{Power per square metre (Earth)}} = \frac{r_{Earth}^2}{r_{Jup}^2} = \frac{(1\,\text{A.U.})^2}{(5.2\,\text{A.U.})^2} = 0.037$$

    Hence, Jupiter receives: $0.037 \times 1380 = 51\,\text{Wm}^{-2}$

    Or, start from the Sun's luminosity and calculate the absolute brightness using $b = \frac{L}{4\pi r^2}$.

    $$b = \frac{L}{4\pi r^2} = \frac{3.85 \times 10^{26}}{4\pi \times (5.2 \times 1.496 \times 10^{11})^2} = 50.6\,\text{Wm}^{-2}. \text{ (It varies from 46 to 56 in the course of its orbit)}$$

10. (a) Alcyone's surface area is: $A = 4\pi r^2 = 4\pi \times (8.2 \times 6.955 \times 10^8)^2 = 4.09 \times 10^{20}\,\text{m}^2$

    Use Stefan-Boltzmann Law: $\sigma T^4 = 5.67 \times 10^{-8} \times 12750^4 = 1.50 \times 10^9\,\text{Wm}^{-2}$

    Multiply to obtain the luminosity: $L = 1.50 \times 10^9\,\text{Wm}^{-2} \times 4.09 \times 10^{20}\,\text{m}^2 = 6.13 \times 10^{29}\,\text{W}$

    (b) Apparent brightness: $b = \frac{L}{4\pi r^2} = \frac{6.13 \times 10^{29}}{4\pi \times (370 \times 9.46 \times 10^{15})^2} = 3.98 \times 10^{-9}\,\text{Wm}^{-2}$

    (c) Apparent brightness obeys the inverse square law of distance. In words, if you decrease the distance by a factor of $\sqrt{2}$, you double the apparent brightness. In symbols:

    $$r \to \frac{r}{\sqrt{2}} \quad \text{then} \quad b \propto \frac{1}{r^2} \to \frac{1}{\left(\frac{r}{\sqrt{2}}\right)^2} = \frac{2}{r^2} \quad \text{hence,} \quad b \to 2b$$

    Or this method: $b = \frac{L}{4\pi r^2} \Rightarrow L = \text{constant} = 4\pi r^2 b$

    $$r_1^2 b_1 = r_2^2 b_2 \Rightarrow r_1^2 b_1 = r_2^2 \times 2b_1 \Rightarrow r_1^2 = 2r_2^2 \Rightarrow r_2 = \frac{1}{\sqrt{2}} r_1$$

    By either method, the distance to the star has to become $1/\sqrt{2}$ of its previous distance of 370ly.

    This gives $\frac{1}{\sqrt{2}} \times 370 = 262\,\text{ly}$. Hence you have to move 108 lightyears towards the star.

11. (a) 10 parsecs (=32.6 lightyears). One parsec is the distance at which 1A.U. would subtend an angle of 1 arc-second (=1/3600°).

    (b) If the star is at a distance of 10pc.

    (c) Amateur astronomers use optical telescopes and observe visually with the human eye, or use cooled charged coupled detectors (CCD's) in the visual / near infrared region. A brightness scale which corresponds to what the human eye can see is more useful to them (and this is the magnitude system). The second reason is that the numbers for the apparent brightnesses of stars are very small, so a system with numbers either side of zero is more convenient. The magnitude system was also devised well before we could calculate the power per square metre reaching us from a star. They retained a well known and useful system rather than adopting something new and inconvenient.

12. With a power law, you add the powers when multiplying two things. Adding the magnitudes means you have to multiply the brightnesses. This gives 100×100=10,000.

13. (a) $M_{ABS} = M_{APP} + 5 - 5\log_{10} d = 8.2 + 5 - 5 \times \log_{10} 15 = 13.2 - 5 \times 1.176 = 7.32$

    (b) Earth to Sun distance is 1.496×10^{11}m. The distance of 32.6 lightyears equals 10 parsecs and this is the standard distance for measuring the absolute magnitude, so can use the above equation.

    One parsec is 3.26 lightyears = $3.26 \times 9.46 \times 10^{15}$m = 3.08×10^{16}m.

    Hence, Earth to Sun distance is $\dfrac{1.496 \times 10^{11}}{3.08 \times 10^{16}} = 4.86 \times 10^{-6}$ pc

    Substitute this value in the equation:

    $M_{ABS} = M_{APP} + 5 - 5\log_{10} d = -26.7 + 5 - 5 \times \log_{10} 4.86 \times 10^{-6} = -21.7 - 5 \times (-5.31) = +4.8$

14. The power output per square metre from a star's surface is accurately expressed by the Stefan-Boltzmann Law and this depends upon the fourth power of the temperature. For example, a star which was twice as hot as another star would output 16 times more power per square metre. For stars of equal size, this means that the higher temperature star uses up its nuclear fuel more rapidly and so has a shorter lifespan.

15. (a) On the y-axis either Luminosity or absolute magnitude

    On the x-axis either the temperature or the spectral type.

    (b) Assume the usual plot which has higher temperatures on the left of the x-axis, and has the luminosity increasing up the y-axis.

    Main trend (called the Main Sequence) runs from bottom right to top left. Half way up is a branch towards the top right (usually red giants). Cluster of stars at bottom left (mainly white dwarfs).

    (c) A typical star would follow the numbered positions one through nine, on the diagram. Time spent on each section varies enormously, from a few years in position 1, to 10 billion years on the main sequence (positions 3 to 4), to trillions of years as a white dwarf at position 9.

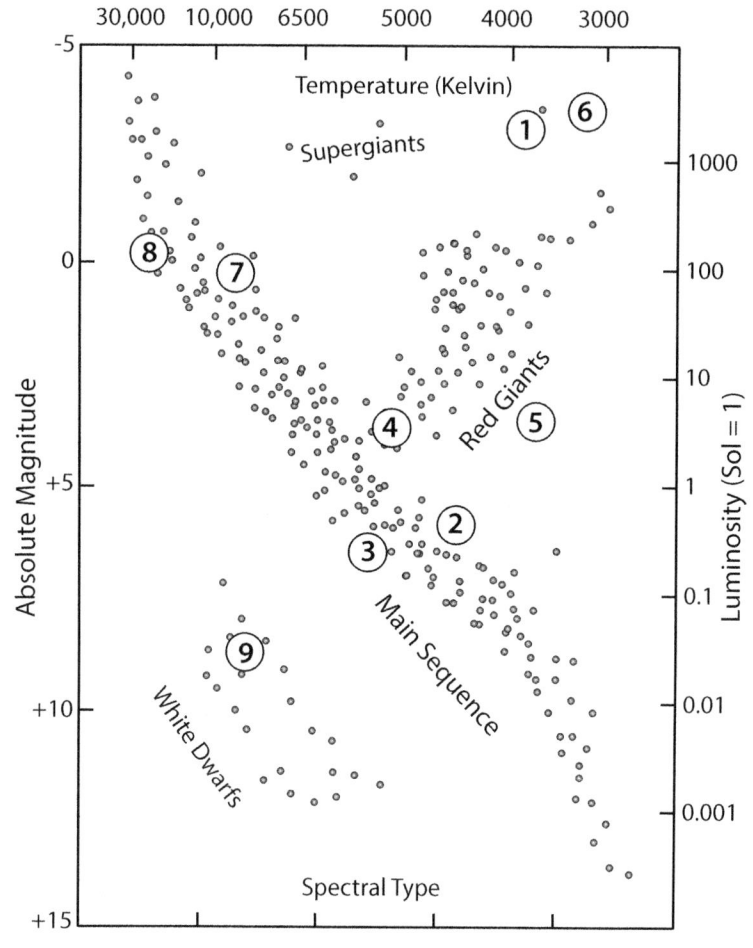

16. (a) Nuclear fusion reactions amongst the basic constituents in the core. These are protons (hydrogen atoms minus the electron), deuterons (heavy hydrogen-deuterium-without the electron) and the helium-3 nucleus. Outwith the core, the temperature isn't high enough for nuclear reactions.

    (b) $E = mc^2 = 4.26 \times 10^9 \times (3 \times 10^8)^2 = 3.84 \times 10^{26}$ Joules. This is the Luminosity.

    (c) The nuclear fusion reactions provide energy to the photons and neutrinos (which escape) and also kinetic energy to the ions and nuclei. This keeps them moving around and resists the attractive force of gravity between the particles. Once the nuclear reactions have stopped, the force of gravity takes over and contracts the star. This results in heating of the star which can produce further brief episodes of expansion and contraction.

17. (a) Helium-4 consists of two protons and two neutrons, so the 4 neutrons will make 2 nuclei.

    (b) The two helium nuclei need 4 protons so that leaves 28 protons.

    (c) There are 28 proton masses and 2 helium masses.

    Helium mass is about 4 proton masses, so ratio is 28 to 8 (which is 3.5:1).

    (d) Protons are used to produce helium so the ratio will decrease (after 5 billion years of burning, the ratio in the Sun's core is now about 2:3).

18. (a) Deuteron (nucleus of the hydrogen isotope deuterium, which is one proton plus one neutron)

    Positron (antiparticle of the electron)

    Neutrino (of the electron-type)

    (b) Total mass on left hand side is 3.34524 × 10⁻²⁷kg.

    Total mass on right hand side is 3.34449 × 10⁻²⁷kg.

    Difference in mass (mass defect) is 7.5 × 10⁻³¹kg.

    $$E = mc^2 = 7.5 \times 10^{-31} \times (3 \times 10^8)^2 = 6.75 \times 10^{-14} \text{ Joules}$$

    Convert to eV: $E = 6.75 \times 10^{-14}$ Joules $= \dfrac{6.75 \times 10^{-14}}{1.6 \times 10^{-19}} = 4.2 \times 10^5$ eV . This is 0.42MeV.

    (c) The e⁻ is an electron and the γ is a gamma ray photon.

    (d) The positron takes part in the reaction in (c) above and disappears. The photons get absorbed in a collision with a charged ion and another different photon gets emitted with a different energy in a random direction. The offspring of the original reaction take about 10,000years to make it to the surface and escape (perhaps ending on your skin on a sunny day).

19. (a) The main production process uses helium-3:

    $$^3_2He + ^3_2He \rightarrow ^4_2He + ^1_1H + ^1_1H$$

    A secondary route is: $^3_2He + ^4_2He \rightarrow ^7_4Be + \gamma$

    $$^7_4Be + e^- \rightarrow ^7_3Li + \nu_e$$

    $$^7_3Li + ^1_1H \rightarrow ^4_2He + ^4_2He$$

    A small amount from: $^3_2He + ^4_2He \rightarrow ^7_4Be + \gamma$

    $$^7_4Be + ^1_1H \rightarrow ^8_5B + \gamma$$

    $$^8_5B \rightarrow ^8_4Be + e^+ + \nu_e$$

    $$^8_4Be \rightarrow 2\,^4_2He$$

    (b) This is the Carbon-Nitrogen-Oxygen (CNO) cycle. A sequence of nuclear fusion reactions and nuclear decays starts from carbon-12 adding a proton to make nitrogen-13 (decay to carbon-13), then adding protons to make nitrogen-14 followed by oxygen-15 (decay to nitrogen-15), another proton added, then final decay to carbon-12 and a helium-4 nucleus. Refer to the companion Theory Book on page 89.

20. (a) There are 3 types. Electron-neutrino, muon-neutrino and tau-neutrino.

   (b) Detectors on Earth recorded reactions initiated by muon-neutrinos coming from the direction of the Sun. The nuclear reactions in the Sun only produce electron-neutrinos. The neutrino reactions on Earth are very rare and many years passed before reliable data could be accumulated. Only about 30% of the expected number of electron-neutrinos were detected. This could have implied that the calculations about the Sun's core were wrong.

   The solution is that the different types of neutrino change back and forth between the three types. Some of the electron-neutrinos changed into muon-neutrinos on the way from the Sun to Earth. This is called neutrino oscillation.

21. (a) The nuclei of the heavier elements are built be adding protons in nuclear reactions in the Sun's core.

   These are sometimes followed by decays where a positron is emitted from the conversion of a proton into a neutron. In this way, the nucleus is always reacting with protons but builds up numbers of protons and neutrons.

   As the nucleus gets heavier, it becomes harder to add more protons due to the greater electrostatic repulsion. The mass defect in the reaction also gets smaller with the creation of larger nuclei, until it becomes energetically 'a waste of time' to make nuclei larger than Iron-56.

   Some stars explode as supernovae and the great energies reached in the explosion can produce heavier nuclei than Iron-56. All elements in the Earth's crust which are larger than Iron-56 were created in supernovae explosions over 5 billion years ago.

   (b) There were no heavier elements like lead, since the first stars didn't get any material from previous supernovae. Heavy elements keep the temperature lower and prolong the lives of stars. Without heavy elements to do this, the first stars burned very hot and had short lives.

22. The fate of a star is determined by the force of gravity. Every particle in a star is attracted by the force of gravity to all the other particles in the star, and if there is a lot of it, that's a lot of attraction. Our Sun is fairly typical and will end its days as a slowly cooling white dwarf. There is a rule in quantum mechanics called the Pauli Exclusion Principle. No two electrons (in general, spin half particles) in a system can occupy the same state. This is what gives atoms their chemical structure, and its what stops gravity crushing the white dwarf to even higher densities. A 1cm^3 cube of white dwarf stuff would have a mass of about 1ton.

   If the Sun had a mass of more than 1.44 its present value, the force of gravity would overpower the outward electron quantum pressure of the Exclusion Principle and squash the star even further. It then is driven towards the next application of the Pauli Exclusion Principle, but this time its the spin-half neutrons which resist being placed in the same state. These neutron stars have high spin rates, diameters of about 12km and densities of 10^{17}kg/m^3.

   Starting with a mass greater than about 3.2 solar masses will defeat the outward neutron quantum pressure and gravity will drive the star towards a supernova explosion, leaving a Black Hole as a remnant.

   And brown dwarfs? They started off as somewhere between very large planets (super Jupiters) and very small stars. During its formation, there wasn't enough mass for gravity to convert the gravitational potential energy of collapse into enough heat to start nuclear burning. Typically, they have a temperature like we have on Earth or a bit hotter, and spend their days cooling slowly out in the vast, lonely, empty spaces of our galaxy.

Unit 2 Quantum Theory.....Answers

Where units have not been given for a quantity, assume that they are in S.I. units.

1. Classical physics assumes that **space** is flat and that time has no **beginning** and will continue on to **eternity**. There are no restrictions on the **magnitudes** of physical quantities. These assumptions give **accurate** results for many applications of physics, like **forces** in bridges or the cooling in a kitchen **refridgerator**. By the end of the **nineteenth** century, problems became apparent.

   The problem was the **emission** of radiation from an ideal radiator called a **Black-body**. Classical Theory could not **predict** the correct emission for **short** wavelengths. This is known as the **ultraviolet catastrophe**. The physicist Max **Planck** tried a new approach and assumed that the objects emitting the **radiation** could only have **discrete** energy values. This was the birth of **Quantum Theory**.

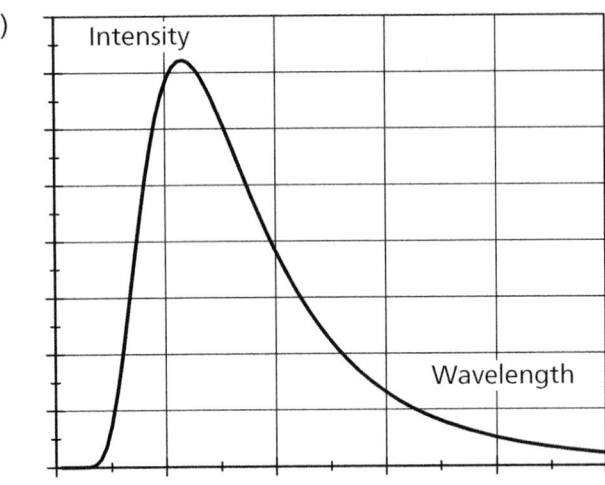

2. (a)

   (b) $\lambda_{Max} T = 2.9 \times 10^{-3} \, \text{m K} \quad \Rightarrow \quad \lambda_{Max} \times 5800 = 2.9 \times 10^{-3} \quad \Rightarrow \quad \lambda_{Max} = 5.0 \times 10^{-7} \, \text{m}$

   (c) The Sun is nearly a black-body and the graph above shows that it emits over a range of wavelengths - not just the region which produces a green sensation inside your head. The overall effect is a slightly yellowish white.

   (d) All thermal radiation hitting a black-body is 100% absorbed. By thermal radiation, we mean all radiation emitted by a body due to its temperature.

3. $E = hf = \dfrac{hc}{\lambda} = \dfrac{6.626 \times 10^{-34} \times 3 \times 10^8}{1200 \times 10^{-9}} = 1.66 \times 10^{-19} \, \text{Joules}$

4. (a) This is the effective black-body temperature of the Sun and it's the Sun's radiation which hits the atmosphere.

   (b) If you multiply the units on the x and y-axes, the micrometers cancels out and you're left with units for the area of kW/m². So the area is the power on a 1m² surface.

   (c) The gases of the atmosphere absorb the radiation. Some wavelengths get absorbed more than others leaving big dips in the graph. Main culprits are ozone for the ultraviolet and water vapour in the infrared.

   (d) Peak for the top of the atmosphere is shifted towards shorter wavelengths. To the human eye, it would be slightly less yellow and slightly more blue (different shades of white to the casual observer).

   (e) (i) strongly absorbs it   (ii) effective absorber   (iii) less effective in far infrared

   (f) It should be 1380W/m².

(g) 1200nm is the same as 1.2μm. Estimate for the ground level reading at this wavelength is 0.4kW m^{-2} μm^{-1}. Wavelength range is 1200 to 1205nm, which is a spread of 5nm = 0.005μm. So if you get 0.4kW m^{-2} from including radiation over a range of 1μm, then by proportion, you get 0.4×0.005=0.002kW m^{-2} over this narrower range. So power received on surface is 2Watts.

5. (a) The scale at which quantum physics begins to operate is too small. Processes which humans can see, feel and experience are many orders of magnitude beyond the interface between classical and quantum physics.

   (b) You would make Planck's constant much bigger. The bigger the better, say h = 100Js.

6. The dispute was over the nature of radiation. The 19TH century had convinced many scientists that radiation was a wave rather than a particle. In 1905 Einstein suggested that electromagnetic radiation had particle properties. This was not taken seriously until 1916 with Millikan's experiment with the photoelectric effect. This confirmed Einstein's predictions, though many still had to wait until the Compton Scattering experiment of 1923 before finally discarding the classical theory.

7. (a) Electrons would be scattered by the air molecules and make calculations impossible.

   (b) $E = hf = h\dfrac{c}{\lambda} = 6.626 \times 10^{-34} \times \dfrac{3 \times 10^8}{380 \times 10^{-9}} = 5.23 \times 10^{-19} \text{J} = \dfrac{5.23 \times 10^{-19}}{1.6 \times 10^{-19}} \text{eV} = 3.27 \text{eV}$

   (c) Plate 'P' is connected to the negative end of the battery and will slow down the electrons as they approach the plate. Increase the potential difference of the battery until the point where electrons are stopped and the current drops to zero.

   (d) The electric field between the plates gets its energy from the battery. A voltage 'V' will do work of 'qV' on each electron of charge 'q'. This will be used to reduce the kinetic energy to zero:

   $qV = \dfrac{1}{2}mv^2 \Rightarrow 1.6 \times 10^{-19} \times 0.22 = \dfrac{1}{2} \times 9.1 \times 10^{-31} \times v^2 \Rightarrow v = 2.8 \times 10^5 \text{m/s}$

   (e) From part (a) the photon energy is 3.27eV. A stopping potential of 0.22volts would mean the electrons started with a kinetic energy of 0.22eV. This leaves an energy of 3.05eV for getting the electrons out of the zinc. This is 4.88 × 10^{-19} Joules. That's the quick way.

   Here's the equation method:

   $hf = W_o + \dfrac{1}{2}mv^2 \Rightarrow W_o = hf - \dfrac{1}{2}mv^2 = 6.626 \times 10^{-34} \times \dfrac{3 \times 10^8}{380 \times 10^{-9}} - \dfrac{1}{2} \times 9.109 \times 10^{-31} \times (2.8 \times 10^5)^2$

   $W_o = 5.23 \times 10^{-19} - 3.57 \times 10^{-20} = 4.87 \times 10^{-19} \text{J}$

8. (a) The energy of a photon is determined by its **frequency**. So increasing the frequency will pass an energy threshold for knocking out an electron. Once the threshold is passed, increasing the intensity will free more electrons. Millikan's experiment showed this to be true.

   (b) In classical theory, the energy is determined by the **amplitude** of the wave (square the amplitude to get the intensity). Increasing the amplitude will increase the energy of the wave and should knock out more electrons. This should happen no matter the frequency of the light. Millikan's experiment showed this to be complete bollocks.

9. $qV = \dfrac{1}{2}mv^2 \Rightarrow V = \dfrac{mv^2}{2q} = \dfrac{9.109 \times 10^{-31} \times (8.6 \times 10^5)^2}{2 \times 1.602 \times 10^{-19}} = 2.1 \text{volts}$

10. (a) $hf = W_o + eV_s$

    (b) From equation in part (a), divide both sides by Planck's constant 'h':

    $f = \dfrac{W_o}{h} + \dfrac{e}{h}V_s$ Part beside V_s is the slope and the other part is the intercept.

(c) Intercept at 7.4 × 10¹⁴Hz (remember it's where it cuts the x = 0 vertical line, the 'y-axis').

Take endpoints for slope: $\dfrac{(9.8-(-2.3))\times 10^{14}}{(1-(-4))} = 2.42\times 10^{14}\,\text{Hz volt}^{-1}$

(d) Slope is $\dfrac{e}{h}$, hence: $\dfrac{e}{h} = 2.42\times 10^{14} \Rightarrow h = \dfrac{1.6\times 10^{-19}}{2.42\times 10^{14}} = 6.61\times 10^{-34}\,\text{Js}$

Intercept is $\dfrac{W_o}{h}$, hence: $\dfrac{W_o}{h} = 7.4\times 10^{14} \Rightarrow W_o = 7.4\times 10^{14} \times 6.61\times 10^{-34} = 4.89\times 10^{-19}\,\text{J}$

(e) Zero volts stopping potential means the electrons didn't need any stopping. This means that they got out the zinc, but didn't have any kinetic energy left over. The energy of the photon was just enough to equal the energy it takes to get an electron out of the zinc. Hence the energy of the photon equals the Work Function (this is what the intercept equation in part (d) is quantifying; it's just $W_o = hf_o$, where f_o is the threshold frequency).

11. (a) Not necessarily so! It could be that the smallest part of matter investigated so far contains an equal number of positive and negative charges. Half of all atoms could be positive and half could be negative negative with them all well mixed. You could test this by experimentally measuring smaller and smaller bits of matter. We now know that atoms are neutral but that their components (electrons and protons) are charged.

(b) An oft-heard quote, but not true. Photons aren't atoms.

(c) In some quarters, this was the biggest objection to the theory of atoms (not so much the theory of the structure of the atom, but that atoms exist). How can complicated objects like people be made from simple basic components? We are alive so the smallest parts of our bodies must also possess the property of 'aliveness'. That was the objection. It rejects the idea that complicated objects can be built from collections of smaller, simpler components. Reductionism is the idea that you can explain the behaviour of complicated objects by understanding their smaller component parts (in theory, you can explain human biochemistry from a knowledge of quantum mechanics).

(d) That the world is split into two substances, mind and body, is a widely held belief. One of the best-kept secrets in science, is that there is only one substance. Modern philosophers even agree! The sensations of thought, love, emotion, grief, anger, curiosity, are all the products of biochemical processes in our brains. Many people reject this, but it's where the evidence leads. Consider, for example, the supposed interface between mind stuff and body stuff. If you have a thought, and it's mind stuff, how does this become a body action. How can non-physical stuff influence physical stuff?

(e) A global property of an object doesn't have to be the same as the local property of its components. For example, the liquid property of water is the result of the forces between the atoms, not of the substance of the atoms themselves.

(f) This is a hot topic in the philosophy of science. A model is something which tries to describe 'what's actually there'. The Böhr model of the atom had small solid electrons orbiting a small solid nucleus. This was refined into a model of probabilities where the small solid things didn't have a definite location. Then into a model where there isn't anything solid at all (called Quantum Field Theory). So what is 'actually there'? Is it capable of description? Do the atoms we model even exist, anymore than the 3D digital model of a house in a computer exists?

The way models are described is through mathematics. Sociologists use it to model human behaviour, but how good is that at describing 'what's actually there'?

12. (a) Positive electric charge at centre. Mostly empty space.

Negative electric charges in orbit. Only allowed orbits of a definite energy.

Angular momentum is quantised.

(b) Electron jumps down from outer to inner orbit.

(c) Each orbit has a definite energy. The energy of the photon is the difference in energy between the two orbitals which the electron jumped between.

(d) There are many (actually an infinite number of) orbits possible. This gives a large number of possible transitions for the electron to go from outer to inner orbits. All those ending on the n = 1 level are grouped into a series called the Lyman Series. All those ending on the n = 2 level are called the Balmer Series. Line spectra of gases exhibit a combination of these transitions depending on how excited the electrons become (giving access to high 'n' orbits). Spectra of glowing hot solids are more complicated due to the forces between the atoms.

(e) The electron is moving in a circle, therefore it's accelerating. Classically, an accelerating electric charge should radiate energy (just as in an aerial). Böhr had to assume that the electron didn't radiate energy in his atomic model, otherwise it would spiral into the nucleus.

The angular momentum was given by $mvr = n\dfrac{h}{2\pi}$. This was used to calculate the energy levels of the orbits and the radii of the orbits, but in fact gives the wrong value for the angular momentum of the ground state of the hydrogen atom (which is zero).

13. (a) Substitute for the wavelength and take n = 3:

$$\dfrac{1}{656.3\times 10^{-9}} = R_H\left(\dfrac{1}{2^2} - \dfrac{1}{3^2}\right) = \dfrac{5}{36}R_H \quad \Rightarrow \quad R_H = 1.097\times 10^7 \text{ m}^{-1}$$

(b) Using n = 5 and the value for the (Rydberg) constant from part (a):

$$\dfrac{1}{\lambda} = R_H\left(\dfrac{1}{2^2} - \dfrac{1}{n^2}\right) \quad \Rightarrow \quad \dfrac{1}{\lambda} = 1.097\times 10^7 \times\left(\dfrac{1}{2^2} - \dfrac{1}{5^2}\right) = \dfrac{21}{100}\times 1.097\times 10^7 \quad \Rightarrow \quad \lambda = 4.34\times 10^{-7}\text{m}$$

2ND line from the left. Using a ruler, I got 15.1cm from the 400 to 700 scale marks and 1.8cm from the 400nm mark to the line, giving 436nm. The correct wavelength is 434.1nm.

14. $\hbar = \dfrac{h}{2\pi} = 1.055\times 10^{-34}\text{ Js}$

15. (a) The electron now had wave properties. An integer number of electron wavelengths fitted into each circumference of the orbit.

(b) Circumference of orbit is: $2\pi r = n\lambda \quad \Rightarrow \quad 2\pi r = n\dfrac{h}{p} = n\dfrac{h}{mv} \quad \Rightarrow \quad mvr = n\dfrac{h}{2\pi}$

16. $\lambda = \dfrac{h}{p} = \dfrac{6.626\times 10^{-34}}{2.2\times 10^{-22}} = 3.0\times 10^{-12}\text{ m}$

17. $p = \dfrac{h}{\lambda} = \dfrac{6.626\times 10^{-34}}{3.2\times 10^{-11}} = 2.07\times 10^{-23}\text{ kg m s}^{-1}$

18. (a) $\lambda = \dfrac{c}{f} = \dfrac{3\times 10^8}{7.5\times 10^{16}} = 4\times 10^{-9}\text{ m}$

(b) $p = \dfrac{h}{\lambda} = \dfrac{6.626\times 10^{-34}}{4\times 10^{-9}} = 1.66\times 10^{-25}\text{ kg m s}^{-1}$

(c) $c = f\lambda \quad E = hf \quad \lambda = \dfrac{h}{p} \quad \Rightarrow \quad E = hf = h\dfrac{c}{\lambda} = \dfrac{hc}{\left(h/p\right)} = pc$

19. Calculate the momentum first: $p = \dfrac{h}{\lambda} = 8.28\times 10^{-21}\text{ kg m s}^{-1} \qquad p = mv \Rightarrow v = \dfrac{p}{m} = 4.94\times 10^6\text{ m s}^{-1}$

20. Calculate its quantum mechanical wavelength: $\lambda = \dfrac{h}{p} = \dfrac{6.626\times 10^{-34}}{9.11\times 10^{-31}\times 200} = 3.6\times 10^{-6}\text{ m}$

This is much smaller than the slit width so it does **not** show obvious diffraction effects.

21. We don't know of any good physics reason why it shouldn't. Experimentally, the jury is OUT.

22. (a) $p = mv = 0.16 \times 50 = 8 \text{ kg m s}^{-1}$ $\lambda = \dfrac{h}{p} = \dfrac{6.626 \times 10^{-34}}{8} = 8.3 \times 10^{-35} \text{ m}$

    (b) $p = \dfrac{h_{Fantasy}}{\lambda} \Rightarrow h_{Fantasy} = p\lambda = 8 \times 0.2 = 1.6 \text{ J s}$ Total nightmare for the batsman.

23. (a) 1   If it started at zero, what would be the implications for 'v' and 'r'?

    (b) $n\dfrac{h}{2\pi} = 2 \times \dfrac{6.626 \times 10^{-34}}{2\pi} = 2.1 \times 10^{-34} \text{ Js}$

    (c) $mvr = n\dfrac{h}{2\pi} = 1 \times \dfrac{6.626 \times 10^{-34}}{2\pi} \Rightarrow mv = \dfrac{1.055 \times 10^{-34}}{5.3 \times 10^{-11}} = 2 \times 10^{-24} \text{ kg m s}^{-1}$

24. (a) Classical physics predicts that it will remain the same.

    (b) On travelling from air to glass, the wavelength will decrease. On emerging back into the air, the wavelength will return to its initial value.

25. (a) The wavelength of the scattered beam has been changed (has increased).

    (b) According to Classical Theory, the wavelength should be unchanged.

    (c) $\Delta\lambda = \dfrac{h}{m_e c}(1 - \cos\theta) = \dfrac{6.626 \times 10^{-34}}{9.109 \times 10^{-31} \times 3 \times 10^8}(1 - \cos 90) = 2.42 \times 10^{-12} \text{ m}$

    (d) An increase in wavelength means the wave has lower energy (from $E = hf$). Losing energy after scattering is a characteristic of a particle interaction (like a ball bouncing off a wall).

    (e) It means that the basic process involves the constituents of the graphite (that is, it's fundamental particles common to all materials, like the electrons), rather than its bulk properties (like density).

26. The equation contains a wave-like property; the wavelength 'λ'. Particle equations (in classical physics) contain properties like the mass, the momentum and moment of inertia.

27. (a) scatter off the crystal randomly / be absorbed by the crystal

    (b) wave effects due to diffraction of waves meeting a regular structure (the crystal lattice).

    (c) Convert the electron's energy into joules: $54 \text{eV} = 54 \times 1.6 \times 10^{-19} = 8.64 \times 10^{-18}$ Joules

    Now calculate its momentum from the kinetic energy:

    $E_k = \dfrac{1}{2}mv^2 = \dfrac{(mv)^2}{2m} = \dfrac{p^2}{2m} \Rightarrow p = \sqrt{2mE_k} = \sqrt{2 \times 9.109 \times 10^{-31} \times 8.64 \times 10^{-18}} = 3.97 \times 10^{-24} \text{ kgms}^{-1}$

    Then use the deBroglie relation: $\lambda = \dfrac{h}{p} = \dfrac{6.626 \times 10^{-34}}{3.97 \times 10^{-24}} = 1.67 \times 10^{-10} \text{ m}$. This is close to the value calculated by Davisson and Germer from the diffraction equation.

28. (a) That it had wave properties.

    (b) Work Done $= Vq = 60000 \times 1.6 \times 10^{-19} = 9.6 \times 10^{-15} \text{ J}$ This equals the kinetic energy.

    Use the classical expression: $E_K = \dfrac{1}{2}mv^2 \Rightarrow v = \sqrt{\dfrac{2E_{Kin}}{m}} = \sqrt{\dfrac{2 \times 9.6 \times 10^{-15}}{9.109 \times 10^{-31}}} = 1.45 \times 10^8 \text{ m s}^{-1}$.

    This is almost half the speed of light. The rule of thumb is to treat speeds as relativistic if they are greater than 10% of the speed of light.

29. A dice has _6_ faces. Throw it a large _number_ of times and each face will come up, on _average_, a fraction of _one-sixth_ of the total number of throws. In theory, according to _Classical_ Physics, you could calculate which face would appear from the _trajectory_ of the throw and the _surface_ on which it _lands_.

On average, a free neutron amongst a large sample of neutrons will last for 15 minutes. In theory, according to _Quantum_ Physics, it is _impossible_ to calculate how long an _individual_ neutron will survive before _decaying_ to a proton, _electron_ and antineutrino.

Classical Physics is called _deterministic_. The future can be _predicted_ to any degree of accuracy if the _initial_ conditions are known to a high degree of _accuracy_. In contrast, _Quantum_ Physics cannot predict the outcome of a _single_ event. The best that can be calculated is the _probability_ of that outcome occuring. It doesn't matter how _accurately_ known are the _initial_ conditions, or how _intelligent_ you are.

30. (a) $\Delta x \Delta p \geq \frac{1}{2}\hbar$ where the Dirac constant $\hbar = \frac{h}{2\pi}$.

    (b) We're looking for an energy, so form a combination containing the units of $\frac{1}{2}mv^2$.

    $\Delta x \Delta p \Rightarrow m \times kg\,m\,s^{-1} = kg\,m^2\,s^{-1} = kg\,m^2\,s^{-2}\,s = kg\left(\frac{m}{s}\right)^2 s = Js$

    (c) For the minimum uncertainty, change the greater or equal sign to an equal sign:

    $\Delta x \Delta p = \frac{1}{2}\hbar = \frac{h}{4\pi} \Rightarrow \Delta p = \frac{h}{4\pi \times \Delta x} = \frac{6.626 \times 10^{-34}}{4\pi \times 7 \times 10^{-24}} = 7.53 \times 10^{-12}\,kg\,m\,s^{-1}$

31. (a) $\Delta x \Delta p \geq \frac{1}{2}\hbar \Rightarrow \Delta x = \frac{h}{4\pi \Delta p} = \frac{6.626 \times 10^{-34}}{4 \times \pi \times 1.67 \times 10^{-27} \times 1.8 \times 10^5} = 1.75 \times 10^{-13}\,m$

    (b) This is about 100 times larger than the proton itself (a hydrogen nucleus) and about 12 times larger than the largest nuclei (like uranium).

32. Böhr radius is 5.29×10^{-11}m, so uncertainty in position Δx is 1.058×10^{-10}m.

    $\Delta x \Delta p = \frac{h}{4\pi} \Rightarrow \Delta p = \frac{h}{4\pi \times \Delta x} = \frac{6.626 \times 10^{-34}}{4\pi \times 1.058 \times 10^{-10}} = 4.84 \times 10^{-25}\,kgms^{-1}$

    Now calculate the uncertainty in the speed:

    $\Delta p = \Delta mv = m\Delta v = 4.84 \times 10^{-25} \Rightarrow \Delta v = \frac{4.84 \times 10^{-25}}{9.109 \times 10^{-31}} = 5.3 \times 10^5\,m/s$

33. (a) Typical walking speed is 1.5m/s, so $\Delta v = \pm 0.15$m/s, and a typical person is 60kg in mass.

    $\Delta x \Delta p \geq \frac{1}{2}\hbar \Rightarrow \Delta x = \frac{h}{4\pi \Delta mv} = \frac{6.626 \times 10^{-34}}{4 \times \pi \times 60 \times 0.15} = 5.9 \times 10^{-36}\,m$

    (b) It's in the equation, so it does make a difference. Heavier people can be more precisely located!

34. (a) 24fs is 24×10^{-15}s. $\Delta E \Delta t \geq \frac{1}{2}\hbar \Rightarrow \Delta E = \frac{h}{4\pi \Delta t} = \frac{6.626 \times 10^{-34}}{4\pi \times 24 \times 10^{-15}} = 2.2 \times 10^{-21}\,J$

    (b) $E = hf = h\frac{c}{\lambda} = \frac{6.626 \times 10^{-34} \times 3 \times 10^8}{780 \times 10^{-9}} = 2.55 \times 10^{-19}\,J \quad (=1.6eV)$

    (c) $(2.55 \pm 0.022) \times 10^{-19}$J is the combined result of parts (a) and (b) above. This is a range from 2.572×10^{-19}J down to 2.528×10^{-19}J and corresponds to wavelengths from 773nm to 786nm.

35. The probability. If the amplitude is a function of the position ψ(x), then the graph of |ψ(x)|² plotted against 'x' represents the probability of finding the object at position 'x'.

36. (a) The only classical way to escape is for the nuclear particle to be given enough energy to raise it above the top of the potential well. There is a thermal distribution of energies of the particles inside the nucleus (according to classical physics) but it's not enough to explain it.

    (b) The square of the probablility amplitude shows how likely it is for the nuclear particle to be found at a certain position 'r' from the centre of the nucleus. The dotted line shows non-zero values outside the nucleus and hence there is a chance that it will be emitted from the nucleus.

    (c) Quantum tunnelling.

    (d) Inside the nucleus it's dominated by the strong interaction.

    Outside the nucleus, it's the electromagnetic interaction

    (e) The strong interaction can't distinguish protons from neutrons, so the shape inside the nucleus stays the same for neutrons. Neutrons have no net electric charge, so there wouldn't be a gently falling curve outside the nucleus due to the electromagnetic potential. The graph for a neutron is shown on the diagram opposite.

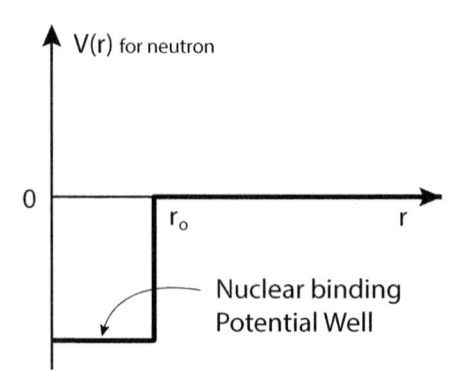

37. (a) Use electrons as incident particles. The 'double slit' isn't a slit. It's a charged thin wire with the electrons passing by on either side. See diagram below.

    (b) (i) One hole open: spread of detected electrons about a central point.

        Two holes open: interference pattern just as in Young's slits using light.

        (ii) The number of electrons detected (obviously) reduces, but the interference pattern remains not matter how low the intensity.

        (iii) Interference is supposed to be an interaction between **two** things. Reducing the intensity to the point where the electrons come out separately means you can't have two things interacting. Yet you still get an interference pattern.

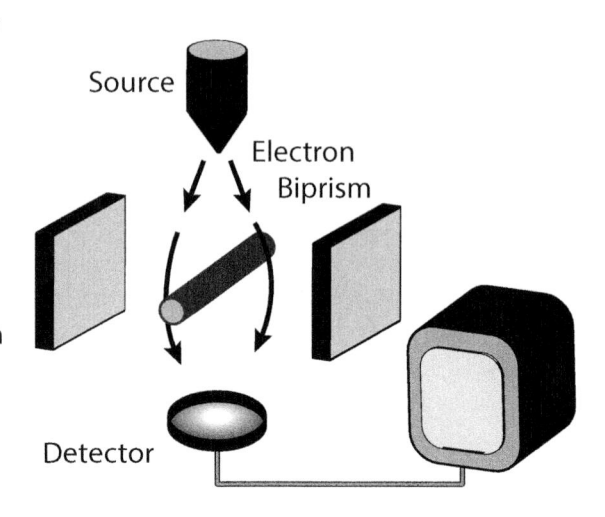

38. The Copenhagen approach is the standard position. The process of measurement is important. Before the measurement is made in an experiment, all outcomes allowed by the theory are possible. The mathematics is precise and deterministic, but it's meaningless to ask what's actually happening (so the question 'is Schroedinger's Cat alive or dead' is meaningless.) One of the possible outcomes 'becomes real' at the point of measurement. This is when the probability amplitude (the wave function) gets squared. The other possible outcomes disappear and don't become part of our universe.

In the Many Worlds approach, it's a similar story to the Copenhagen one, except that at the point of measurement, the other possible outcomes don't disappear. The universe branches at the point of measurement. If the experiment had 5 possible outcomes before measurement by the experimenter, then the universe divides into 5 universes with 5 experimenters, all with identical pasts but different futures. You can see why it's called 'Many Worlds' (and a favourite of Sci-Fi authors).

Unit 2 Particles from Space.....Answers

1. The word 'cosmic' is correct since this correctly describes their origin, and most of them come from outside our Solar System.

   The word 'ray' is incorrect since very few of them are rays (as in electromagnetic radiation). They are almost all particles. The Cosmic Microwave Background isn't thought of as 'cosmic rays'.

2. Primary cosmic rays are the particles which arrive at the top of the atmosphere.

   Secondary cosmic rays are the particles (and gamma rays) which reach the Earth's surface and derive from the interaction of the primary cosmic rays with the atmosphere.

3. Primary cosmic rays have travelled many lightyears to reach Earth and they have to be stable to do that (things like protons, electrons, alpha particles and heavy nuclei). Any short-lived particles produced when the cosmic rays were born, have long since decayed.

   The high energy collisions of the primary cosmic rays with the atmosphere produce a wide range of particles. Dependent upon the energy and the rules of the Standard Model of particle physics being obeyed, all possible particles will be produced and that includes various short-lived mesons (like the pion and kaon), and the heavier version of the electron (the muon). Gamma rays are also produced and are stable, but they don't get far in the atmosphere before being bagged by a nearby nucleus.

4. Convert energy in electron-volts into joules: $3 \times 10^{20} \, \text{eV} = 3 \times 10^{20} \times 1.6 \times 10^{-19} = 48 \, \text{J}$.

   Equate it to the kinetic energy of the golfball: $\frac{1}{2}mv^2 = 48 \Rightarrow v = \sqrt{\frac{2 \times 48}{0.04}} = 49 \, \text{m/s} \; (\approx 110 \, \text{mph})$

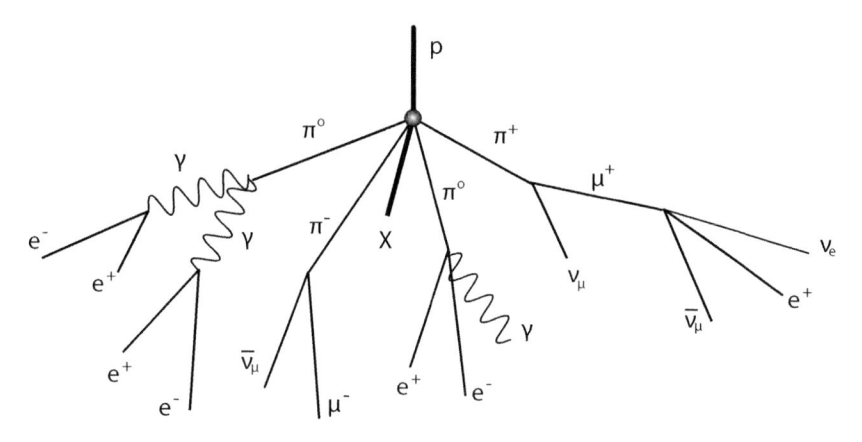

5. (a)

   (b) Conservation of electric charge (and conservation of lepton number).

   (c) Left alone, positrons are stable. But it's fatal to encounter their antiparticle (the electron). The bad news for positrons is that the universe isn't short on electrons. Imagine the platform of a London Tube station at rush-hour without touching anyone. It's goodbye positron and electron; hello two gamma rays: $e^+ + e^- \rightarrow \gamma + \gamma$.

   (d) The gamma ray must pass near a nucleus and have an energy greater than the combined rest energy of the electron/positron pair (1.02 MeV). Look up 'pair production'.

6. (a) $s = vt = 3 \times 10^8 \times 2.2 \times 10^{-6} = 660 \, \text{m}$ (b) close to zero

   (c) $t' = \dfrac{t}{\sqrt{1 - \dfrac{v^2}{c^2}}} = \dfrac{2.2 \times 10^{-6}}{\sqrt{1 - 0.99995^2}} = \dfrac{2.2 \times 10^{-6}}{0.01} = 2.2 \times 10^{-4} \, \text{s}$

   (d) This is 100 times longer-lived than in the rest frame so it travels 66000 m = 66 km.

   (e) Yes, many more will be observed (it's about one hundred per square metre each second).

125

7. About 90 would be protons, about 9 alpha particles, about 1 would be a heavier nucleus and about 1 would be an electron. It doesn't add up to 100, but that's what the 'abouts' are about.

8. A photon from the cosmic microwave background can collide with the ultrahigh energy cosmic proton and excite the three quarks of the proton into a higher energy state (a baryon resonance called a 'Delta' particle). The higher energy state then decays into lower energy products. The CMB photon has a very low energy (it's microwave, remember) so its a bit like a midge colliding with an express train. This imbalance in 'combatants' pushes up the energy threshold for triggering the resonance, to a very high level ($\approx 10^{20}$ eV).

9. (a) The secondary cosmic ray shower is spread over a large area (like square miles). Gathering data on the group of particles detected allows estimates of the original primary cosmic ray's energy. Detection of a single particle in a single detector only provides limited information (was it from a cosmic event or just local; did it have average energy etc.)

    (b) The speed of light in water is reduced due to the refractive index of water being greater than 1 (it's 1.33, so the speed of light is 2.25×10^8 m/s). The secondary cosmic ray (particle) enters the water faster than light can travel through it. The surrounding water molecules along the track are excited by the fast moving electric charge and emit a bluish coloured light (known as Cherenkov radiation). The light is detected by photomultiplier tubes surrounding the water vessel. It travels slower than the particle and fans out in a pattern like the sonic boom of a jet fighter.

10. The Sun is our major source of _energy_. It is in the shape of a _sphere_ of radius _6.96×10^8 m_ and is at a mean distance from Earth of _1.496×10^{11} m_. As well as providing us with _heat_ and _light_ energy, it also sends out charged _particles_. This is known as the _solar wind_. It can produce beautiful colours in the night sky known as the _aurora borealis_, but can also cause _disruption_ to communication satellites and _knock-out_ power grids. The Sun goes through a _cycle_ with a period of about _11 (or 22)_ years. Dark areas on the surface known as _sunspots_ become more common for certain periods during the _solar cycle_ and it is these phenomena which are largely responsible for the effects seen high up in the _atmosphere_.

    The dark _sunspots_ are areas of reduced _temperature_ and are produced by the interplay of the movement of hot volumes of _plasma_ and of the _magnetic_ fields due to these moving charges. The _magnetic_ fields produced by the Sun can extend out over large _distances_, as far as _Earth_ and beyond. The Sun's field and the Earth's own field combine around our planet to produce the _magnetosphere_, a region where the _charged_ particles from the _solar wind_ are trapped. These particles move along the _field_ lines in _spirals_ and are directed towards the _north_ and _south_ poles.

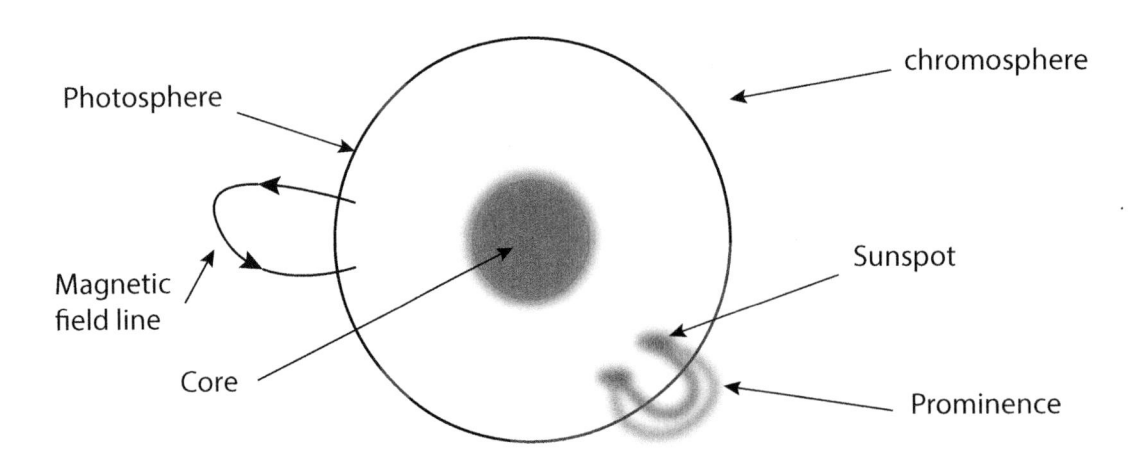

11.

12. (a) The energy range of cosmic rays is much wider (from very low up to 10^{20} eV). The Sun rarely emits particles over 1GeV in energy.

    The Solar Wind reflects the composition of the Sun's Chromosphere (more heavy ions present) while the composition of primary cosmic rays is mostly the simple elements of protons and helium-4 nuclei.

    (b) If the Sun emitted an excess of one type of electric charge over the other (say more positive charge than negative charge), it would itself become charged. This would create an electric field which would attract or repel the particles of the Solar Wind and restore balance.

13. (a) Distance from Sun to Earth is 1A.U. = 1.496×10^{11}m. Three days is 3×24×60×60=259200s.

    $$v = \frac{s}{t} = \frac{1.496 \times 10^{11}}{2.592 \times 10^5} = 5.77 \times 10^5 \text{ m/s} = 577 \text{km/s}$$

    (b) Mass of a proton = 1.67×10^{-27}kg. and the speed is non-relativistic.

    $$E_k = \frac{1}{2}mv^2 = \frac{1}{2} \times 1.67 \times 10^{-27} \times (5.77 \times 10^5)^2 = 2.78 \times 10^{-16} \text{J} = \frac{2.78 \times 10^{-16}}{1.6 \times 10^{-19}} = 1740 \text{eV} = 1.74 \text{keV}$$

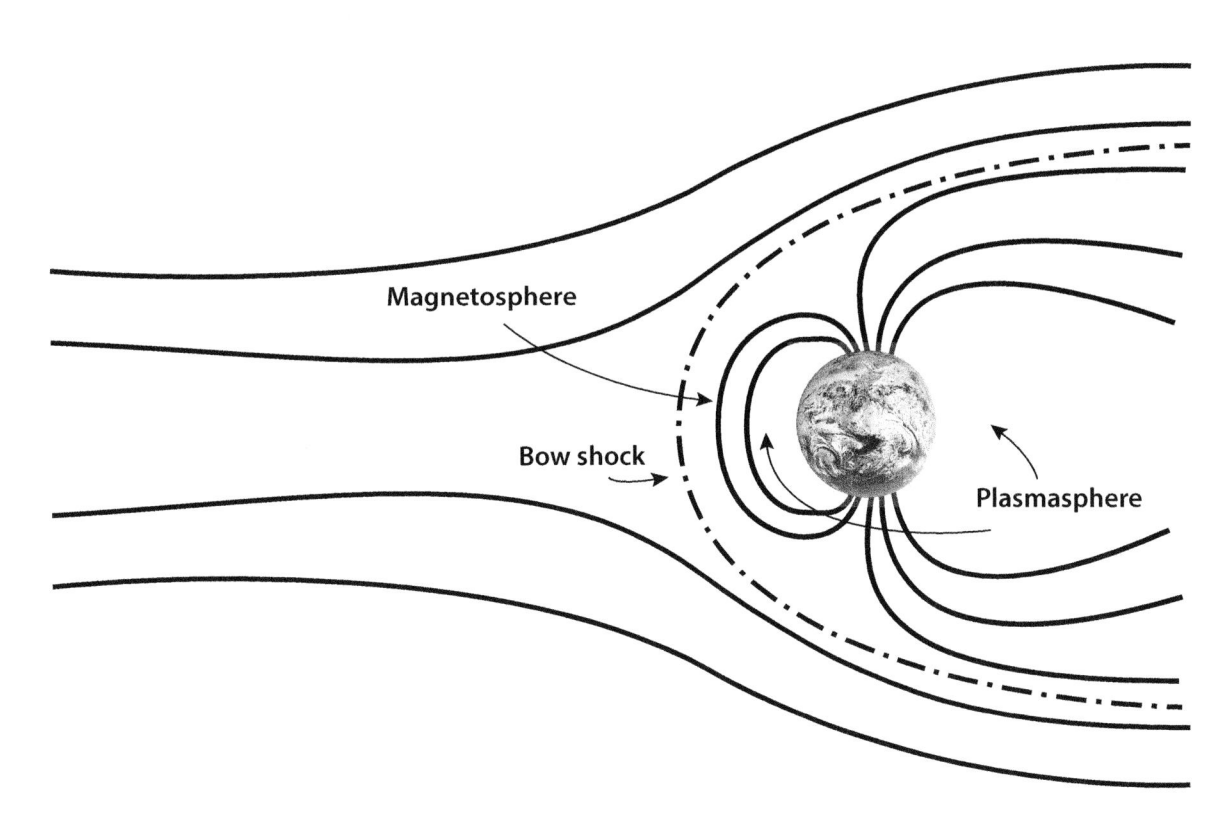

14.

15. (a) Under normal conditions, astronauts in orbit receive enhanced levels of radiation (about ten times the ground level dose), but still within safety guidelines. Most of the Solar Wind is deflected by the magnetosphere, but during solar flares the radiation levels can increase by ten to one hundred times. The worst case could cause radiation sickness and death. The only preventive routines are to shelter behind thick (low atomic mass) materials in the spacecraft or ingest foods with high concentrations of non-radioactive isotopes of the radioactive elements produced by the flare.

    (b) Electronic equipment is becoming smaller and smaller and thus more suseptible to disruption by single charged particles. In some cases this will corrupt an instruction and in others, destroy a component. The spacecraft itself can become electrically charged and thus cause sparks and subsequent burnout of components. Radiowaves bend in the upper atmosphere due to the fields in the ionosphere and can distort GPS signals when solar activity is high. To protect against disruption requires clever software routines and backup systems. Duplicate rather than protect (and don't make components too small). Has anyone designed a purely mechanical spacecraft?

(c) Changing magnetic fields due to rough space weather can induce currents to flow in the Earth's surface and also in metal pipelines and electrical subsystems of power grids. These can trip safety switches and temporarily close down electrical supply to communities and businesses. Reduce effects by installing smoothing capacitors, having reserve supplies or using non-conducting materials (eg in pipelines).

(d) There have been suggestions of a connection between the Solar Cycle of 11 years and the Earth's climate. This may be connected to cloud formation where the passage of charged particles induces tiny water droplets to form in the moist atmosphere. The science is speculative, and there's not a lot we can do about it if it's true.

16. (a) Symbols: 'q' is the electric charge of the particle (usually in units of Coulombs), 'v' is its velocity (that'll be in m/s), and 'B' is the magnetic induction (in Tesla).

    Objects: the shiny sphere is the electrically charged particle, and the circle with the cross inside denotes the magnetic field. These circles with crosses are evenly spaced, showing a uniform magnetic field (same value everywhere). Crosses inside the circle indicate the direction of the field as 'into the page' (a dot inside would show coming 'out of the page').

    (b) It doesn't act along the direction of the magnetic field lines, and it doesn't act along the direction of the velocity of the particle.

    (c) It has no electric charge, is stationary relative to the magnetic field, or moves along a field line.

17. (a) Here's the most common configuration: use the right hand for negatively charged particles like electrons (they are the most common particle used in these calculations).

    There are other systems in use. Discuss with your teacher.

    (b) With the above rule: First finger is the magnetic field arrow direction, Second finger is the direction in which the negative charges move, Thumb shows the direction of the force on the charged particle.

    (c) Using the above rule, the right hand is configured correctly (okay the second finger is not quite coming straight out of the page), so the force is to the top of the page.

18. (A) $F = qvB\sin\theta = 4 \times 0.25 \times 0.65 \times \sin 45° = 0.46\text{N}$ out of page

    (B) $F = qvB\sin\theta = 0.03 \times 0.06 \times 0.015 \times \sin 90° = 2.7 \times 10^{-5}\text{N}$ into page

    (C) $F = qvB\sin\theta = 0.75 \times 3.2 \times 0.03 \times \sin 90° = 0.072\text{N}$ out of page

    (D) $F = qvB\sin\theta = 0.12 \times 500 \times 0.08 \times \sin 120° = 4.16\text{N}$ into page

    (E) $F = qvB\sin\theta = 8 \times 10^{-6} \times 0.03 \times 0.025 \times \sin 90° = 6 \times 10^{-9}\text{N}$ towards bottom of page

19. (a) Horizontal component: $v_H = 20\cos 30° = 17.32\text{m/s}$

    Vertical component: $v_V = 20\sin 30° = 10\text{m/s}$

    (b) In direction of magnetic field lines: $v_{\|B} = 7\cos 50° = 4.5\text{m/s}$

    At right angles to magnetic field lines: $v_{\perp B} = 7\sin 50° = 5.36\text{m/s}$ towards the top of the page.

20. (A) $v_{\|B} = 8 \times 10^5 \cos 35° = 6.55 \times 10^5 \text{ m s}^{-1}$

    (B) $v_{\|B} = 2.5 \times 10^3 \cos 105° = -647 \text{ m s}^{-1}$ (the angle is the one between the field line and the velocity).

21. (a) A positive electric charge will feel an initial force in the direction of the electric field lines. It's always parallel to the field lines.

    (b) At right angles to both the magnetic field lines and the velocity of the particle possessing the charge.

    (c) The electric charge must be moving in the magnetic field. It doesn't have to be moving in the electric field.

22. (a) $\dfrac{mv^2}{r} = qvB\sin\theta = qvB\sin 90° = qvB \quad\Rightarrow\quad r = \dfrac{mv^2}{qvB} = \dfrac{mv}{qB}$

    (b) $v = \omega r \quad r = \dfrac{mv}{qB} = \dfrac{m\omega r}{qB} \quad\Rightarrow\quad 1 = \dfrac{m\omega}{qB} \quad\Rightarrow\quad \omega = \dfrac{qB}{m}$

    (c) $\omega = 2\pi f = \dfrac{qB}{m} \quad\Rightarrow\quad f = \dfrac{qB}{2\pi m}$

    (d) $T = \dfrac{1}{f} \quad\Rightarrow\quad T = \dfrac{2\pi m}{qB}$

23. (a) Using the right-hand rule (in this drawing, it's: first finger into page, second finger pointing to top of page, thumb pointing rightwards to provide the centripetal force) gives a drawing consistent with a negative charge.

    (b) $r = \dfrac{mv}{qB} = \dfrac{0.18 \times 3}{0.07 \times 0.74} = 10.4\,\text{m}$

    (c) $\omega = \dfrac{qB}{m} = \dfrac{0.07 \times 0.74}{0.18} = 0.288\,\text{rad/s}$ or $\omega = \dfrac{v}{r} = \dfrac{3}{10.4} = 0.288\,\text{rad/s} \quad f = \dfrac{\omega}{2\pi} = \dfrac{0.288}{2\pi} = 0.0458\,\text{Hz}$

    (d) $T = \dfrac{1}{f} = \dfrac{1}{0.0458} = 21.8\,\text{s}$

    (e) The radius is given by $r = \dfrac{mv}{qB}$ so doubling the speed doubles the radius.

    The period is given by $T = \dfrac{2\pi m}{qB}$. There's no speed term in the equation so the period remains the same as before.

    These two are consistent since doubling the radius will double the circumference, and if the speed is doubled, the time for one orbit will remain constant.

24. Calculate the electron's speed: 1keV = 1000×1.6×10⁻¹⁹=1.6×10⁻¹⁶ Joules.

    $E_k = \dfrac{1}{2}mv^2 \quad\Rightarrow\quad v = \sqrt{\dfrac{2E_k}{m}} = \sqrt{\dfrac{2 \times 1.6 \times 10^{-16}}{9.1 \times 10^{-31}}} = 1.88 \times 10^7\,\text{m/s}$

    Then the force: $F = qvB\sin\theta = 1.6 \times 10^{-19} \times 1.88 \times 10^7 \times 50 \times 10^{-6} \times \sin 90° = 1.5 \times 10^{-16}\,\text{N}$

    The weight of an electron near the surface is negligible: $W = mg = 9.1 \times 10^{-31} \times 9.8 = 8.9 \times 10^{-30}\,\text{kg}$

25. $r = \dfrac{mv}{qB} \quad\Rightarrow\quad B = \dfrac{mv}{qr} = \dfrac{9.11 \times 10^{-31} \times 2.19 \times 10^6}{1.6 \times 10^{-19} \times 5.29 \times 10^{-11}} = 2.36 \times 10^5\,\text{T}$ (Böhr radius used for 'r').

26. (a) The speed is given by: $r = \dfrac{mv}{qB} \quad\Rightarrow\quad v = \dfrac{qBr}{m}$. The speed stays constant since the track is circular so all quantities stay constant on the right hand side.

    Here is a qualitative, alternative explanation. The (magnetic) force on the ion is at right angles to its velocity and the work done on the ion is the vector dot product of the force and displacement. The displacement is in the same direction as the instantaneous velocity so the work done is zero since force and displacement are at 90° to each other (since the cosine of 90° is zero).

(b) There are a few ways to do it. This way rearranges the two equations to get the speed squared on its own on the left side (first line), then equates them (second line):

$$\frac{1}{2}mv^2 = qV \Rightarrow v^2 = \frac{2qV}{m} \qquad r = \frac{mv}{qB} \Rightarrow v = \frac{qBr}{m} \Rightarrow v^2 = \left(\frac{qBr}{m}\right)^2$$

$$\frac{2qV}{m} = \left(\frac{qBr}{m}\right)^2 \Rightarrow m = \frac{qB^2r^2}{2V}$$

(c) At 'P': $r = 0.14 \div 2 = 0.07\,\text{m} \Rightarrow m = \frac{qB^2r^2}{2V} = \frac{1.6 \times 10^{-19} \times 0.12^2 \times 0.07^2}{2 \times 350} = 1.61 \times 10^{-26}\,\text{kg}$

At 'Q': $r = 0.15 \div 2 = 0.075\,\text{m} \Rightarrow m = \frac{qB^2r^2}{2V} = \frac{1.6 \times 10^{-19} \times 0.12^2 \times 0.075^2}{2 \times 350} = 1.85 \times 10^{-26}\,\text{kg}$

27. (a) The electric field is supplied by the oscillator and accelerates the particles during the straight sections between the 'dees'. The magnetic field makes the particles move in circles.

(b) Section AB increases speed, section BC keeps constant speed, section CD increases speed. During the passage 'B' to 'C' the polarity of the 'dees' must change. For section AB, the 'B' side Dee must be negative to speed up the protons. By the time the protons reach, 'C', the bottom Dee must become negative. The protons will always be accelerated when between the Dees.

(c) Into the page

(d) The equation for the half-period $T = \frac{1}{2} \times \frac{2\pi m}{qB}$ doesn't depend on the speed or the radius so the time for each half orbit is the same. Hence the frequency applied by the oscillator stays constant.

(e) The deflector attracts the beam towards the experiment. For protons, it's negative.

28. (a) Looking from the left, it would move in an anticlockwise direction.

(b) $f = \frac{qB}{2\pi m} = \frac{1.6 \times 10^{-19} \times 0.28}{2\pi \times 9.1 \times 10^{-31}} = 7.8 \times 10^9\,\text{Hz}$

(c) It is the component of velocity along the direction of the magnetic field lines. The electron moves in a circle but the circle is drifting to the left with a constant speed (the component just mentioned). The result is a helix (a spiral of constant radius).

29. (a) The nucleus moves in a helix, a drawn-out circle of constant radius.

(b) Parallel: $v_{\parallel B} = v\cos 80° = 0.04 \times 3 \times 10^8 \times \cos 80° = 2.08 \times 10^6\,\text{m/s}$

At right angles: $v_{\perp B} = v\sin 80° = 0.04 \times 3 \times 10^8 \times \sin 80° = 1.18 \times 10^7\,\text{m/s}$

(c) $r = \frac{mv_{\perp B}}{qB} = \frac{2.0 \times 10^{-26} \times 1.18 \times 10^7}{6 \times 1.6 \times 10^{-19} \times 35 \times 10^{-6}} = 7.02 \times 10^3\,\text{m}$

(d) $T = \frac{2\pi m}{qB} = \frac{2\pi \times 2.0 \times 10^{-26}}{6 \times 1.6 \times 10^{-19} \times 35 \times 10^{-6}} = 3.7 \times 10^{-3}\,\text{s}$

(e) Sideways drift speed is 2.08×10^6 m/s, so 1km of distance takes a time of 4.8×10^{-4} s.

Period is 3.7×10^{-3} s, so in 4.8×10^{-4} s it will turn only a fraction of one orbit: $\frac{4.8 \times 10^{-4}}{3.7 \times 10^{-3}} = 0.13$. This is about 47°.

(f) The pitch (sideways distance for one turn) of the helix is $s = v_{\parallel B} t = 2.08 \times 10^6 \times 3.7 \times 10^{-3} = 7.7\,\text{km}$.

30. (a) Out of the page. Don't dislocate your shoulder. With the page flat on the table, your right hand should have the first finger pointing at the ceiling with your thumb pointing left.

   (b) It has no electric charge. It's shown as a dotted line on the analysis but leaves no track on the photograph. Charged particles ionise the liquid along the track and (with a sudden release of pressure from 5atm to 1atm) cause localised boiling to produce mm size bubbles. Neutral particles like the Lambda and the neutrino don't cause ionisation so don't leave a track.

   (c) The radius of the track is given by $r = \dfrac{mv}{qB}$. The charged particles have the same '|q|' and are in the same uniform magnetic field 'B', so the radius is proportional to the product 'mv'. The masses of a pion and a muon are over 200 times more than the electron, so for roughly similar speeds, the lighter electron would have a smaller track radius.

   (d) Conservation of momentum.

   (e) The collision is: $v_\mu + p \to 3\pi^+ + \pi^- + \mu^- + \Lambda^0$.

   The electric charges are: 0 + 1 = +3 – 1 – 1 + 0. This is true, so electric charge is conserved.

For more info, this is an excellent resource:

http://teachers.web.cern.ch/teachers/archiv/HST2005/bubble_chambers/BCwebsite/about.htm

Unit 2 Simple Harmonic Motion.....Answers

1. (a) The particle undergoing SHM has to return to the equilibrium position (the rest position, usually taken as the origin) so a force must always be applied towards the origin. The direction of the force is opposite to the displacement of the particle.

   (b) $F = -kx$ where 'k' is the spring constant and the minus sign indicates the direction.

2. (a) 8N at 2m, 12N at 3m and 16N at 4m. All pointing leftwards.

   (b) Same magnitude (8N), opposite direction (to the right)

3. (a) To be **Simple** Harmonic Motion the restoring force has to be directly proportional to the negative of the displacement. A relationship like $F = -kx^2$ wouldn't be Simple HM, just HM.

   (b) The restoring force decreases as the particle moves further from the origin, so it must be an inverse relationship. Trying an inverse square gets the correct relationship $F = -\dfrac{k}{x^2}$.

4. (a) the amplitude   (b) read off the frequency then use $T = \dfrac{1}{f}$

   (c) the speed at any time 't'   (d) the acceleration at any time 't'

5. (a) We match terms against: $y = A\cos \omega t = A\cos 2\pi ft = A\cos\left(\dfrac{2\pi t}{T}\right)$ to give an amplitude of A = 5m, a frequency of f = 4Hz, a period of T = 0.25s, and an angular frequency of ω = 8π rad s⁻¹.

   (b) $\dfrac{dy}{dt} = v = -40\pi \sin 8\pi t$. Maximum value is the number outside the sine: $v_{max} = 40\pi = 125.7$ m/s.

   (c) It's fastest at the origin y = 0.

6. The '7' is the 'A'. Period 'T' of 0.2s is a frequency of 5Hz, so match with $x = A\sin 2\pi ft$.

   This gives: $x = 7\sin 10\pi t$ (or, $x = 7\cos 10\pi t$ if you start your clock at maximum displacement).

7. (a) $x = \int v\,dt = \int -24\sin 30t\,dt = -24\int \sin 30t\,dt = -24\left[-\dfrac{1}{30}\cos 30t\right] = 0.8\cos 30t$

131

(b) $x = 0.8\cos 30t = 0.8\cos\left(2\pi \times \dfrac{30}{2\pi}t\right) = A\cos 2\pi ft$. Reading off: A = 0.8m   f = 30/2π = 4.77Hz

(c) $x = 0.8\cos 30t = 0.8\cos 0 = +0.8$m

8. For the cosine solution: $x = A\cos\omega t$. At t = 0, x = +A (maximum displacement, on the 'right')

   For the sine solution: $x = A\sin\omega t$. At t = 0, x = 0 (at the origin)

9. (a) $m\dfrac{d^2}{dt^2}(A\sin\omega t) = -kA\sin\omega t$ ⇒ $-m\omega^2 A\sin\omega t = -kA\sin\omega t$ ⇒ $\omega^2 = \dfrac{k}{m}$

   (b) It comes from $F = -kx$ ⇒ $k = -\dfrac{F}{x}$, so units are Nm⁻¹.

   (c) If you have the mass in an equation, you can rearrange it to put the 'm' on the left hand side. Then go and measure the quantities on the right hand side. This gives you a way of measuring the mass of an object by oscillating it. Why do this when you can just stick it on a balance? Well a balance measures weight, not mass. And it wouldn't be any use in a low-g environment out in space, or where things are weightless (they'd still have mass, which you measure by oscillating it in an SHM experiment).

10. (a) Time for two cycles is 4s, so period is 2s and $f = \dfrac{1}{T} = 0.5s$ $\omega = 2\pi f = \pi$ rad s⁻¹

    (b) $y = A\sin 2\pi ft = 0.08\sin(2\pi \times 0.5 \times t) = 0.08\sin\pi t$

    (c) $v = \dfrac{dx}{dt} = \dfrac{d}{dt}(0.08\sin\pi t) = 0.08\pi\cos\pi t$ ⇒ $v_{max} = 0.08\pi = 0.25$ m s⁻¹

    (d) From Q9a, $\omega^2 = \dfrac{k}{m}$ ⇒ $k = m\omega^2 = 0.06\pi^2 = 0.59$ Nm⁻¹

11. Amplitude 'A' = 0.09m, frequency 'f' = 5Hz, so: $y = A\sin 2\pi ft = 0.09\sin 10\pi t$ or $y = 0.09\cos 10\pi t$

12. (a) amplitude = 3m   (b) 2πf = 200, giving a frequency of 31.8Hz   (c) T = 1/f = 0.0314s

    (d) Differentiate the displacement: $v = \dfrac{dx}{dt} = 600\cos 200t$ to give a maximum value of 600m s⁻¹

    (e) $E_{Kin} = \dfrac{1}{2}mv^2 = \dfrac{1}{2} \times 0.05 \times 600^2 = 9000$J

13. (a) Differentiate the displacement:
    $v = \dfrac{dx}{dt} = \dfrac{d}{dt}(3\sin 8\pi t) = 24\pi\cos 8\pi t$

    Differentiate the velocity:
    $a = \dfrac{dv}{dt} = \dfrac{d}{dt}(24\pi\cos 8\pi t) = -192\pi^2\sin 8\pi t$

    (b) This is a long-winded way of asking for **half** a period,

    2πf = 8π, so f = 4Hz and T = 0.25s

    So time = 0.125s

    (c) From part (a) above, maximum acceleration is 192π² = 1895m/s².

    See graphs opposite. It follows the same pattern as minus displacement. The acceleration is most positive at x = -A.

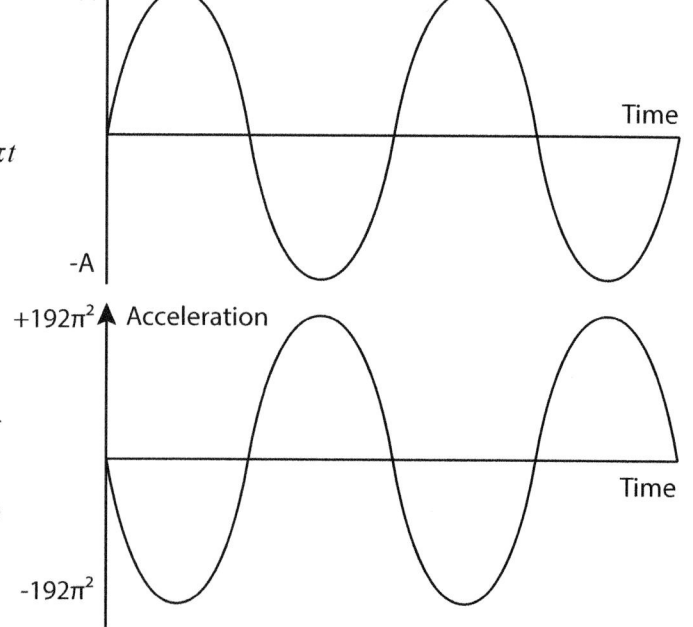

14. (a) The term outside the sine is $0.72\pi^2$. This is $7.1 m/s^2$.

(b) The sequence of differentiating the displacement gives the velocity then the acceleration:

$$x = A\sin 2\pi ft \qquad v = \frac{dx}{dt} = 2\pi fA\cos 2\pi ft \qquad a = \frac{dv}{dt} = -4\pi^2 f^2 A \sin 2\pi ft$$

Matching up the equation in the question gives: $2\pi f = 6\pi$ and $-4\pi^2 f^2 A = -0.72\pi^2$. Solving for the frequency and amplitude gives: $f = 3Hz$ and $A = 0.02m$.

(c) From part (b) above, the velocity is given by: $v = \frac{dx}{dt} = 2\pi fA\cos 2\pi ft$. The maximum speed is the bit outside the cosine: $2\pi fA = 2\pi \times 3 \times 0.02 = 0.377 m/s$.

Nerdy note: I said 'speed' in the second sentence since the sign of the velocity (its directional behaviour) is controlled by the cosine function.

15. (a) $x = A\sin 2\pi ft \qquad v = v_o\cos 2\pi ft = \frac{dx}{dt} = 2\pi f \times A\cos 2\pi ft \qquad \therefore v_o = 2\pi fA = \omega A$

(b) Start by squaring the expressions for the displacement and velocity:

$$x^2 = A^2 \sin^2 \omega t \quad \Rightarrow \quad \sin^2 \omega t = \frac{x^2}{A^2} \qquad v^2 = (\omega A)^2 \cos^2 \omega t \quad \Rightarrow \quad \cos^2 \omega t = \frac{v^2}{(\omega A)^2}$$

$$\sin^2 \omega t + \cos^2 \omega t = 1 \quad \Rightarrow \quad \frac{x^2}{A^2} + \frac{v^2}{(\omega A)^2} = 1 \quad \Rightarrow \quad v^2 = \omega^2 (A^2 - x^2) \quad \Rightarrow \quad v = \pm \omega \sqrt{A^2 - x^2}$$

The ± is there since for every 'x' position, the particle can pass in either direction.

16. (a) Maximum kinetic energy is where it's fastest, when it flies past the origin.

Imagine the motion was generated by the particle on a spring. Maximum potential energy is where the spring is at maximum extension, $x = \pm A$.

(b) Undamped means no energy loss, so the total energy is constant.

(c) $E_{Kin} = \frac{1}{2}mv^2 = \frac{1}{2}m\omega^2(A^2 - x^2)$

(d) At the origin (x = 0): $E_{Kin} = \frac{1}{2}m\omega^2(A^2 - x^2) = \frac{1}{2}m\omega^2(A^2 - 0^2) = \frac{1}{2}m\omega^2 A^2$ At $x = \pm A$, $E_{Kin} = 0$.

(e) Conservation of energy at the origin and at maximum extension gives:

$(E_{Kin} + E_{Pot})_{at\, x=0} = (E_{Kin} + E_{Pot})_{at\, x=A}$

The potential energy at the origin is zero and the kinetic energy at maximum extension is zero.

$\left(\frac{1}{2}m\omega^2 A^2 + 0\right)_{at\, x=0} = (0 + E_{Pot})_{at\, x=A} \quad \Rightarrow \quad E_{Pot\, x=A} = \frac{1}{2}m\omega^2 A^2$

(f) The total energy is constant so there won't be an 'x' in the expression. You can choose any position; take x = 0 to make things easy.

$E_{Total} = E_{Pot} + E_{Kin} = 0 + \frac{1}{2}m\omega^2 A^2 = \frac{1}{2}m\omega^2 A^2 \quad \left(= \frac{1}{2}kA^2 \text{ using } k = m\omega^2\right)$

17. (a) Amplitude = 3m (b) the dotted line (c) a horizontal line passing through 9 Joules

(d) $\frac{1}{2}m\omega^2(A^2 - x^2) = \frac{1}{2}m\omega^2 x^2 \quad \Rightarrow \quad A^2 = 2x^2 \quad \Rightarrow \quad x = \pm\frac{1}{\sqrt{2}}A = \pm 2.12m$ (where the graphs cross)

(e) Use the potential energy expression and evaluate at x = +A to obtain:

$E_p = \frac{1}{2}m\omega^2 x^2 = \frac{1}{2}kx^2 \quad \Rightarrow \quad 9 = \frac{1}{2}k \times 3^2 \quad \Rightarrow \quad k = 2 Nm^{-1}$

18. First integration to obtain the velocity:

$$\frac{d^2x}{dt^2} = \frac{dv}{dt} = \frac{qE_o}{m}\sin\omega t \Rightarrow \int dv = \frac{qE_o}{m}\int_{t=0}^{t=t}\sin\omega t\, dt \Rightarrow v = \frac{qE_o}{m}\left[-\frac{1}{\omega}\right][\cos\omega t]_0^t = -\frac{qE_o}{m\omega}[\cos\omega t - 1]$$

Integrate again to obtain the displacement:

$$v = \frac{dx}{dt} = -\frac{qE_o}{m\omega}[\cos\omega t - 1] \Rightarrow \int dx = -\frac{qE_o}{m\omega}\int_0^t(\cos\omega t - 1)dt = -\frac{qE_o}{m\omega}\left[\frac{1}{\omega}\sin\omega t - t\right]_0^t$$

Then substitute the limits:

$$x = -\frac{qE_o}{m\omega}\left[\frac{1}{\omega}\sin\omega t - t\right]_0^t = -\frac{qE_o}{m\omega}\left[\left(\frac{1}{\omega}\sin\omega t - t\right) - \left(\frac{1}{\omega}\sin 0 - 0\right)\right] \Rightarrow x = \frac{qE_o}{m\omega}t - \frac{qE_o}{m\omega^2}\sin\omega t$$

This is the displacement 'x' of a particle which drifts to the side (the first term) as it oscillates back and forth (the second term with the sine function). An observer moving along at the velocity of the first term would only observe the oscillating component and declare it to be Simple Harmonic Motion. That drift velocity is read-off from the first term: $\frac{qE_o}{m\omega}$.

19. (a) At the equilibrium level x = 0 (same level in both tubes).

    (b) about: 0.9m : 0.65m : 0.48m : 0.35m

    (c) Six complete periods is about 18.8s. So period = 3.13s and frequency = 0.32Hz. It does remain constant (judged by eye).

    (d) The liquid occupies all the space over a range of x-values, so it's like having particles at many places all at once. Taking a single particle (the one at the top of a column) means one particle at one place at one time (and that one gives the graph).

    Think about the energy. Taking a single particle at the top of the column is just an interplay of kinetic and (gravitational) potential energy as it bobs up and down. If you take the **whole** liquid, how does its potential energy change (does it change?). Consider other quantities like air pressure on the top surfaces. Discuss amongst your group!

    (e) Energy is being 'lost' to the surroundings (as heat energy due to friction with the walls).

    (f) At a peak, the potential energy of a particle of the liquid (same as total energy since its kinetic energy is zero here) at the top of the column is: $E_{pot.} = \frac{1}{2}kx^2$. The energy is proportional to the displacement squared, so the ratio of the energies for the first two peaks will be $0.65^2 : 0.9^2$. This is a ratio of 0.52 to 1, hence, the total energy is about halved.

20. (a) The angle of swing has to be small, the smaller the better. The approximation compares the angle in radians with the sine of the angle eg 10° is 0.1745rad and sin10° is 0.1736.

    (b) $T = 2\pi\sqrt{\frac{L}{g}} = 2\pi\sqrt{\frac{1.5}{9.8}} = 2.46s$

    (c) $T = 2\pi\sqrt{\frac{L}{g}} \Rightarrow L = g\left(\frac{T}{2\pi}\right)^2 = 9.8\times\left(\frac{1}{2\pi}\right)^2 = 0.248m$

    Depends upon the local 'g' value. Unsuitable in an accelerating environment. The pendulum will lose energy and require 'winding-up'.

21. (a) Period is 2s. $T = 2\pi\sqrt{\frac{L}{g}} \Rightarrow L = g\left(\frac{T}{2\pi}\right)^2 = 9.8\times\left(\frac{2}{2\pi}\right)^2 = 0.993m$

(b) The angle subtended from the vertical, 'θ' is given by: $\theta = \theta_{Max} \cos \omega t$. The maximum angle subtended is given in the problem as $4° = 0.0698$ radians.

The arc length is $s = L\theta$, and the velocity is given by:

$$v = \frac{ds}{dt} = \frac{d(L\theta)}{dt} = L\frac{d\theta}{dt} = L\frac{d}{dt}(\theta_{Max} \cos \omega t) = -\omega L \theta_{Max} \sin \omega t$$

The part outside the sine is the maximum speed:

$$v_{Max} = \omega L \theta_{Max} = \frac{2\pi}{T} L\theta_{Max} = \frac{2\pi}{2} \times 0.993 \times 0.0698 = 0.218 \text{m/s}$$

(Why did I drop the minus sign? It attaches itself to the sine part to correctly describe the phase difference between the displacement (a cosine) and the velocity (a negative sine)).

22. Typical neutron star has 12km radius with twice the mass of the Sun.

First calculate the 'g' value: $g = \frac{GM}{R^2} = \frac{6.67 \times 10^{-11} \times 2 \times 2 \times 10^{30}}{12000^2} = 1.85 \times 10^{12} \text{Nkg}^{-1}$

Then the period: $T = 2\pi\sqrt{\frac{L}{g}} = 2\pi\sqrt{\frac{1}{1.85 \times 10^{12}}} = 4.62 \times 10^{-6}$s. It swings at about 200kHz.

23. It wouldn't oscillate back and forth. The 'g' value at the ISS isn't zero, it's about 8.6Nkg⁻¹, so using the formula, you'd expect it to oscillate with a period slightly more than on Earth's surface. So why doesn't it swing? The satellite is in freefall and its contents are 'weightless' even though they are in a locally strong gravitational field. The pendulum bob needs a restoring force, and it won't get one if the pendulum bob is 'weightless'.

You could also look at it from Einstein's perspective. The Equivalence Principle from the General Theory of Relativity says that an accelerating frame of reference is identical in its physics with the effect of a gravitational field. To Newton, the spacecraft is in a circular orbit so it's accelerating. To Einstein it's not accelerating (it's following a geodesic), so there is no gravitational field inside the spacecraft (g = 0 and so the period of the pendulum is infinite).

Unit 2 Waves.....Answers

1. (a) 1.8×10^8m s⁻¹   (b) 0.045m   (c) 3.2Hz   (d) 0.04s   (e) 5.7×10^{-3}s

2. **Transverse Wave**: particles of the medium vibrate at 90° to the direction of the disturbance e.g. the flick of a rope, or the bobbing of a cork in water.

   Longitudinal Wave: particles of the medium vibrate in the same direction as the disturbance e.g. sound wave.

3. (a) Graph 'A'   (b) Amplitude = 8cm   Period = 4.8s   Frequency = 0.208Hz
   (c) 8cm   (d) 3.6s   (e) No. Nature isn't interested at what time you started your clock.

4. (a) Amplitude = 4m   Frequency= 3Hz   Period = 0.333s
   (b) Form a bracket with the 6π outside: $6\pi t \pm 3\pi T = 6\pi(t \pm \tfrac{1}{2}T)$. This shows what the displacement of the particle would be half a period before time 't' or half a period after time 't'.

5. Fit to the equation: $y = A \sin 2\pi f t$.   (a) $y = 0.03 \sin 24\pi t$ (b) $y = 0.15 \sin 8\pi t$

6. (a) They have the same frequency of oscillation.
   (b) When 'P' is at the top; 'Q' is at the bottom etc.

(c) (i) 90°

(ii) A travelling wave

(iii) Diagram on the right. The disturbance is 'travelling' to the left (the way the peak goes). You can see this by comparing the position of the peak on the original diagram (particle 'B') with the position of the peak at the later time in the above diagram (particle 'A').

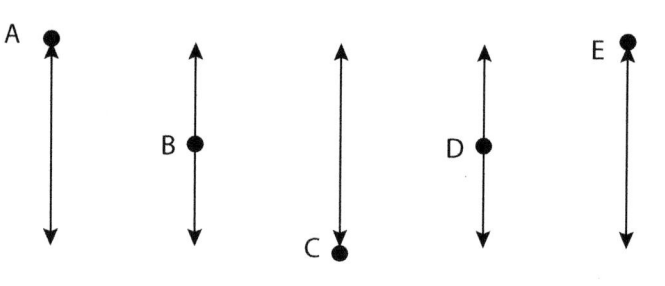

7. **A travelling wave consists of a line of particles each vibrating under the action of Simple Harmonic Motion with each particle being slightly out of phase with its neighbour.**

8. (a) Amplitude = 0.3m   Frequency = 50Hz   Period = 0.02s λ = 0.8m   v = 40m s^{-1}

    (b) [Graph: Displacement (m) vs Distance (m), sine wave starting negative]

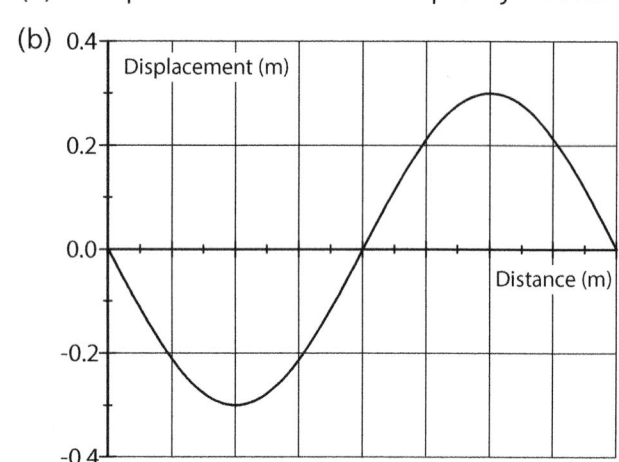

    (c) [Graph: Displacement (m) vs Distance (m), sine wave starting positive going negative]

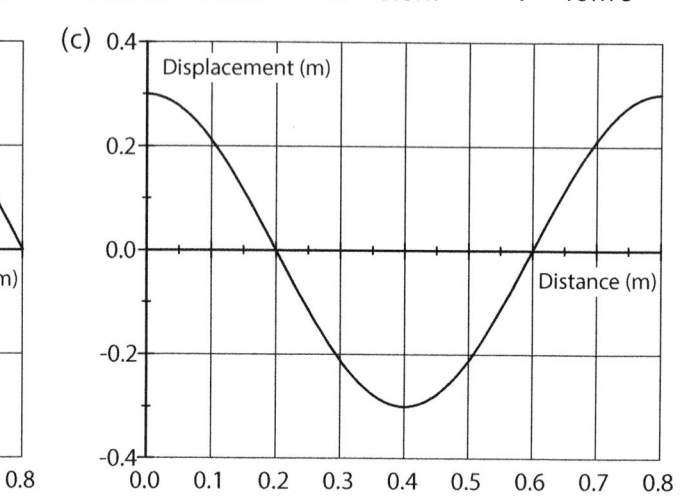

    (d) The disturbance would go in the opposite direction. The expression with (t – x) goes in the positive x-direction and the one with (t + x) goes in the negative x-direction.

    Note that when you express the wave equation with time first followed by the distance as in $y = \sin 2\pi \left(\dfrac{t}{T} \pm \dfrac{x}{\lambda} \right)$, the shape of the wave at time = 0 is like answer (b), an upside down sine wave. If your equation is $y = \sin 2\pi \left(\dfrac{x}{\lambda} \pm \dfrac{t}{T} \right)$, then at t = 0 you start with the usual sine wave.

9. The Intensity is proportional to the square of the amplitude, so Intensity = 80W m^{-2}.

10. $I = kA^2 = 3.5 \times 0.075^2 = 0.0197 \text{ W m}^{-2}$

11. (a) Both graphs have a wavelength of 8 units of distance. The two curves are 1 unit apart and this corresponds to a phase difference of ⅛th of 360°. So it's 45° = π/4 radians. Graph 'B' is the same, so it's also 45° = π/4 radians.

    (b) $f = 96\text{Hz} \Rightarrow T = \dfrac{1}{f} = \dfrac{1}{96} = 0.0104\text{s}$. The curves are ⅛th of a wave out so this is 0.0013s.

    (c) They must have the same frequency.

12. (a) Amplitude = 2.4m   Frequency = 20Hz   Period = 0.05s λ = 0.2m   v = 4m s^{-1}

    (b) Amplitude = 0.04m   Frequency = 800Hz   Period = 0.00125s λ = 0.008m   v = 6.4m s^{-1}

    (c) Amplitude = 95m   Frequency = 1.11Hz   Period = 0.9s λ = 15.7m   v = 17.4m s^{-1}

    (d) Amplitude = 0.8m   Frequency = 0.00398Hz Period = 251s λ = 12πm   v = 0.15m s^{-1}

13. (a) - (d) [Displacement vs Distance graphs]

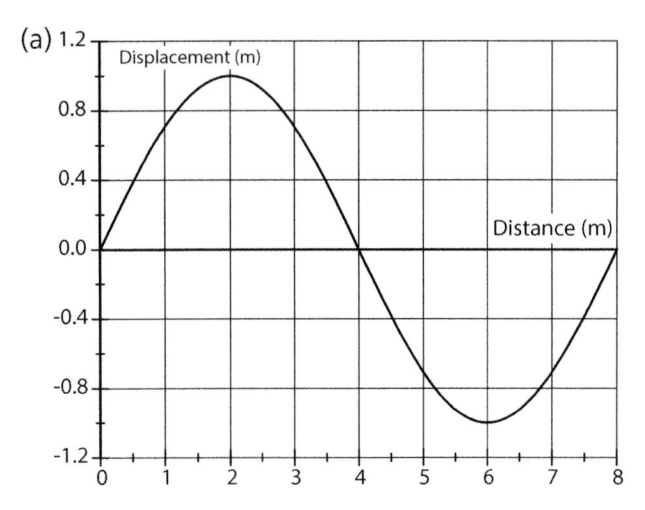

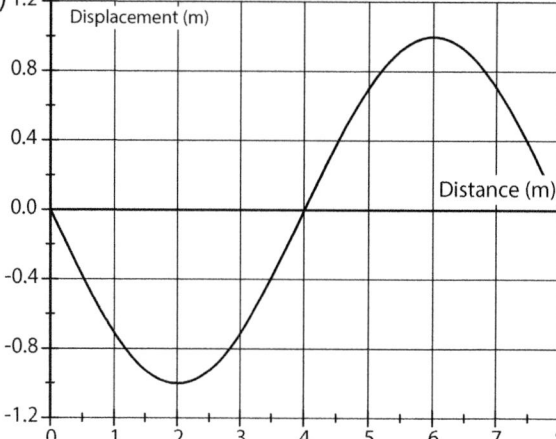

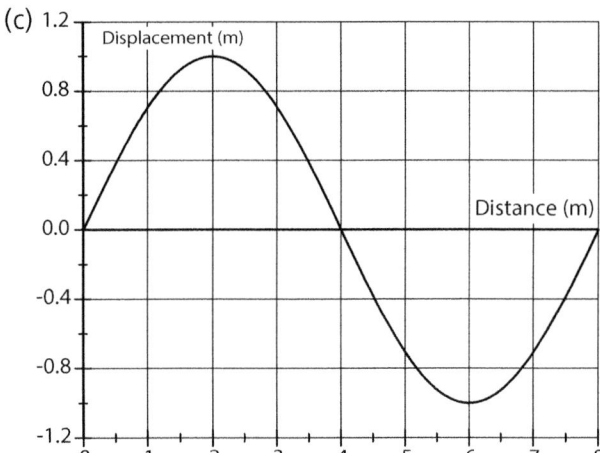

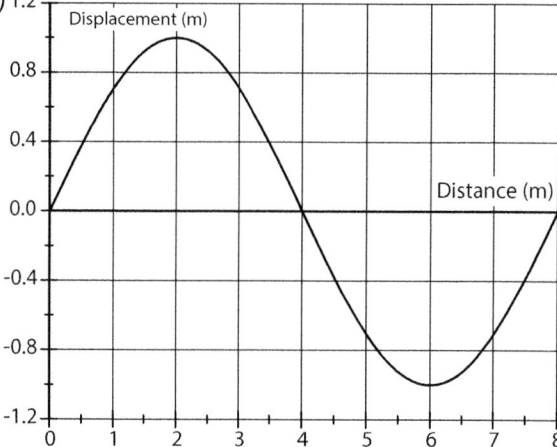

14. (a) $y = \sin 2\pi \left(\dfrac{t}{T} - \dfrac{x}{\lambda} \right)$ (b) $y = \sin \omega \left(t - \dfrac{x}{v} \right)$

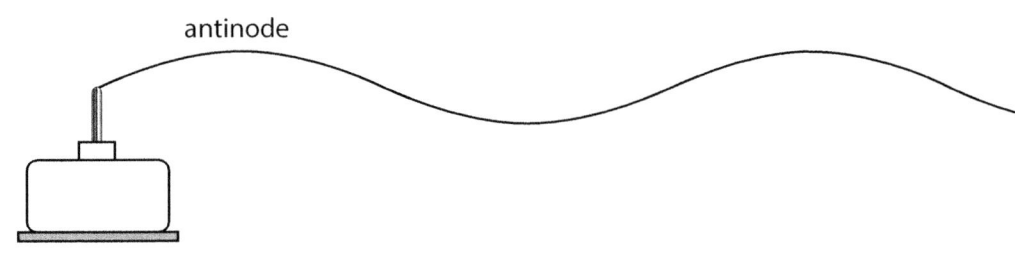

15. (a) [Diagram of standing wave on string with antinode labelled, vibrator on left, fixed end on right]

    (b) It travels in the opposite direction: $y = \sin 2\pi \left(ft + \dfrac{x}{\lambda} \right)$

    (c) The distance from node to neighbouring node is **half** a wavelength. So one wavelength is the distance from first node to third node etc.

    (d) 0.72m is two complete wavelengths, so wavelength is 0.36m.

    $v = f\lambda = 18 \times 0.36 = 6.48 \text{m s}^{-1}$

16. (a) The Principle of Superposition (you add the individual displacements to get the total).

    (b) (i) Graph 'C' (two lots of the same thing give you twice the thing)

    (ii) Graph 'D'.

    (iii) Graph 'B' (three lots of the same thing give you thrice the thing)

    (iv) Graph 'A'.

137

17. (a) The oscilloscope's timebase is switched off so a vertical line indicates the signal strength. As the detector is moved from one generator towards the other, the height of the line increases to a maximum then decreases to a minimum, then repeats the pattern.

(b) Nodes are half a wavelength apart so wavelength is 8cm. The microwaves travel at (nearly) the speed of light in a vacuum, so:

$$v = f\lambda \quad \Rightarrow \quad f = \frac{v}{\lambda} = \frac{3 \times 10^8}{0.08} = 3.73 \times 10^9 \, Hz = 3.73 \, GHz$$

The idealised signal looks like this (antinodes are the peaks):

Oscilloscope voltage

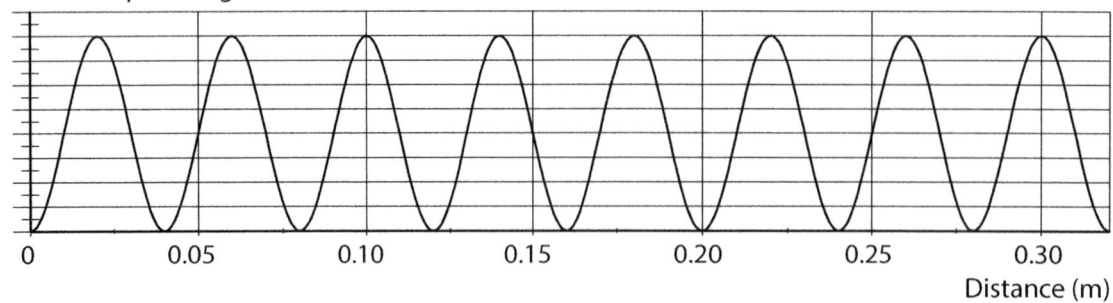

[Graph showing sinusoidal oscillations from 0 to 0.30 m on Distance axis]

The above display assumes equal amplitudes from both waves at all positions between them. In reality, the amplitude from each generator decreases with the distance from the generator. As a result, the nodes don't drop to zero, and the antinode peaks don't keep the same height.

Unit 2 Interference by Division of the Amplitude.....Answers

1. The two beams must have a constant phase difference between them and to ensure this they must have the same frequency.

2. (a) The phase difference at the meeting point will change continuously. At one instant, the waves constructively interfere, then destructively interfere the next instant, then do something in between. The frequency of light waves is so high that it changes much too rapidly for instruments to record the phase difference.

   (b) The two beams should have a constant phase difference between them (be coherent). For example a point where the combination cycles through: big crest → zero → big trough →zero etc. would yield a consistent measurement (brighter) on an instrument.

   (c) Square first then add: $1 \times 3^2 + 1 \times 5^2 = 34$

   Add first then square: $1 \times (3+5)^2 = 64$

   (d) For coherent sources, you add the amplitudes then square (like the 64 in (c)).

3. It stays constant.

4. (a) Wavelength, wavespeed and direction.

   (b) Geometric path length is the distance along the ray measured using a ruler.

   Optical path length is the geometric path length multiplied by the refractive index of the medium.

   (c) (A) Geometric Path = 26cm Optical Path = 26cm

   (B) Geometric Path = 26cm Optical Path = (4 x 1 + 8 x 1.5 + 14 x 1) = 30cm

   (C) Geometric Path = 26cm Optical Path = (10 x 1 + 8 x 1.5 + 8 x 1) = 30cm

   (Why must the answers to (B) and (C) be the same?)

5. (a) There are 6 waves within the 18cm length of block giving a wavelength of 3cm. In air, the wavelength is 4.5cm, so refractive index: $n = \dfrac{\lambda_{air}}{\lambda_{block}} = \dfrac{4.5}{3} = 1.5$

    (b) Block in place gives a total of: $4 + 6 + 2 = 12$ waves

    Block removed gives $4 + (18/4.5) + 2 = 10$ waves

    So 2 waves difference means no change in phase.

    (c) Phase change of 180° means additional optical path of half a wavelength

    So with the old block, a total of 12 waves changes to a total of 12½ waves with the new block in place. This would be made up of 6 waves in the air (as before) and 6½ waves in the new 18cm block. The wavelength in the new block has to be $18/6.5 = 2.769$cm. This gives a refractive index of: $n = \dfrac{\lambda_{air}}{\lambda_{block}} = \dfrac{4.5}{2.769} = 1.625$.

6. (a) Add an additional 180° if reflecting off a material of higher refractive index.

    (b) The wavelength is 3cm in air and it travels through $18 + 18 = 36$cm of air. This is 12 complete wavelengths so there is no change in phase due to the geometric path length. It reflects off a material of higher refractive index, so gets an additional 180°. Total phase difference is 180°.

7. (a) Interference by division of the amplitude.

    (b) **P to A:** 8cm   **P to Q to A':** $4 \times 1.375 + 4 \times 1.375 + 5 = 16$cm.

    This is an optical path difference of 8cm which is exactly 4 wavelengths. There is a 180° phase shift added at **both** reflecting surfaces at points 'P' and 'Q', so the phase difference is unaffected. The result is that the two rays are in phase as they cross line AA'.

    (c) As in part (b) the optical path difference is 4 wavelengths. The phase shift of 180° occurs at the air/film reflection 'P', but not 'Q'. Hence the two rays are 180° out of phase along BB'.

    (d) Consider the incident beam striking point 'P' at right angles to the thin film (angle of incidence is zero). Calculate the thickness of the film using trigonometry: $4\cos 30° = 3.464$cm. For normal incidence, both rays emerge from the same point, so the optical path difference is just through the film and straight back up: $2nt = 2 \times 1.375 \times 3.464 = 9.53$cm. Previously, when crossing the line AA', the optical path difference was 8cm (part (b), above). It is now 9.53cm, so has increased.

8. (a) The equation for destructive interference contains the wavelength so it only works (exactly) for that wavelength. If the wavelength is slightly different, cancellation of the beams due to destructive interference is not complete.

    Using white light gives cancellation of one region of colour. Most thin film thicknesses are calculated to give destructive interference in the middle of the visible spectrum. This allows some reflected light from the blue and red ends of the spectrum (resulting in a purple caste).

    (b) It has no effect. The 'n' in the formula is for the thin film, not the glass.

9. For destructive interference, the phase difference of the emerging beams should be 180°.

    This is satisfied by: $2nt = \dfrac{1}{2}\lambda \Rightarrow t = \dfrac{\lambda}{4n} = \dfrac{600 \times 10^{-9}}{4 \times 1.35} = 1.1 \times 10^{-7}$m.

    What about any phase shifts on reflection? It doesn't alter the answer in this example since both reflections take place against surfaces of higher refractive index (so they both get a 180° phase shift which makes no overall difference).

10. (a) The reflection from the bottom of the thin film will not have a phase shift of 180°.

(b) In question 9, we used the formula $2nt = \frac{1}{2}\lambda$. It's correct when no other phase shifts of 180° are needed. In this example, a phase shift of 180° occurs at the top surface but not at the bottom surface. So that formula would give us constructive interference. The left hand side (2nt) is the optical path difference and we require it to be one wavelength, λ. Adding in the additional 180° will then give us destructive interference:

$$2nt = \lambda \quad \Rightarrow \quad \lambda = 2 \times 1.25 \times 2 \times 10^{-7} = 5 \times 10^{-7} \text{m} = 500\text{nm}$$

(c) The new material has a higher refractive index than the thin film so gives an additional phase shift of 180° at the lower reflection. Both reflections get a phase shift of 180°, so:

$$2nt = \frac{1}{2}\lambda \quad \Rightarrow \quad t = \frac{\lambda}{4n} = \frac{500 \times 10^{-9}}{4 \times 1.25} = 1 \times 10^{-7} \text{m}$$

11. (a) Interference by division of the wavefront and interference by division of the amplitude

 (b) Left diagram: division of amplitude.   Right diagram: division of wavefront.

 (c) (i) Point source. (ii) Extended source (can also use a 'point' source).

  (iii) A pinhole. Place it between the extended source and the double slit. The pinhole will act like a point source.

12. The frequency is the same in air and in the calcite so: $T = \frac{1}{f} = \frac{1}{5.09 \times 10^{14}} = 1.96 \times 10^{-15}$ s.

 Calculate the wavelength in air, then use the refractive index to calculate the wavelength in calcite:

$$\lambda_{air} = \frac{v_{air}}{f} = \frac{3 \times 10^8}{5.09 \times 10^{14}} = 5.89 \times 10^{-7} \text{m} \qquad n = \frac{\lambda_{air}}{\lambda_{calcite}} \Rightarrow \lambda_{calcite} = \frac{5.89 \times 10^{-7}}{1.658} = 3.55 \times 10^{-7} \text{m}$$

13. (a) Interference by division of the amplitude.

 (b) The upper surface of the flat glass plate, and internally off the lower surface of the lens.

 (c) The fringes are circles centred on the point of contact of the two glass surfaces. The circles get closer together as you go out. If the convex surface was flat instead of curved, the fringes would be evenly spaced (you don't have to go so far out to get an additional optical path of one wavelength due to the glass curving up). At the point of contact at the centre you would have no geometric path difference and expect a bright spot but the 180° phase shift at the lower air to glass surface makes it a dark spot.

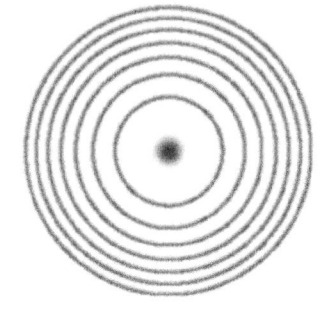

14. (a) A semi-silvered mirror is constructed to allow half a beam to be reflected and half to be transmitted. The incident rays reflect off the mirror (which is set at 45°) to strike glass slide at 90°. The rays reflected from the slides pass up through the semi-silvered mirror into microscope.

 (b) (i) 10 fringe spacings give 4.7mm, so fringe spacing is 0.47mm = 4.7 x 10⁻⁴m.

  (ii) $\tan\alpha = \frac{\lambda}{2nd} = \frac{5.89 \times 10^{-7}}{2 \times 1.0 \times 4.7 \times 10^{-4}} \Rightarrow \alpha = 6.26 \times 10^{-4}$ radians = 0.036°

  (iii) The glass slide is 8cm long, so hair diameter is: $0.08 \times \tan\alpha = 5 \times 10^{-5}$ m

 (c) Fringe spacing $d = \frac{\lambda}{2n\tan\alpha}$, so increasing 'n' decreases the fringe spacing.

15. Optical Path Length = (1 × 5) + (1.5 × 4) + (1.3 × 10) + (2.4 × 6) + (1 × 4) = 42.4cm. Number of waves is 42.4cm ÷ 3cm = 14.133 waves = 14 waves + 0.1333 waves. One wave is 360°, so 0.1333 wave is 48°. Note that there are no 180° phase shifts for transmissions, just for some reflections.

Unit 2 Interference by Division of the Wavefront.....Answers

1. A point source. The two small gaps have to act as sources in phase. The rays behind the gaps have to reach them with a constant phase relation (eg. always in phase). You achieve this from a point source since the two rays came from the same place. An extended source like a fluorescent strip light emits light rays from its entire length, all of them out of phase (the light reaching the gaps will not be coherent).

2. (a) Both rays come from the same point (the source), so the optical path difference will be constant. If the point source was the same distance to each slit (midway between the slits and at right angles to the barrier), the phase difference at the slits would be zero.

   (b) (i) Q is the first bright fringe out from the centre so there must be an optical path difference of one wavelength from the two sources.

   (ii) P is the second bright fringe out so has an optical path difference of two wavelengths from the two sources.

   (c) Point 'O' is equidistant from the two sources. There is an optical path difference of zero, so constructive interference occurs.

   (d) Simplest way is to put in two numbers. For example n = 5 and n = 6. This gives:

   $$6\lambda = \frac{x_6 d}{D} \Rightarrow x_6 = \frac{6\lambda D}{d} \qquad 5\lambda = \frac{x_5 d}{D} \Rightarrow x_5 = \frac{5\lambda D}{d}$$

   The fringe separation is: $\Delta x = (x_6 - x_5) = \left(\frac{6\lambda D}{d} - \frac{5\lambda D}{d}\right) = \frac{\lambda D}{d}$. This works for any neighbouring pair.

   (e) Typical numbers in a real experiment are: screen distance D of 1m to 2m, and fringe separation Δx of a few millimetres. So the angles up to 'P' and 'Q' should be much smaller.

3. (a) 20 fringe spacings is a distance of 65mm, so Δx = 3.25mm = 3.25 × 10⁻³m.

   (b) $\Delta x = \frac{\lambda D}{d} \Rightarrow d = \frac{\lambda D}{\Delta x} = \frac{624 \times 10^{-9} \times 1.5}{3.25 \times 10^{-3}} = 2.88 \times 10^{-4}\,\text{m}$ (= 0.288mm)

4. (a) 'n' is the fringe number (n = 0 is the centre fringe).

   'λ' is the wavelength.

   'x' is the distance to the nᵗʰ fringe measured from the centre.

   'Δx' is the distance between neighbouring fringes on the screen.

   'd' is the separation of the slits.

   'D' is the distance between the slits and the screen.

   (b) The fringe separation Δx should be much less than the screen distance 'D'.

   (c) Using the equation with the 'n' in it requires you to locate the centre fringe, and they all look much the same around the middle. Using the Δx equation allows you to take any neighbouring pair of fringes.

   (d) In most experiments, the fringe separation Δx is too small to measure directly. Measure across a large number of fringe spacings and divide by the number of spacings. Ensure that the screen is at right angles to the beam direction.

5. Fringe spacing Δx = 2.4 / 5 = 0.48cm = 4.8 × 10⁻³m   Slit separation d = 4.6 × 10⁻⁴m   D = 4.09m

   $$\Delta x = \frac{\lambda D}{d} \Rightarrow \lambda = \frac{d \Delta x}{D} = \frac{4.6 \times 10^{-4} \times 4.8 \times 10^{-3}}{4.09} = 5.4 \times 10^{-7}\,\text{m} \quad (= 540\text{nm})$$

6. (a) From the equation: $n\lambda = \dfrac{xd}{D} \Rightarrow x = \dfrac{n\lambda D}{d} \Rightarrow x \propto D$, the fringe distance will double.

   (b) From the equation: $n\lambda = \dfrac{xd}{D} \Rightarrow x = \dfrac{n\lambda D}{d}$. The only variable left to adjust is the slit separation 'd'. It's inversely proportional to the fringe distance. Halving the fringe distance from 1.76cm to 0.88cm requires doubling the slit separation.

   (c) The question gives us the distance 'x' to the third bright fringe (1.76cm) and the wavelength 'λ' of the light (620nm). We aren't given the screen distance 'D', or the slit separation 'd'.
   The appropriate formula is: $n\lambda = \dfrac{xd}{D}$. The 'D' and 'd' stay constant in the experiment, so rewrite the formula as: $\dfrac{n\lambda}{x} = \dfrac{d}{D}$, and equate the two different wavelengths:

   $$\dfrac{d}{D} = \dfrac{n\lambda_{red}}{x_{red}} = \dfrac{n\lambda_{blue}}{x_{blue}} \Rightarrow \dfrac{3 \times 620 \times 10^{-9}}{1.76 \times 10^{-2}} = \dfrac{3 \times 440 \times 10^{-9}}{x_{blue}} \Rightarrow x_{blue} = 1.25 \times 10^{-2}\,\text{m}$$

   From the formula, you could have stated that the distance to the fringe, 'x' is proportional to the wavelength 'λ' and calculated: 1.76×440÷620.

7. (a) The centre fringe is bright since the optical path length is the same from both slits.

   (b) $x = \dfrac{n\lambda D}{d} = \dfrac{1 \times 420 \times 10^{-9} \times 2.4}{1.5 \times 10^{-4}} = 6.7 \times 10^{-3}\,\text{m}$

   (c) $x = \dfrac{n\lambda D}{d} = \dfrac{1 \times 630 \times 10^{-9} \times 2.4}{1.5 \times 10^{-4}} = 10.1 \times 10^{-3}\,\text{m}$

   (d) The position of the fringe depends on the wavelength, so a range of wavelengths will spread out the fringe on the screen. The blue wavelengths will be at the smaller angle and the red wavelengths will be at the greater angle (like a little spectrum).

   (e) The red area from the 'n' fringe is far enough out to reach the blue area of the (n+1) fringe:

   $$x_{n+1}^{420nm} = \dfrac{(n+1)\lambda_{420}D}{d} \qquad x_n^{630nm} = \dfrac{n\lambda_{630}D}{d} \Rightarrow \dfrac{(n+1)\lambda_{420}D}{d} = \dfrac{n\lambda_{630}D}{d}$$

   Simplify by cancelling the 'D' and 'd', put in the wavelengths and solve for n. It's n = 2.

   It's independent of 'D' and 'd' since they both cancelled in the equation!

8. (a) With microwaves, the fringe spacing is much larger compared with the slit-detector distance. With light, the first fringe will make an angle of much less than one degree.

   The barrier with the two gaps has to be a conductor to prevent microwaves passing straight through it (what's transparent to the electromagnetic spectrum depends on the wavelength).

   The much bigger angles means you can't assume the previous formulas will be accurate. In the example below, the accurate answers are: 17.6cm and 40.7cm.

   (b) Position 'B' is the first bright fringe n = 1: $x = \dfrac{n\lambda D}{d} = \dfrac{1 \times 2.8 \times 60}{10} = 16.8\,\text{cm}$

   Position 'A' is the second bright fringe n = 2: $x = \dfrac{n\lambda D}{d} = \dfrac{2 \times 2.8 \times 60}{10} = 33.6\,\text{cm}$

9. (a) The refracted rays seem to be coming from these points, so act like a pair of 'slits'

   (b) The region of overlap of the two light beams where interference occurs.

   (c) Screen at far right side. You see a series of straight bright/dark fringes in the shaded region.

Unit 2 Polarisation.....Answers

1. (a) The vibrations in a transverse wave have the freedom to vibrate in any direction on a two dimensional plane while the vibrations in a longitudinal wave can only vibrate in one direction.

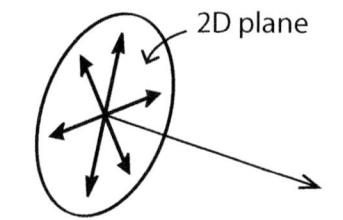

   (b) Air molecules.

   (c) The displacement from the middle is the electric field strength 'E'.

2. (a) Diagram 1 shows polarised rays since the vibrations are all in the same direction.

   Diagram 2 shows unpolarised rays since the vibration directions are randomly aligned.

   (b) **Set (A)** is polarised since the arrows are all parallel to each other. They are not coherent since they are out of step and reach a peak at different times.

   Set (B) is polarised / coherent.

   Set (C) is unpolarised / not coherent.

   Set (D) is unpolarised / coherent.

   (c) Set (C). Each emission of a photon of light from a filament bulb does its own thing.

3. It sounds plausible because you can do things like pass a sheet of paper between the bars if you hold it vertically, but not horizontally. But electromagnetic waves don't behave like sheets of paper. A plane polarised microwave with its electric field vector vibrating up and down will excite the free electrons in the conducting bars and have its energy removed from it. Hence, no microwave gets through. All its energy has been absorbed by the bar. Turn the microwave generator through 90° with its plane of polarisation horizontal and much less energy is extracted from it since the electrons in the bar can only move through the width of the bar (it's a resonance thing with the energy transfer inefficient for short lengths of conductor).

4. (a) The intensity is proportional to the square of the amplitude, so the intensity is 1 before entering the sheet and $\cos^2\theta$ on leaving the sheet.

   (b) Graph on right.

   (c) The intensity is proportional to the cosine squared: $\cos^2 20° = 0.883$.

   Intensity on exit is: $0.883 \times 2.75 = 2.43 \, W/m^2$

   It's the 'maximum' since some light may also be absorbed by the usual scattering process.

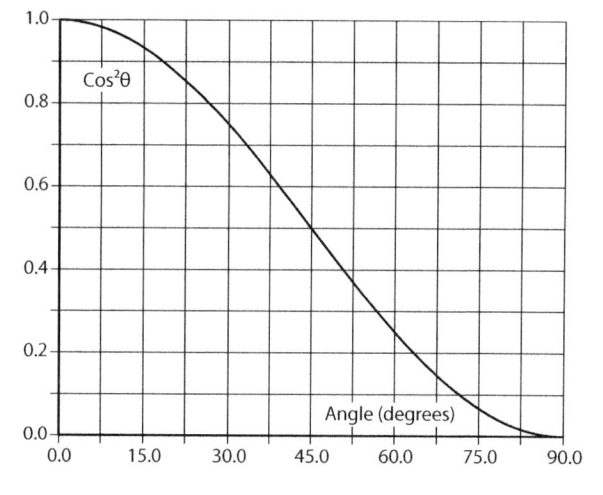

5. (a) Maximum light is transmitted at 0° and at 180°. Minimum light at 90° and 270°. The intensity transmitted follows $\cos^2\theta$.

   (b) The function of the first sheet is to make the light plane polarised for the second sheet. So it doesn't matter if the light is polarised or unpolarised on entry to the first sheet; it'll still be plane polarised for the second sheet. The assumption is that if the incident light is polarised, its plane of polarisation is lined up with the first sheet. The overall magnitude of the transmitted intensities may be different depending on whether the incident light is polarised or unpolarised (unpolarised incident light will have a high fraction of it removed by the first sheet).

   (c) $\cos^2 45° = 0.5$ so the fraction transmitted is ½.

6. (a) The sheets are identical and the polarising directions are parallel. If the intensity is reduced by the fraction 'p' on going from 'A' to 'B', it will be reduced by the same fraction 'p' on going from 'B' to 'C'. In symbols this is:

    $$I_B = pI_A \qquad I_C = pI_B \quad \Rightarrow \quad I_C = p^2 I_A \quad \Rightarrow \quad p^2 = \frac{I_C}{I_A} = \frac{0.8}{6} \quad \Rightarrow \quad p = 0.365$$

    The intensity at 'B' is: $I_B = pI_A = 0.365 \times 6 = 2.19 \, W/m^2$

    Remember that this reduction in intensity isn't to do with polarisation. It's simply because polarising sheets aren't perfectly transparent.

    (b) The intensity varies as the cosine squared of the angle: $\cos^2 40° = 0.587$. The intensity when the sheets are aligned is $0.8 \, W/m^2$, so it's reduced to $0.587 \times 0.8 = 0.469 \, W/m^2$.

7. (a) Apply Snell's Law to the angles of incidence and refraction: $n = \dfrac{\sin \theta_i}{\sin \theta_r}$

    We have the special case of 90° between reflected and transmitted rays:

    $$n = \frac{\sin \theta_i}{\sin \theta_r} = \frac{\sin \theta_i}{\sin(90 - \theta_i)} = \frac{\sin \theta_i}{\cos \theta_i} = \tan \theta_i$$

    Substitute values: $1.58 = \tan \theta_i \Rightarrow \theta_i = 57.7°$

    (b) The reflected beam is plane polarised with the plane at 90° to the page. The vibration direction is in and out of the page.

    (c) If the incident beam is polarised with the vibrations along the direction of the diagram on the right, then there won't be a reflected beam.

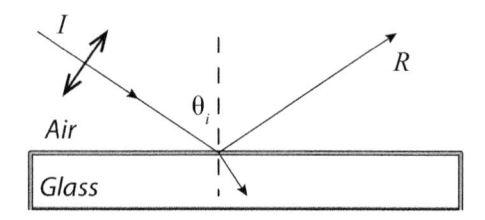

8. (a) $n = \tan \theta_i \Rightarrow 1.48 = \tan \theta_i \Rightarrow \theta_i = 55.95°$

    (b) $n = \tan \theta_i \Rightarrow 2.41 = \tan \theta_i \Rightarrow \theta_i = 67.46°$

    (c) $n = \tan \theta_i \Rightarrow 1.68 = \tan \theta_i \Rightarrow \theta_i = 59.2°$

9. With only two sheets at right angles to each other, the component transmitted to the second sheet gets absorbed by the second sheet since it is at 90° to the transmission direction.

    If you place a third sheet between the other two, then the third sheet will transmit a component at an angle to the second sheet. This angle isn't at 90° to the second sheet, so the second sheet will transmit a component of it and some light gets through. Amazing but true. Try it!

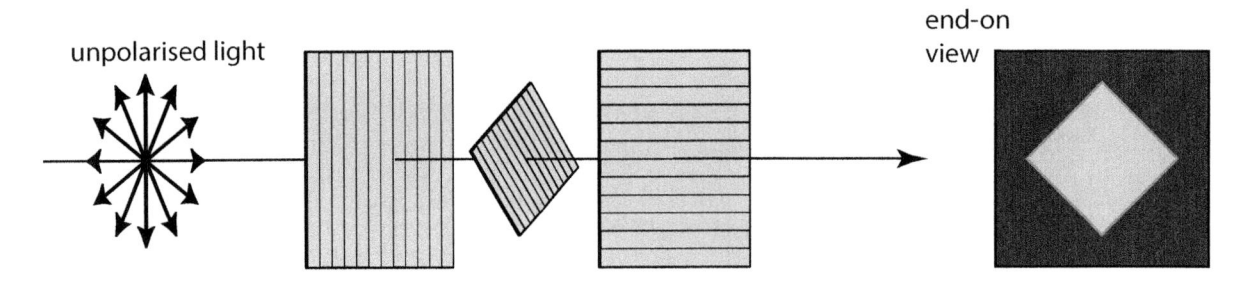

Unit 3 Electric Fields............Answers

1. (a) 9×10^9

   (b) The permittivity of free space (also known as the electric constant).

   From the definition: $F = \dfrac{1}{4\pi\varepsilon_o}\dfrac{Qq}{r^2}$ $\Rightarrow$ $\varepsilon_o = \dfrac{1}{4\pi}\dfrac{Qq}{Fr^2}$ $\Rightarrow$ Coulombs^2 Newtons^{-1} metres^{-2}

   Newtons (from F = ma) are kg m s^{-2}, so this gives ε_o in Coulomb^2 kg^{-1} m^{-3} s^2 (basic SI units).

   It's simpler in terms of derived units (that's things like joules, ohms, volts):

   Using the unit for capacitance, ε_o can be expressed simply as Farads per metre (F m^{-1})

   (c) It's all 1's: $F = \dfrac{1}{4\pi\varepsilon_o}\dfrac{Qq}{r^2} = \dfrac{1}{4\pi \times 8.854 \times 10^{-12}} \times \dfrac{1 \times 1}{1} = 9$ billion newtons.

   Lifting a mass of 1 ton at the Earth's surface requires 'only' 9800N of force, so facing north would see your right arm heading towards Russia with your left arm high over the Atlantic.

2. (a) $F = \dfrac{1}{4\pi\varepsilon_o}\dfrac{Qq}{r^2} = \dfrac{1}{4\pi \times 8.854 \times 10^{-12}} \times \dfrac{15 \times 10^{-6} \times 12 \times 10^{-6}}{0.25^2} = 25.9$N (repulsion)

   (b) $F = \dfrac{1}{4\pi\varepsilon_o}\dfrac{Qq}{r^2} = \dfrac{1}{4\pi \times 8.854 \times 10^{-12}} \times \dfrac{15 \times 10^{-6} \times 12 \times 10^{-6}}{0.5^2} = 6.48$N

   So, doubling the distance for point charges gives one quarter of the force: 25.9/4 = 6.48N.

   (c) $F = \dfrac{1}{4\pi\varepsilon_o}\dfrac{Qq}{r^2} = \dfrac{1}{4\pi \times 8.854 \times 10^{-12}} \times \dfrac{1.6 \times 10^{-19} \times 1.6 \times 10^{-19}}{(5.3 \times 10^{-11})^2} = 8.2 \times 10^{-8}$N

   (d) $F = \dfrac{1}{4\pi\varepsilon_o}\dfrac{Qq}{r^2} = 9 \times 10^9 \times \dfrac{5000 \times 5000}{(3.85 \times 10^8)^2} = 1.52$N

3. (a) $W = mg = 0.002 \times 9.8 = 0.0196$N

   (b) The downwards force of gravity and the upwards electrostatic force.

   (c) $F = mg = Eq$ $\Rightarrow$ $q = \dfrac{mg}{E} = \dfrac{0.002 \times 9.8}{5 \times 10^3} = 3.92 \times 10^{-6}$C

4. (a) The charges must be of opposite sign to provide an attractive upwards force to balance the downwards force of gravity. Assume a mass of 60kg for the person. This requires an upwards force of about 600N (we can take 'g' to be 10N/kg since the mass is only an example). Your button and the harness are at about the same vertical height, so the separation of the electric charges is about 10m.

   $F = \dfrac{1}{4\pi\varepsilon_o}\dfrac{Q_1Q_2}{r^2}$ $\Rightarrow$ $600 = 9 \times 10^9 \times \dfrac{Q_1Q_2}{10^2}$ $\Rightarrow$ $Q_1Q_2 = 6.7 \times 10^{-6}$

   If the charges were of equal magnitude (take the square root) we get 2.6×10^{-3}C each charge.

   (b) You start to spin and topple. The weight of the potatoes provides a torque.

   (c) The upwards attractive force becomes a repulsive force pushing you down. It would feel as if you have twice your weight (with the numbers we've used, you'd be a 60kg person with an apparent weight of 1200N). As they say on the sports channels, 'questions would be asked about his legs'.

5. An inverse square law is used with point electric charges (or point masses as in Newton's Law of Gravitation). It means that if you double the distance 'r', you quarter the force 'F' between them. It's a consequence of us living in a three dimensional space.

6. (a) Diagram on the right. By 'tension', we mean the force of the string on the sphere (tension really describes the force on the molecules within the string).

   (b) From the diagram, the tension arrow heads off at about the 1 o'clock direction. Resolve this into a vertical component going in the 12 o'clock direction (which must equal the weight mg), and a horizontal component heading at 3 o'clock. Using simple trig. the horizontal component is $mg\tan\theta$.

   (c) The sphere is stationary, so the vertical forces are balanced and the horizontal forces are balanced. Taking the horizontal forces, we have:

   $$mg\tan\theta = \frac{1}{4\pi\varepsilon_o}\frac{q^2}{r^2} \Rightarrow r^2 = \frac{1}{4\pi\varepsilon_o}\frac{q^2}{mg\tan\theta} = 9\times10^9 \times \frac{(0.25\times10^{-6})^2}{5\times10^{-3}\times9.8\times\tan20°} = 0.0315\,\text{m}^2$$

   Take the square root: $r = 0.178\,\text{m}$

7. Write down the force expressions for the two cases then put them equal:

   $$F_{Qq} = \frac{1}{4\pi\varepsilon_o}\frac{Qq}{0.8^2} \qquad F_{3Q5q} = \frac{1}{4\pi\varepsilon_o}\frac{(3Q)(5q)}{r^2} \qquad \frac{1}{4\pi\varepsilon_o}\frac{Qq}{0.8^2} = \frac{1}{4\pi\varepsilon_o}\frac{(3Q)(5q)}{r^2} \Rightarrow r = 3.1\,\text{m}$$

8. It's called the electric field. Does it answer the question as to how it's done? The electric field is the effect on the surrounding space of placing an electric charge within it. If you think of a vacuum as 'nothing at all' then it's still a mystery and all you're doing is modelling the effect (like a wax model at Madame Tussauds models a real person; it looks good, but....). If you think of a vacuum as 'nothing that shows up on our instruments', then the electric charge can influence the behaviour of what's there. This is the view of quantum mechanics where a vacuum is turning out to be more complicated than was once thought.

9. (a) The direction of the arrow (out from the positive charge and into the negative charge).

   (b) • Direction of arrows as above.
       • Lines cannot cross each other (if they did, a charge placed there would have a choice of routes).
       • Lines cannot come to a stop. They must start on a positive charge and end on a negative charge.

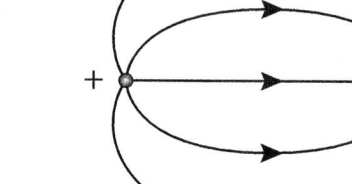

   (c) Diagram on the right.

10. (a) Positive (since arrows come out).

    (b) The charges try to get as far away as they can from each other due to electrostatic repulsuion.

    (c) In practice, all charges distort the field pattern. A test charge is an ideal charge (a physicist's dream charge) which doesn't do this, so you can draw it without altering the pattern.

    (d) Use $F = Eq$ where 'F' is the force in newtons and 'q' is the charge in coulombs.

    (e) The spacing of the lines is a measure of the electric field strength, so it's **not** uniform.

    (f) $E = \dfrac{F}{q} = \dfrac{180}{0.02} = 9000\,\text{N C}^{-1}$

11. **In common**: infinite range and can operate in a vacuum.

    Different: vastly different in strength, one type of mass / two types of charge.

146

12. (a) Radial.
    (b) No. The separation of the lines indicates the electric field strength. These lines get further apart and hence the electric field strength decreases.
    (c) $E = \dfrac{1}{4\pi\varepsilon_o}\dfrac{Q}{r^2}$
    (d) It reduces to one quarter of its initial value due to the inverse square law.
    (e) It doubles since the field strength 'E' is proportional to the charge 'Q'.

13. (a) $F = qE \Rightarrow 24 = 0.2 \times E \Rightarrow E = 120\,\text{N C}^{-1}$
    (b) The equation in part (a) works for any field. This alternative only works for uniform fields:
    $E = \dfrac{V}{d} = \dfrac{6}{0.05} = 120\,\text{Vm}^{-1}$

14. Physicist's way: $E = \dfrac{1}{4\pi\varepsilon_o}\dfrac{Q}{r^2} = 9\times 10^9 \times \dfrac{4\times 10^{-3}}{25^2} = 57600\,\text{N C}^{-1}$

    Pedant's way: $E = \dfrac{1}{4\pi\varepsilon_o}\dfrac{Q}{r^2} = \dfrac{1}{4\pi \times 8.854\times 10^{-12}} \times \dfrac{4\times 10^{-3}}{25^2} = 57600\,\text{N C}^{-1}$

15. (a) The electric field must be uniform (field lines all parallel with the same distance apart)
    (b) This must be a radial field since the electric field strength decreases according to the inverse square law (doubling the distance quarters the result). The reference position must be at the position of the point charge responsible for producing the field.

16. At 'A' Due to Q1: $E = \dfrac{1}{4\pi\varepsilon_o}\dfrac{Q}{r^2} = 9\times 10^9 \times \dfrac{5\times 10^{-4}}{8^2} = 7.03\times 10^4\,\text{N C}^{-1}$ ←

    Due to Q2: $E = \dfrac{1}{4\pi\varepsilon_o}\dfrac{Q}{r^2} = 9\times 10^9 \times \dfrac{5\times 10^{-4}}{36^2} = 3.47\times 10^3\,\text{N C}^{-1}$ ←

    Total electric field strength: $E = 7.38 \times 10^4$ N C^{-1} to the left.

    At 'B' $E = 0$ (since the fields are equal in magnitude but opposite in direction, and so cancel).

    At 'C' Due to Q1: $E = \dfrac{1}{4\pi\varepsilon_o}\dfrac{Q}{r^2} = 9\times 10^9 \times \dfrac{5\times 10^{-4}}{48^2} = 1.95\times 10^3\,\text{N C}^{-1}$ →

    Due to Q2: $E = \dfrac{1}{4\pi\varepsilon_o}\dfrac{Q}{r^2} = 9\times 10^9 \times \dfrac{5\times 10^{-4}}{20^2} = 1.125\times 10^4\,\text{N C}^{-1}$ →

    Total electric field strength: $E = 1.32 \times 10^4$ N C^{-1} to the right.

17. (a) Taking them as point objects allows us to use the formula: $E = \dfrac{1}{4\pi\varepsilon_o}\dfrac{Q}{r^2}$. This is simple to use. If the charges had a size, you'd have to use calculus and perform difficult integrations to sum the overall effect of the distributed charges.
    (b) At 'A'

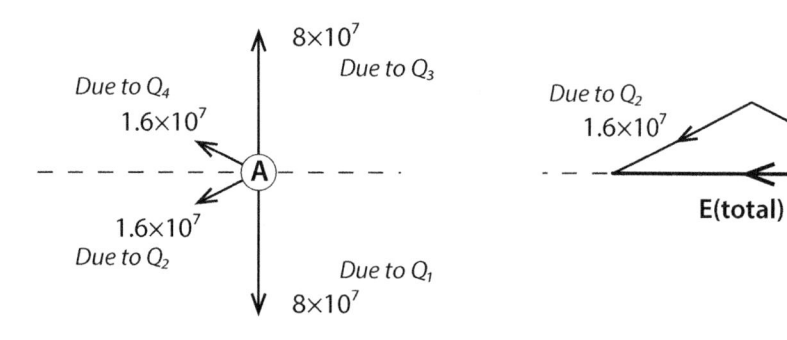

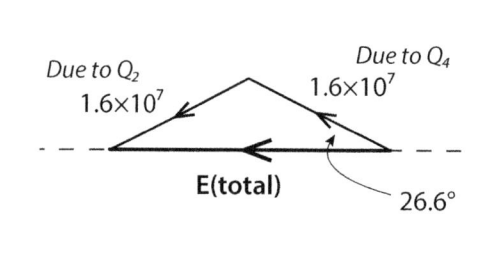

    Due to Q4: 1.6×10^7
    Due to Q3: 8×10^7
    Due to Q2: 1.6×10^7
    Due to Q1: 8×10^7

    Due to Q2: 1.6×10^7
    Due to Q4: 1.6×10^7
    E(total) at $26.6°$

147

The angle of 26.6° comes from the trigonometry of the square (tan⁻¹ 15/30), and the resultant is calculated using the cosine rule: $a^2 = b^2 + c^2 - 2bc \cos A$.

$$E_{res}^2 = (1.6 \times 10^7)^2 + (1.6 \times 10^7)^2 - 2 \times 1.6 \times 10^7 \times 1.6 \times 10^7 \times \cos 126.8 \quad \Rightarrow \quad E_{res} = 2.86 \times 10^7 \, \text{NC}^{-1}$$

The direction is to the left.

(c) At 'B'

Point 'B' is equidistant from all four charges. The contributions all cancel to give an electric field strength of zero.

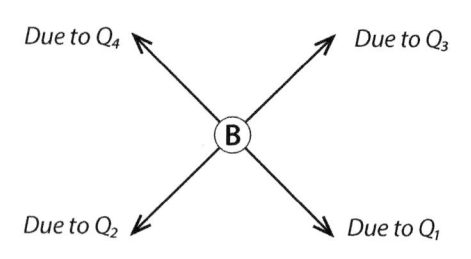

(d) Contributions due to Q_2 and Q_3 cancel as before, but the contributions due to Q_1 and Q_4 now point in the same direction on a bearing of 135°. The resultant electric field strength is:

$$E = 2 \times \frac{1}{4\pi\varepsilon_o} \frac{Q}{r^2} = 2 \times 9 \times 10^9 \times \frac{2 \times 10^{-4}}{(0.15\sqrt{2})^2} = 8 \times 10^7 \, \text{NC}^{-1}$$

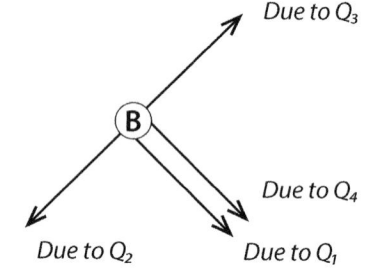

(e) Assuming all charges are non-zero and equal in magnitude, the top two charges Q_1 and Q_2 should be negative and the bottom two charges Q_3 and Q_4 should be positive.

18. (a) The electric field is uniform with the electric field lines equally spaced ('E' is constant).

(b) There are no horizontal forces so the horizontal component of the velocity is constant:

$$t = \frac{S_{hor}}{v_{hor}} = \frac{0.08}{1.68 \times 10^7} = 4.76 \times 10^{-9} \, \text{s}$$

(c) $E = \dfrac{V}{d} = \dfrac{500}{0.05} = 10000 \, \text{V m}^{-1} \quad (= 10000 \, \text{NC}^{-1})$

(d) The electron experiences a constant force of $F = Eq$ towards the positive plate. Equate this with Newton's 2nd Law to obtain the upwards acceleration (gravity can be neglected):

$$F = ma = Eq \quad \Rightarrow \quad a = \frac{Eq}{m} = \frac{10000 \times 1.6 \times 10^{-19}}{9.1 \times 10^{-31}} = 1.76 \times 10^{15} \, \text{ms}^{-2}$$

The acceleration is constant, so the vertical displacement is given by:

$$s_{vert} = ut + \frac{1}{2}at^2 = 0 + \frac{1}{2} \times 1.76 \times 10^{15} \times (4.76 \times 10^{-9})^2 = 0.02 \, \text{m}$$

The plates are 5cm apart and the electron was aimed along the mid-point of the plates, so it emerges ½cm below the top right corner.

Unit 3 Electrostatic Potential............Answers

1. (a) The charge is positive since the arrows are pointing outwards from it.

(b) $|E| = \dfrac{1}{4\pi\varepsilon_o} \dfrac{Q}{r^2} = 9 \times 10^9 \times \dfrac{4 \times 10^{-5}}{0.28^2} = 4.59 \times 10^6 \, \text{NC}^{-1} \quad V = \dfrac{1}{4\pi\varepsilon_o} \dfrac{Q}{r} = 9 \times 10^9 \times \dfrac{4 \times 10^{-5}}{0.28} = 1.29 \times 10^6 \, \text{V}$

(c) Magnitudes stay the same. The electrostatic potential changes sign to -1.29 × 10⁶ volts. The electric field strength changes direction.

(d) Anywhere on the surface of the sphere of radius 28cm centred on the electric charge 'Q'.

2. You don't have any directions to worry about. So no sine rule or cosine rule to calculate resultants; just adding and subtracting simple numbers.

3. (a) Electrostatic potential in volts. Energy in joules.

   (b) At 'A': $V = \frac{1}{4\pi\varepsilon_o}\frac{Q}{r} = 9\times10^9 \times \frac{8\times10^{-4}}{40} = +1.8\times10^5$ volts

   At 'B': $V = \frac{1}{4\pi\varepsilon_o}\frac{Q}{r} = 9\times10^9 \times \frac{8\times10^{-4}}{60} = +1.2\times10^5$ volts

   Electrostatic potential difference = 1.8 x 10⁵ – 1.2 x 10⁵ = 60,000 volts.

   (c) Asking for the energy required is the same as asking for the Work Done in moving from 'B' to 'A'. From Higher Physics, Work Done = Vq where 'V' is the potential difference and 'q' is the electric charge moved. This gives 60,000 × 3 × 10⁻⁶ = +0.18J.

   When calculating a difference in physics, you always take it this way around: (final - initial) value. In our example (from 'B' to 'A'), this makes the potential difference positive. The charge moved is positive so the answer for the work done is positive. This means that external forces (that's you) have to do work **on** the system (put in energy and increase the internal energy of the system).

4. (a)

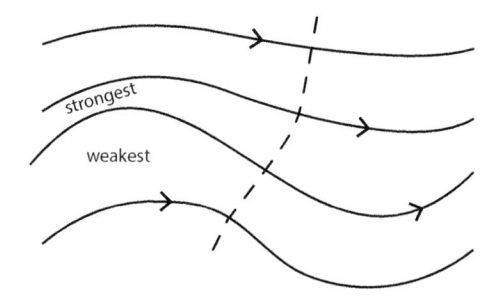

   (b) It's called an equipotential line. The electrostatic potential has a constant value all along the dotted line eg. +82volts. No work is done in moving an electric charge between any two points on the dotted line regardless of the route taken (you can go via. Neptune if you feel so inclined, though gravity would have to be considered).

   (c) No arrow on the dotted line. It represents a scalar quantity (electrostatic potential).

   (d) None.

5. The shape is the surface of a sphere. The potential for a point charge $V = \frac{1}{4\pi\varepsilon_o}\frac{Q}{r}$ only depends upon the distance 'r' and does not contain angles (like the (r,θ,ϕ) of spherical co-ordinates).

6. (a)

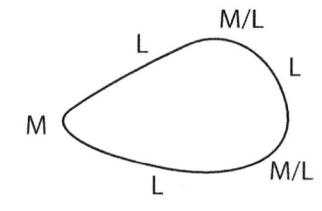

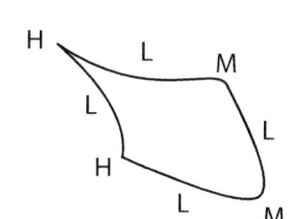

   (b) Electric field 'E' inside is zero. Electrostatic potential 'V' inside is +350volts.

7. (a)

r(m)	±0.2	±0.4	±0.6	±0.8	±1.0	±1.2	±1.4
V(volts)	90000	45000	30000	22500	18000	15000	12857

(b)

[Graph: Potential (V) vs Distance (m), positive peak around 0, values from 0 to 100000, x-axis from -1.2 to 1.2]

(c)

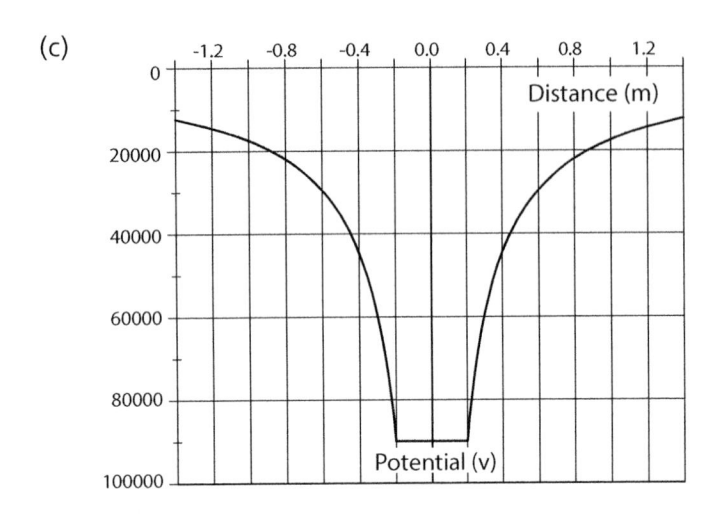

[Graph: Potential (V) vs Distance (m), negative peak (inverted) around 0, values from 0 to -100000, x-axis from -1.2 to 1.2]

8. One of the charges is larger in magnitude and positive so will produce relatively large positive numbers for the electrostatic potential. The other charge is smaller and negative so will produce smaller negative numbers. If they were equal in magnitude, there would be a zero point midway between the charges. We expect to find a zero point between them and off-centre. Remember that the electrostatic potential is a scalar so it's just the numbers with their signs that matter. Adding the individual contributions gives:

$$V_P = \frac{1}{4\pi\varepsilon_o}\frac{(+6\times10^{-6})}{x} + \frac{1}{4\pi\varepsilon_o}\frac{(-4\times10^{-6})}{(0.8-x)}$$

Now put this equal to zero and solve to give x = 0.48m.

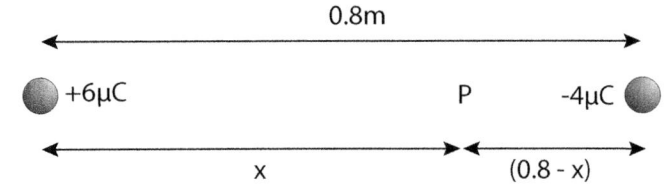

There is another solution to the right of the -4μC charge at point 'P':

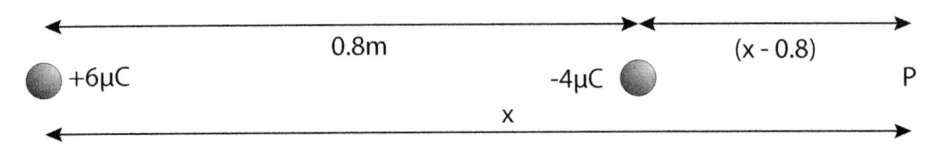

As above, just add the two individual contributions:

$$V_P = \frac{1}{4\pi\varepsilon_o}\frac{(+6\times10^{-6})}{x} + \frac{1}{4\pi\varepsilon_o}\frac{(-4\times10^{-6})}{(x-0.8)}$$

Put this equal to zero and solve for 'x' to give x = 2.4m.

Here is a graph of the electrostatic potential against distance along the straight line through the centre of the charges. The two charges are shown with the left hand charge at the origin. As calculated, the zeroes of potential are at x = 0.48m and x = 2.4m.

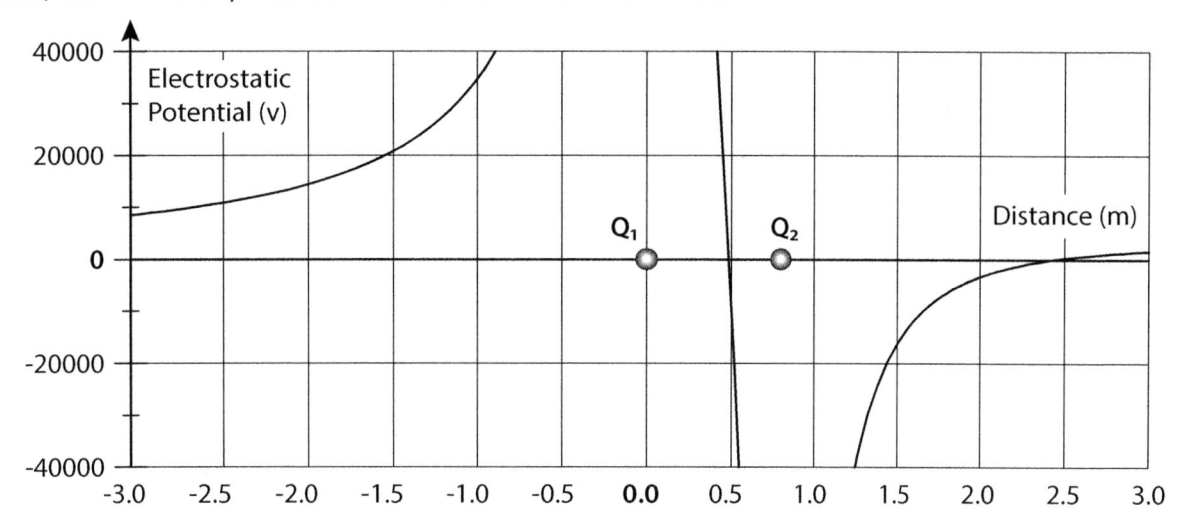

9. (a) By Pythagoras Theorem, the length of a side is 2m, point 'H' is 1m from the left pair and $\sqrt{5}$m from the right pair. Calculate each potential separately then add them to give:

At 'G': $V_G = 9\times10^9 \times \dfrac{2\times10^{-6}}{\sqrt{5}} + 9\times10^9 \times \dfrac{2\times10^{-6}}{\sqrt{5}} + 9\times10^9 \times \dfrac{(-2\times10^{-6})}{1} + 9\times10^9 \times \dfrac{(-2\times10^{-6})}{1}$

The total is: $V_G = +8050 + 8050 - 18000 - 18000 = -19900$ volts

At 'H': $V_H = 9\times10^9 \times \dfrac{2\times10^{-6}}{1} + 9\times10^9 \times \dfrac{2\times10^{-6}}{1} + 9\times10^9 \times \dfrac{(-2\times10^{-6})}{\sqrt{5}} + 9\times10^9 \times \dfrac{(-2\times10^{-6})}{\sqrt{5}}$

A total of: $V_H = +18000 + 18000 - 8050 - 8050 = +19900$ volts

(b) The charge 'q' is positive. You're moving it nearer the two positive charges and further away from the negatives, so you'll have to put **in** energy ('do work **on** the system'). The work done is given by qV where 'V' is the potential difference (final minus initial values) of +19900-(-19900). This is 39800volts. Hence work done is qV = 5 × 10⁻⁶ ×39800 = 0.2J.

(c) To the right.

10. (a) Uniform (same 'E' value everywhere, magnitude and direction).

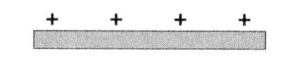

(b) Parallel to the plates (horizontal lines) and evenly spaced

(c) 0volts at bottom plate and +80volts at top plate. By proportion, the 48v line is 48/80ths of the way up. Dotted line on the diagram.

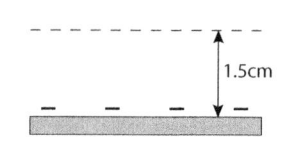

11. It is uniform at all points above it (constant magnitude and always pointing away from the plane for a positively charged surface). If you are above an infinite plane sheet of charge, it doesn't matter how far above it you are, or how far sideways you travel, you always get the same view (of a flat plane receeding to infinity in all directions).

12. $V = \dfrac{1}{4\pi\varepsilon_o}\dfrac{Q}{r}$ ⇒ $3000 = \dfrac{9\times10^9 \times 5\times10^{-6}}{r}$ ⇒ $r = 15$m

13. (a) Equipotential lines (the locus of points intersecting the equipotential surfaces). Points at the same voltage is okay by me.

(b) $V_a = \dfrac{1}{4\pi\varepsilon_o}\dfrac{Q}{r} = 9\times10^9 \times \dfrac{3\times10^{-6}}{5} = +5400$ volts

$$V_b = 9 \times 10^9 \times \frac{3 \times 10^{-6}}{10} = +2700 \text{ volts}$$

$$V_c = 9 \times 10^9 \times \frac{3 \times 10^{-6}}{15} = +1800 \text{ volts}$$

(c) $V_{surface} = 9 \times 10^9 \times \frac{3 \times 10^{-6}}{2.5} = +10800 \text{ volts}$

(d) E = 0   V = +10800 volts

(e) 90°

14. (a) You can only use Fr if the force is constant. You need to push harder as you bring them closer due to the greater force of repulsion so the integral form is necessary.

(b) $-\int_\infty^r F dr = -\int_\infty^r \frac{1}{4\pi\varepsilon_o} \frac{Qq}{r^2} dr = -\frac{1}{4\pi\varepsilon_o} Qq \int_\infty^r \frac{1}{r^2} dr = -\frac{1}{4\pi\varepsilon_o} Qq \left[-\frac{1}{r} \right]_\infty^r = \frac{1}{4\pi\varepsilon_o} Qq \left[\frac{1}{r} - \frac{1}{\infty} \right] = \frac{1}{4\pi\varepsilon_o} \frac{Qq}{r}$

(c) $E_p = \frac{1}{4\pi\varepsilon_o} \frac{Qq}{r} = 9 \times 10^9 \times \frac{28 \times 10^{-6} \times 4 \times 10^{-6}}{0.5} = 2.016 \text{ J}$ (should you round off this answer?)

15. (a) 350 volts per metre means 350 volts potential difference if they were 1m apart. By proportion, 20cm corresponds to 70 volts potential difference.

(b) $F = Eq = 350 \times 80 \times 10^{-6} = 0.028 \text{ N}$

16. (a) By proportion, 150Vm⁻¹ is 18 volts over 12cm.

(b) Constant force giving uniform acceleration.

(c) Work Done $= Vq = 18 \times 1.6 \times 10^{-19} = 2.88 \times 10^{-18} = \frac{1}{2} mv^2$ ⇒ $v = 2.51 \times 10^6 \text{ m s}^{-1}$

17. (a) **AB** and **CD** show constant velocity since there is no electric field outside the plates and hence no force on the electron.

BC has constant horizontal speed and constant vertical acceleration since the electric field is constant and points from the top plate to the bottom plate (negative charges like electrons are forced in the opposite direction to the field lines, since by definition the field line arrows show the direction of the force on a positive test charge).

(b) A parabola.

(c) (15cm, 2cm) = (0.15m, 0.02m)

(d) Use the co-ordinates at position 'C':

$y = \left(\frac{Vq}{2mv^2 d} \right) x^2$ ⇒ $0.02 = \left(\frac{200 \times 1.6 \times 10^{-19}}{2 \times 9.1 \times 10^{-31} \times v^2 \times 0.06} \right) \times 0.15^2$ ⇒ $v = 1.82 \times 10^7 \text{ m s}^{-1}$

(e) From the equation: $y = \left(\frac{Vq}{2mv^2 d} \right) x^2$ ⇒ $y \propto \frac{1}{v^2}$, doubling 'v' will quarter 'y'. It was originally at 2cm up from the centre so will change to ¼ of this, giving 0.5cm.

18. (a) The electron-volt (eV). It's the energy gained by an electron in travelling through a potential difference of 1 volt. 1eV = 1.6 × 10⁻¹⁹ J.

(b) 50mph is 50×1609m/3600s = 22.35 m s⁻¹.

$E = \frac{1}{2} mv^2 = \frac{1}{2} \times 0.4 \times 22.35^2 = 99.9 \text{ J} = \frac{99.9}{1.6 \times 10^{-19}} \text{ eV} = 6.24 \times 10^{20} \text{ eV}$

- (c) The highest energy primary cosmic rays have energies of about this magnitude.
- (d) Semiconductor processes like the mechanism for producing light in LEDs involve energies of the order of eV.

19. (a) Bombardment of the oil drops with ionising radiation.
    (b) Watch the falling charged oil drop through the microscope. Adjust the p.d. across the charged plates until the oil drop is stationary.
    (c) $m = \rho V = 860 \times \frac{4}{3}\pi r^3 = 860 \times \frac{4}{3}\pi (6 \times 10^{-7})^3 = 7.78 \times 10^{-16} \text{kg}$
    (d) Weight of the oil drop is balanced by the upwards electrostatic force:
    $mg = Eq \Rightarrow q = \frac{mg}{E} = \frac{7.78 \times 10^{-16} \times 9.8}{5280} = 1.44 \times 10^{-18} \text{C}$
    (e) Electric charge is quantised (comes in multiples of a basic amount).

20. (a) $E = \frac{V}{d} = \frac{27500}{0.08} = 343750 \text{Vm}^{-1}$

    (b) **Gamma ray:** Travels a distance of 4cm at the speed of light so hits the negative plate after a time of: $t = \frac{s}{v} = \frac{0.04}{3 \times 10^8} = 1.33 \times 10^{-10} \text{s}$

    Alpha particle: The alpha particle is accelerated to the right (electric field lines go to the right and the alpha particle has a positive charge).

    $F = Eq = ma \Rightarrow a = \frac{Eq}{m} = \frac{343750 \times 2 \times 1.6 \times 10^{-19}}{6.64 \times 10^{-27}} = 1.66 \times 10^{13} \text{m/s}^2$

    Speed at which it hits the cathode:
    $v^2 = u^2 + 2as = (1.2 \times 10^6)^2 + 2 \times 1.66 \times 10^{13} \times 0.04 \Rightarrow v = 1.66 \times 10^6 \text{m/s}$

    Time taken: $t = \frac{v-u}{a} = \frac{1.66 \times 10^6 - 1.2 \times 10^6}{1.66 \times 10^{13}} = 2.77 \times 10^{-8} \text{s}$

    Beta particle: The force on the beta particle (electron) is to the left.

    $F = Eq = ma \Rightarrow a = \frac{Eq}{m} = \frac{343750 \times 1.6 \times 10^{-19}}{9.11 \times 10^{-31}} = 6.04 \times 10^{16} \text{m/s}^2$ (will be -ve in calculations).

    Will it reach the cathode before coming to rest? Calculate the distance to come to rest:
    $v^2 = u^2 + 2as \Rightarrow 0 = (1.2 \times 10^6)^2 + 2 \times (-6.04 \times 10^{16}) \times s \Rightarrow s = 1.19 \times 10^{-5} \text{m}$

    This is short of the cathode; so it comes to rest in a time of: $t = \frac{v-u}{a} = \frac{0 - 1.2 \times 10^6}{-6.04 \times 10^{16}} = 1.99 \times 10^{-11} \text{s}$.

    It then reverses direction and hits the anode with a speed of:
    $v^2 = u^2 + 2as = (1.2 \times 10^6)^2 + 2 \times (-6.04 \times 10^{16}) \times (-0.0400119) \Rightarrow v = 6.95 \times 10^7 \text{m/s}$

    This takes a total time of: $t = \frac{v-u}{a} = \frac{-6.95 \times 10^7 - 1.2 \times 10^6}{-6.04 \times 10^{16}} = 1.17 \times 10^{-9} \text{s}$.

    (c) $v^2 = u^2 + 2as \Rightarrow a = \frac{v^2 - u^2}{2s} = \frac{0 - (1.2 \times 10^6)^2}{2 \times 0.04} = -1.8 \times 10^{13} \text{m/s}^2$

    $ma = Eq \Rightarrow E = \frac{ma}{q} = \frac{9.11 \times 10^{-31} \times 1.8 \times 10^{13}}{1.6 \times 10^{-19}} = 102.5 \text{V/m} \Rightarrow V = Ed = 102.5 \times 0.08 = 8.2 \text{V}$

21. (a) The electrostatic force of repulsion is infinite in range, so strictly speaking we should specify the speed of the alpha particle at infinity. Any closer than infinity and the nucleus slows it down. 'Very far away' is a good approximation.

(b) $E_K = \frac{1}{2}mv^2 = \frac{1}{2} \times 6.64 \times 10^{-27} \times (7.2 \times 10^5)^2 = 1.72 \times 10^{-15} \text{J} \; (=10.76 \text{keV})$

(c) It's been converted into the electrical potential energy of the system of two charges and is stored in the electric field.

(d) Equate the kinetic energy of the alpha particle with the electrostatic potential energy:

$\frac{1}{4\pi\varepsilon_o}\frac{Qq}{r} = 1.72 \times 10^{-15} \Rightarrow r = \frac{9 \times 10^9 \times (12 \times 1.6 \times 10^{-19})(2 \times 1.6 \times 10^{-19})}{1.72 \times 10^{-15}} = 3.2 \times 10^{-12} \text{m}$

(e) An assumption is that the magnesium nucleus stays fixed in position. In reality it will be slightly pushed back as the alpha particle approaches. Another assumption is that the expression for point particles was used for the electrostatic potential energy. This will be very accurate.

Unit 3 Magnetic Fields............Answers

1. James Clerk Maxwell. His synthesis of electricity and magnetism ('electromagnetism') contained within it the secrets of Einstein's Special Relativity, though nobody was clever enough at the time to spot it. Electromagnetism and the Weak Interaction were unified a century after Maxwell's work and are key ingredients of the Standard Model of particle physics SU(2)$_L$×U(1).

2. (a) The magnetic field. (b) The magnetic field becomes zero.

   (c) Special Theory of Relativity. Magnetism is a relativistic effect of moving charges.

3. (a) The 'q' in $F = qE$ is a single isolated electric charge. There are no single magnetic poles found in nature.

   (b) Magnetic Induction. Symbol 'B'.

4. (a) Hold thumb and first two fingers of **right** hand at right angles to each other. The first finger is the direction of the magnetic field arrows, the second finger is the direction that the electrons move and the thumb is the direction of the force on the electrons. Note: I use true electron flow as the current direction in a circuit; the way that the real charges move (though slowly). Some teachers use what's called conventional current. This pretends that positive charges move in a circuit (look for the direction of the current arrows, if it comes out of the long end of the battery then they are using conventional current). So my left hand grip rule and right hand rule would become the right hand grip rule and the left hand rule in the other system. (I know what you're thinking ... pass the revolver).

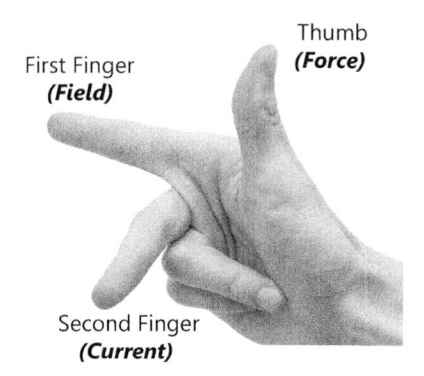

   (b) Use the rule with the **left** hand.

5. (a) (A) $F = BIl \sin\theta = 0.5 \times 4 \times 1 \times \sin 90° = 2\text{N}$ **Into** the page

   (B) $F = BIl \sin\theta = 0.2 \times 6 \times \sin 90° = 1.2\text{N}$ **Out** of the page

   (C) $F = BIl \sin\theta = 0.03 \times 0.8 \times \sin 65° = 0.0218\text{N}$ **Out** of the page

   (D) $F = BIl \sin\theta = 0.025 \times 12 \times \sin 135° = 0.212\text{N}$ **Into** the page

   (E) $F = BIl \sin\theta = 0.025 \times 12 \times \sin 45° = 0.212\text{N}$ **Out** of the page

   (F) $F = BIl \sin\theta = 0.08 \times 1.5 \times \sin 90° = 0.12\text{N}$ To **Top** of the page

   (b) The force acts on the electric charges so the wire is unnecessary.

6. (a) To the right (from north pole to south pole)

    (b) Y. This book always uses current arrows which show true electron flow. Negative electrons are repelled out of the negative side and attracted to the positive side of a battery.

    (c) **AB** up   **BC** no force   **CD** down   **AD** no force

    There isn't a force on sections BC and AD since the field lines and the current direction are parallel (so giving sin0° for BC and sin180° for AD)

    (d) For any position of the rectangle, the force on each of the long sides of the wire is always **vertical**. If the rectangle itself is in the vertical position, the vertical forces will not produce a turning effect (so no torque).

    (e) AB $l = 0.06$m $m = 9\text{g/m} \times 0.06\text{m} = 0.54$g $mr^2 = 5.4 \times 10^{-4} \times (0.02)^2 = 2.16 \times 10^{-7}$ kg m^2

    Moment of inertia is mr^2 since all parts of that section are equidistant from the spin axis.

    BC $l = 0.04$m $m = 9\text{g/m} \times 0.04\text{m} = 0.36$g $\frac{1}{12}mr^2 = \frac{1}{12} \times 3.6 \times 10^{-4} \times (0.04)^2 = 4.8 \times 10^{-8}$ kg m^2

    Moment of inertia is $\frac{1}{12}mr^2$ since this is a 4cm length spinning about its centre.

    CD $l = 0.06$m $m = 9\text{g/m} \times 0.06\text{m} = 0.54$g $mr^2 = 5.4 \times 10^{-4} \times (0.02)^2 = 2.16 \times 10^{-7}$ kg m^2

    AD $l = 0.04$m $m = 9\text{g/m} \times 0.04\text{m} = 0.36$g $\frac{1}{12}mr^2 = \frac{1}{12} \times 3.6 \times 10^{-4} \times (0.04)^2 = 4.8 \times 10^{-8}$ kg m^2

    Total Moment of Inertia is 5.28×10^{-7} kg m^2.

    (f) A force is only applied to the two long sections AB and CD:

    $F = BIl\sin\theta \quad \Rightarrow \quad (0.15 \times 0.25 \times 0.06 \times \sin 90°) + (0.15 \times 0.25 \times 0.06 \times \sin 90°) = 4.5 \times 10^{-3}$ N

    That force supplies the torque:

    $T = rF = 0.02 \times 4.5 \times 10^{-3} = 9 \times 10^{-5}$ Nm

    Giving an instantaneous angular acceleration of:

    $T = I\alpha \quad \Rightarrow \quad \alpha = \frac{T}{I} = \frac{9 \times 10^{-5}}{5.28 \times 10^{-7}} = 170\,\text{rad s}^{-2}$

7. (a) It produces a uniform magnetic field over a volume large enough to include the horizontal section of wire.

    (b) Using the righthand rule, the force on the vertical sections of wire point horizontally (the way it's set-up, the two vertical sections are pulled together). These side pieces have no downward component of force on them so don't contribute.

    (c) The difference in readings on the balance (in grams) is equivalent to a force of:

    $F = (\Delta m)g = (0.48564 - 0.48303) \times 9.8 = 0.0256$ N

    Use it to calculate the magnetic induction:

    $B = \frac{F}{Il\sin\theta} = \frac{0.0256}{8 \times 0.04 \times \sin 90} = 0.08\,\text{Tesla}$

8. (a) $F = BIl\sin\theta = 0.3 \times 2.4 \times \sin 60° = 0.624$ N   Direction is **out** of the page.

    An angle of 60° is used since it's the angle between the way the current flows and the direction of the arrows on the magnetic field lines.

    (b) Same size of force but pointing **into** the page.

155

9. (a) $\dfrac{4}{1.6\times 10^{-19}} = 2.5\times 10^{19}$ (b) $I = \dfrac{Q}{t} = \dfrac{28}{60} = 0.47\text{A}$

10. (a) **Out** of the page (use right hand rule for electrons and take the opposite for the result, **or** use your left hand).

    (b) $F = BIl\sin\theta = 2.5\times 0.006\times 1\times \sin 90° = 0.015\text{N}$ Note the connection with the LHC at Cern.

11. (a) Looking down from above the wire, the arrows go clockwise.

    (b) The magnetic field gets weaker ('B' decreases).

    (c) The permeability of free space (or permeability of the vacuum) is the usual phrase though 'magnetic constant' is becoming the accepted term. Value is $\mu_o = 4\pi \times 10^{-7}$ m kg s^{-2} A^{-2}.

    (d) $B = \dfrac{\mu_o I}{2\pi r} = \dfrac{4\pi \times 10^{-7} \times 2}{2\pi \times 0.1} = 4\times 10^{-6}\text{T}$

12. (a) $B = \dfrac{\mu_o I}{2\pi r} \Rightarrow r = \dfrac{\mu_o I}{2\pi B} = \dfrac{4\pi \times 10^{-7}\times 0.75}{2\pi \times 6\times 10^{-6}} = 0.025\text{m}$

    (b) 'B' is inversely proportional to 'r', so doubling 'r' halves the above answer to give 0.0125m.

    (c) 2×10^{-7}. The 2π crops up due to integrations along the circumference of closed circles.

13. Currents are equal in size but opposite in direction so produce magnetic fields at any point which are equal in size but opposite in direction. The fields cancel (though not quite in practice, since the wires are separated). The earth wire only carries a current if there's a fault.

14. $B = \dfrac{\mu_o I}{2\pi r} = \dfrac{4\pi \times 10^{-7}\times 3}{2\pi \times 20} = 3\times 10^{-8}\text{T}$

15. (a) $F = BIl\sin\theta = 50\times 10^{-6}\times 2\times 1\times \sin 90° = 1\times 10^{-4}\text{N}$

    (b) The direction of the Earth's field is tilted off the vertical, so it depends on the angle you hold the wire. For maximum force, the field lines should cut the wire at right angles.

16. (a) They come out of the geographic south pole and into the geographic north pole.

    (b) The North geographic pole (at the arctic) is a magnetic south pole!! It's all a question of choosing a convention and applying it consistently. Originally, the end of a magnetised compass needle which pointed towards the geographic north pole was painted red and called the *north-seeking-pole*. Over the years, this was shortened to *north pole*, so the convention is that the end of a compass needle which points to the arctic is a magnetic north pole.

    (c) Compasses for navigation are held horizontally in the hand and the field lines are pointing almost vertically downwards near the poles. The horizontal component of the field is the part which makes the needle rotate and it's very small.

17. $B = \dfrac{\mu_o I}{2\pi r} = \dfrac{4\pi \times 10^{-7}\times 250}{2\pi \times 10} = 5\times 10^{-6}\text{T} \equiv 5\mu\text{T}$ This is about one-tenth of the Earth's field at the UK.

    The direction of the field vertically below the cable is horizontal and at right angles to the cable. Real transmission lines carry several conductors with the currents out of phase with each other, and the field direction (the tip of the vector) traces out an ellipse. The electric field strengths are typically several thousand volts per metre.

18. (a) At 'P', into page. At 'Q', out of page.

    (b) A magnetic field coming out of the page intersecting a current flowing to the top of the page will produce a force (on wire 'B') to the left (towards wire 'A').

(c) Wire 'B' would be repelled to the right.

(d) $F = \dfrac{\mu_o I_1 I_2 l \sin\theta}{2\pi r} = \dfrac{4\pi \times 10^{-7} \times 2.5 \times 1.5 \times 1 \times \sin 90°}{2\pi \times 0.08} = 9.4 \times 10^{-6}\,N$

19. $F = \dfrac{\mu_o I_1 I_2 l \sin\theta}{2\pi r} = \dfrac{4\pi \times 10^{-7} \times 3 \times 5 \times 0.25 \times \sin 90°}{2\pi \times 0.15} = 5 \times 10^{-6}\,N$ Towards the other wire.

20. (a) In both cases, it's to the right. Just use your right hand rule for the electrons (first finger into the page, second finger pointing to the top of the page for the right hand diagram, and your thumb will be pointing to the right). Use your left hand for the positive holes, and your thumb will also point to the right.

(b) No, polarity is opposite. For holes the positive charge builds up on the right. For electrons the negative charge builds up on the right. Connect a voltmeter across the opposite faces (left-right on the diagrams). The sign of the voltmeter reading will tell you if the dominant process is hole movement or electron movement.

21. (a) A magnetic domain is a small volume within a sample of a ferromagnetic material where the north-south directions of all the millions of atomic dipoles point in the same direction. It is caused by the spin-spin interaction of neighbouring unpaired electrons.

(b) Each domain starts out with its own magnetic alignment. As the applied magnetic field from the coil is increased, the domain directions are gradually forced into alignment with the applied magnetic field (along the central axis of the coil). Physics-speak would describe this as a torque applied to each dipole. A sufficiently strong applied field will result in all the domains pointing along the coil axis. A further increase in the current will have no additional effect (the magnetisation of the sample is described as being *saturated*).

(c) Yes, it's different from what it was at the start. Refer to the diagram. The unmagnetised sample starts at 'A' and the field from the coil is applied. This takes the magnetic state of the sample to point 'B' where the domains are all aligned. Now reduce the applied field to zero. This takes us to point 'C'. The 'y' axis is the combined magnetic field from the coil and the sample. The applied field is zero but a magnetic field remains from the sample. The domains started to reform as before, but get stuck in position and the material remains magnetic. The above graph is part of what's called a 'hysteresis' curve. The area between the two curves is a measure of the heat generated within the sample, so as well as becoming magnetised, the sample also heats up slightly.

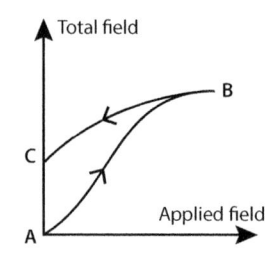

22. (a) Common ones are: iron, nickel, cobalt.

(b) As the temperature increases, the thermal energy of vibration of the atoms increases. This randomises the directions of the magnetic fields in the domains. At the Curie temperature, the domain structure of the sample has been dismantled, resulting in no overall magnetism at any scale larger than a single atom.

23. (a) A 'soft' magnetic material can be magnetised and demagnetised using little energy. As a result, there is only a small increase in temperature after many magnetise/demagnetise cycles.

A 'hard' magnetic material requires a significant amount of energy to magnetise/demagnetise it. Heat is generated within it.

(b) 'Soft' magnetic materials are used for electrical transformers where energy losses should be reduced to a minimum.

'Hard' magnetic materials are used when information needs to be retained such as magnetic tape, disc drives and swipe cards.

Unit 3 Capacitors............Answers

1. $Q = CV = 64 \times 10^{-6} \times 12 = 7.68 \times 10^{-4}$ coulombs, (that quantity on the positive plate and the same magnitude but negative on the negative plate).

2. $E = \frac{1}{2}CV^2 = \frac{1}{2} \times 2000 \times 10^{-6} \times 240^2 = 57.6$ joules, (stored within the electric field between the plates).

3. (a) The graph is heading smoothly towards 9volts

   (b) (i) Smaller capacitance or smaller resistance. *Nerdy note*: Don't say 'smaller resistor' since it's not the physical size of the resistor which should be smaller, it's the property of the resistor (its resistance) which should be smaller.

   (ii) Larger resistance or capacitance.

   (c) A 9volt battery driving current through a 2000Ω resistance will produce a current of:
   $$I = \frac{V}{R} = \frac{9}{2000} = 0.0045\text{A} = 4.5\text{mA}$$

   (d) Adding the voltages across the resistor and capacitor will give the battery voltage of 9volts. So at any instant, the graph of voltage across the resistor versus time, is 9volts minus the voltage across the capacitor.

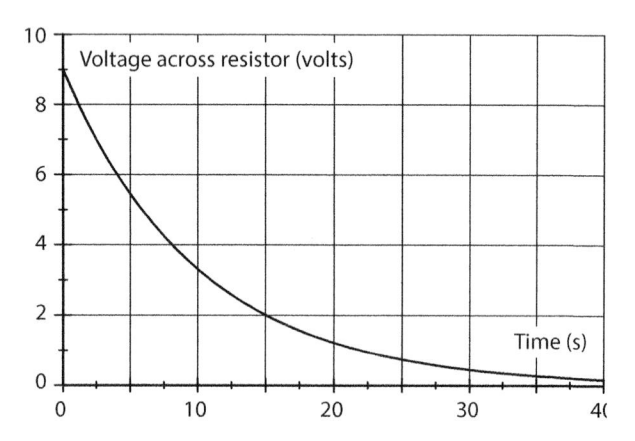

4. (a) Switch on an LED after a time delay.

   (b) The switch is closed and the voltage across the capacitor increases. A certain minimum voltage is required at the base of the transistor to allow current to flow from $+V_S$ through the LED and transistor to the zero volt line. The capacitor will pass this voltage level and switch on the LED.

   (c) The time delay can be adjusted by varying the resistance of R_1 and/or the capacitance of C.

   (d) Limits the current flowing through the LED when the transistor switches on.

   (e) Replace R_2 and the LED with a relay which switches on the more powerful circuit containing the lamp and its own power supply.

5. (a) Seconds (for capacitance in farads and resistance in ohms).

   (b) (i) $CR = 2 \times 8 = 16$s

   (ii) $CR = 32 \times 10^{-6} \times 15 \times 10^3 = 0.48$s

   (iii) $CR = 80 \times 10^{-9} \times 22 \times 10^6 = 1.76$s

6. $V_C = V_S\left(1 - e^{-\frac{t}{CR}}\right) = 12\left(1 - e^{-\frac{CR}{CR}}\right) = 12(1 - e^{-1}) = 12\left(1 - \frac{1}{e}\right) = 12(1 - 0.368) = 7.59$volts

7. (a) 12volts

   (b) The fraction is $\left(1 - \frac{1}{e}\right) = \left(1 - \frac{1}{2.718}\right) = 0.632$. This gives a voltage of 12 × 0.632 = 7.59volts.

   Reading from the graph gives about 0.25s.

   (c) $CR = 0.25 \Rightarrow R = \frac{0.25}{C} = \frac{0.25}{47 \times 10^{-6}} = 5300\Omega$

(d) No effect. The time constant depends upon the product of capacitance and resistance. It is independent of the supply voltage.

8. (a) A charging circuit.

    (b) The initial current is controlled by the supply voltage and the resistance.

    $I = \dfrac{V}{R} = \dfrac{6}{940} = 0.00638\text{A} = 6.38\text{mA}$

    (c) The time constant is $CR = 25 \times 10^{-6} \times 940 = 0.0235\text{s}$.

    At the time constant, the initial current has dropped to $I = I_o e^{-\frac{t}{CR}} = 6.35 \times e^{-1} = 2.34\text{mA}$. Read across from this value on the y-axis to the curve then drop down to the x-axis. That value will be 0.0235s. You can then calculate the 't' position by proportion, or just assume that the time-axis ticks don't have whacky values. You obtain a 't' value of 40ms.

9. (a) This is a charge/discharge circuit. At position S_1 the capacitor charges-up. At position S_2 the capacitor discharges through the resistor.

    (b) **At S_1** There is no resistance in the charging circuit so the time constant is zero seconds.

    At S_2 There is a resistance of 82Ω. This gives: $CR = 250 \times 10^{-6} \times 82 = 0.021\text{s}$.

    (c) The time constant is very short at position S_1 so the capacitor is charged to the supply voltage of 3 volts. At position S_2 the initial current is $I = \dfrac{V}{R} = \dfrac{3}{82} = 0.037\text{A}$.

    (d) The easy answer is 'after an eternity'. But this isn't maths, it's the real world and that's the kind of question real people ask. Usually it's a safety question; you set a safe voltage level and calculate how much time it takes to drop below it. As a rule of thumb, after four or five time constants, the voltage drops to about 1% of its initial value. This gives a time of about one-tenth of a second (still quicker than the blink of an eye, so that's the smart answer).

10. (a) Just before switch-off, the indicated voltage of the supply is across the output capacitor. At switch-off, the capacitor starts to discharge but the 'live' terminal is still at a level sufficient to give the user a shock.

    (b) (i) $20 = 50 \times e^{-\frac{t}{CR}} \Rightarrow e^{-\frac{t}{CR}} = \dfrac{20}{50} = 0.4 \Rightarrow -\dfrac{t}{CR} = \text{Log}_e 0.4 = -0.916$

    The time constant is $CR = 2700 \times 10^{-6} \times 680 = 1.836\text{s}$.

    This gives: $-\dfrac{t}{CR} = -0.916 \Rightarrow t = 1.836 \times 0.916 = 1.68\text{s}$.

    (ii) $20 = 40 \times e^{-\frac{t}{CR}} \Rightarrow e^{-\frac{t}{CR}} = \dfrac{20}{40} = 0.5 \Rightarrow -\dfrac{t}{CR} = \text{Log}_e 0.5 = -0.693$

    The time constant is $CR = 400 \times 10^{-6} \times 5000 = 2\text{s}$.

    This gives: $-\dfrac{t}{CR} = -0.693 \Rightarrow t = 2 \times 0.693 = 1.39\text{s}$.

    The second arrangement reaches 'safety' first.

11. Ben Nevis is 1344m high (you had to look that up). Energy needed: $mgh = 0.045 \times 9.8 \times 1344 = 592.7\text{J}$

    This energy must be stored by the capacitor: $\dfrac{1}{2}CV^2 = 592.7 \Rightarrow V = 344\text{volts}$.

12. (a) At switch position S_1, the circuit should be charging. You must arrange the timing such that the switch is at S_1 when the voltage supply is at 5volts.

    At switch position S_2, the circuit should be discharging the capacitor. When the supply is at zero volts, the switch should be at S_2.

    Ideally, the switch position should copy the square wave shape of the supply at the same frequency. Unrealistic, but it should take no time to change positions.

(b) The time constants are controlled by the capacitance and resistance values. They share a part of the circuit common to both charging and discharging processes.

$$CR = 25 \times 10^{-6} \times 80 = 0.002\text{s}$$

(c) **At 0s:** Capacitor starts charging, switch at S_1.

   At 10ms: Charging stops, discharge begins. Switch moves across to position S_2 (very quickly!)

   At 20ms: Discharging stops, charging begins. Switch flashes back across to position S_1.

(d) Charging lasts for 10ms. The time constant is 0.002s, so this is 5 time constants.

(e) $V_C = V_S\left(1-e^{-\frac{t}{CR}}\right) = 5\left(1-e^{-\frac{0.01}{0.002}}\right) = 5(1-e^{-5}) = 5(1-0.006738) = 4.966\text{volts}$

(f) The time constant would ideally reduce to zero, thus taking no time to charge and no time to discharge. The graph would follow the square wave shape of the supply.

13. (a) For the new Dyson hand dryers where the hands pass into a slot of fast moving air, an infrared beam on one side with a sensor on the other side can switch on/off the system. For older systems where the hands come up under the device, a capacitor can be used as a proximity sensor. The hand acts as one plate of a capacitor, with the air in between the hand and the device acting as the insulator. The capacitance of the system (hand-air-dryer) will depend on the separation of the 'plates' (hand and dryer), and a current will flow between dryer and earth if this changes. Amplify this current and use a transistor as a switch together with a relay to operate the 1-2kW heater (though there are more modern ways to do it).

    If the separation of the hands and the dryer makes the capacitance drop below a certain level, you assume that the person has left the building and you can switch off the heater/blower. Older models left the hand dryer operating for a fixed time (up to 45s in some cases). This was controlled by a CR circuit where the potential difference across a capacitor would reach a threshold value and switch off the system. Fixed time dryers are now considered wasteful of energy.

    (b) Capacitance resistance product of 20s could be a 10kΩ resistance and a 2,000μF capacitance.

14. (a) The symbol is X_C and its unit is the ohm (it must be since it's the ratio volts/amps).

    (b) Left circuit: $X_C = \dfrac{1}{2\pi fC} = \dfrac{1}{2\pi \times 50 \times 32 \times 10^{-6}} = 99.5\Omega$

    Mid circuit: $X_C = \dfrac{1}{2\pi fC} = \dfrac{1}{2\pi \times 1000 \times 2000 \times 10^{-6}} = 0.08\Omega$

    Right circuit: $X_C = \dfrac{1}{2\pi fC} = \dfrac{1}{2\pi \times 18000 \times 68 \times 10^{-9}} = 130\Omega$

    (c) Left circuit: $X_C = \dfrac{V}{I} \Rightarrow I = \dfrac{V}{X_C} = \dfrac{3}{99.5} = 0.030\text{A}$

    Mid circuit: $X_C = \dfrac{V}{I} \Rightarrow I = \dfrac{V}{X_C} = \dfrac{230}{0.08} = 2875\text{A}$ (why is this so large?)

Right circuit: $X_C = \dfrac{V}{I}$ ⇒ $I = \dfrac{V}{X_C} = \dfrac{12}{130} = 0.092\text{A}$

15. (a) As the frequency increases, the current increases in proportion. From the reactance definition:

    $X_C = \dfrac{V}{I}$ ⇒ $I = \dfrac{V}{X_C} = \dfrac{V}{\frac{1}{2\pi fC}} = 2\pi CVf$ ⇒ $I \propto f$

    (b) Changing the supply voltage changes the current. This is why it's much much more sensible to plot the reactance against the frequency, and why you see it in all grown-up textbooks.

    (c) $X_C = \dfrac{V}{I} = \dfrac{3}{0.015} = 200\Omega$

    (d) $X_C = \dfrac{1}{2\pi fC}$ ⇒ $f = \dfrac{1}{2\pi X_C C} = \dfrac{1}{2\pi \times 200 \times 8 \times 10^{-6}} = 99.5\text{Hz}$

16. (a) $X_C = \dfrac{1}{2\pi fC}$ ⇒ $f = \dfrac{1}{2\pi X_C C} = \dfrac{1}{2\pi \times 50 \times 400 \times 10^{-6}} = 7.96\text{Hz}$

    $X_C = \dfrac{V}{I}$ ⇒ $I = \dfrac{V}{X_C} = \dfrac{12}{7.96} = 1.51\text{A}$

    (b) For a constant supply voltage and an unchanged frequency, the current is proportional to the capacitance (similar to the Q15a relationships above), so halving the capacitance halves the current to 0.75A.

    (c) Current at 12volts was 1.51A. From: $X_C = \dfrac{V}{I}$ ⇒ $V = IX_C = \dfrac{I}{2\pi fC}$ we see that the voltage is proportional to the current (when the frequency and capacitance are held constant). Doubling the supply voltage will double the current to 3.02A.

    (d) $X_C = \dfrac{V}{I}$ ⇒ $I = \dfrac{V}{X_C} = \dfrac{V}{\frac{1}{2\pi fC}} = 2\pi CVf$ ⇒ $I \propto CVf$

    Proportional in each case, so halving, halving again, and halving again gives a current of 0.19A.

    Note: In the above, I've used the potential difference across the capacitor and the supply voltage, as interchangeable quantities. This is okay in the present circuit where the ammeter has negligible resistance (as a good ammeter should).

17. (a) The potential difference across the capacitor is no longer equal to the supply voltage. We need separate voltmeters to record the different values and determine the relationship governing them.

    (b) The current. It flows through the wires on and off the plates, but not between them.

    (c) All three pointers oscillate back and forwards with a frequency of 0.5Hz but they are out of step with each other.

    (d) $V_S^2 = V_R^2 + V_C^2$

18. (a) $V_S^2 = V_R^2 + V_C^2 = 1.25^2 + 2.6^2$ ⇒ $V_S = 2.88\text{volts}$

    (b) $X_C = \dfrac{1}{2\pi fC} = \dfrac{1}{2\pi \times 1800 \times 4 \times 10^{-6}} = 22.1\Omega$

    (c) (i) $X_C = \dfrac{V_C}{I}$ ⇒ $I = \dfrac{V_C}{X_C} = \dfrac{2.6}{22.1} = 0.118\text{A}$ (ii) $R = \dfrac{V_R}{I} = \dfrac{1.25}{0.118} = 10.6\Omega$

161

19. (a) The period of the supply is 4 squares of time and the peaks are 1 square out of step, so the phase difference is 90°.

   (b) The current is at its peak at the origin (0.00s) and the voltage reaches its peak at the **later** time of 0.01s. So current leads voltage (by 90°).

   (c) Peak voltage is 4volts and peak current is 1amp, so: $X_C = \dfrac{V}{I} = \dfrac{4}{1} = 4\Omega$

   (d) Period is 0.04s so frequency is 25Hz.

   $$X_C = \dfrac{1}{2\pi fC} \Rightarrow C = \dfrac{1}{2\pi fX_C} = \dfrac{1}{2\pi \times 25 \times 4} = 1.59 \times 10^{-3}\,\text{F}$$

20. Current flows in the circuit and the charge builds up on each plate. When the current reduces to zero (a quarter of a period after reaching its peak value), the capacitor is fully charged and is at its peak potential difference. Hence the voltage lags the current by 90°.

21. (a) $\sin\theta = \dfrac{2.5}{5.0} = \dfrac{1}{2} \Rightarrow \theta = 30°$

   (b) First, calculate the p.d. across the resistor.

   Either, $V_R = \sqrt{V_S^2 - V_C^2} = \sqrt{5.0^2 - 2.5^2} = 4.33\,\text{volts}$ or, $\cos\theta = \dfrac{V_R}{V_S} \Rightarrow V_R = 5\cos 30 = 4.33\,\text{volts}$

   $R = \dfrac{V_R}{I} = \dfrac{4.33}{3.8 \times 10^{-3}} = 1140\Omega$

   (c) $X_C = \dfrac{V_C}{I} = \dfrac{2.5}{3.8 \times 10^{-3}} = 658\Omega$

   (d) $X_C = \dfrac{1}{2\pi fC} \Rightarrow C = \dfrac{1}{2\pi fX_C} = \dfrac{1}{2\pi \times 484 \times 658} = 5 \times 10^{-7}\,\text{F} = 0.5\mu\text{F}$

   (e) $Z = \dfrac{V_S}{I} = \dfrac{5}{3.8 \times 10^{-3}} = 1316\Omega$

   $Z^2 = R^2 + X_C^2 \Rightarrow 1316^2 = 1140^2 + 658^2$ (which is about right).

22. (a) The resistance of the resistor stays constant. The reactance of the capacitor decreases in inverse proportion to the frequency (double the frequency gives half the reactance).

   (b) The reactance drops to zero, leaving only the resistance of the resistor (about 50Ω).

   (c) The impedance the graph tends towards at high frequency is due to the resistance of the resistor. Estimate this as 50Ω.

   Now take a convenient point on the graph, say an impedance of 200Ω at a frequency of 100Hz.

   Use the relation: $Z^2 = R^2 + X_C^2 \Rightarrow 200^2 = 50^2 + X_C^2 \Rightarrow X_C = 194\Omega$.

   Then the capacitance: $X_C = \dfrac{1}{2\pi fC} \Rightarrow C = \dfrac{1}{2\pi fX_C} = \dfrac{1}{2\pi \times 100 \times 194} = 8.2 \times 10^{-6}\,\text{F} = 8.2\mu\text{F}$.

23. (a) The output is still high (about 90%) at 100Hz but drops to about 20% at 1kHz. This would dampen even voice frequencies and anything with a highish frequency would be very quiet. The overall sound is one of bass frequencies dominant.

   (b) The graph exhibits the opposite behaviour. It passes high frequencies and dampens low frequencies. That mp3 track would sound shrill.

Unit 3 Inductors............Answers

1. $I = \dfrac{V}{R} = \dfrac{12}{220} = 0.055\text{A}$

2. (a) $P = VI \Rightarrow V = \dfrac{P}{I} = \dfrac{3.1}{1.26} = 2.46\text{volts}$

   (b) Heat energy. Resistors take all the energy they get from the supply and convert it into heat energy. Capacitors store the energy in the electric field between the plates, and inductors store their energy in the magnetic field, but both of them always return some energy back to the supply.

3. (A) 0.8A in both   (B) 3A (in 3Ω)   1.5A (in 6Ω)

   (C) Resistance of parallel section: $\dfrac{1}{R_\parallel} = \dfrac{1}{2000} + \dfrac{1}{1500} \Rightarrow R_\parallel = 857\Omega$.

   Total resistance is 750+857 = 1607Ω.

   Current from supply is: $I = \dfrac{V}{R} = \dfrac{24}{1607} = 0.0149\text{A}$. This is the current through the **750Ω** resistor.

   The p.d. across the 750Ω resistor is $V = IR = 0.0149 \times 750 = 11.175\text{volts}$. This leaves a potential difference of 24 - 11.175 = 12.825volts across the parallel section. This is the p.d. across both the 2kΩ and the 1.5kΩ resistors. This gives:

   $I = \dfrac{V}{R} = \dfrac{12.825}{2000} = 0.0064\text{A}$ through the **2kΩ** resistor.

   $I = \dfrac{V}{R} = \dfrac{12.825}{1500} = 0.0086\text{A}$ through the **1.5kΩ** resistor.

4. (a) The supply voltage is = 2 + 2 − 1 = 3volts. This gives a current of 0.25A.

   (b) The p.d. of the 'funny' cell drops uniformly to zero in 15s. After 3s, the p.d. will be 0.8volts. This gives a supply voltage of 3.2volts driving a current of 0.267A.

Time (s)	3	6	9	12	15
Current (A)	0.267	0.283	0.3	0.317	0.333

5. 3.5A

6. (a) For a straight line graph, the gradient at any point is constant. So:

   $\dfrac{dI}{dt} = \dfrac{\Delta I}{\Delta t} = \dfrac{(0.70 - 0.25)}{5} = 0.09\text{As}^{-1}$

   (b) It must be increasing.

   (c) At start: $V = IR = 0.25 \times 6 = 1.5\text{volts}$ At end: $V = IR = 0.70 \times 6 = 4.2\text{volts}$

7. $I = 3e^{-0.4t} \Rightarrow \dfrac{dI}{dt} = -0.4 \times 3e^{-0.4t} = -1.2e^{-0.4 \times 5} = -1.2 \times e^{-2} = -0.162\text{As}^{-1}$

   The minus sign means the current is decreasing.

8. (a) Graph on next page.

   (b) 2A

   (c) (i) The rate of change of current levels off at 0A s⁻¹.

       (ii) The maximum value is at the start (it's 0.4A s⁻¹).

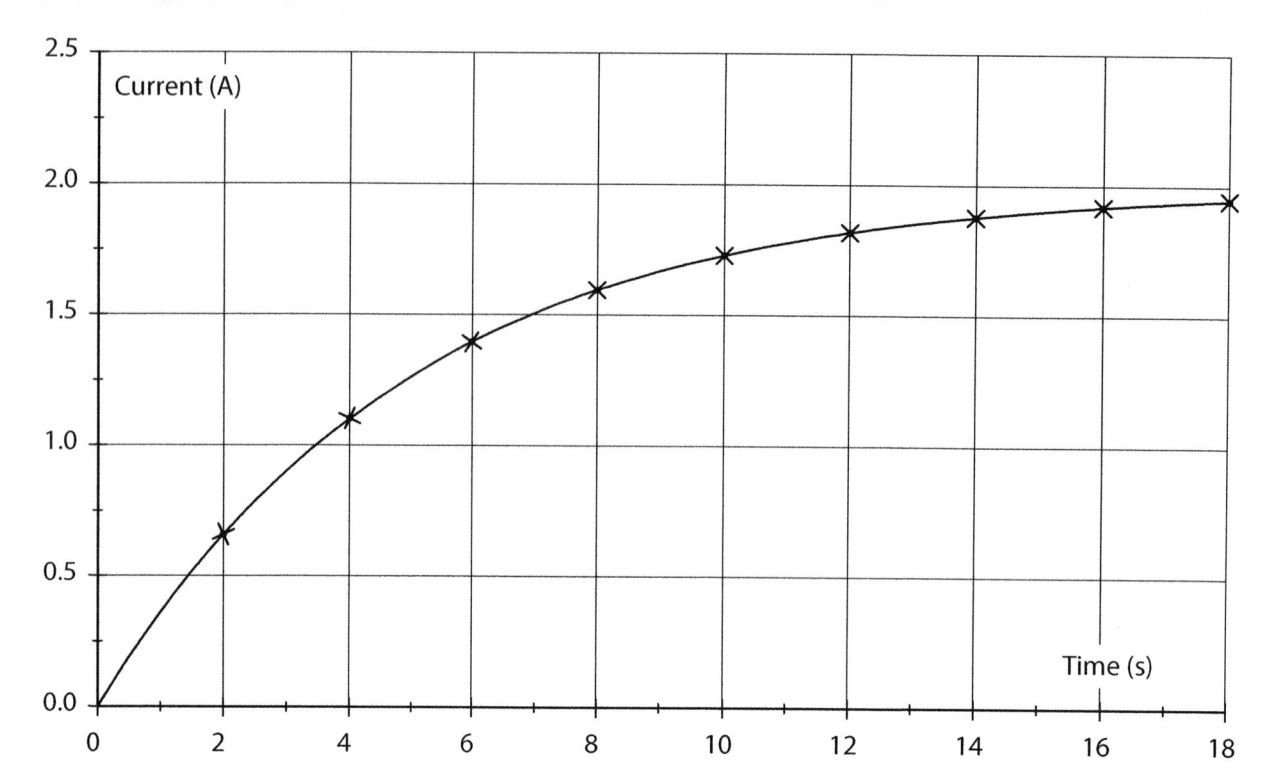

(d) At time zero: 12 volts

At level-off: 0 volts

(e) From the table, at a time of 2s the current is 0.66A.

So voltage across resistor is $V = IR = 0.66 \times 6 = 3.96$ volts.

Voltage across coil is: $12 - 3.96 = 8.04$ volts.

9. (a) $emf = -L\dfrac{dI}{dt} = -3 \times 1.6 = -4.8$ volts

(b) $emf = -L\dfrac{dI}{dt} \Rightarrow -4.5 = -0.06\dfrac{dI}{dt} \Rightarrow \dfrac{dI}{dt} = 75 \text{As}^{-1}$

(c) $emf = -L\dfrac{dI}{dt} \Rightarrow -2.5 = -L \times 6.4 \Rightarrow L = 0.39$ H

10. (a) $CR \Rightarrow \dfrac{Q}{V} \times \dfrac{V}{I} \Rightarrow \dfrac{Q}{I} = t \Rightarrow$ seconds

(b) $\dfrac{L}{R} \Rightarrow \dfrac{e}{dI/dt} \times \dfrac{1}{V/I} \Rightarrow$ seconds

(c) $LC \Rightarrow \dfrac{e}{dI/dt} \times \dfrac{Q}{V} \Rightarrow \dfrac{It}{I/t} \Rightarrow t^2 \Rightarrow$ seconds^2

Note: that these combinations always occur in circuits where changes take time e.g. CR sets the time scale for charging a capacitor and $\dfrac{1}{\sqrt{LC}}$ is the resonance frequency in LC circuits.

11. (a) The steady value of current is reached when there is no back emf across the coil. The supply voltage will then all be across the resistor, giving a current of 2A.

(b) (i) Current is halved.

(ii) Changing the inductance makes no difference to the final steady current.

12. Refer to the diagram on the right. We produce a large voltage across an inductor using the expression $emf = -L\dfrac{dI}{dt}$. The right hand side should be as large as possible, so we need a large inductance, and we need the current to change rapidly. Opening the switch will produce a large change in current (as opposed to closing the switch where the current build-up is slow). With a suitable coil (10,000 turns and thickish wire) you will exceed the 70 volts for a brief moment and make the neon bulb flash.

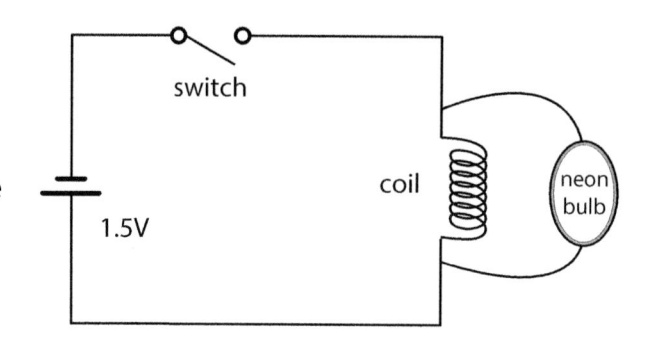

    It can't be lit continuously since the voltage depends upon a large change in current.

13. (A) $B \times A = 0.35 \times \pi \times 0.028^2 = 8.6 \times 10^{-4}\,\text{Tm}^2$

    (B) $B \times A = 0.8 \times \pi \times 0.02^2 = 1.0 \times 10^{-3}\,\text{Tm}^2$

    (C) There are five geometric areas but in terms of the magnetic induction, there are only two areas (ones with 0.6T and ones with 0.4T).

    0.6T section size is 0.04m x 0.04m giving flux of $B \times A = 0.6 \times 0.04 \times 0.04 = 9.6 \times 10^{-4}\,\text{Tm}^2$

    0.4T section has area: $(0.08^2 - 0.04^2) = 4.8 \times 10^{-3}\,\text{m}^2$.

    This gives a flux of: $B \times A = 0.4 \times 4.8 \times 10^{-3} = 1.92 \times 10^{-3}\,\text{Tm}^2$

    Total flux = 2.88 x 10⁻³Tm².

    Nerdy Note: the unit for flux Tm² (tesla times metres squared) is called the 'weber' (pronounced vayber).

14. (a) Steady current means no back emf so it's just a 12 volt battery and a resistor. With a steady current of 6A, this is a resistance of 2Ω.

    (b) The current through the resistor at the start is zero. This gives a potential difference across the resistor of zero volts. What does the world look like from the resistor's point of view? Either there's no battery out there or there **are** batteries but their p.d.s cancel. There **are** 'batteries': the chemical battery of 12volts, and the back emf of -12volts. So the emf across the inductor at time zero is -12volts.

    (c) At the start, the rate of change of current is 3As⁻¹.

    $\dfrac{dI}{dt} = 3 \quad e = -L\dfrac{dI}{dt} \quad \Rightarrow \quad -12 = -L \times 3 \quad \Rightarrow \quad L = 4\text{H}$

    (d) From solid line: $I = 3.75\text{A} \quad V_R = IR = 3.75 \times 2 = 7.5\,\text{volts}$

    From dotted line: $\dfrac{dI}{dt} = 1.1\text{As}^{-1} \quad V_L = -L\dfrac{dI}{dt} = -4 \times 1.1 = -4.4\,\text{volts}$

    Sum of emfs = emf of supply + back emf of coil = 12 + (-4.4) = 7.6volts and this agrees with the voltage driving the current (7.5V from above).

15. (a) The resistor. The current levels off at different values (3A and 5A) and the resistance of the circuit controls the steady current.

    (b) At origin: $e = -L\dfrac{dI}{dt} \quad \Rightarrow \quad -1.5 = -L \times 7.5 \quad \Rightarrow \quad L = 0.2\text{H}$

    At level off: $V = IR \quad \Rightarrow \quad R = \dfrac{V}{I} = \dfrac{1.5}{5} = 0.3\,\Omega$ and $R = \dfrac{V}{I} = \dfrac{1.5}{3} = 0.5\,\Omega$

    Top graph is (0.3Ω : 0.2H)   Bottom graph is (0.5Ω : 0.2H)

16. (a) $E = \frac{1}{2}LI^2 = \frac{1}{2} \times 0.25 \times 3.6^2 = 1.62\text{J}$

(b) $E = \frac{1}{2}LI^2 = \frac{1}{2} \times 75 \times 10^{-3} \times 1.5^2 = 0.084\text{J}$

(c) $E = \frac{1}{2}LI^2 = \frac{1}{2} \times 6 \times 2.15^2 = 13.9\text{J}$

17. $E = \frac{1}{2}LI^2 \Rightarrow I = \sqrt{\frac{2E}{L}} = \sqrt{\frac{2 \times 0.28}{0.8}} = 0.84\text{A}$

18. $E = \frac{1}{2}LI^2 \Rightarrow L = \frac{2E}{I^2} = \frac{2 \times 0.065}{0.92^2} = 0.15\text{H}$

19. (a) It creates the magnetic field of the coil (plus heat energy to any resistance in the wires).

(b) $E = \frac{1}{2}LI^2 = \frac{1}{2} \times 0.4 \times 2.7^2 = 1.46\text{J}$

(c) The energy from the battery to the coil creates the magnetic field and is a 'one-off' process. The resistor is continually producing heat energy and receives a steady supply of energy from the battery.

When the current is switched off, the coil returns the energy to the battery. The heat energy in the resistor goes into the surroundings.

(d) Heat energy.

20. When switching off, the circuit is broken immediately and the current must collapse extremely quickly. So $\frac{dI}{dt}$ is very high and the back emf is large. When switching on, the circuit is complete and $\frac{dI}{dt}$ can be small(ish). This is why electric shocks from inductors are greater at switch-off.

21. (a) **At 'A'** The resistor and coil are in series with the supply and the current builds-up.

At 'B' The emf of the coil drives current through the resistor.

(b) The graphs below show the general shape.

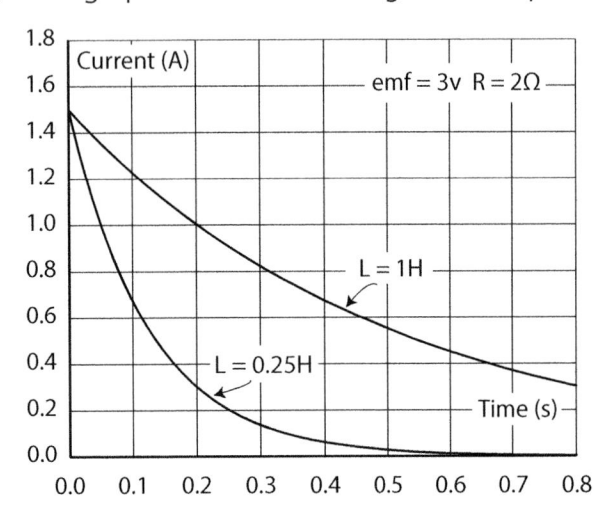

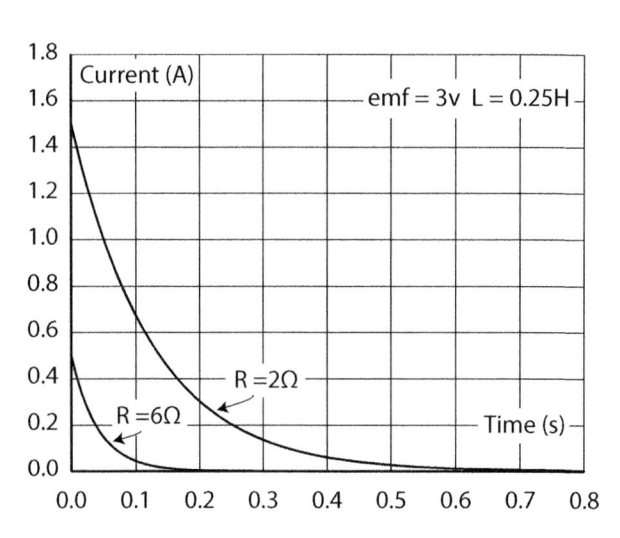

(c) Either increasing the inductance 'L' (left graph), or decreasing the resistance 'R' (right graph).

22. (a) The secondary voltage is greater than the primary voltage.

(b) The voltage ratio equals the turns ratio $\frac{V_S}{V_P} = \frac{N_S}{N_P}$. The 'S' stands for 'secondary, the 'P' stands for 'primary', and 'N' is the number of turns.

(c) The back emf blip across the primary coil is magnified by the step-up turns ratio to give a high voltage blip in the secondary coil.

(d) An example is a car ignition system where a 12volt battery produces a brief potential difference of over 20kV at the spark plugs. The 'coil' as it's usually known, is a cylinder shaped canister about 5 to 6cm in diameter (also called the 'magneto' by those of a certain personality).

23. (a) $V_{rms} = \dfrac{V_p}{\sqrt{2}} \Rightarrow V_p = \sqrt{2} \times V_{rms} = 6\sqrt{2} = 8.49 \text{Volts}$

(b) 0.02s. It reverses polarity every half cycle (0.01s).

24. (a)

(b) The current drops as you increase the frequency with a constant r.m.s. supply, so it becomes more difficult.

(c) The reactance increases with frequency.

(d) (i) Take the first pair of readings (100Hz, 0.238A):

$\dfrac{V}{I} = \dfrac{6}{0.238} = 2\pi fL \Rightarrow L = \dfrac{6}{0.238 \times 2 \times \pi \times 100} = 0.04 \text{H}$

(ii) Plot a graph of 'V/I' against 'f'. It will be a straight line passing through the origin with a slope of 2πL.

25. (a) **Resistor:** The resistance of a resistor is unaffected by a change in frequency so the bulb brightness is unchanged.

Capacitor: The current is proportional to the frequency so the bulb gets brighter.

Inductor: The current is inversely proportional to the frequency so the bulb gets dimmer.

(b) 'Choke' means 'reduce' or 'cut off', so an inductor will choke **high** frequencies.

(c) A capacitor 'blocks' **low** frequencies.

26. (a) $X_L = \omega L = 2\pi fL = 2 \times \pi \times 50 \times 0.35 = 110\Omega$

(b) $X_L = \dfrac{V}{I} = \dfrac{4}{0.12} = 33.3\Omega$

(c) $X_L = 2\pi fL = 2 \times \pi \times 1750 \times 0.008 = 88\Omega$

27. Refer to the circuits below:

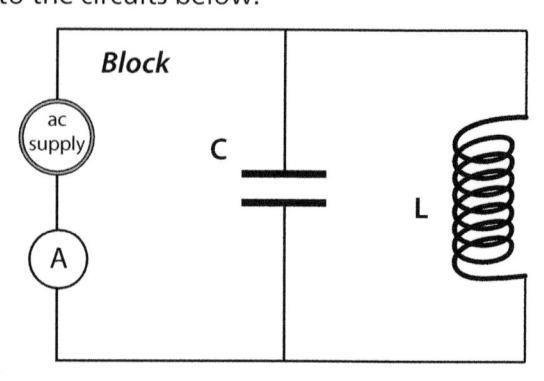

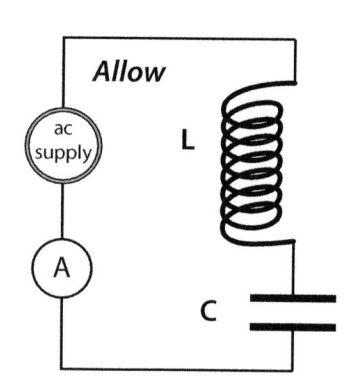

(a) The left circuit blocks the current over a range of frequencies. At low frequencies, current can't flow in the capacitor branch, but can flow in the inductor branch. This gives a decent current reading on the ammeter. At high frequencies, the inductor blocks the current but the current can still flow in the capacitor branch. This gives a decent reading on the ammeter. At in-between frequencies, they both do a bit of blocking / choking and the ammeter reading is small.

(b) The right circuit allows the current to flow over a range of frequencies. At low frequencies, the capacitor reduces the current and at high frequencies the inductor blocks the current. For in-between frequencies, a decent current flows.

28.

Component	Value	Setting 1 Frequency (Hz)	Setting 1 V/I (Ω)	Setting 2 Frequency (Hz)	Setting 2 V/I (Ω)
Resistor	15Ω	20	15	800	15
Capacitor	32μF	20	249	800	6.2
Inductor	60mH	20	7.5	800	302

29. (a) Calculate the reactances:

$X_L = 2\pi fL = 2\pi \times 50 \times 20 \times 10^{-3} = 6.28\Omega$ $X_C = \dfrac{1}{2\pi fC} = \dfrac{1}{2\pi \times 50 \times 80 \times 10^{-6}} = 39.8\Omega$

Then the impedance: $Z = \sqrt{R^2 + (X_L - X_C)^2} = \sqrt{10^2 + (6.28 - 39.8)^2} = 35\Omega$

(b) $Z = \sqrt{R^2 + (X_L - X_C)^2} = \sqrt{10^2 + (0)^2} = 10\Omega$

(c) The impedance is equal to the resistance. In practice, this would also include the resistance of the coils of the inductor.

(d) $X_L = X_C \Rightarrow 2\pi fL = \dfrac{1}{2\pi fC} \Rightarrow f = \dfrac{1}{2\pi \sqrt{LC}} = \dfrac{1}{2\pi \sqrt{20 \times 10^{-3} \times 80 \times 10^{-6}}} = 125.8 \text{Hz}$

(e) The resistance is at its minimum (10Ω), so the current will be at its maximum.

Unit 3 Electromagnetic Radiation..........Answers

1. (a) James Clerk Maxwell.
   (b) ε_o is the permittivity of free space. μ_o is the permeability of free space. $c = \dfrac{1}{\sqrt{\varepsilon_o \mu_o}}$
   (c) A light ray is a bundle of energy consisting of vibrating electric and magnetic fields.

2. (a) Mass of 60mg has a weight of 5.88×10^{-4}N.

   $F = \dfrac{\mu_o I_1 I_2 l}{2\pi r} \Rightarrow \mu_o = \dfrac{2\pi rF}{I_1 I_2 l} = \dfrac{2\pi \times 0.008 \times 5.88 \times 10^{-4}}{9.5 \times 9.5 \times 0.25} = 1.31 \times 10^{-6} \text{Hm}^{-1}$ (about 4% too big).

   (b) $B = \dfrac{\mu_o I}{2\pi r} = \dfrac{4\pi \times 10^{-7} \times 9.5}{2\pi \times 0.008} = 2.38 \times 10^{-4} \text{T} = 238\mu\text{T}$. This is much bigger so no sweat.

Unit 4 Units & Uncertainties............Answers

1. (a) Seconds, minutes, hours, days, months, years, centuries, millenia

   (b) Kilogram, ton, gram, pound, stone, hundredweight

   (c) Metres per second, miles per hour, lightseconds per month, centimetres per year. The last one is used in geology with ocean floor spreading. The Mid-Atlantic Ridge is spreading apart at a rate of 2.5cm/yr where it passes through Iceland.

   (d) $[L^3 M^{-1} T^{-2}]$

2. No, it could be greater than 50 or less than 40, though this is unlikely. The uncertainty is only a probability of being within the quoted values. It's usually expressed as ± 1 standard deviation 'σ' (a 68% probability of being within the limits). The Higgs Boson detected at Cern in 2012 was announced as being 'certain at the 4-sigma level', meaning that they were 99.994% certain it was a real effect. That's a 1 in 15,800 chance that they are wrong.

3. (a) 12.5% (b) 0.57% (c) 11% (d) 0.02% (e) 5.3% (f) 26%

4. (a) It's probably a digital ammeter with the last digit (the 5 or 0) giving discrete jumps. It may be an analogue ammeter with the experimenter estimating anything between scale marks as ½.

   (b) 4 + 10 + 16 + 10 + 4 = 44

   (c) The middle three bars contain 36 out of the 44 readings. This is 82% and is greater than one standard deviation's worth (68%). But this isn't a precision game, so 0.25 ± 0.05A will suffice.

5. (a) 0.23 (b) 0.007 (c) 0.019 (d) 0.014 (e) 0.00014 (f) 0.015

6. (a) Mean = 1.415   Random uncertainty = (1.46 – 1.38) / 15 = 0.005

   (b) 1.415 ± 0.005

7. (a) (i) 6.254×10^4 (ii) 2.7×10^{-4} (iii) 2.5×10^0 (iv) 9.4×10^{-1}

   (b) (i) 490 (ii) 16,000 (iii) 30,000 (iv) 8.21

8. (a) $\dfrac{\Delta I}{I} = \dfrac{0.1}{3.15} = 0.032$ $\dfrac{\Delta R}{R} = \dfrac{5}{47} = 0.11$

   (b) Ignore the fractional uncertainty of the current. It's less than ⅓rd of the fractional uncertainty of the resistance.

   (c) If using Pythagoras Theorem (the root sum of squares, RSS rule), then ignore it if its fractional (or %) uncertainty is less than ⅓rd of the largest fractional uncertainty.

   (d) If you missed it, here's the derivation:

   $$V = IR \Rightarrow (V + \Delta V) = (I + \Delta I)(R + \Delta R) = IR + I\Delta R + R\Delta I + \Delta I \Delta R$$

   The last term multipies two small quantities, so ignore it. This gives:

   $$V + \Delta V = IR + I\Delta R + R\Delta I \Rightarrow \Delta V = I\Delta R + R\Delta I$$

   Divide both sides by 'V':

   $$\dfrac{\Delta V}{V} = \dfrac{I\Delta R + R\Delta I}{V} = \dfrac{I\Delta R + R\Delta I}{IR} = \dfrac{\Delta R}{R} + \dfrac{\Delta I}{I}$$

   The current term (0.032) is less than ⅓rd of the resistance term (0.11), so drop it.

   $$\dfrac{\Delta V}{V} = \dfrac{\Delta R}{R} = 0.11 \Rightarrow \Delta V = 0.11 \times V = 0.11 \times 3.15 \times 47 = 16.3 \Rightarrow V = (148 \pm 16) \text{ volts}$$

9. (a) $F = ma = 3.3 \times 0.932 = 3.076 \text{N}$

   (b) $F = ma = 3.26 \times 0.918 = 2.993 \text{N}$

   (c) $F = (3.034 \pm 0.042) \text{N} \Rightarrow (3.03 \pm 0.04) \text{N}$ Some scientists would round up to ±0.05.

   (d) $\dfrac{\Delta m}{m} = \dfrac{0.02}{3.28} = 0.0061 \qquad \dfrac{\Delta a}{a} = \dfrac{0.007}{0.925} = 0.0076$

   (e) $\left(\dfrac{\Delta F}{F}\right)^2 = \left(\dfrac{\Delta m}{m}\right)^2 + \left(\dfrac{\Delta a}{a}\right)^2 \Rightarrow \dfrac{\Delta F}{F} = \sqrt{0.0061^2 + 0.0076^2} = 0.0097$

   Calculate the uncertainty in the force: $\Delta F = 3.03 \times 0.0097 = 0.03$.

   Final answer: $F = 3.03 \pm 0.03 \text{N}$.

   The uncertainty is smaller than the answer in part (c) since it takes into account the low probability of both results being crap.

10. (a) Mean value of current is 3.64A. For voltage it's 5.217volts. (Totals were 101.91 and 146.09)

    (b) It's near the centre of the spread of dots.

    (c) 28 pupils. Pattern is a circular disc with greatest density of dots near the centre.

11. $\dfrac{\Delta E_k}{E_k} = \sqrt{\left(\dfrac{\Delta m}{m}\right)^2 + \left(\dfrac{2\Delta v}{v}\right)^2} = \sqrt{\left(\dfrac{5}{362}\right)^2 + \left(\dfrac{2 \times 0.04}{1.46}\right)^2} = 0.056$

    The '2' in the above expression is often placed (erroneously) outside the bracket. This would be the case if (from $v^2 = v \times v$) the separate v's were uncorrelated. They are the same 'v' and are obviously completely correlated. Also, deduce the implications if the mass uncertainty was zero.

    $E_k = \dfrac{1}{2}mv^2 = \dfrac{1}{2} \times 0.362 \times 1.46^2 = 0.386 \text{J} \Rightarrow \Delta E_k = 0.386 \times 0.056 = 0.02 \text{J}$

    Round-off to: $E_k = (0.39 \pm 0.02) \text{J}$

12. $\left(\dfrac{\Delta E_P}{E_P}\right)^2 = \left(\dfrac{\Delta m}{m}\right)^2 + \left(\dfrac{\Delta g}{g}\right)^2 + \left(\dfrac{\Delta h}{h}\right)^2 \Rightarrow \left(\dfrac{9}{99.5}\right)^2 = \left(\dfrac{2}{29}\right)^2 + \left(\dfrac{0.1}{9.8}\right)^2 + \left(\dfrac{\Delta h}{h}\right)^2 \Rightarrow \dfrac{\Delta h}{h} = 0.058$

    $h = \dfrac{E_P}{mg} = \dfrac{99.5}{29 \times 9.8} = 0.35 \Rightarrow h = (0.35 \pm 0.02) \text{m}$

13. (a) 4nA   (b) 7mm   (c) 28pJ   (d) 49.8nkg !!! (the odd one)

    (e) 32TW   (f) 16.1GK   (g) 700ns   (h) 293kV

14. (a) 14.2 is 1DP and 3 sig. figs.   (b) 395.28 is 2DPs and 5 sig. figs.

    (c) 0.275 is 3DPs and 3 sig. figs.   (d) 0.00048 is 5DPs and 2 sig. figs.

15. $r = \dfrac{\varepsilon_o h^2}{\pi m_e e^2} = \dfrac{8.854 \times 10^{-12} \times (6.626 \times 10^{-34})^2}{\pi \times 9.109 \times 10^{-31} \times (1.602 \times 10^{-19})^2} = 5.293 \times 10^{-11} \text{m}$

16. (a) $1+2+3+6+4+2+1 = 19$

    (b) Mean $= (1\times4.1 + 2\times4.2 + 3\times4.3 + 6\times4.4 + 4\times4.5 + 2\times4.6 + 1\times4.7)/19 = 4.405$

    Random uncertainty $=(4.7-4.1)/19 = 0.032$

    (c) Calibration uncertainty (the manufacturer is telling you how well its been designed and built).

    (d) Yes. This is usually taken as ±½ of the right-most digit, so its ± 0.05.

(e) Divide each of the uncertainties by the mean value and convert to a percentage:

Calibration: 0.05/4.4 is 1.1%   Reading: 0.05/4.4 is 1.1%   Random: 0.032/4.4 is 0.7%

They're all comparable in magnitude so we must retain all of them. Using the 'root sum of squares' method for combining uncertainties gives:

$$\sqrt{1.1^2 + 1.1^2 + 0.7^2} = 1.7\% \quad \Rightarrow \quad t = 4.405 \pm 0.075 \quad \Rightarrow \quad t = 4.41 \pm 0.08 \text{s}$$

17. (a) $(\Delta P)^2 = (0.2)^2 + (0.1)^2 \Rightarrow \Delta P = 0.22 \Rightarrow P = 7.6 \pm 0.2$. Some would round-up to ± 0.3.

(b) $(\Delta F)^2 = (0.5)^2 + (0.5)^2 \Rightarrow \Delta F = 0.71 \Rightarrow F = 5.5 \pm 0.7$

(c) $(\Delta V)^2 = (0.08)^2 + (0.22)^2 \Rightarrow \Delta V = 0.23 \Rightarrow V = -0.79 \pm 0.23$

(d) $(\Delta T)^2 = (0.4)^2 + (0.2)^2 + (0.3)^2 \Rightarrow \Delta T = 0.54 \Rightarrow T = 6.1 \pm 0.6$

You probably noticed the rounding-off on the uncertainty is a bit odd. It doesn't follow the same rule as '5 and above, round-up'. It's not an exact science, but most good experimenters get trigger happy with the rounding button when it gets to 3.

18. (a) 0.15, 15%   (b) 0.0033, 0.33%   (c) 0.043, 4.3%   (d) 0.059, 5.9%

19. $\dfrac{\Delta T}{T} = \dfrac{0.2}{2.7} = 0.074 \qquad \dfrac{\Delta(T^2)}{T^2} = 2T\dfrac{\Delta T}{T^2} = \dfrac{2\Delta T}{T} = 2 \times 0.074 = 0.148$

The small change 'Δ' is handled like differentiation (recall differentiating x^2, that's where the '2' comes from).

20. (a) $\left(\dfrac{\Delta V}{V}\right)^2 = \left(\dfrac{\Delta I}{I}\right)^2 + \left(\dfrac{\Delta R}{R}\right)^2 = \left(\dfrac{0.01}{0.18}\right)^2 + \left(\dfrac{20}{275}\right)^2 = 0.0031 + 0.0053$

Remember the rule about discarding fractional uncertainties if one is more than three times the other? When things are squared, like the above, it translates into the square of one being more than ten times the square of the other. To a physicist, three squared is ten (okay, only when dealing with uncertainties!) Looking at the two numbers, we keep them both. Now calculate the fractional uncertainty in the answer.

$$\left(\dfrac{\Delta V}{V}\right)^2 = 0.0084 \quad \Rightarrow \quad \dfrac{\Delta V}{V} = 0.092$$

Calculate the central value, then the absolute uncertainty:

$$V = IR = 0.18 \times 275 = 49.5 \quad \Rightarrow \quad \Delta V = 0.092V = 0.092 \times 49.5 = 4.6$$

Final answer: $V = (49.5 \pm 4.6)$ volts. Rounding to (50 ± 5) volts would show good judgment.

(b) $\left(\dfrac{\Delta E_P}{E_P}\right)^2 = \left(\dfrac{\Delta m}{m}\right)^2 + \left(\dfrac{\Delta g}{g}\right)^2 + \left(\dfrac{\Delta h}{h}\right)^2 = \left(\dfrac{0.02}{4.45}\right)^2 + \left(\dfrac{0.01}{9.81}\right)^2 + \left(\dfrac{0.01}{17.62}\right)^2 = (202 + 10.4 + 3.2) \times 10^{-7}$

Remember this is squares, so the rule is 'if ten times greater then dump'. This is the case here, so just take the fractional uncertainty from the mass reading.

$$\dfrac{\Delta E_P}{E_P} = \dfrac{\Delta m}{m} = \dfrac{0.02}{4.45} = 0.0045$$

Central value then absolute uncertainty:

$$E_P = mgh = 4.45 \times 9.81 \times 17.62 = 768.4 \quad \Rightarrow \quad \Delta E_P = 0.0045 \times 768.4 = 3.5$$

Final answer is $E_P = (768 \pm 4)$ joules.

(c) $$\left(\frac{\Delta E_K}{E_K}\right)^2 = \left(\frac{\Delta\frac{1}{2}}{\frac{1}{2}}\right)^2 + \left(\frac{\Delta m}{m}\right)^2 + \left(\frac{2\Delta v}{v}\right)^2 = \left(\frac{0}{\frac{1}{2}}\right)^2 + \left(\frac{0.01}{1.53}\right)^2 + \left(\frac{2\times 0.03}{0.82}\right)^2 = (0+4.3+535)\times 10^{-5}$$

I've left the half in the above expression to show that you just ignore any fixed constants (things like ½'s and π's). From the two remaining numbers, we can take the fractional uncertainty in the kinetic energy from the speed term.

$$\left(\frac{\Delta E_K}{E_K}\right)^2 = \left(\frac{2\Delta v}{v}\right)^2 \Rightarrow \frac{\Delta E_K}{E_K} = \frac{2\Delta v}{v} = \frac{2\times 0.03}{0.82} = 0.073$$

Central value then absolute uncertainty:

$$E_K = \frac{1}{2}mv^2 = \frac{1}{2}\times 1.53\times 0.82^2 = 0.514 \text{ J} \Rightarrow \Delta E_K = 0.073\times 0.514 = 0.038 \text{ J}$$

Final answer is $E_K = (0.514 \pm 0.038)$ J $\Rightarrow$ (0.51 ± 0.04) J

The above three examples all use the squaring of the fractional uncertainties. You use this method if the measurements of each of the variables are unrelated to each other (so a bad mass measurement doesn't also give a bad speed measurement in the last one). If for some weird reason good measurements are followed by other good measurements, and bad measurements are followed by other bad measurements, then don't use the squares. Just use fractional uncertainties unsquared.

21. (a) Error bars.

    (b) Mean value of acceleration is 0.898 m/s² and for the force it's 6.06N.

    (c) The graph plots force against acceleration and they are related by $F = ma$. With the force on the 'y' axis, the slope will be equal to the mass. I got 4.7kg for the slope. The slope doesn't pass through the origin due to friction. To get a non-zero value for the acceleration you need a force of at least 1.8N (my value for the intercept). This is the frictional force.

22. (a) Calibration uncertainty.

    (b) Reading uncertainty.

    (c) Calibration uncertainty: 0.1% + ½ smallest division = (0.1% of 835mm) + 0.5mm is ± 1.3mm

    Reading uncertainty: ½ smallest division at both ends gives a total of (just add): ± 1mm

    Use Pythagoras Theorem with absolute uncertainties:

    $(\Delta L)^2 = 1.3^2 + 1.0^2 \Rightarrow \Delta L = 1.64$ mm $\Rightarrow L = 835 \pm 1.7$ mm

    Round off to (835 ± 2)mm.

23. (a) Random uncertainty, since there is no human error.

    (b) 0.5% of 0.86s is 0.0043s.

    Smallest division is 0.01s, so ½ smallest division is 0.005s.

    Total is 0.0043 + 0.005 = approx 0.01, giving 0.86 ± 0.01s

    (c) No, the uncertainty has no statistical component.

24. (a) Mean = 10.73s   Random uncertainty = (10.9 - 10.3)/10 = 0.06s   (b) Yes

    (c) No, the sprinter would run a different race (might be slower or faster).

    (d) Ignore the 10.3 reading. Recalculating gives: 10.78s and 0.03s.

25. (a) No, there is too much chance of an odd reading influencing the result.

(b) It gets smaller. Doubling the number of readings doesn't usually double the spread of the readings, so the ratio decreases.

(c) No. A single odd reading unduly influences the random uncertainty (it's one of only two numbers in the formula) but has little effect on the mean (where the odd reading is only one amongst many readings). It's reckoned that about ten to a dozen readings is optimal for the procedure.

26. **Calibration**: 1% of 1.87 amps is 0.0187 (round to 0.019A)

Smallest division is 0.01A, so ½ smallest division is 0.005A.   Total is ±0.024A

Reading: ±0.005A

Random: ±0.02A

All these uncertainties are associated with the same quantity, so use absolute uncertainties:

$$\Delta I = \sqrt{0.024^2 + 0.005^2 + 0.02^2} = 0.032 \implies I = 1.87 \pm 0.03\text{A} \quad \text{(could also choose } \pm 0.04\text{)}.$$

27. (a)

Voltage (volts)	Current (amps)
1.87 ± 0.07	0.046 ± 0.002
4.01 ± 0.16	0.11 ± 0.004
6.08 ± 0.24	0.15 ± 0.006
8.07 ± 0.32	0.21 ± 0.008
10.4 ± 0.42	0.25 ± 0.01
12.0 ± 0.48	0.31 ± 0.012
14.3 ± 0.57	0.35 ± 0.014
16.0 ± 0.64	0.40 ± 0.016
18.3 ± 0.73	0.45 ± 0.018
20.1 ± 0.8	0.50 ± 0.02

(b) The uncertainty is a percentage of the reading, so a bigger reading gives a bigger uncertainty.

(c) My result was $R = 40.6\Omega$.

(d) The bottom part of the line has less room for adjustment and you only have to waggle the top end. Usually you would locate the centroid from the means of the voltage and current, then pivot your attempt at a best line about this point.

(e) My result was $R = 40 \pm 2\Omega$.

28. $$\frac{\Delta s}{s} = \sqrt{\left(\frac{\Delta a}{a}\right)^2 + \left(\frac{2\Delta t}{t}\right)^2} = \sqrt{\left(\frac{0.02}{0.31}\right)^2 + \left(\frac{2 \times 0.05}{1.15}\right)^2} = \sqrt{0.0117} = 0.108$$

Now calculate the central value and its absolute uncertainty:

$$s = \frac{1}{2}at^2 = \frac{1}{2} \times 0.31 \times 1.15^2 = 0.205\text{m} \quad \Delta s = 0.205 \times 0.108 = 0.022 \implies s = 0.205 \pm 0.022\text{m}$$

The raw data requires rounding to 2 decimal places, but how do we round off the 0.205? Up to 0.21 or down to 0.20? With a rounded uncertainty of ±0.02, the rounding on the central value is significant. There's no correct answer, but $s = (0.205 \pm 0.02)$m will do fine. The LHCb experiment at Cern quoted the mass of the Omega 'b' (a bottom quark and 2 strange quarks) as (6046±2.2±0.6)MeV, so don't get too hung-up on rounding.

29. It's inappropriate since there is a gross mismatch of decimal places, three on the result and one on the uncertainty. It's 'bad form' since it matches a pure (unitless) number with a number which has a unit. Tidier to wrap it in brackets (6.237±0.2)J to correct the bad form, then finally (6.2±0.2)J.

30. (a) $\dfrac{\Delta V}{V} = \sqrt{\left(\dfrac{2\Delta I}{I}\right)^2 + \left(\dfrac{\Delta R}{R}\right)^2} = \sqrt{\left(\dfrac{2\times 1}{38}\right)^2 + \left(\dfrac{1}{10}\right)^2} = 0.113$

    Now calculate the central value and its absolute uncertainty:

    $V = I^2 R = 0.038^2 \times 4700 = 6.78 \text{ volts}$ $\quad \Delta V = 6.79 \times 0.113 = 0.77$ $\Rightarrow$ $V = 6.79 \pm 0.77$

    Round off to obtain $V = (6.8 \pm 0.8)$ volts.

    (b) This is a mixture of an addition with a product. Strategy is to calculate the uncertainty in the 'at' part first, then use absolute uncertainties for the addition.

    The 'at' bit: $\dfrac{\Delta(at)}{(at)} = \sqrt{\left(\dfrac{\Delta a}{a}\right)^2 + \left(\dfrac{\Delta t}{t}\right)^2} = \sqrt{\left(\dfrac{0.1}{1.5}\right)^2 + \left(\dfrac{0.4}{6}\right)^2} = 0.09$

    Now calculate the central value for the 'at' and its absolute uncertainty:

    $at = 1.5 \times 6 = 9$ $\quad \Delta(at) = 0.09 \times 9 = 0.81$ $\Rightarrow$ $at = (9.0 \pm 0.8) \text{ m s}^{-1}$

    The 'u+at' bit: $(\Delta v)^2 = (\Delta u)^2 + (\Delta(at))^2 = 2^2 + 0.8^2 = 4.64$ $\Rightarrow$ $\Delta v = 2.2 \text{ m s}^{-1}$

    Now calculate the central value for 'v' and its absolute uncertainty:

    $v = u + at = 27 + 1.5 \times 6 = 36 \text{ m s}^{-1}$ $\Rightarrow$ $v = (36 \pm 2) \text{ m s}^{-1}$

    (c) This one is very tricky since it's got a square on the left hand side. First, the good news; the % error in the displacement 's' (0.12%) is much smaller than the rest, so ignore it and take the uncertainty in the '2as' term as due to the acceleration.

    Rewrite the formula $v^2 = u^2 + 2as$ as a power: $v = (u^2 + 2as)^{\frac{1}{2}}$.

    Apply the rules of differentiation: $y = x^n$ $\quad \dfrac{dy}{dx} = nx^{(n-1)} = nx^n x^{-1} = nyx^{-1}$ $\Rightarrow$ $\dfrac{dy}{y} = n\dfrac{dx}{x}$

    With finite sized Δ's, this gives: $\dfrac{\Delta y}{y} = n\dfrac{\Delta x}{x}$ $\Rightarrow$ $\dfrac{\Delta v}{v} = \dfrac{1}{2}\dfrac{\Delta(u^2 + 2as)}{(u^2 + 2as)}$

    Now tackle the $\Delta(u^2 + 2as)$ bit using Pythagoras with absolute uncertainties:

    $(\Delta(u^2 + 2as))^2 = (\Delta(u^2))^2 + (\Delta(2as))^2 = (2u\Delta u)^2 + (2s\Delta a)^2$ (differentiation on the first bit).

    Put in values: $(2 \times 12.8 \times 1.0)^2 + (2 \times 415 \times 0.02)^2 = 655 + 276 = 931$ $\Rightarrow$ $\Delta(u^2 + 2as) = 30.5$

    Work out the central value: $v^2 = u^2 + 2as = 12.8^2 + 2 \times 0.27 \times 415 = 388$ $\Rightarrow$ $v = 19.7 \text{ m s}^{-1}$

    Now bring it together: $\dfrac{\Delta v}{v} = \dfrac{1}{2}\dfrac{\Delta(u^2 + 2as)}{(u^2 + 2as)} = \dfrac{1}{2} \times \dfrac{30.5}{388} = 0.039$

    Calculate the absolute uncertainty: $\Delta v = 19.7 \times 0.039 = 0.77$

    Final answer: $v = (19.7 \pm 0.8) \text{ m s}^{-1}$ (itchy trigger finger on the uncertainty).

    Pretty desperate problem and far harder than you're expected to achieve!

Printed in Great
Britain
by Amazon

30248672R00102